Richard Verdi was Professor of Fine Art and Director of the Barber Institute of Fine Arts at the University of Birmingham, England until 2007. He organized the exhibition 'Cézanne and Poussin: The Classical Vision of Landscape' held at the National Gallery of Scotland in 1990, for which he wrote the catalogue and received an Art Fund Award for an 'Outstanding Contribution to the Visual Arts'. He is also the author of *Klee and Nature* (1984), *Rembrandt's Themes: Life Into Art* (2014), *Poussin as a Painter: From Classicism to Abstraction* (2020) and *Cézanne* (2022).

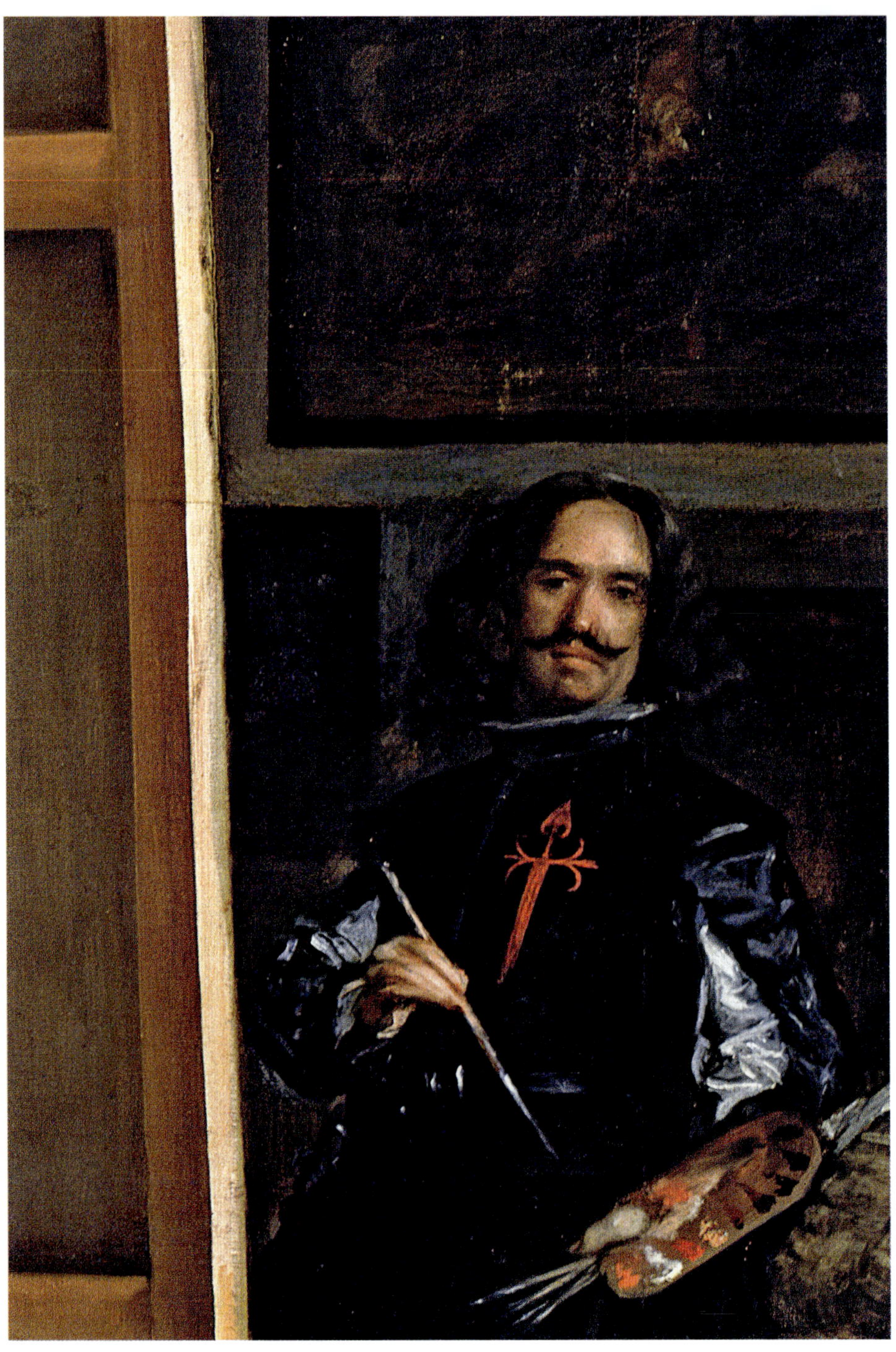

1 *Las Meninas*, 1656, detail

Velázquez
Richard Verdi

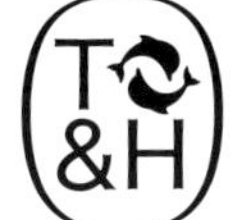

T&H

First published in 2023 in the United Kingdom
by Thames & Hudson Ltd, 181A High Holborn,
London WC1V 7QX

www.thamesandhudson.com

First published in 2023 in the United States
of America by Thames & Hudson Inc.,
500 Fifth Avenue, New York, New York 10110

www.thamesandhudsonusa.com

Art direction and series design by Kummer & Herrman
Layout by Adam Hay Studio

British Library Cataloguing-in-Publication Data
A catalogue record for this book is available from the
British Library

Library of Congress Control Number 2022931221

ISBN 978-0-500-20474-0

Printed and bound in China through Asia Pacific
Offset Ltd

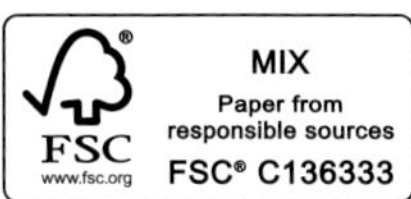

Contents

Chapter 1
6   **A Teenage Prodigy**

Chapter 2
38   **Painter to the King**

Chapter 3
70   **A New Prince and a New Palace**

Chapter 4
111   **Entertaining the King**

Chapter 5
143   **Consolidating his Style**

Chapter 6
169   **Serving the Court and Painting the Pope**

Chapter 7
194   **'The Painter of Painters'**

Chapter 8
223   **After Velázquez**

265   Select Bibliography
267   List of Illustrations
275   Index

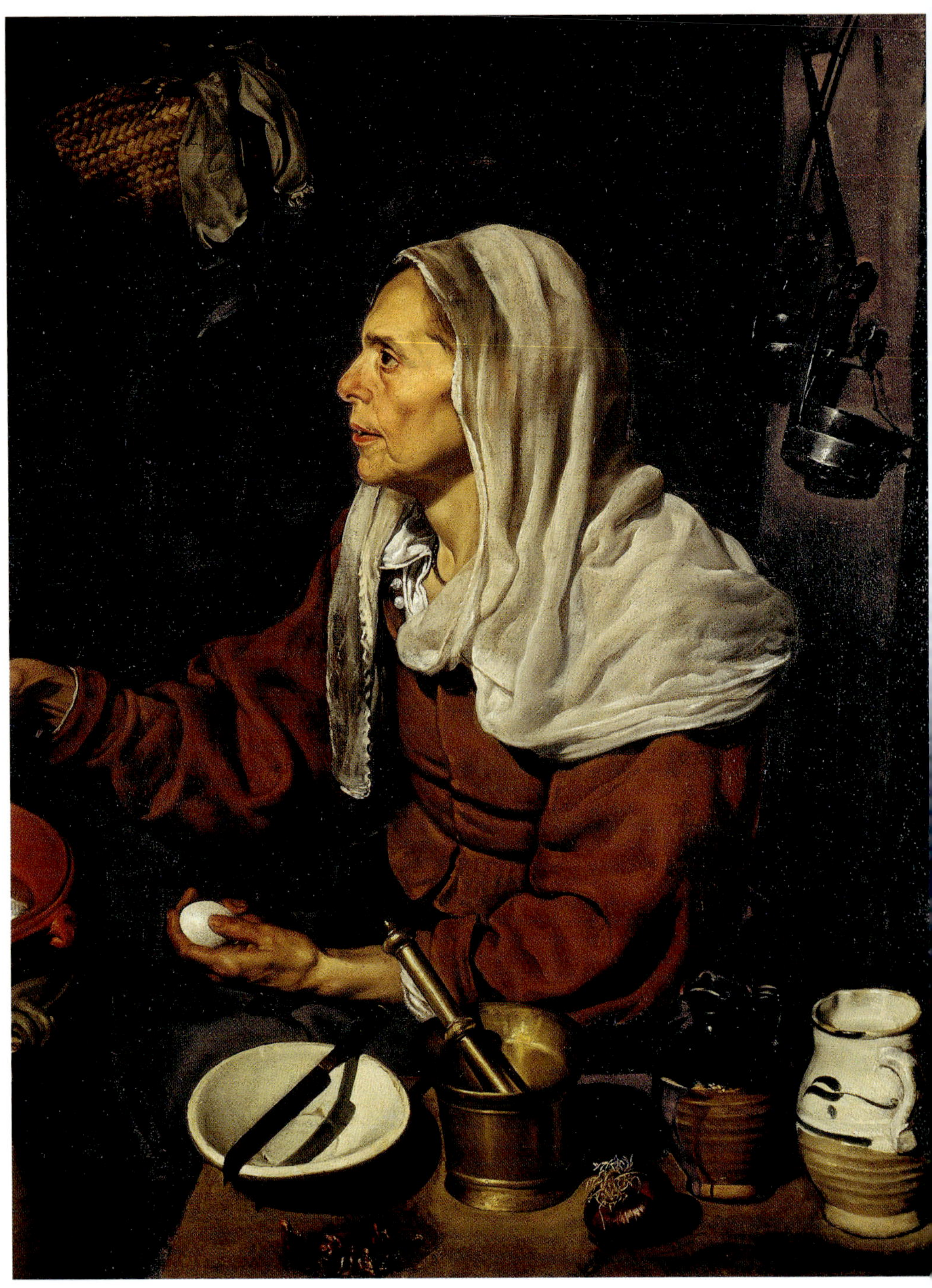

2 *Old Woman Cooking Eggs*, 1618, detail

Chapter 1
A Teenage Prodigy

Nature and circumstance looked favourably upon Velázquez from the very start. Nature gifted him with genius as a painter, so much so that he was already attracting acolytes and imitators from his earliest years, while circumstances closely aligned his birth with that of the future Spanish king Philip IV (1605–65), whose appetite for art would prove insatiable and at whose court Velázquez would serve for nearly four decades of his career. The two were well matched, Philip primarily desiring portraits of himself, his family and other members of the royal household, and Velázquez having already proven himself to be an expert painter of people. But such royal requests were also to place severe constraints upon the artist, except in those rare instances when he was working for others, or for himself. As a result, more than half of his surviving pictures consist of single figures formally posed. Yet if Velázquez was to enjoy relatively little freedom in his choice of subjects, his style would be entirely his own, and here he effected a revolution in painting that was to reverberate for three centuries after his death, from Goya to the Impressionists and Picasso to Francis Bacon.

*   *   *

Diego de Velázquez was baptized on 6 June 1599, the eldest of seven children of Juan Rodríguez de Silva, a notary, and Jerónima Velázquez, whose surname he adopted. Both parents claimed descent from the minor nobility – a distinction that the artist would succeed in turning to his advantage in later life. The family were natives of Seville, then the largest city

in Spain – and one of the largest in Europe – and a major
maritime and trading centre with both the East Indies and
the New World. It was also a flourishing cultural centre,
where an informal academy of poets, scholars and artists had
existed since the 1560s. In Velázquez's youth this was led by
the foremost painter in the city, Francisco Pacheco (1564–1644),
who specialized in religious paintings and portraits. After an
early education in which he showed a particular inclination
for art, Velázquez was apprenticed to Pacheco late in 1610, a
relationship that was to prove fruitful for both master and
pupil. Although Pacheco was certainly not a great painter, in
the words of Velázquez's later biographer Antonio Palomino,
'Pacheco's house was a gilded cage of art, the academy and
school of the greatest minds in Seville'. Here the young artist
was trained in the practice of painting and drawing and early
on revealed a distinct preference for studying life models.
According to Pacheco himself, who also wrote an early life of
the artist, Velázquez 'hired a little country boy to serve him
as a model in different attitudes and poses – be it crying or
laughing – without shrinking from any difficulty, and he did
many drawings in charcoal heightened with white on blue
paper after this boy and after many other subjects from nature,
so that he gained assurance in portraiture'. Although none of
these drawings survive, Velázquez's earliest paintings testify to
his dedication to working from nature and created a sensation
in Seville and beyond, marking a turning point in Spanish art.

Religious themes, portraits and (to a lesser extent) still life
painting were all practised in early seventeenth-century Spain
but scenes from everyday life (or genre paintings) existed
almost entirely in the form of imported examples, largely from
Italy and Flanders. The young Velázquez was doubtless familiar
with such works either through originals or engravings and,
in a radical departure from Pacheco's practice, set out to rival
them. In March 1617 he was granted his licence to practise
painting and a year later he married Pacheco's daughter, Juana.
By this time he had become a master at depicting scenes from
everyday life – or *bodegones* – in the just words of his master
and (now) father-in-law, 'surpassing in that genre every other
painter without exception'.

Bodegón is the Spanish for still life but, by the early
seventeenth century, it was also used to designate compositions
that combined figures with prominent still life elements,
invariably in humble settings such as a market stall, a kitchen
scene or the interior of a tavern. Velázquez was among the first
artists to depict such subjects, in seven canvases of his Sevillian
years. Their novelty and fame is apparent from the number of

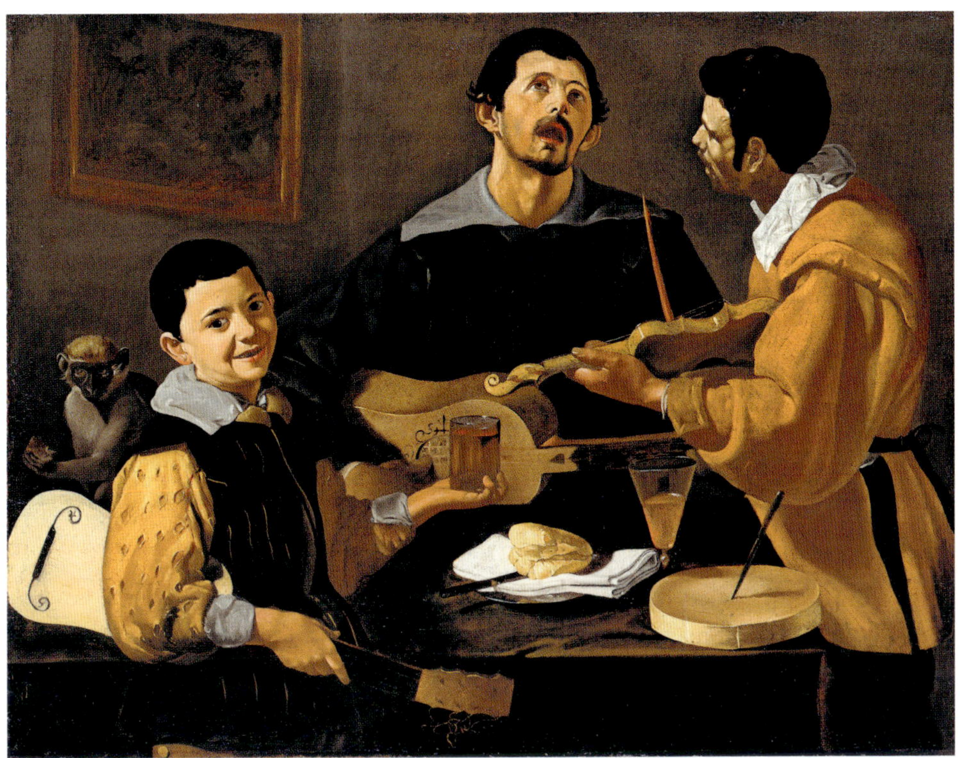

3 *The Musical Trio, c.* 1617

copies and pastiches that exist after certain of them, together
with the testimony of his early biographers.

The earliest of these is probably *The Musical Trio* of about
1617, which depicts a group of strolling players performing
around a table set out with a simple meal. Posed frontally in
the centre is a man singing and strumming a guitar. Turning
towards him on the right, another man plays the violin while,
opposite him, a youth holding a mandolin and a filled glass
stares out at the viewer with a fixed smile. Behind him sits
a monkey and above them both hangs a landscape painting
awkwardly angled on the back wall. On the table a loaf of bread,
a knife and a napkin rest on a pewter plate accompanied by
a half-filled wine glass and a round cheese stuck with a knife.
Space is weakly defined and the composition overcrowded,
but the picture leaves one in no doubt of the youthful artist's
ambition. Three figures with diverse and highly animated
poses and expressions are connected in the centre through
their converging gestures. As in all of the artist's *bodegones*

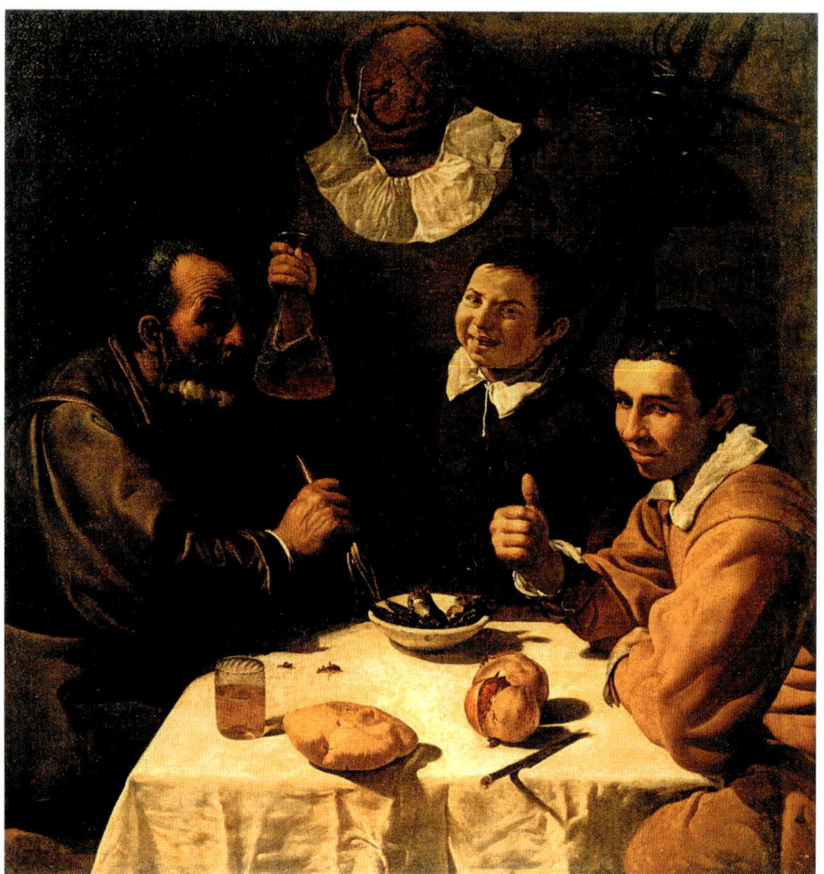

4 *Three Men at a Table*, 1617–18

the colours are earthy but subtly differentiated, ranging from black to white through grey, brown, beige and yellow. Two other Velázquez trademarks are already apparent here, which will persist throughout the artist's career. The figures have clearly been studied from life, even if they were not posed together, and the artist made changes to the painting as he went along. Beneath the broad collar of the central musician is a much narrower one which Velázquez increased in size to accentuate his prominence.

Still in a tavern setting, but now minus music and monkeys, is *Three Men at a Table*, where the poses are more restrained, the composition more cohesive and the meal marginally more generous. Three different ages come together: an old man seated in profile and holding a spring onion on the left,

a mischievously grinning youth in the centre proudly raising
a flask of wine and a roguish young man seated on the right
staring out at the viewer and giving the thumbs-up to his
cohorts' indulgences. On the table are a bowl of small fish,
two pomegranates, a loaf of bread, a glass of wine and a knife
protruding over the edge of the tablecloth. On the back wall
hang a cap and collar artfully arranged to centralize the design.
Here more than in *The Musical Trio*, still life elements assume
an even greater prominence in relation to the figures, the artist
deliberately setting himself the task of depicting different
textures and shapes, colours and light effects, from the slimy
sheen on the fish to the crusty surface of the loaf and the juicy
innards of the fruit. The result understandably strikes one as
a self-conscious demonstration piece. Velázquez has staged a
scene made up of real people and things and challenged himself
to imitate it, his discerning eye even registering the crumpled
creases in the tablecloth.

In the *Old Woman Cooking Eggs*, which is dated 1618, still
life and stilled lives are brought together in equal measure.
Arguably the most ambitious of the artist's *bodegones*, this
depicts a seated old woman preparing a meal for a youth who
enters the scene on the left bearing a flask in one hand and a
melon in the other. Accompanying the figures is the still life: an
onion and some chillies, a mortar and pestle, two glazed jugs
and a gleaming brass pot. On the back wall hang some oil lamps
and, in the centre, a basket and piece of grey cloth, pinning
the design into place much as Velázquez had done with the
cap and collar in *Three Men at a Table*. The two figures appear
in a state of suspended animation, their hands in motion but
their gazes not meeting. In place of their interaction is that of
the artist's own eyes with this scene. The shadow cast by the
knife on the bowl, the discolorations on a melon or stains in a
glaze, the striking reflections off glass, pewter and brass and
(most wondrous of all) the coagulation of the egg whites as they
cook and the glimpse of the old woman's left ear as it peers
through her headscarf – what a tour de force of observation and
execution. To be sure, the picture is very busy and overcrowded
and the viewer given a lot of work to do. But no one could fault
its ambition or mastery, or Velázquez's youthful desire to grasp
and conquer so much at once.

Also dated 1618 is *Christ in the House of Martha and Mary*,
which introduces a new feature to Velázquez's art, and one that
would re-emerge at the end of his career: that of a picture within
the picture. In the foreground a sullen young kitchen maid
pauses while grinding a pestle and mortar. She is preparing
a simple meal of a plate of fish, two eggs, chillies and garlic.

6

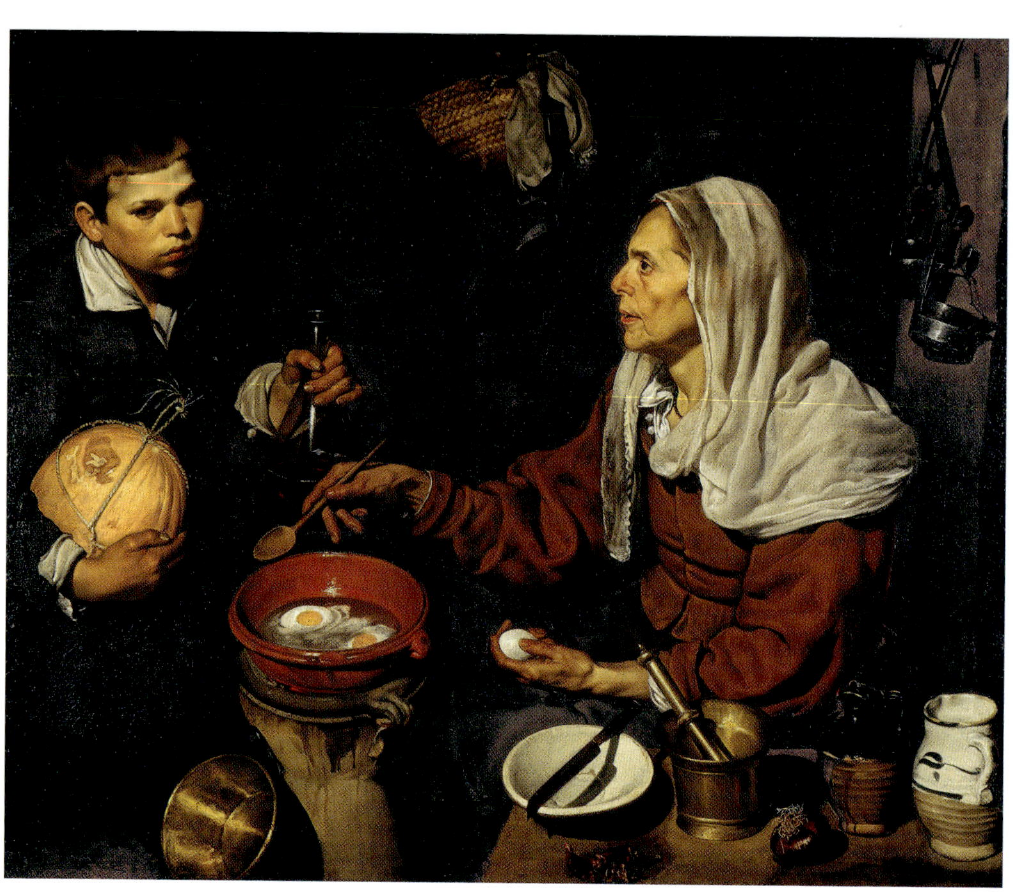

5 *Old Woman Cooking Eggs*, 1618

Behind her is an old woman – perhaps the same model previously depicted cooking eggs – who raises her right hand either to admonish her youthful companion to get on with her task or to direct her to the scene visible through a hatch in the background. Here Christ visits the house of Mary and Martha, an event recounted in Luke 10:38–42. While Martha busied herself serving him, Mary sat at his feet and listened to his words. When Martha complained to Jesus that her sister was not helping her, Christ replied:

> *Martha, Martha, thou art careful and troubled about many things: But one thing is needful: and Mary hath chosen that good part which shall not be taken away from her.*

The differing roles of the two sisters later came to symbolize the active and contemplative life, Martha's service to the Lord being great but Mary's absorption in his teachings even greater.

8   Closely related to this painting is the *Kitchen Maid with the Supper at Emmaus*, where another episode from Luke's gospel (24:30–31) is depicted at the rear. The risen Christ and two disciples are seated at a table. When the Lord breaks bread, he is recognized by them, and suddenly vanishes. (The picture has been cut at the left, removing one of the disciples.) In the foreground is another kitchen scene. A serving maid pauses meditatively from her labours amidst a discreet arrangement of crockery and utensils.

Velázquez derived the idea of inserting a biblical scene into the background of one from everyday life from the Netherlandish artists Pieter Aertsen (1508/9–1575) and his pupil Joachim Beuckelaer (*c*. 1533–1573/4), both of whom had popularized such compositions in the late sixteenth century. Paintings and engravings of these are already recorded in Spain in Velázquez's day and he may well have caught sight of
7   a print after Aertsen's *Kitchen Scene with the Supper at Emmaus* in Pacheco's studio. But at least two questions remain. How do the biblical and kitchen scenes relate to each other in both the northern examples and Velázquez's reinterpretation of them, and how does he modify and improve upon them?

In Aertsen's example a biblical supper scene provides a scriptural precedent for the meal being prepared in the foreground, thereby bestowing historical legitimacy on an everyday act. At a time when religious art was still dominant and genre subjects becoming increasingly popular the artistic and commercial sense of combining the two is readily understandable. But was a moral connection also intended?

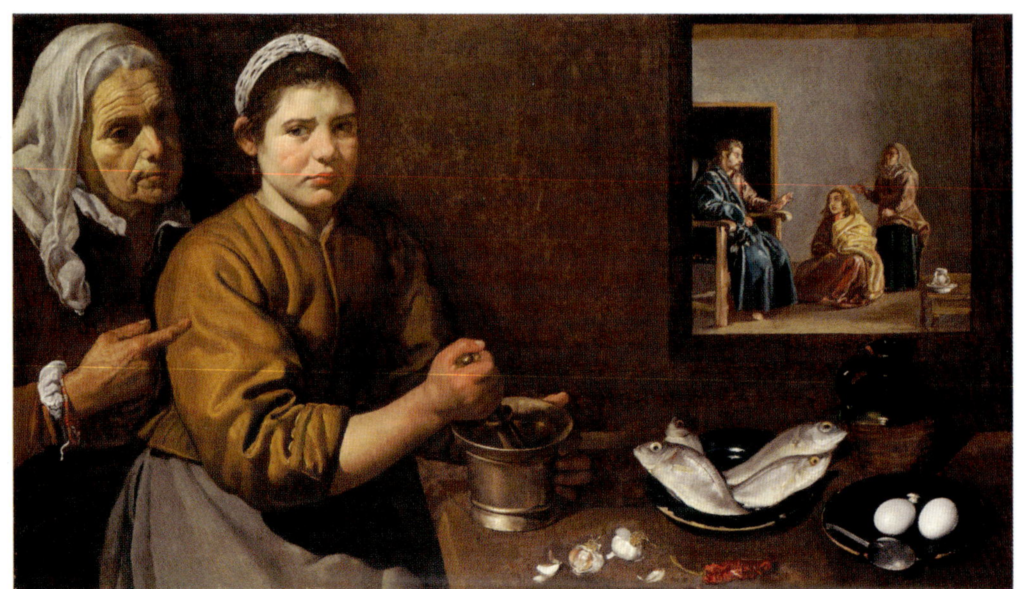

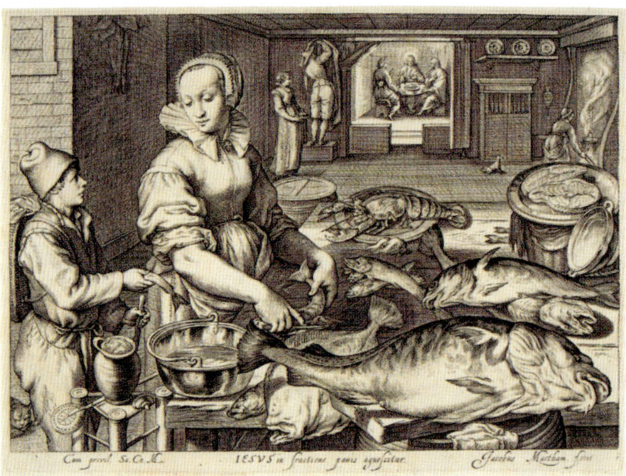

6 TOP *Christ in the House of Martha and Mary*, 1618
7 ABOVE Jacob Matham after Pieter Aertsen, *Kitchen Scene with the Supper at Emmaus*, c. 1603
8 OPPOSITE *Kitchen Maid with the Supper at Emmaus*, 1618–19

Christ's meal at Emmaus was humble whereas Aertsen's
worktable is overflowing. Velázquez alters this, his still life
objects being spare, separated, serious and decidedly meagre.
But these features are common to all of his *bodegóns* and are
unlikely to carry hidden significance. Moreover, a painted
replica of the *Kitchen Maid* exists that is probably also by the
artist but lacks the biblical scene. This strongly suggests that
no necessary symbolic connection exists and that both versions
were regarded as equally marketable. What is beyond dispute,
however, is the care and scrutiny with which Velázquez has
rendered the still life objects. From the surface discolourations
in the design on a water jug to the internal anatomy of a garlic
bulb, nothing escapes Velázquez's eye. The youthful master
of the *bodegón* has already revealed himself to be a born
portraitist, even of inanimate things.

Velázquez's only upright *bodegón*, *The Waterseller of Seville*, is
also his most celebrated and well documented. Perhaps prompted
by the vertical format, the artist here treats a genre scene almost
like a portrait. Its focus is a raggedly clad old man seen in profile
who has filled a glass with water for a youth standing next to him.
Behind them is another man, shown frontally and now much
darkened, drinking from a jug, having already been served by the
old man. In the foreground on the left is a table atop which sits
a greyish-green glazed vessel with a white cup inside.

The illusionism is masterly, from the weathered and leathery
features of the waterseller to the stains and striations on his
jug and the drops of water trickling down it. The subtle and
graduated play of light and shade over the faces of both him
and the youth make those of their counterparts in the *Old
Woman Cooking Eggs* look harsh, even flat, by comparison.
And the rendering of the glass is nothing short of miraculous.

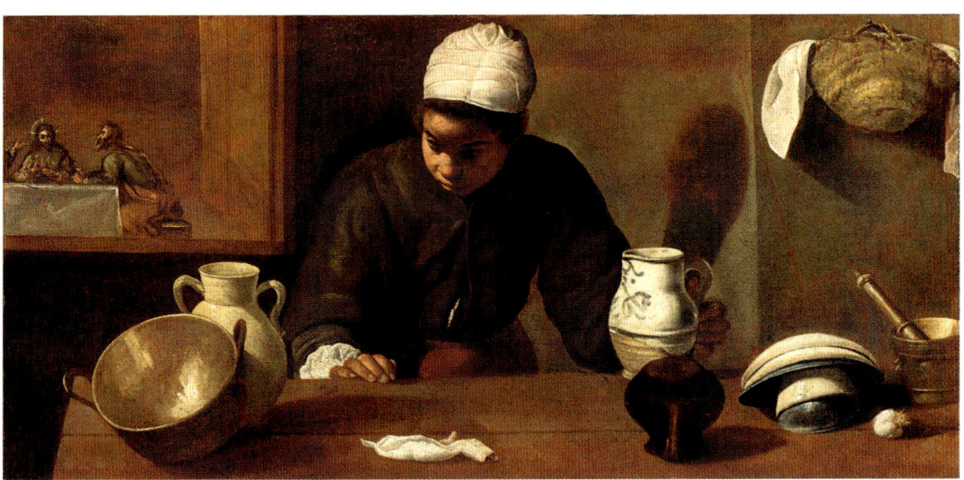

Holding a fig or glass bubble within it, its form and contents
appear conjured forth onto the canvas as though in defiance
of the pigments out of which they are made.

Velázquez took this picture with him on one of his visits
to the court in Madrid in either 1622 or 1623 and gave or sold
it to Juan de Fonseca y Figueroa, chaplain to the King. When
Figueroa died in 1627, Velázquez was called upon to value his
collection and gave the *Waterseller* his highest valuation. The
picture's later fame confirms that he had judged wisely.

The remarkable compositional coherence of the *Waterseller*
owes itself to the fact that the three still life vessels in it are
positioned exactly as are the figures, the glass mediating
between left and right as does the man drinking in the shadows
between the youth and waterseller. A similar device occurs
in another of the artist's most mature *bodegones*, *Two Young
Men at a Table*, where the men drinking form a mirror image
of the still life objects alongside them. This is Velázquez's
most hermetic and mysterious early work, the two figures
communicating scarcely more than the objects themselves.
One, with his back to the viewer, is drinking from a bowl, the
tips of his fingers around it echoing the curls of hair on his
neck and his torn sleeve attesting to his humble station. Is
his companion slumped in a drunken stupor or is he merely
drowsing? It is impossible to be sure. But the fall of the napkin
on which he leans provides a seamless transition between the
two halves of the picture, the silence of the figures matched
by the solemnity of the still life of upturned plates, mortar
and pestle and ceramic jugs. Certain of these appear exactly
as in other of the artist's early paintings, but not the most
breathtaking one of all. This is the orange set into the lip of a
jug, which gathers together the reddish browns of the table top,
the ceramic vessels and the seated man's jerkin into a brilliant
accent of colour – the boldest in any of Velázquez's *bodegones*
and a foretaste of the great colourist to come.

The young Velázquez's decision to begin his painting career
with a group of works combining ordinary figures with still
life was both pioneering and pragmatic. No other Spanish
artist had produced such a body of works before and the
painter cannot have been sure that there would be a market
for them. But given that he was instinctively drawn to working
from nature, what better way to begin than by depicting the
people and things immediately around him, at least until more
lucrative commissions for portraits and religious paintings
came his way.

9 OPPOSITE *The Waterseller of Seville, c.* 1620

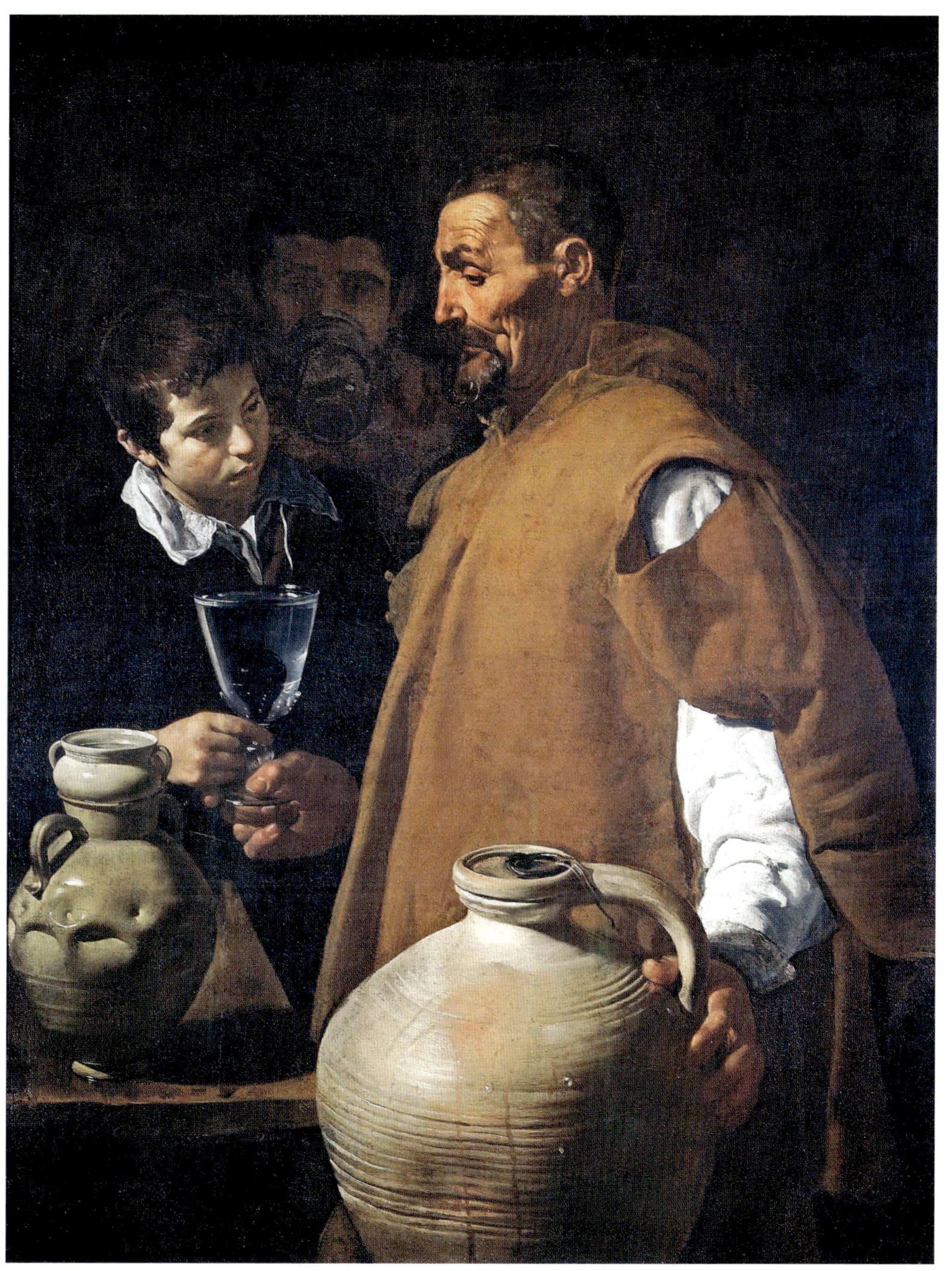

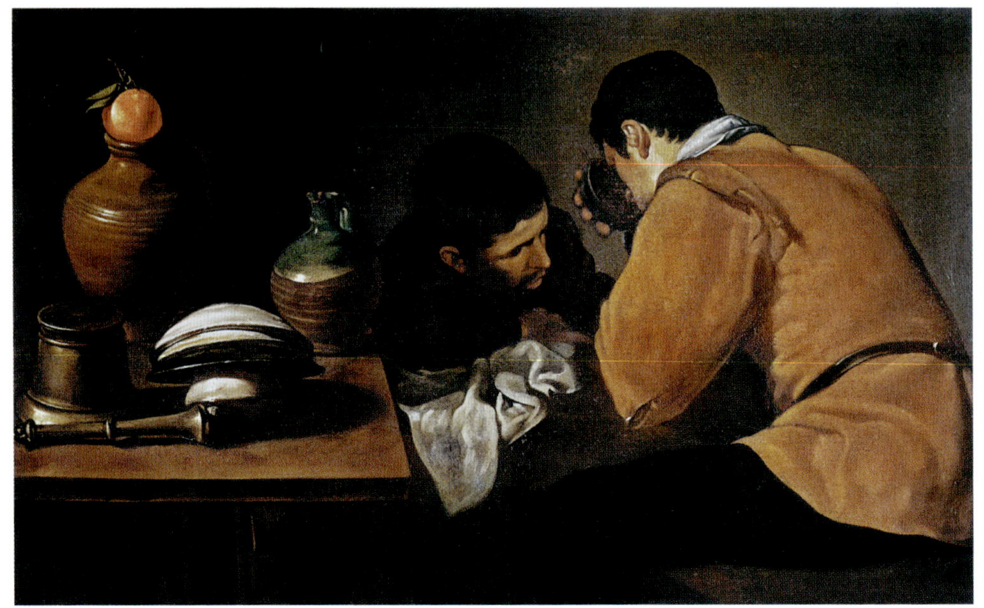

10 *Two Young Men at a Table, c. 1620*

He did not have to wait long, for about one year after being granted his licence to practise as a painter, in 1618–19, Velázquez received a commission for a pair of paintings depicting the *Immaculate Conception* and *St John the Evangelist on the Island of Patmos*, probably from the Convent of the Shod Carmelites, Nuestra Señora del Carmen, in Seville, where these pictures are first recorded in the chapter house in 1800. Both are virtually the same size and confined to a single figure, and they are also thematically related, the Virgin's purity linked to St John's vision of her in the book of Revelation. Velázquez depicts him seated and accompanied by his eagle, his pen upraised before an open book as he gazes up at 'a woman clothed with the sun, and the moon under her feet, and upon her a crown of twelve stars'. Beside her is the dragon threatening 'to devour her child as soon as it was born' (Revelation 12:1, 4). In the background on the right the artist has scored the canvas with seemingly random strokes of colour, probably cleaning his brush at the end of a painting session.

Although Pacheco and other commentators recommended that the Evangelist here be portrayed as a 'venerable old man', Velázquez depicts him as a raw-boned youth in his late teens and clearly based his likeness on the study of a life model. The same may be said for the image of the Virgin in the *Immaculate*

Conception, which would appear to be an attractive young girl also in her teens, standing and praying on a crescent moon backed by the sun and billowing clouds. Crowning her are the twelve stars mentioned in Revelation and visible in the landscape below are attributes associated with the Virgin in the Song of Songs, Ecclesiasticus and elsewhere in the Bible, among them the fountain, temple and enclosed garden – all allusions to her purity.

So, too, is Velázquez's depiction of this figure, which is immaculate in its own conception and handling. The Virgin is framed by a blue mantle which was once much lighter in tone and originally billowed across her lower legs – an alteration made by the artist himself in the course of painting in order to enhance the solemnity and statuesque nature of her pose. The modelling of her form is so sculpturesque that it is hard to believe that she is not really there, and in this she invites comparison with such polychromed wooden sculptures of the artist's native city as Juan Martínez Montañés's *Virgin of the Immaculate Conception* of 1606, where the polychromer was Pacheco himself, who often undertook such commissions. Yet the latter's own painting of this subject of about 1616 indicates that such undertakings did little to bolster the realism and immediacy of his own style. Compared with his future son-in-law's *Immaculate Conception*, that by Pacheco appears lifeless and desiccated rather than in full bloom.

Similar in size to these pictures is the recently authenticated *Tears of St Peter*, of which four painted copies are known, making it the most popular of Velázquez's early religious paintings. St Peter is shown seated and weeping in the wilderness following his denial of Christ. By his side lie the keys to the kingdom of heaven that Christ had entrusted to him, and the scene opens up at the left to reveal a distant vista similar to that seen in the *St John*.

Velázquez follows tradition in depicting St Peter as an elderly, balding man whose furrowed brow and imploring gaze reveal the extent of his guilt. Following his early practice, Velázquez clearly based this figure on the study of a life model, and what is perhaps most uncanny is how little he chose to deviate from his source. Peter is posed in a casual, workaday manner, his legs crossed and knobbly feet thrust forward. Were it not for his tearful expression and heavenward gaze he might easily be mistaken for a tired traveller taking a break from a trek through the woods. Even more defiantly earthbound is Velázquez's treatment of his hands. Clasped or joined hands are traditional in depictions of the penitent St Peter, but they are normally joined in a prayer for forgiveness rather than rested on the saint's knees, as here.

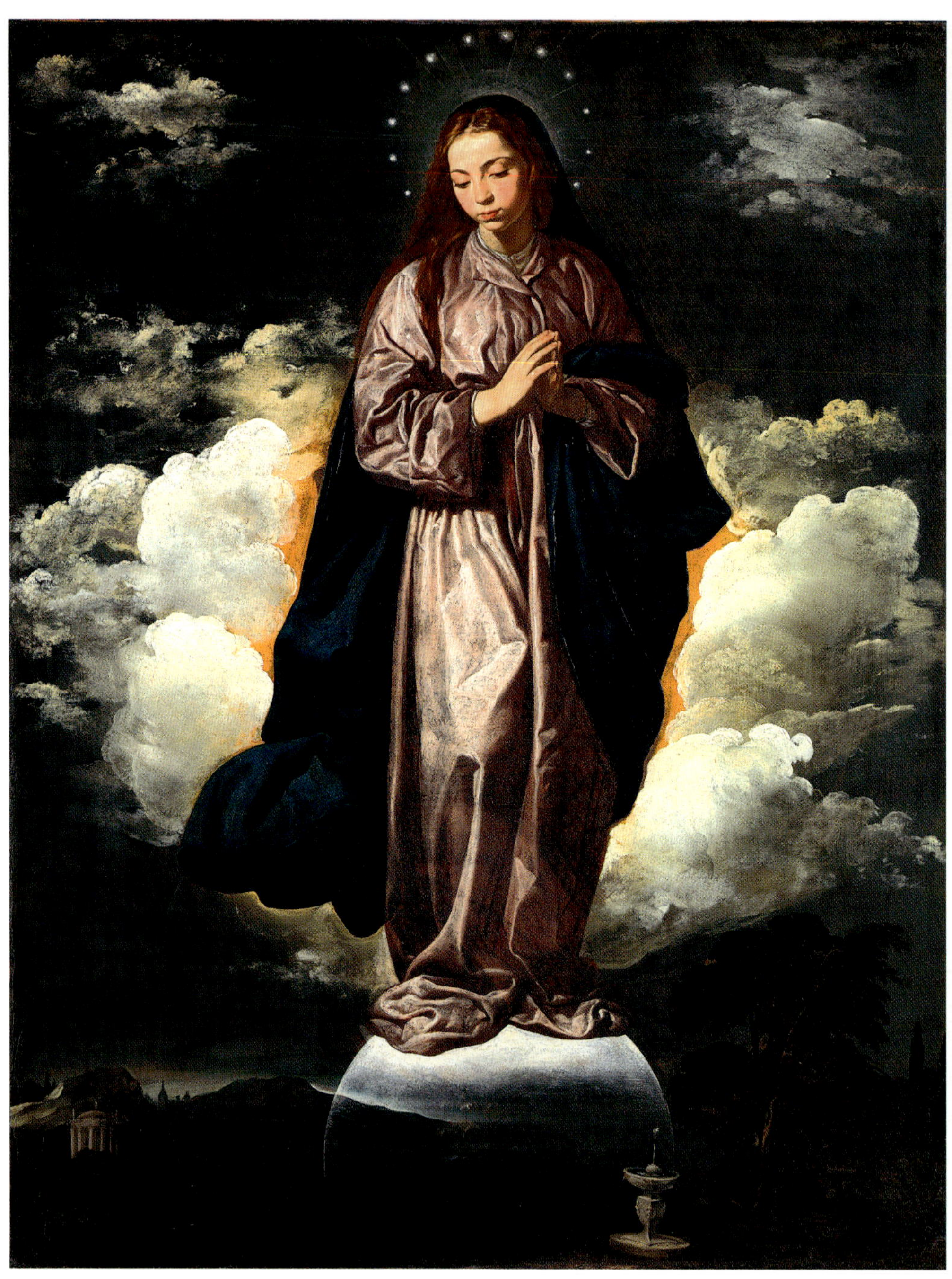

11 *The Immaculate Conception*, c. 1619

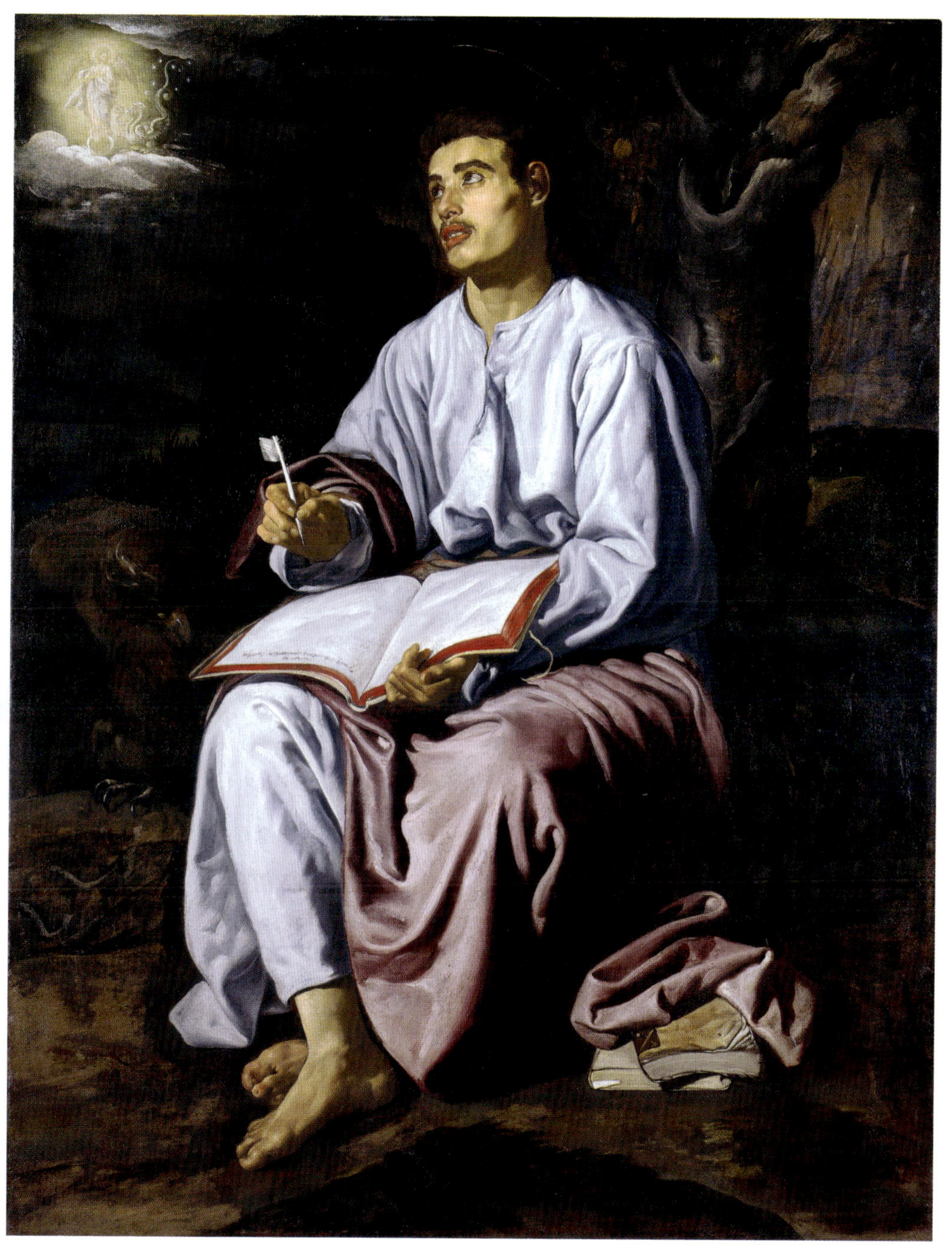

12 *St John the Evangelist on the Island of Patmos, c.* 1619

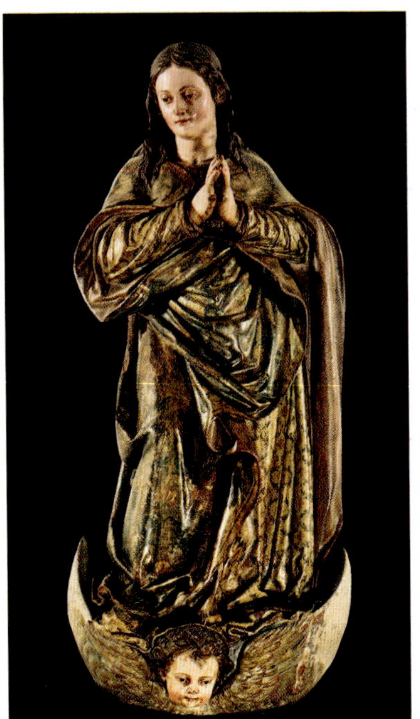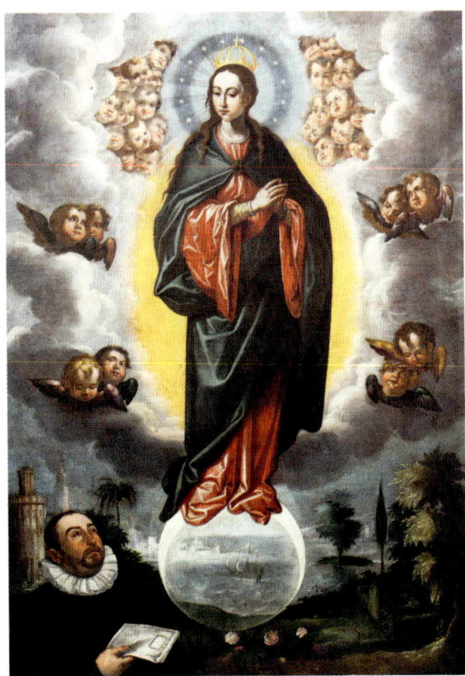

13 ABOVE LEFT Juan Martínez Montañés, *The Virgin of the Immaculate Conception*, 1606
14 ABOVE RIGHT Francisco Pacheco, *Immaculate Conception with Miguel del Cid*, c. 1616

In 1619 Velázquez was commissioned to paint an *Adoration of the Magi* for the Jesuit Noviciate of San Luis in Seville, where it was probably intended to serve as an altarpiece in the Chapel of the Novices. This was his most ambitious work to date, involving multiple figures and still life objects in an architectural and landscape setting. The result is only a qualified success as all of these elements have been slotted into their positions on the canvas in a tiered and overcrowded arrangement in which spatial reality scarcely figures. Instead it seems the higher up the heads of the figures are, the further back they must be. But where is there room for their bodies?

The figures themselves, however, are intensely realistic, with the artist again basing them on life models. The three Magi are accompanied by a young servant who bears more than a passing resemblance to the youth in the *Waterseller*. The three kings are all strikingly differentiated in age and appearance, and if it is hard to imagine where the body of the eldest Magus might fit, it is easy to admire the sweeping and voluminous folds of the garment worn by the kneeling king in the foreground. On the right a youthful Joseph, seen in profile,

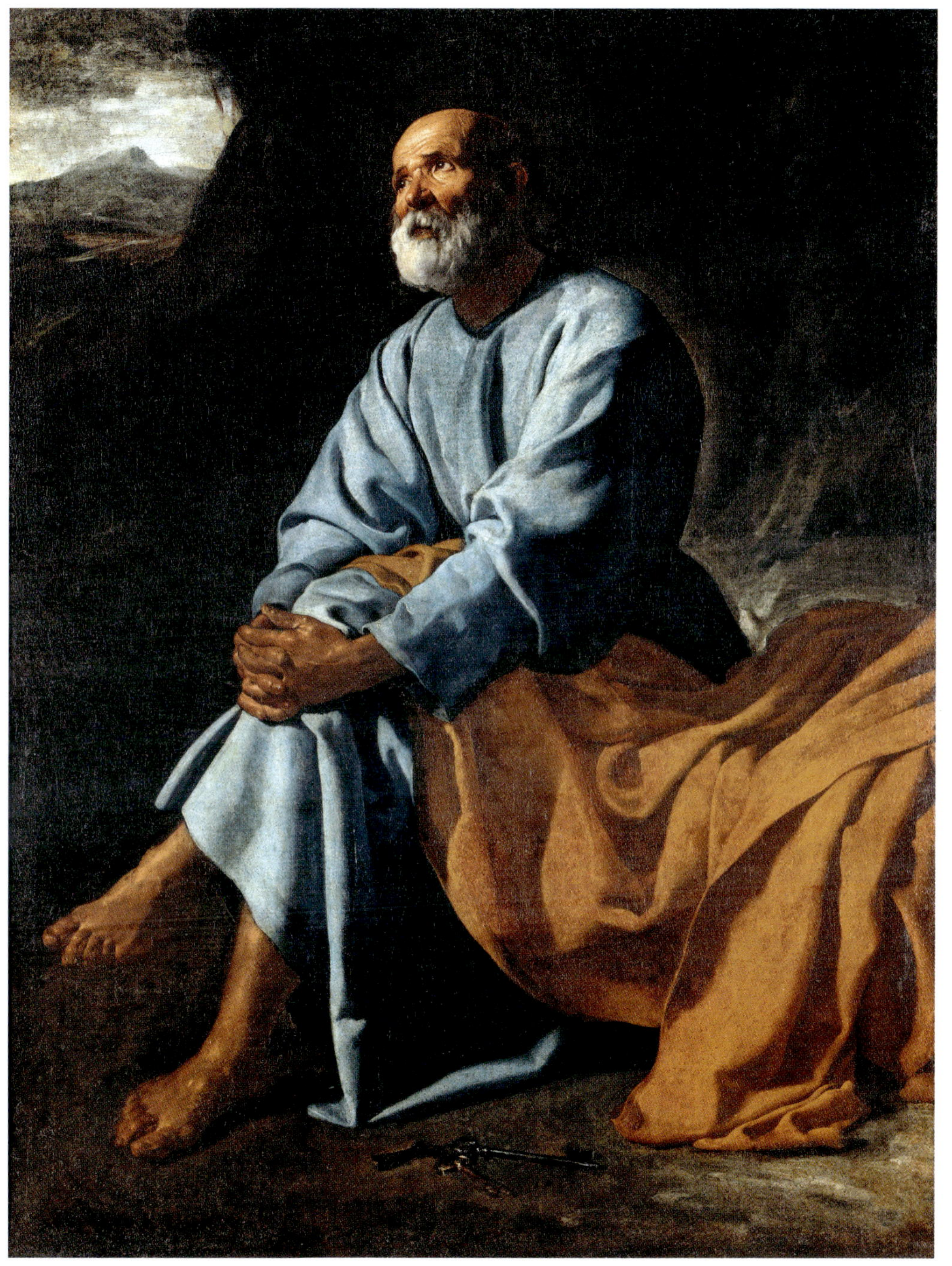

15 *The Tears of St Peter*, 1618–19

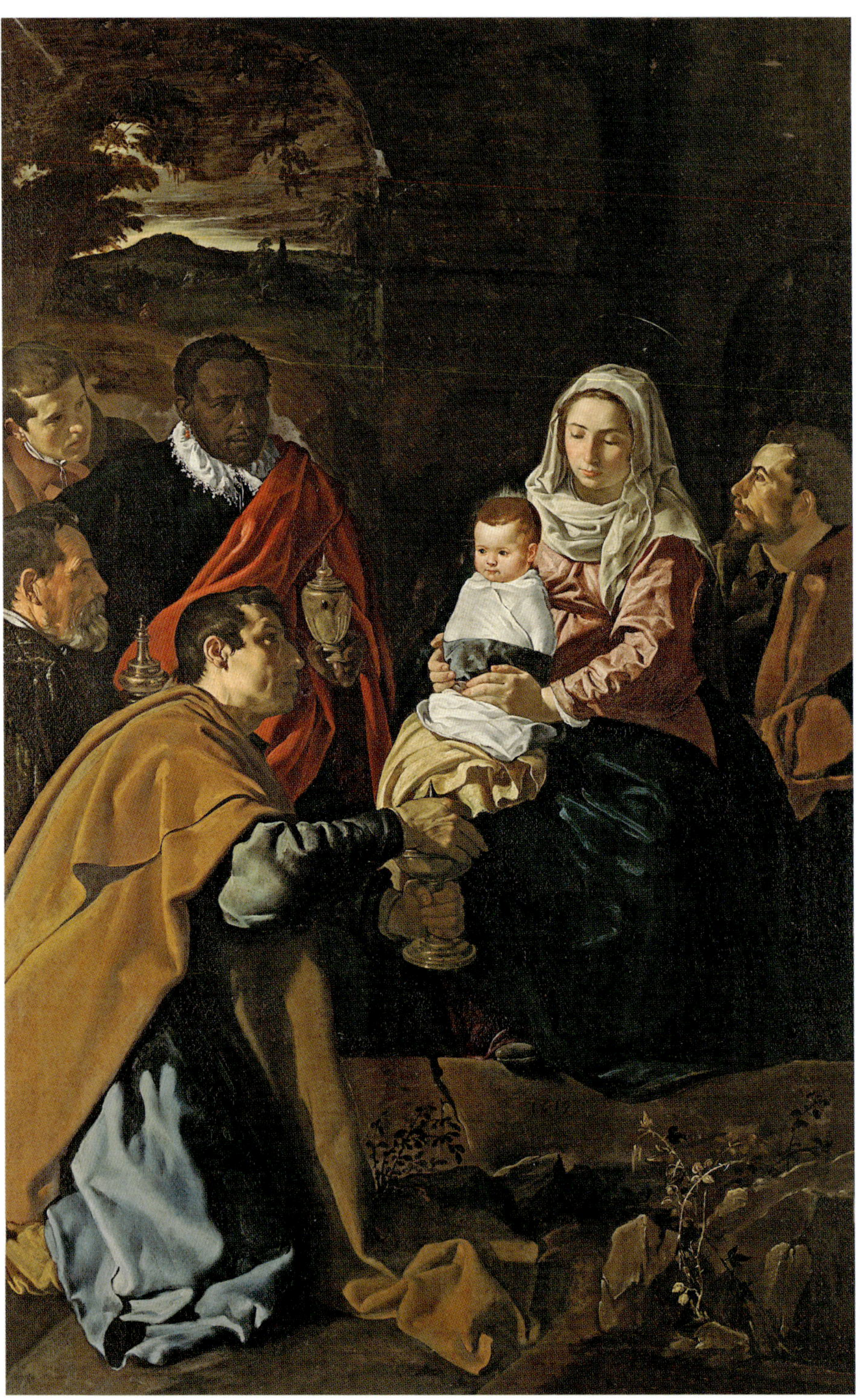

gazes up at the Virgin, who is proudly presenting the swaddled
Christ child to the Magi. He is portrayed as a beaming baby boy
consisting largely of a head and torso, whose legs must be taken
for granted. Above the group is the much darkened arch of a
building and a landscape lit by early morning light, which may
allude to the coming of a new dawn with the birth of Christ.
On the bottom right the Virgin rests her foot on a ledge bearing
the picture's date and a sprig of thorn, a clear reference to
the Crown of Thorns and the Passion.

The earthy realism with which Velázquez depicts this
scene – the Virgin's halo barely visible, the Christ child as a
bandaged baby, and the kings with no crowns – would be a
hallmark of the artist's treatment of biblical and mythological
subjects throughout his career. For him, the imaginary world
could only be conceived in terms of what he knew – and could
see. Thus, when he was commissioned for paintings of two of the
apostles during these same years, he again had them posed for
him. Inscribed at the upper left with the names of St Paul and
St Thomas, these three-quarter-length canvases probably formed
part of a series of the twelve apostles of which nothing more is
known. St Paul is depicted as a pensive and sensitive old man,
his gaze distant and brow furrowed. He holds a large volume of
his Epistles but is lacking his usual sword, the instrument of his
martyrdom. Although the lower portion of his torso is somewhat
weakly defined, the tenebrous colour and lighting coupled with
his introspective demeanour anticipate comparable figures by
Rembrandt, who repeatedly painted the apostles.

St Thomas is cast as a handsome youth shown in profile
and leaning forward, bearing his attributes of a large book
and a lance, symbolic of his evangelical teachings and of his
martyrdom in India. Posed against a dark background and
powerfully lit, the broad heavy folds of his cloak appear as
tangible as those in the *Waterseller*, further proof that for this
young painter the divine and the mundane could co-exist.

The most daring demonstration of this from Velázquez's
Sevillian years is *St Ildefonso Receiving the Chasuble from the Virgin*,
a much damaged picture which, judging by its freer handling
and more atmospheric lighting, probably dates from about 1622–
23. This commemorates a miracle that occurred to the Archbishop
of Toledo, St Ildefonso, in the seventh century. As a reward for
his many writings attesting to the virginity of the Mother of
Christ, she appeared to him one night in the city's cathedral and
bestowed upon him a chasuble as a measure of her gratitude.

16 OPPOSITE *The Adoration of the Magi*, 1619

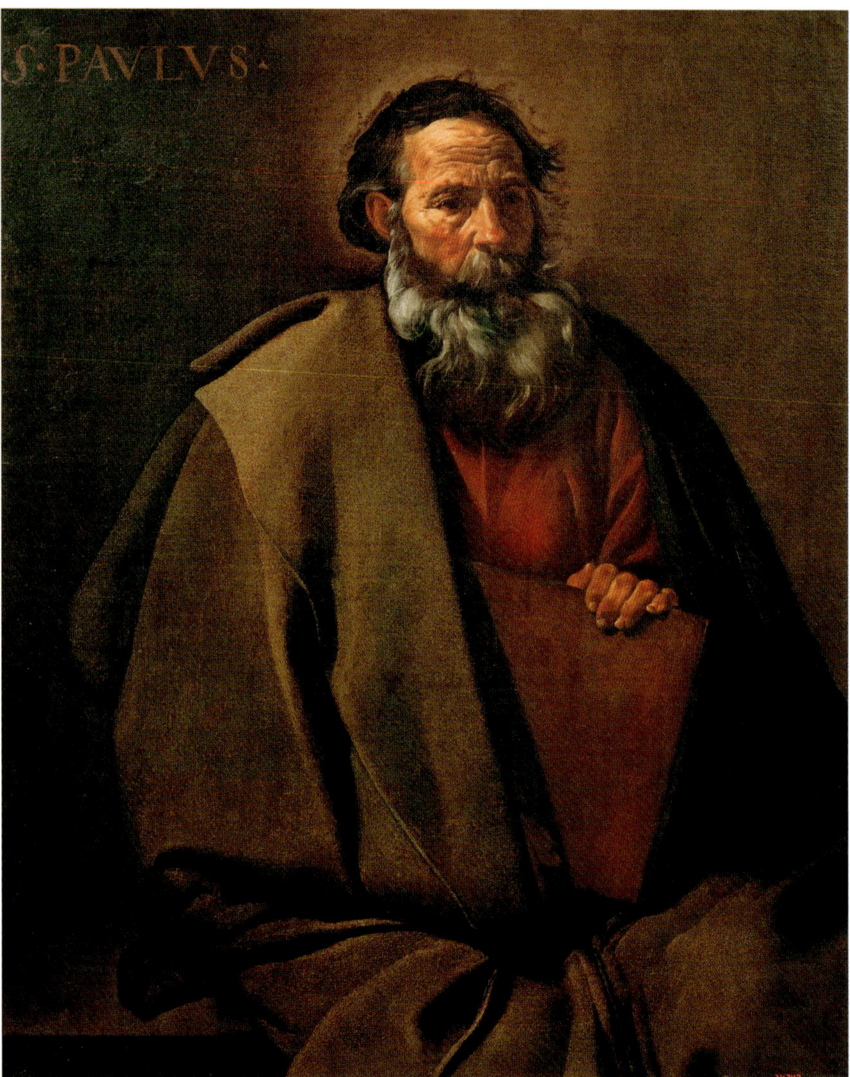

17 *St Paul*, 1619–20

In Velázquez's picture the chasuble itself separates the divine from the human. Seated on a bank of cloud and accompanied by maiden angels, the Virgin envelops the kneeling archbishop with her divine gift. She is portrayed as a shy young girl with her eyes downcast and lacks either a halo or an aureole. Similarly, the angels have no wings and do not hover or float but sit quietly and converse in the clouds, their

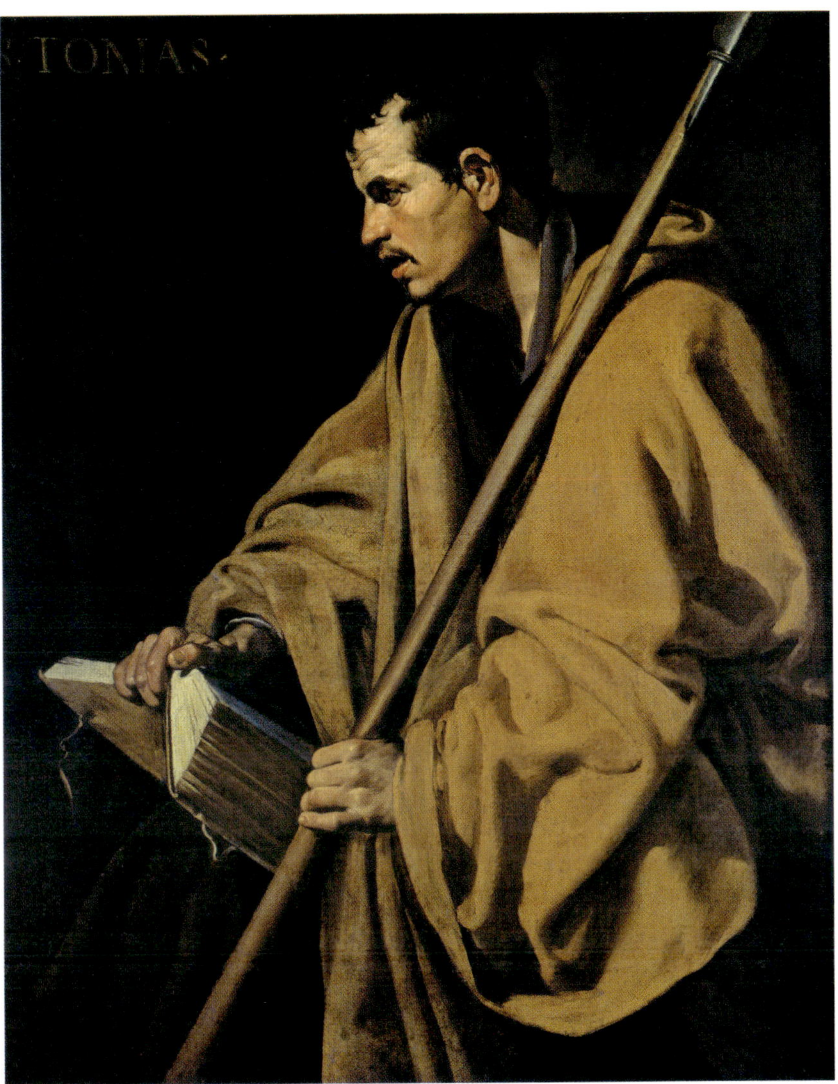

18 *St Thomas*, 1619–20

hairstyles subtly differentiated like those of ordinary humans. Even more down to earth is the portrayal of the archbishop. Wearing none of the regalia of his office nor the habit of the Benedictine order to which he belonged, he is depicted as a humble cleric, whose soulful expression and gaunt, ascetic features (as so often in early Velázquez) belong to the world of the portrait.

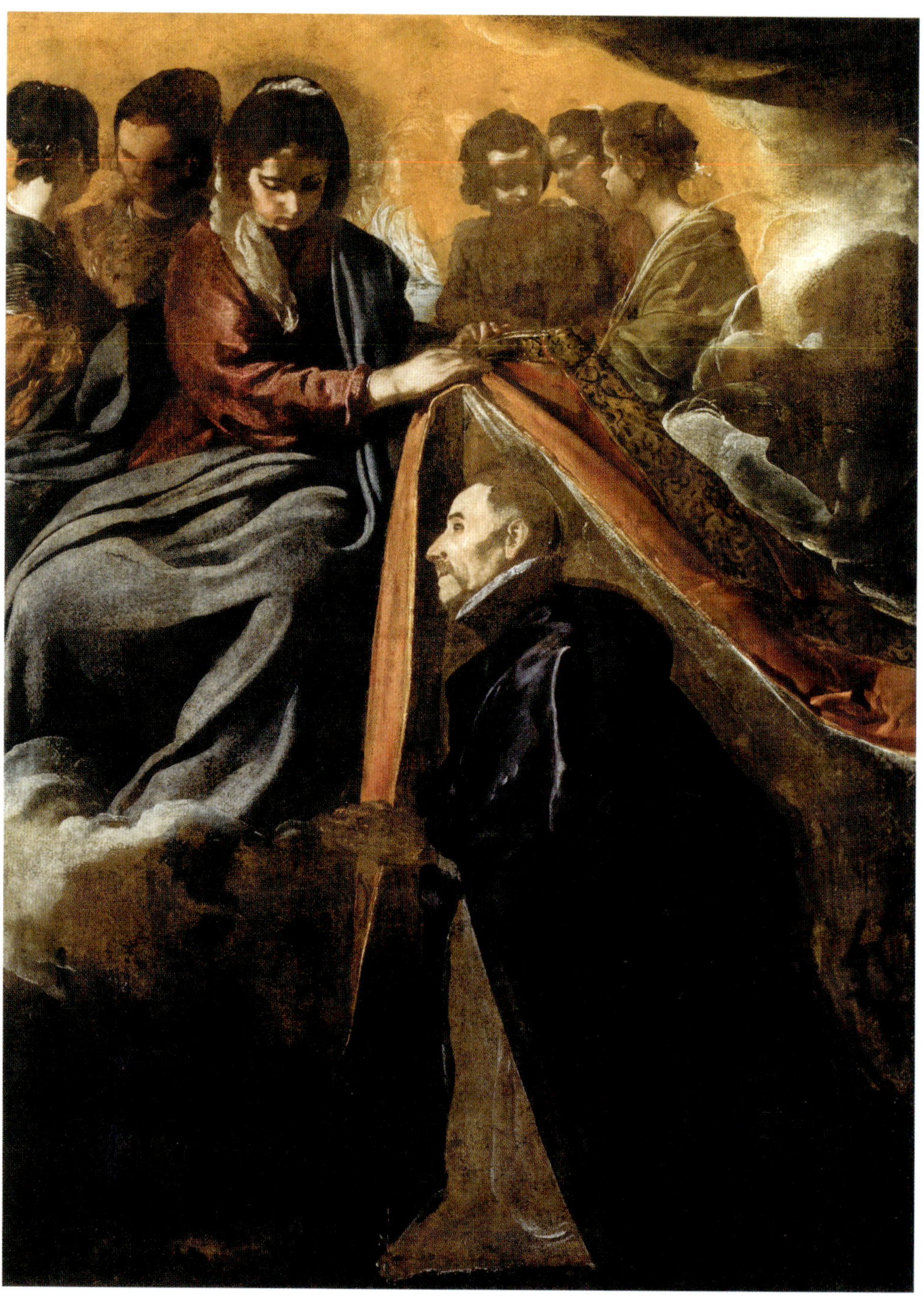

The young artist received his first two portrait commissions in 1620, both full length and depicting ecclesiastical sitters but otherwise strongly contrasting. One was destined to be displayed above the tomb of an already deceased cleric and the other to commemorate the departure of a formidable nun on a mission to the Philippines to win converts to the faith.

20

Cristóbal Suárez de Ribera was a priest who had acted as godparent to Pacheco's daughter Juana, born in 1602. As Velázquez was to marry her in 1618, it is likely that the artist received this commission through the auspices of his teacher and father-in-law. The portrait was intended to hang in the funerary chapel of the sitter, who had died in 1618 at the age of sixty-eight. Since Suárez de Ribera looks younger than this in Velázquez's picture, the artist may have relied on a much earlier likeness when devising this work.

The sitter is depicted kneeling and holding a book as he points towards the high altar of the Chapel of San Hermenegild in Seville, which is believed to have once contained a statue of this martyred sixth-century Spanish saint by Montañés. Suárez de Ribera had built this chapel between 1606 and 1616 and was especially devoted to the cult of this saint, whose emblems of a hatchet, palm and cross crowned with a wreath of roses are visible on the cartouche hanging at the upper left of the work. The cypresses and cedars seen through a window on the opposite side may be an allusion to death and resurrection. As befits the setting and function of the picture it is solemn, serious and plain. Its purpose, after all, was to introduce the viewer to a sculpture of the chapel's patron saint. As was so often to be the case with Velázquez, however, its power derives from its sheer ineloquence.

21, 22

Mother Jerónima de la Fuente was a nun in the Convent of the Poor Clares, Santa Isabel de los Reyes, in Toledo, which she entered at the age of fourteen and which was pledged to silence. In April 1620 she left Toledo on a journey to Manila to found a sister convent in the Spanish Philippines, stopping en route in Seville for two months beginning in June of that year, when Velázquez painted two nearly identical versions of her portrait silhouetted against a plain dark background. Staring us straight in the eye and with her lips pursed, she wields the crucifix like a weapon, bent on compelling the viewer to adopt her faith. The banderole on the left speaks for her with the words: 'I shall be satisfied, when I awake, with thy likeness' (Psalm 17:15). (This was mistakenly removed from the version in the Prado.) Above is a quotation in Latin aimed

19 OPPOSITE *St Ildefonso Receiving the Chasuble from the Virgin*, 1622–23

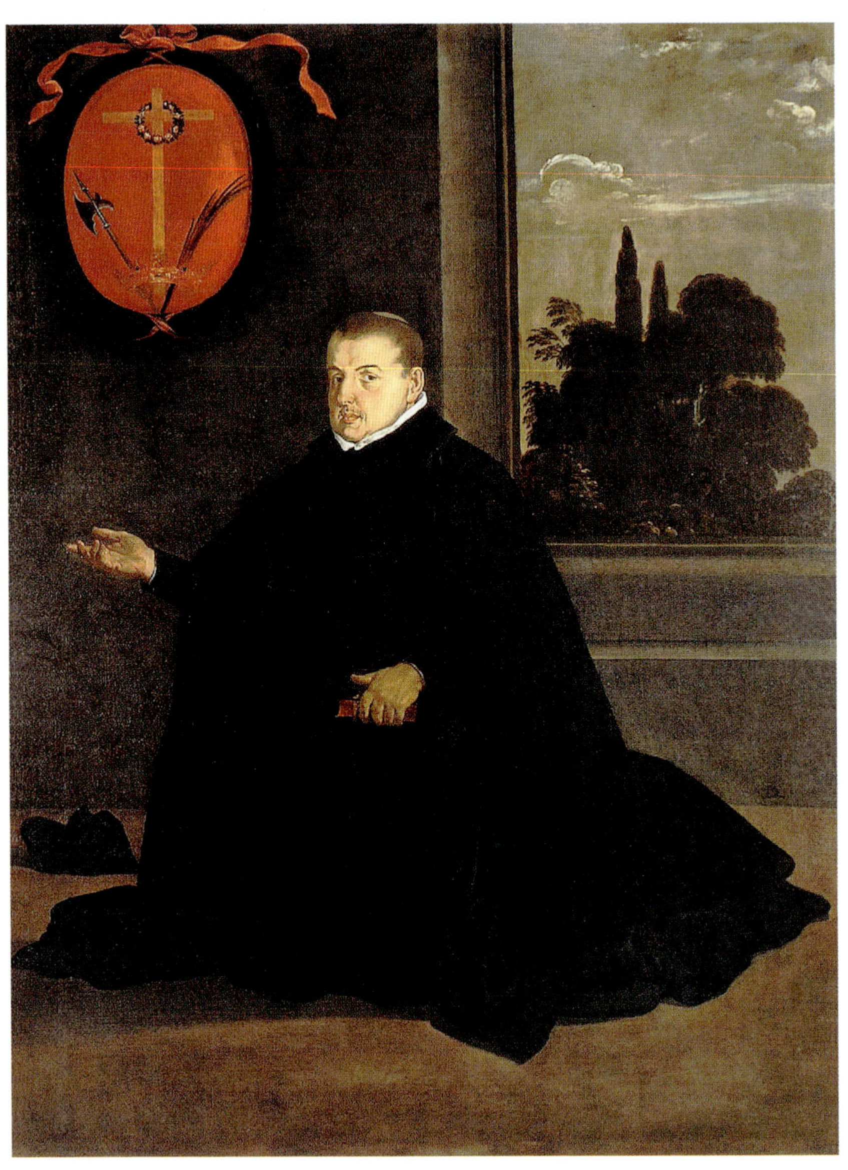

20 *Don Cristóbal Suárez de Ribera*, 1620

at anyone daring to contradict this: 'It is good that a man should both hope and quietly wait for the salvation of the Lord' (Lamentations 3:26). The long inscription in Spanish at the bottom of both works was added later, once the two canvases had travelled to the convent in Toledo and after de la Fuente had successfully founded one in Manila, where she died in 1630. Although the two versions are nearly identical, there are subtle differences between them, most notably the angle at which the crucifix is held in the second version, which renders it more visible – and formidable. In addition, pentimenti are visible in the outlines of the nun's cloak in the original canvas, as are Velázquez's characteristic wipings of his brush at the upper right.

Here, at the outset of his career as a portraitist, Velázquez reveals his unflinching determination to tell the truth. A single, full-length figure posed frontally and centrally against a plain background; no fuss or flourishes, and no distractions for the eye save for a snatch of rope that has escaped from under her gown, together with the vice-like grip of her hands on the crucifix and book. Who would dare to cross her, or to doubt that her mission would succeed?

The Venerable Mother Jerónima de la Fuente is the most ambitious and original of Velázquez's Sevillian portraits, but it was not the last. In the early 1620s he also executed a bust-length portrait of an unknown man wearing a moustache and goatee and a ruff collar that is striking for the plasticity of its modelling and its dramatic play of light and shade. With a thoughtful and intense expression, his brow slightly troubled and his thoughts seemingly elsewhere, he bears further testimony to the extent to which the young artist was increasingly concerned to explore his sitters' inner lives.

This is the most striking difference between Velázquez's early portrait style and that of Pacheco, on which it was modelled. The latter executed a series of portrait drawings in the course of his career that comprised a *Libro de retratos*, or *Book of Portraits*, of eminent scholars, artists and theologians, among them a chalk drawing of an anonymous man wearing a laurel wreath around his forehead which identifies him as a poet. It is conscientiously drawn and shaded and the man's features are carefully described, but it penetrates little deeper than his outward appearance, ignoring the soul within. Velázquez's *Portrait of a Man with a Ruff Collar* is not as painstakingly descriptive, foregoing details of the sitter's costume and shrouding his facial features in shadow and mystery. Yet, if it shows less, it tells more.

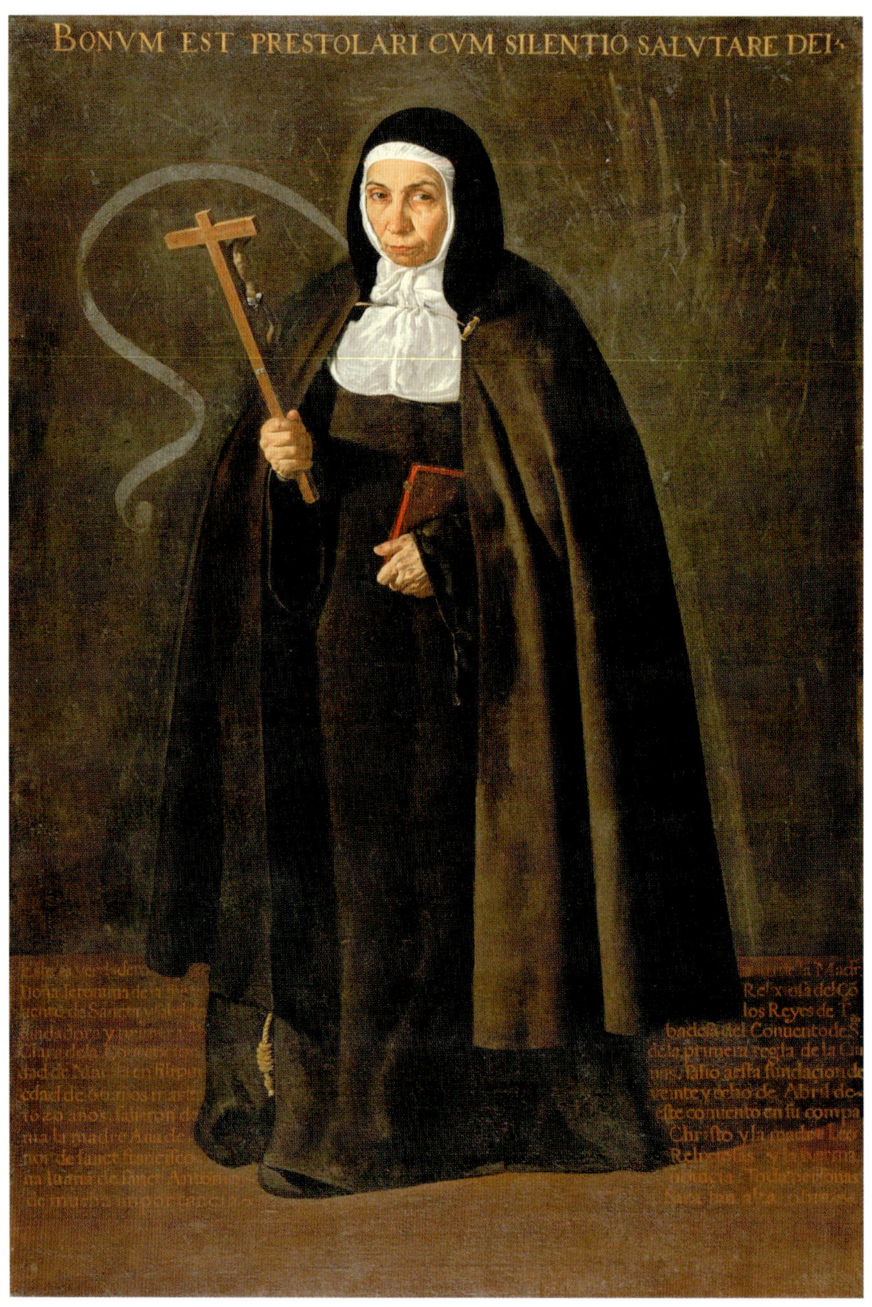

21 *The Venerable Mother Jerónima de la Fuente, 1620*

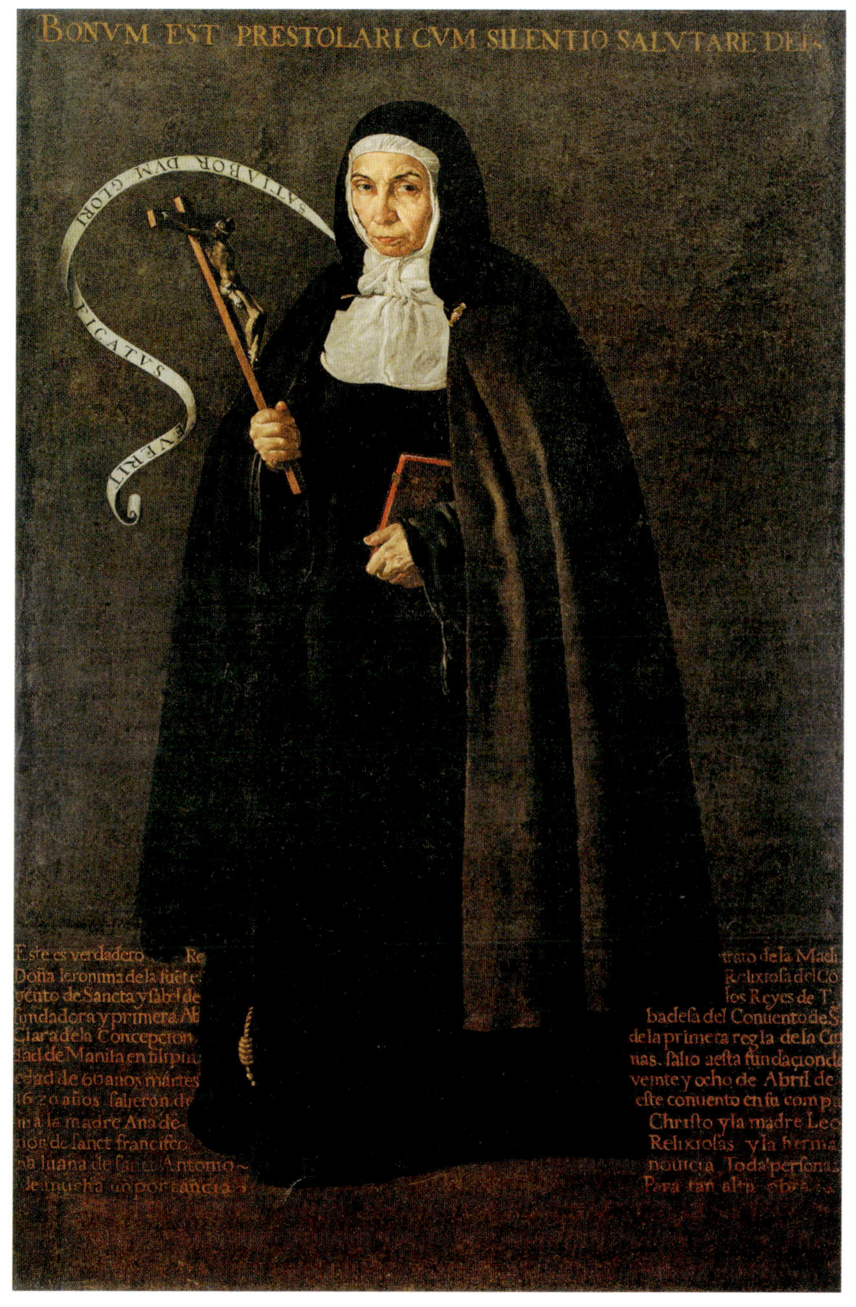

22 *The Venerable Mother Jerónima de la Fuente*, 1620

A Teenage Prodigy

33

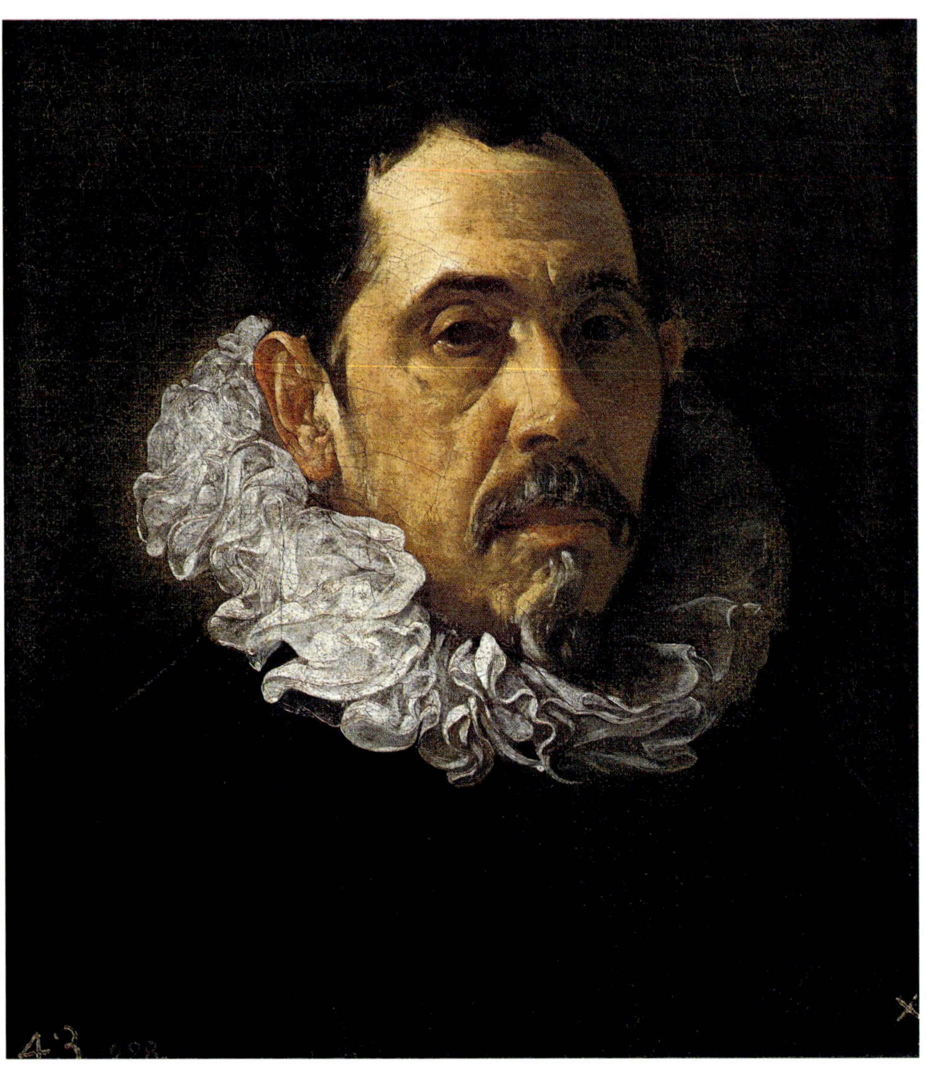

23 ABOVE *Portrait of a Man with a Ruff Collar*, 1620–22
24 OPPOSITE Francisco Pacheco, *Man Wearing a Laurel Wreath*

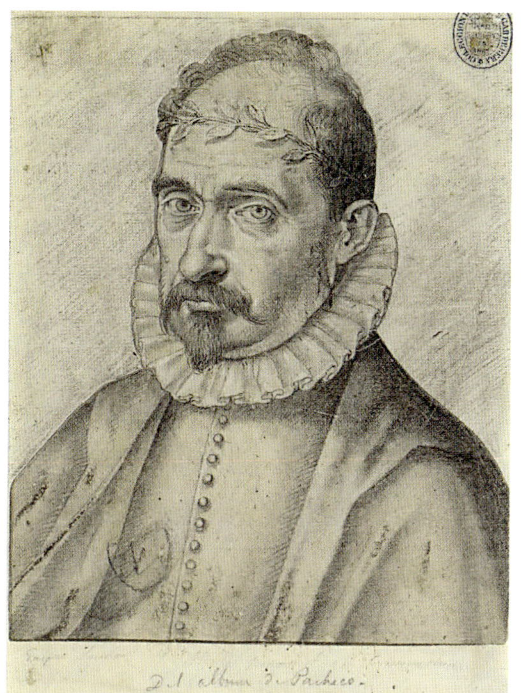

In spring 1622 Velázquez paid a visit to the court at Madrid, hoping to paint a portrait of the King and Queen, which never came to pass, and also armed with a request from Pacheco. This was to paint a likeness of the celebrated poet from Cordoba, Luis de Góngora, who was then chaplain to the King. Pacheco doubtless wished to add this to his *Libro de retratos*, although no such drawing of the poet survives. But several painted copies of Velázquez's bust of Góngora do exist and it also furnished the source for engraved portraits of him. Given the strength of the characterization, this is hardly surprising.

Góngora stares out at the viewer, his brow tensed and mouth downturned. The broad and bony expanse of his forehead, his hooked nose and the slightly suspicious nature of his gaze – all of these bring the poet masterfully to life. So, too, does the powerful modelling, a darker background on the left throwing the lit half of Góngora's face into sharp relief and complementing the tonal contrasts on the opposite side. Again, simplicity speaks volumes, but it nearly did not. Initially, Velázquez painted a laurel wreath crowning Góngora, a learned allusion to his profession of which Pacheco would doubtless have approved. But the artist

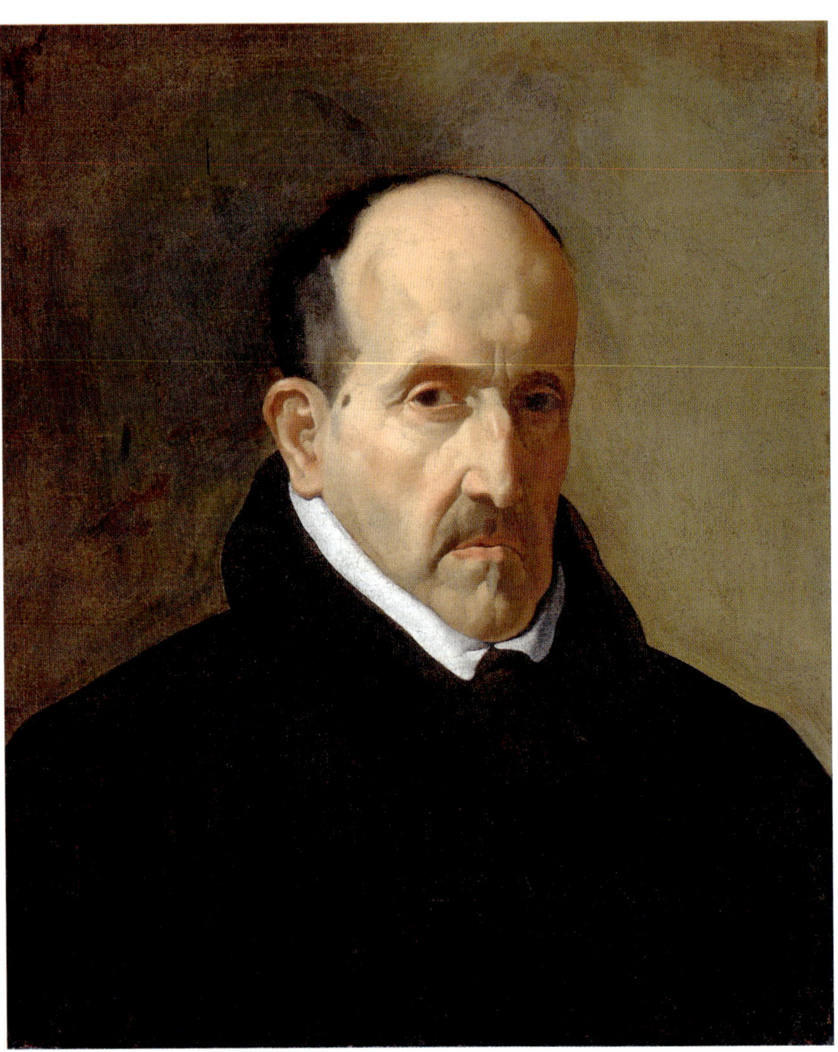

25 *Portrait of Don Luis de Góngora, 1622*

eventually painted this out, leaving only the bare truth
to prevail, devoid of allegorical frippery.

Since the portrait of Góngora had been requested by
Pacheco, Velázquez must have taken it back to Seville with
him on his return there, leaving behind no evidence of his
prowess as a portraitist in the Spanish capital. According
to Pacheco, however, he did leave behind 'an admirer of his
painting'. This was Don Juan de Fonseca, Chief Officer of his
Majesty's Chapel, who was asked to summon him back to
Madrid in 1623 by the Count-Duke of Olivares, minister to the
recently crowned King Philip IV. Olivares had close contacts
with Seville, including members of Pacheco's academy, which
may help to explain his invitation to the young painter, who
returned to the capital in that year, where he was a guest at the
house of Fonseca. There, Pacheco relates, 'he was feted and
served, and painted [Fonseca's] portrait'. When this picture,
which is now lost, was taken to the palace, it immediately
impressed all who saw it, including the King, 'which was
the greatest distinction it could receive'. It was then decided
that he should next paint a portrait of the King, which was
accomplished on 30 August 1623. Upon seeing this, Olivares
summoned Velázquez, promising him that from then on
'he alone would portray His Majesty, and that [all] the other
portraits [of him] would be removed'.

Chapter 2
Painter to the King

On 6 October 1623 Velázquez was appointed painter to the royal household on a salary of twenty ducats a month, free access to doctors and medications, royal lodging and additional payments for the works he produced. Soon after he was requested to summon his family from Seville to the capital and given the title of Painter to the Bedchamber. After a precocious start in the city of his birth, where he had already eclipsed all of his rivals, a new chapter in his life and painterly progress had begun.

In retrospect, it began somewhat inauspiciously, with no more than a dozen works by the artist surviving from the next six or so years. But at least four more are lost and only known from descriptions, two of them his most ambitious and highly praised works of this period and all but one amongst his very earliest. These include the aforementioned portrait of his host in Madrid, Don Juan de Fonseca, which first brought him to royal attention. An even greater loss is a portrait of the Prince of Wales (soon to become King Charles I), who was visiting Madrid at the time on an abortive mission to arrange a marriage with the King's sister, Maria. Had this picture survived, we would be able to compare how two of the greatest portraitists of the time – Velázquez and Van Dyck – had immortalized the same royal sitter.

But the most significant loss of all is an equestrian portrait of King Philip IV 'done entirely from nature, even the landscape', according to Pacheco, who tells us that it was so highly regarded by the monarch himself that 'it was set up with his consent and pleasure, in the Calle Mayor in front of San Felipe, to the admiration of the entire court and the envy of fellow artists'. Such a prestigious location testifies not only to the painting's merits but probably also to its large scale. Like the artist's only other equestrian portrait of the King of 1634–35, it may also have been life-size and comparably majestic, though it would not

have been as fluidly handled or so shimmering in colour as
the later work.

We are on firmer ground when we come to other portraits
of the King from these years. These consist of two full-length
and two bust-length likenesses of Philip, all of which exist in
numerous copies and variants, indicating that the court had
access to assistants from the beginning of the King's reign.
The earliest of these is a bust of the King executed in 1623 in
preparation for a full-length version of the same which the artist
subsequently painted over about three or four years later. The
King is posed in what would become his standard position,
three-quarters to his left (our right) – a viewpoint from which
Velázquez would deviate in only one later portrait. Many of his
distinctive facial features are apparent – the heavily lidded eyes,
thick lips and bulbous nose – although his protruding jaw and
elongated head are underplayed. And crowning them all is the
prominent forehead and curlicued coiffure.

This bust-length portrait of the King served as a study for
the first full-length treatment of him, which dates from 1624
and was executed for a family in Zarautz. The King is posed
formally and turned to his left beside a table bearing his hat.
He wears a black cape and is decorated with a chain of the
Order of the Golden Fleece. While one hand rests on his sword,
the other holds a letter or petition and his legs are spread widely
apart and somewhat awkwardly planted on the ground. The
background is uniformly handled in a murky brownish grey
shade which differs noticeably from Velázquez's next – and
more successful – full-length portrait of the King.

This was painted over the master's initial portrait of Philip,
which Pacheco dates to 30 August 1623. Originally, the King
was shown as squatter, his face much fleshier, his hands and
legs positioned differently and his cloak billowing. Around
1628, Velázquez revised this work, improving upon both its
predecessors of 1623 and 1624. The King's body is now extended,
tapered and more elegantly posed, his left hand resting on
the table beside him and one leg placed behind the other,
stabilizing his balance and enhancing his contour. Moreover,
the background here is subtly differentiated in tone throughout,
with the King's shadow on the bottom right providing an artful
complement to the table and hat, which mimics its shape.
Most notably of all, his head is narrower and more elongated
and his jaw more pronounced. These alterations accord with
another bust of the King of these years, which is a fragment
of a larger painting and shows him identically posed but now
wearing armour. This change of costume required Velázquez
to introduce a more varied range of colours and more readily

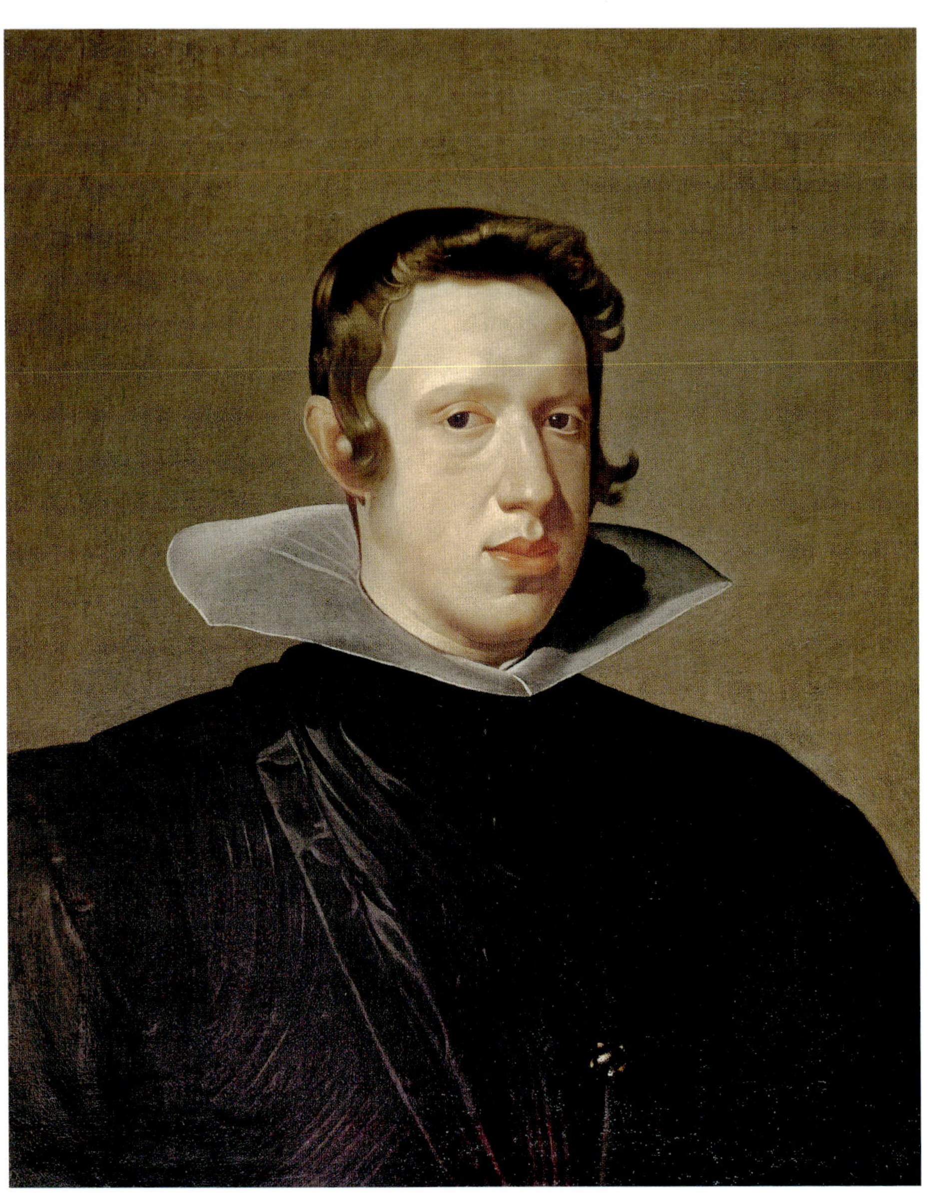

26 ABOVE *Philip IV*, 1623–24
27 OPPOSITE *Philip IV*, 1624

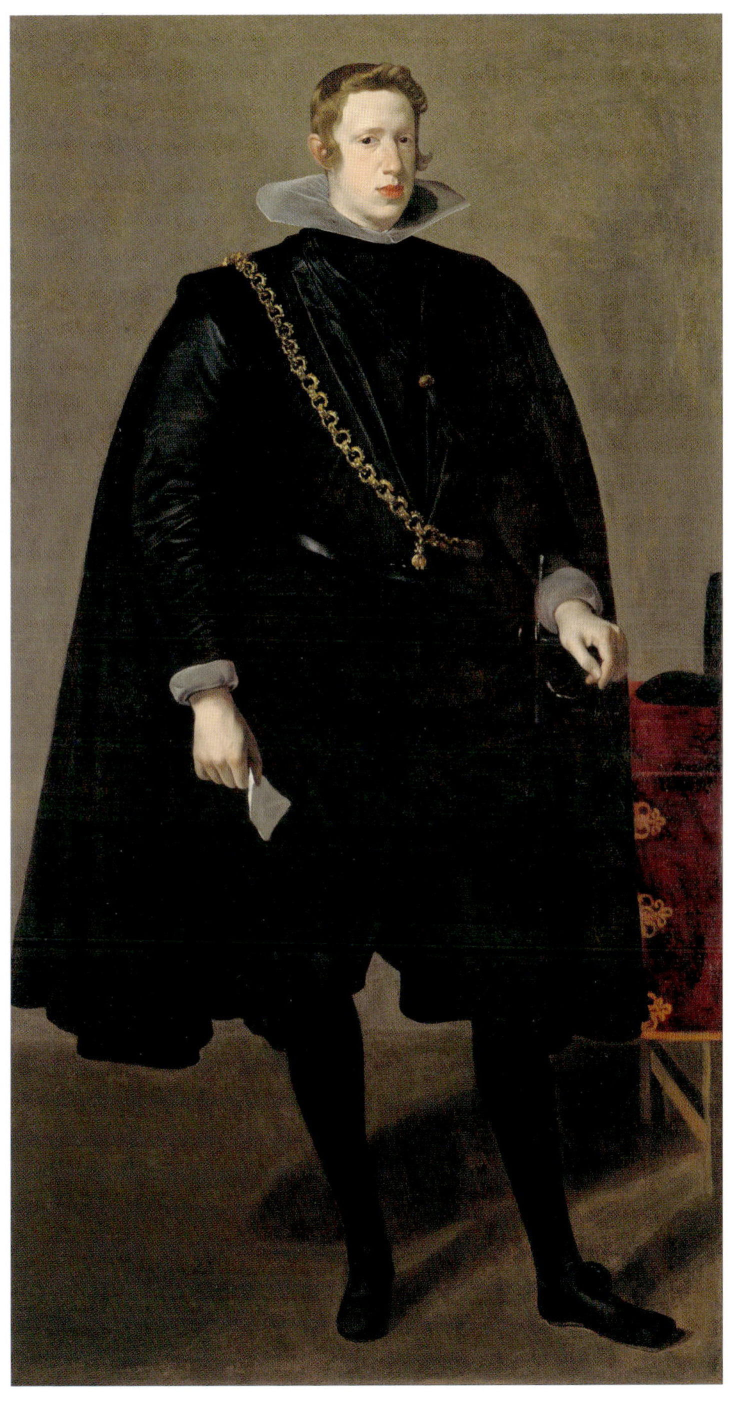

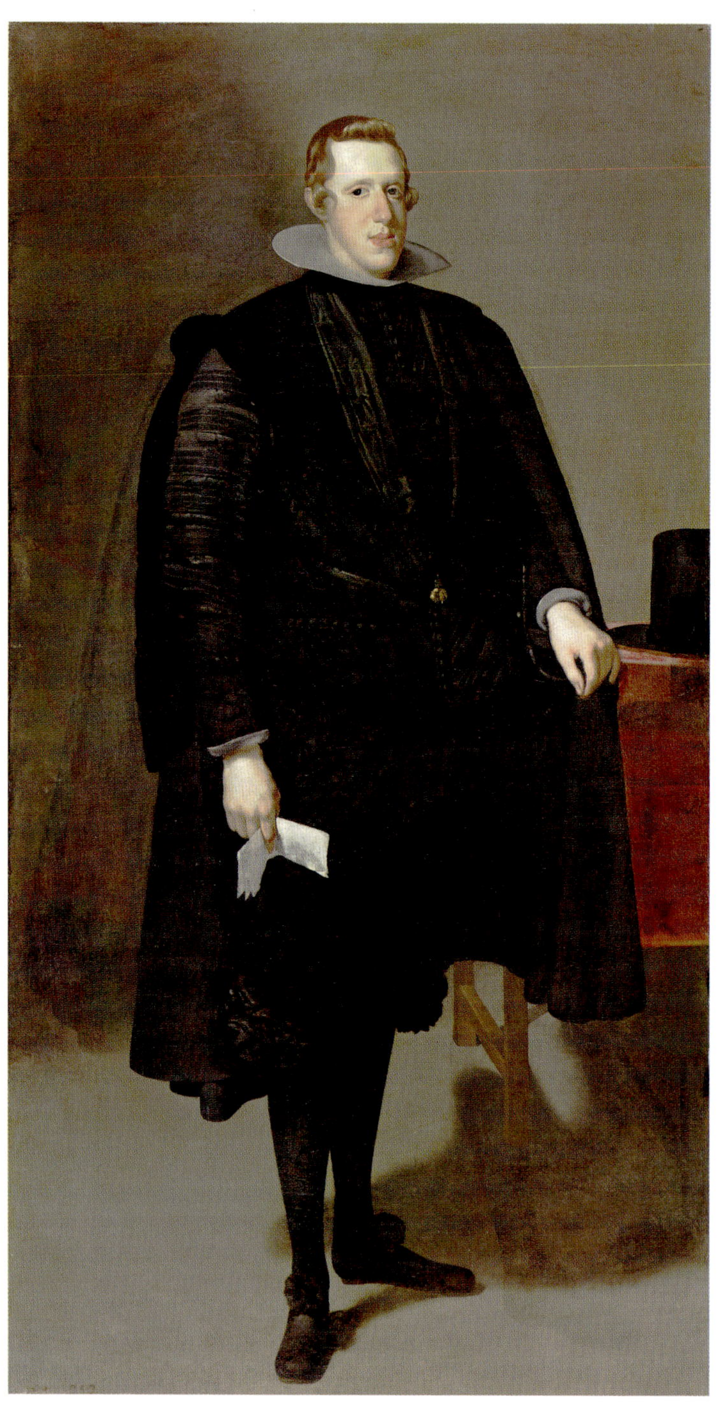

28 ABOVE *Philip IV, 1623–28*
29 OPPOSITE *Portrait of Philip IV in Armour, c. 1628*

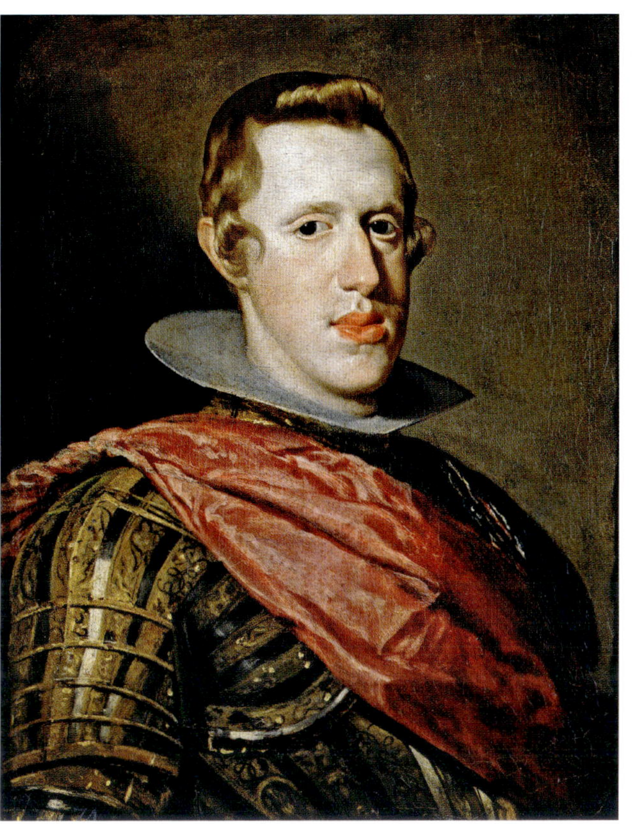

visible brushwork. The latter reveals early signs of what would increasingly develop into the artist's daringly abbreviated technique. Light playing over the King's scarlet sash of office elicits a medley of haltering and zigzagging strokes, some blended with one another and others standing out. Highlights on the armour are reduced to pinpoints of gold paint which appear willy-nilly, exactly as the fleeting eye might perceive them. Most evocative of all are the multicoloured strokes of bright paint running down the King's left shoulder, which tell us that something is catching the light at this point, but little more.

The King's first minister, Don Gaspar de Guzmán, Count-Duke of Olivares, is the subject of two portraits of these years, both of them full length and not for the faint-hearted. In one, which probably dates from 1624, he stands gripping the edge of a table, his imposing bulk filling the picture frame. He wears the red cross of the Order of Calatrava and the regalia of office, the golden key, spurs and chain. The pent-up energy of this portrait,

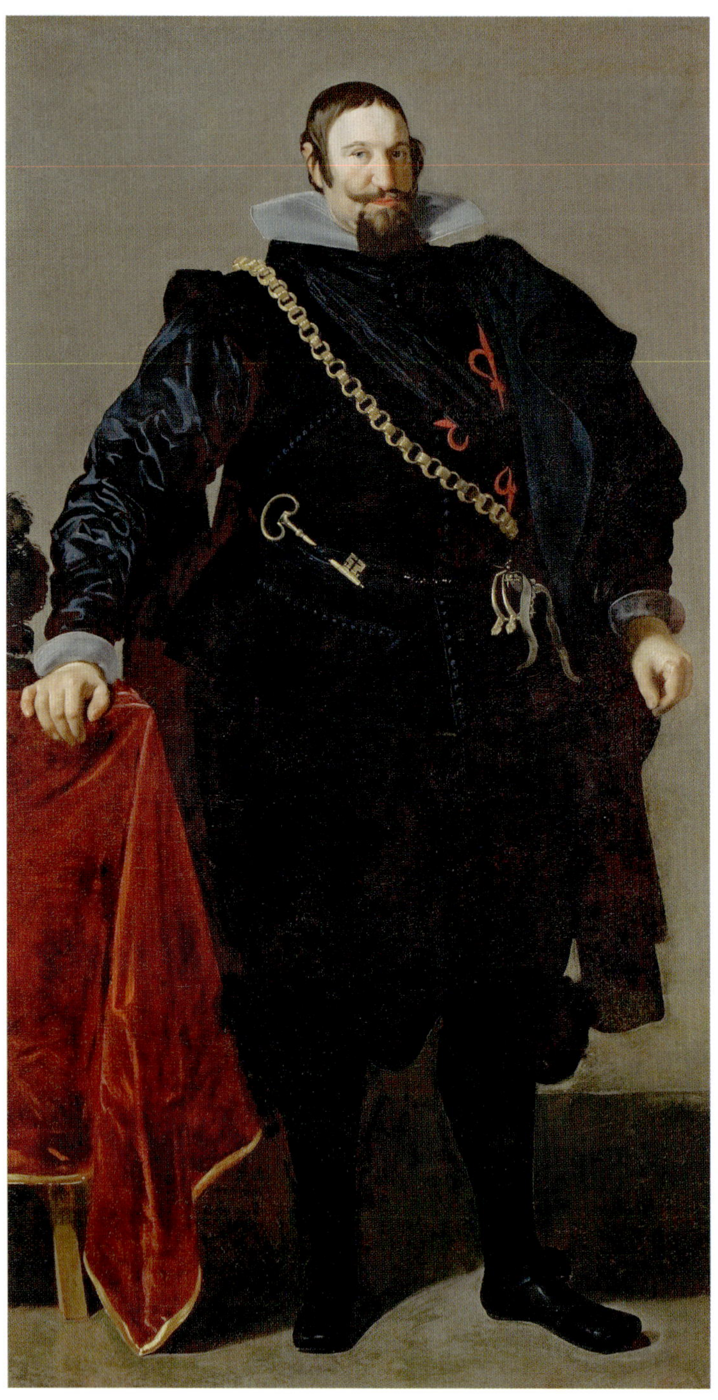

30 ABOVE *Portrait of the Count-Duke of Olivares*, 1624
31 OPPOSITE *The Count-Duke of Olivares*, c. 1625–26

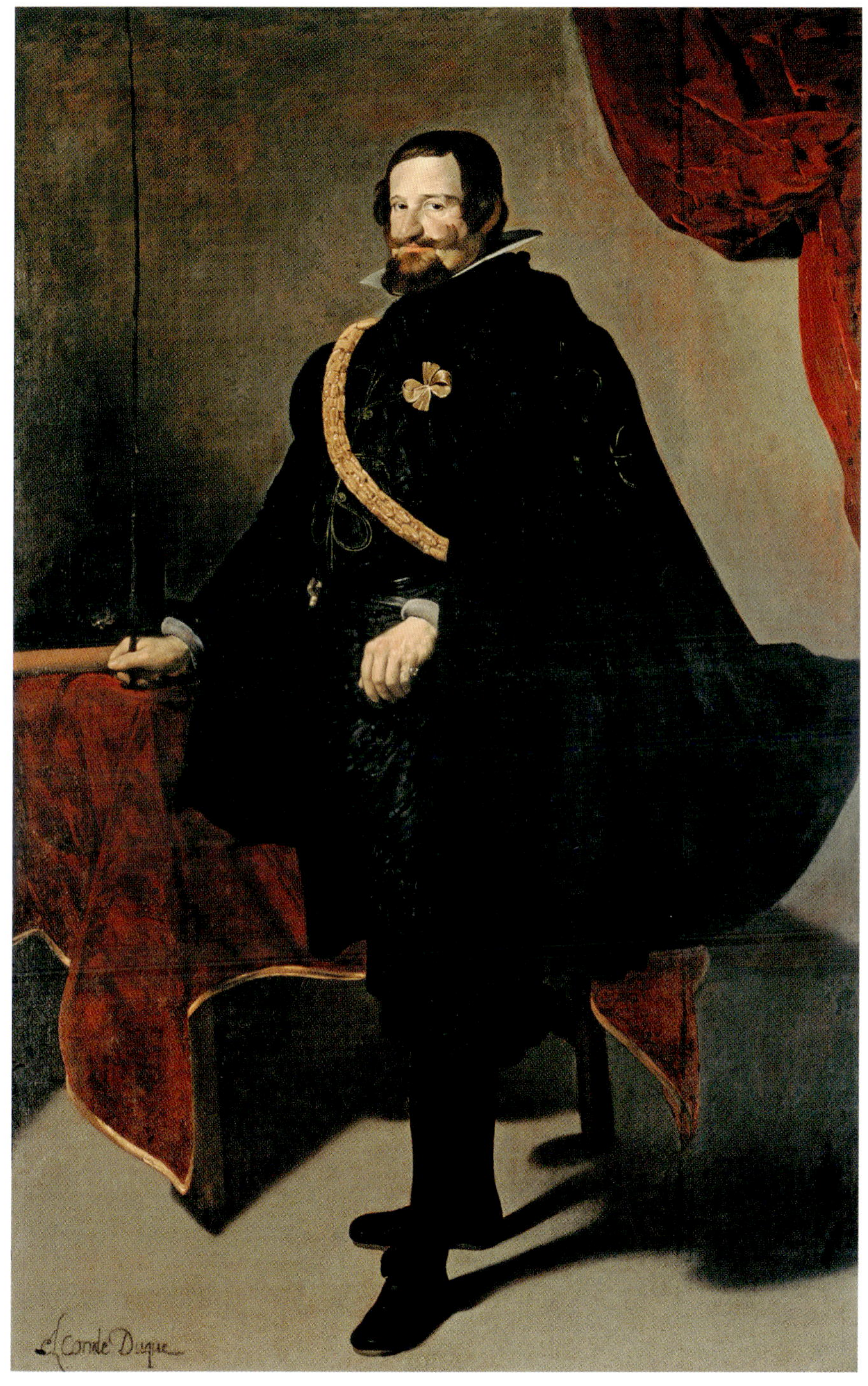

El Conde Duque

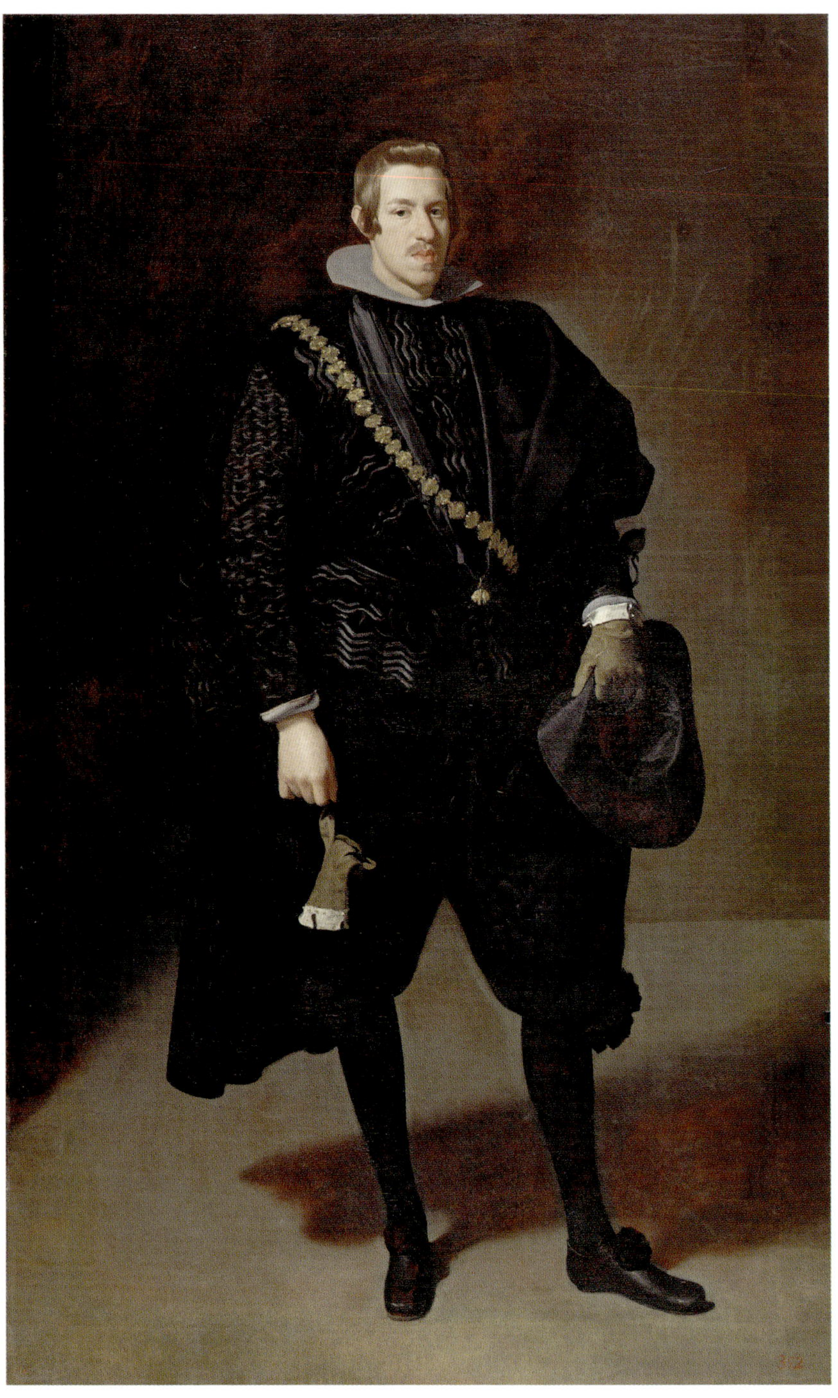

32 ABOVE *Portrait of the Infante Don Carlos, 1626–27*
33 OPPOSITE *Portrait of St Simon de Rojas Dead, 1624*

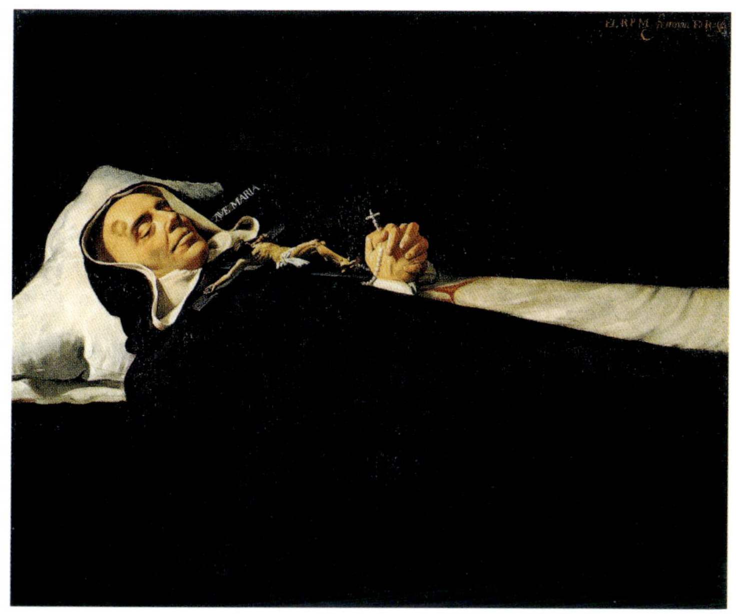

evident in the twist of his body and the spread of his legs, leaves little doubt that he is a man of purpose, but a semblance of humility is apparent in the picture's destination. It was painted not for the Count-Duke himself, nor for the King, but for the family of Doña Antonia de Ipeñarrieta, later to become governess of the King's son Balthasar Carlos.

The second portrait of Olivares, datable to a year or so later, shows him more formally – even regally – posed. Framed by a deep red curtain and tablecloth, his feet together and stance balanced, he grasps the hilt of his sword with one hand and, with the other, holds a riding crop aloft, as though it were a weapon of state. Adorning his chest is the green cross of the Order of Alcántara, to which he was appointed in 1624. In contrast to the artist's previous portrait of him, his granite-like countenance appears squarer and more assertive here, and the way in which his cloak fans out behind him leaves one in no doubt of his sweeping powers of self-assertion.

In contrast to the austere formality of the portraits of Olivares and the King is the more relaxed deportment in the painting of the King's younger brother, the Infante Don Carlos, which dates from around the same time. He holds his hat in one hand and dangles a glove in the other, his legs parted, as though poised to step out. Velázquez added strips of canvas to the bottom and side of this picture to set the Infante further back in space

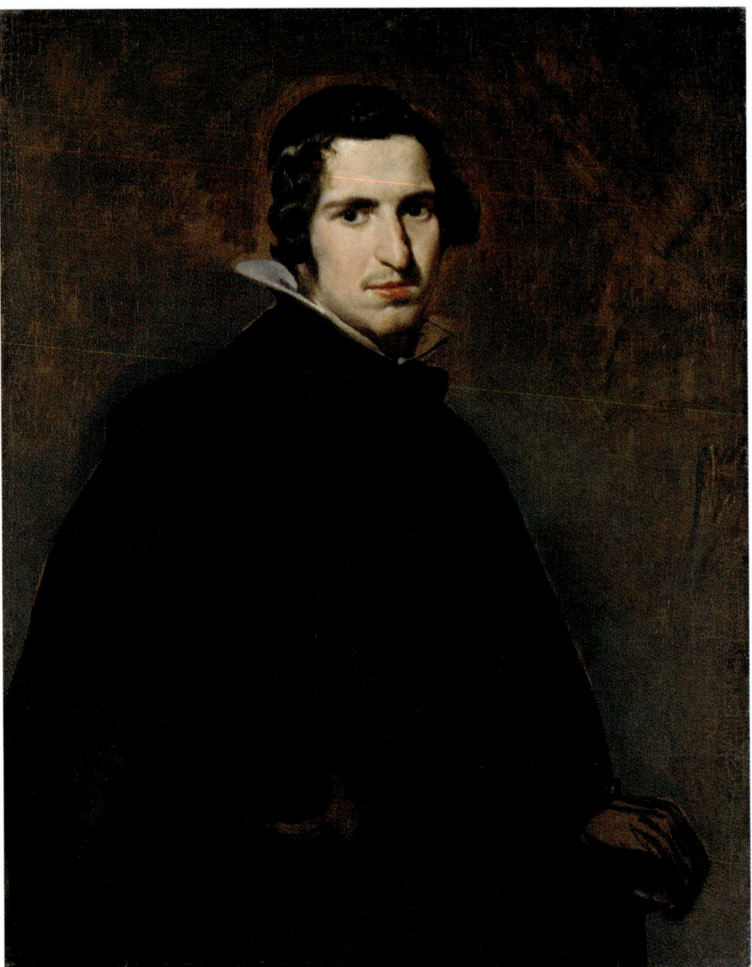

34 ABOVE *Portrait of a Young Man*, 1627–28
35 OPPOSITE *Democritus*, 1628–29

and stressed the familial resemblance between him and the King by setting their heads at exactly the same angle in both. But the absence of a table to support the figure, the prominent floor line on the right and the lighter tonality of the background all lend a more animated quality to the portrait – and not least the sweeping strokes of paint which radiate out from the Infante's left arm, where the artist has wiped his brush while working.

The chiselled clarity of Velázquez's draughtsmanship in these portraits is also seen in a newly discovered painting of these same years which is otherwise unique in the artist's

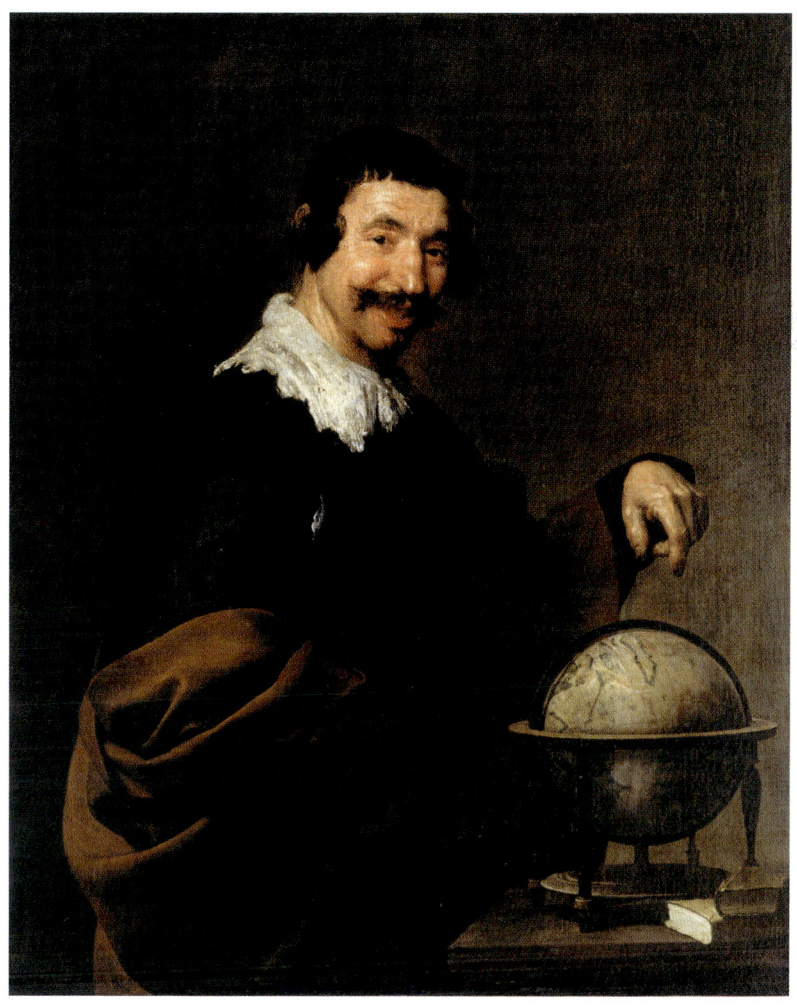

career. Palomino informs us that Velázquez executed 'the portrait of the venerable Father Master Fray Simón de Rojas, outstanding man in learning and virtue, done after his death'. This took place in Madrid in 1624 and the artist's portrayal of de Rojas bears all of the hallmarks of an eye-witness account. Simón de Rojas, who was subsequently canonized, is laid out on his deathbed in the robes of the Trinitarian Order to which he belonged and holding a rosary in his joined hands. Across his chest lies a large sculpted image of Christ on the cross and a phylactery issuing from his lips is inscribed *Ave Maria*.

The picture is marked by an almost unbearable honesty
and truth in its rendering of the deceased monk, from
his sallow skin tones and sunken cheeks to the tumour of
coagulated blood (or haematoma) on his right temple – a
disfigurement from which most other artists would shrink.
In the caressing curves of the cowl around his head, however,
may be found a semblance of peace.

34 The unfinished *Portrait of a Young Man* whose sombre
palette also dates it to this period is one of Velázquez's
most haunting early works and its nonchalant pose marks
a new departure in his portrait style. Hitherto content
to face his subjects head-on, the artist now adopts a sideways
position facing to our right, the sitter's head turned towards
the viewer and his right hand resting on his hips. Although the
face, with its dreamy, unfocused gaze, is fully and sensitively
modelled, the lower portions of the figure and especially
the hands are left barely sketched in. Velázquez was to leave
a number of other works unfinished, notably the later portraits
of Juan Mateos and Juan Martínez Montañés. But rather than
inciting the viewer to imagine the painting's completion,
this draws attention instead to the processes of its very
creation. From the random brushstrokes at the right margin
to the smoky reddish browns of the surrounding atmosphere,
the paint surface of this picture is captured in a condition
of ferment and flux out of which the sitter's hands have yet
to emerge.

Although Velázquez's appointment as royal painter
inevitably placed its greatest demands on his outstanding gifts
as a portraitist, he also found opportunities to tackle other
subjects from the Bible, history and mythology throughout
35 the rest of his career. One such is his *Democritus* of about
1628. The legendary laughing philosopher of ancient Greece
(460–370 BC) is here depicted as an amiable rustic grinning
out of the picture as he points to his traditional attribute,
a terrestrial globe. X-rays and copies of the picture reveal
that his left hand was originally shown holding a filled wine
glass, making him a Spanish counterpart of the many merry
drinkers of these years by Velázquez's Dutch contemporary
Frans Hals. Velázquez later repainted the hand and collar and
added the table, book and globe to convert it into an equally
merry philosopher akin to his paintings of jesters and courtly
'buffoons' of the 1630s. And brilliantly echoing Democritus's
ruddy complexion are the madder and deep green colours of
his costume and of the land masses on the globe.

By the mid-1620s Velázquez's meteoric rise to favour in court
circles was fomenting intense jealousy and rivalry among other

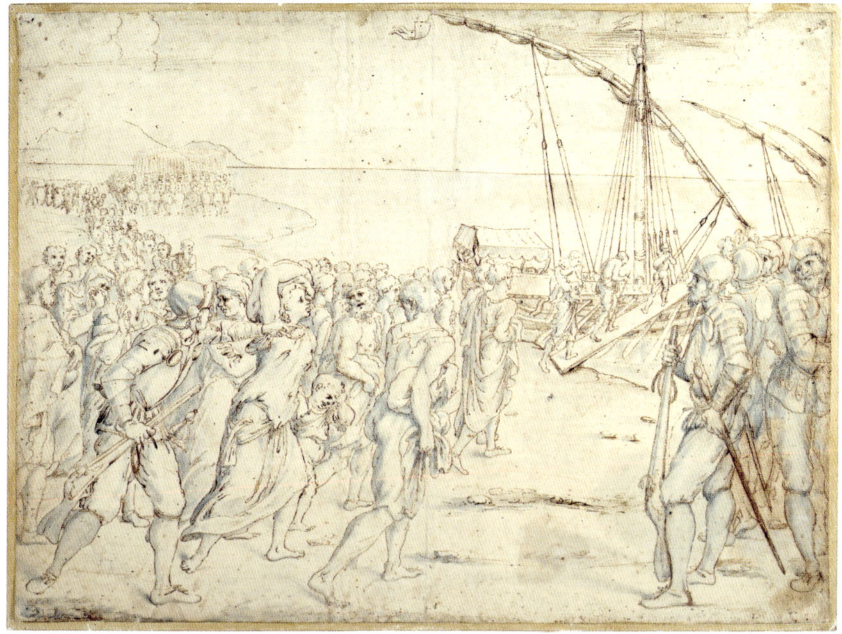

36 Vicente Carducho, drawing for *The Expulsion of the Moriscos*, 1627

painters working for the King, among them Eugenio Cajés, Vicente Carducho and Angelo Nardi. All three of them were of Italian descent and practised a conservative style of painting that placed much emphasis upon elaborate preparatory stages when devising a painting, as well as rejecting the realism of the art of Caravaggio and his followers, which was increasingly gaining favour among the most progressive painters in Europe. Velázquez was to be counted among these and his practice of working directly from life without idealizing his models was anathema to his competitors at court.

In response to these rivalries, the King initiated a competition in 1627 amongst the four for a painting to hang in the Salón Nuevo of the Alcázar Palace in Madrid, which was dedicated to celebrating the achievements of the Spanish Habsburgs, not least as defenders of the faith. The subject chosen was the Expulsion of the Moriscos from Spain in 1603 by Philip III and the chosen judges were two modernists, Fray Juan Bautista Maino and Juan Bautista Crescenzi, the former of whom practised a highly individual version of Caravaggism and the latter of whom was an architect.

Velázquez was voted the winner of the competition but his submitted canvas no longer survives. Along with the other three works it perished in a fire in the Alcázar in 1734 and all the evidence that remains of the project is a squared drawing by Carducho for his own submitted work and a description by Palomino of Velázquez's winning canvas:

'In the centre of this picture is King Philip III in armour, pointing with the baton in his hand to a troop of men, women and children being led away in tears by some soldiers; in the distance are some carts and a stretch of seascape with some vessels to transport them... to the right of the King is Spain, represented by a majestic matron seated at the foot of a building, holding in her right hand a shield and some arrows, and in the left some blades of wheat. She is dressed in Roman armour.'

Palomino then proceeds to cite an elaborate and laudatory inscription to both Philip III and Philip IV on the socle beneath her feet and adds that it bears Velázquez's signature and the date 'on a piece of simulated parchment that he painted on the bottom step'.

Even from this description alone it is clear that Velázquez's art had broken new ground with this work. For one, he had

37 BELOW *Christ after the Flagellation Contemplated by the Christian Soul*, 1626–28
38 OPPOSITE *The Supper at Emmaus*, 1628–29

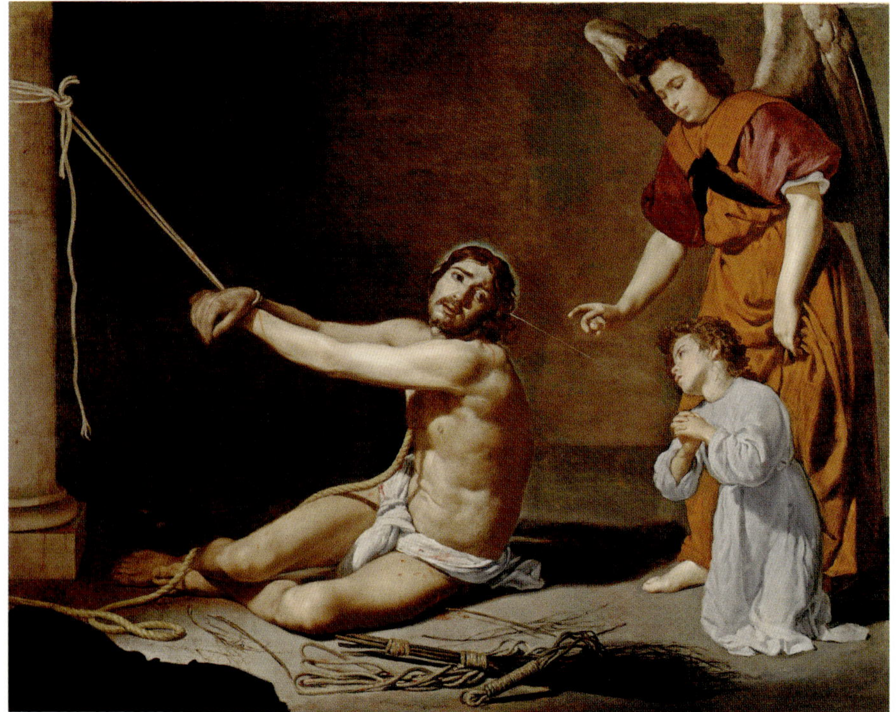

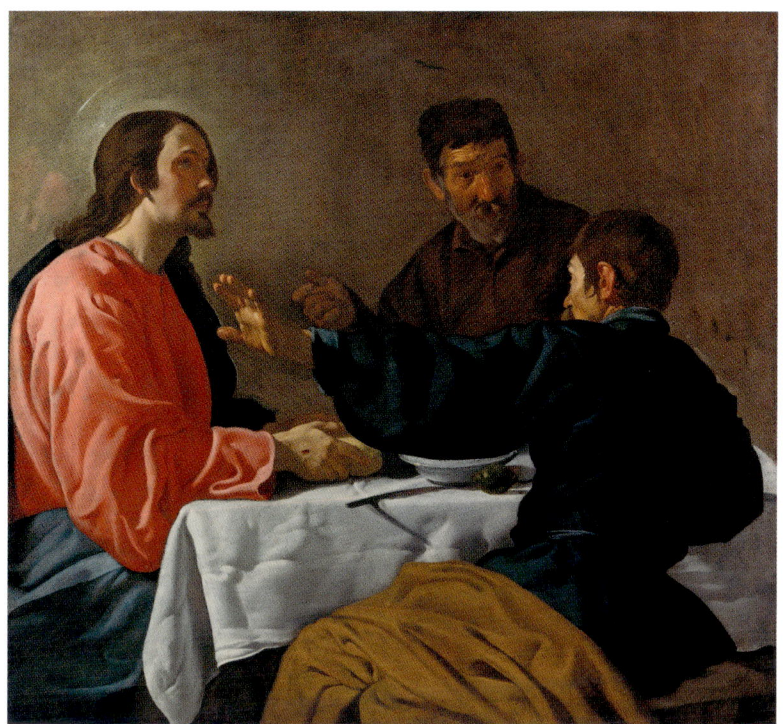

attempted his most expansive multifigure composition, with
the figures evidently in action, and his first (and only) seascape
background and allegorical figure, not to mention the ships
and carts. How much of all of this was painted from life we
shall never know, but it would have been wholly out of character
for the artist if much of it had not been. What is indisputable,
however, is that the competition and the resulting picture
provided Velázquez with the ideal preparation for his next great
history painting, *The Surrender of Breda*, of eight years later.

Velázquez also executed two religious pictures during the
late 1620s, neither of them apparently royal commissions.
*Christ after the Flagellation Contemplated by the Christian
Soul* treats a rare Counter Reformation subject intended to
induce the faithful to seek redemption and salvation through
the contemplation of Christ's sufferings during the Passion.
Christ has fallen to the ground after being bound to a column
and beaten with the twigs and scourges that now lie scattered
around him. Still tied to the column, with the wounds on his
body dripping with blood, he directs his supplicating gaze
towards the praying figure of the Christian soul, personified

by a young child who mournfully returns his gaze. A ray of
light emanating from Christ's head pierces the air to enflame
the contemplative soul, who is directed to reach over to Christ
by a guardian angel standing beside it in a protective pose.

The design could not be more eloquent or emblematic,
two intersecting diagonals meeting with the tender and
beautiful head of Christ, the left side reminding the viewer
of his sufferings and physical torments and the right of his
redemptive powers. In keeping with the sombre and symbolic
tone of the whole, the setting is spacious and spare and the
colours muted. But were the figures actually studied from
life? Although this was certainly the case during Velázquez's
Sevillian period, it may be less so now. Models may have been
used to pose for all three figures, but not necessarily with
the facial features one sees here. The tender and soulful face
of Christ in this painting especially strikes one as a filtered
rather than a faithful version of reality, albeit without a
trace of sentimentality.

The Christ in Velázquez's other religious canvas of these
years, *The Supper at Emmaus*, leaves fewer grounds for doubt,
for he is now a more purely idealized and ethereal figure who
is arguably less moving. Traditionally, when this subject was
depicted by artists such as Dürer, Titian or Caravaggio, it was
arranged symmetrically around a table with Christ in the
centre and the disciples to either side. Velázquez opts for a more
dynamic composition, separating the spiritual presence from
the earthly contingent. Christ has just blessed and is breaking
the bread, his true identity suddenly revealed to the disciples
at Emmaus. In the next moment he will vanish. The aureole
of light around him already anticipates this.

Velázquez's decision to place the disciples to one side of
his picture is not entirely successful, especially when both
are made to perform the same action, their hands raised in
recognition of Christ's identity. The awkward result of this
is the meeting of three hands near the centre of the picture,
Christ's holding the bread below those of his companions. It is
a case of compositional congestion rather than coordination,
made worse by the awkward arrangement of the disciples
themselves. One, shown behind the table and facing forwards,
has to be raised in order to be seen above his companion, who
is seated in the front with his back to us. The space occupied by
the table itself thereby collapses and the whole picture becomes
somewhat of an assemblage of striking but disunified parts.
For all his remarkable powers of observation and execution,
Velázquez had yet to develop skills in choreographing a
composition. But that was soon to come.

38

In September 1628, Peter Paul Rubens, widely regarded as the greatest painter in Europe, arrived in Madrid. The purpose of his visit was not artistic but diplomatic, for amongst his myriad other talents Rubens was renowned as a political negotiator too. He had been sent at the request of the Infanta Isabella, Governor of the Netherlands, to negotiate a peace treaty between Spain and England through an exchange of ambassadors between the two countries. This was intended as a precondition to establishing a reunification of the Netherlands, which had been divided since 1579 with the secession of the seven northerly republics of the United Provinces.

During his seven-month stay in the Spanish capital Rubens also found time to indulge in many artistic pursuits. He studied avidly the great works of art in the royal collection and reputedly copied all of the pictures in it by his favourite artist, Titian. He also painted numerous portraits of the King, including one of him on horseback, thereby infringing upon Velázquez's ostensibly exclusive right to do so. But although Rubens had little contact with other artists, he established a close friendship with Velázquez himself, the two painters visiting the Escorial together to admire not only the monastery but also the outstanding paintings to be seen there. According to Palomino, 'their example served Velázquez as a new stimulus to arouse the desire he had always had to go to Italy'.

Rubens's visit undoubtedly provided a catalyst to that ambition, which was to be fulfilled in the following year. But the immediate impact of the great Flemish master's visit – of witnessing him copy and admire the great works of religious and mythological painting of the past – was to prompt Velázquez to emulate Rubens's achievement by embarking on his own first work of this kind.

39   *The Triumph of Bacchus* was painted in 1628, perhaps when the Flemish master was still in Madrid, and paid for by the King in the following year. It was Velázquez's first attempt at a mythological subject. There can be little doubt that the initiative behind it was the example of Rubens, both in presence and in paint. Rubens was an acknowledged master of mythological subjects and, in the 1630s, would paint his own *Triumph of Bacchus* for the Spanish King. He was also a genius at devising large, complex multifigure compositions such as Velázquez was here attempting for the first time. But this initial effort at emulating the Flemish master shows how much the Spanish novice had yet to learn.

Seated in the centre of his picture is a podgy and decidedly adolescent youth crowned with vine leaves and playing at being Bacchus as he crowns his latest initiate, who kneels before him.

Gathered around them is a group of would-be acolytes – be they local peasants, farm hands or labourers – all of them celebrating the pleasures and benefits of Bacchus's gift. Two of them, on the left, have already been crowned, while those on the other side await their turn. At the top right a beggar seeking alms doffs his hat, only to be rebuffed by one of the revellers. The figures are arranged in a shallow space, which scarcely leaves room for their bodies, and crowded together as though posing for a group photograph. All of their heads are masterfully executed and highly individualized – indeed, one of them may also have posed for the older disciple in *The Supper at Emmaus*. The ever-inquisitive eye of the early *bodegones* – which was equally at home with still life and low life – re-emerges here, after five years of painting the King and his court.

But it comes at a cost. Even the most fervent admirers of *The Triumph of Bacchus* (or the *Borrachos* as it has come to be known) acknowledge that the composition is crowded and somewhat repetitive, the figures all individually studied and painted and then stuck together piecemeal. But consider their poses. Barring our way in the front of the picture are two back views, the one on the left much darkened as a result of fire damage in the early eighteenth century. Then there are three successive frontal views, those of Bacchus and the two drinkers to the right of him; and x-rays reveal that the kneeling man on the far right was originally also looking out of the picture before Velázquez altered his head position to respond to the beggar. But that in turn resulted in two profile poses on the right, one next to the other, with neither colour, gesture, nor costume sufficiently varied to diversify the group.

Now consider how Rubens approaches a similar challenge. On his visit to Madrid the Flemish master extended and extensively reworked an *Adoration of the Magi* he had originally painted in 1609 to celebrate the twelve-year truce between Spain and the Netherlands, which was now in Philip IV's possession. Rubens's scene is crowded to bursting point and alive with colour and action. Among his cluster of Magi, soldiers and followers, heads are directed every which way, no two identical, plumes follow flames, conversations are struck up and glances exchanged, and although the faces are all varied, they strike one as types rather than distinct individuals. The result is that they form part of an ensemble rather than an assemblage of disparate parts. How to achieve this in his own art was the next lesson that Velázquez would learn.

In 1629 Velázquez at last obtained the King's permission to fulfil his longstanding ambition and visit Italy. Provided with 600 ducats from the King and Olivares and a portrait

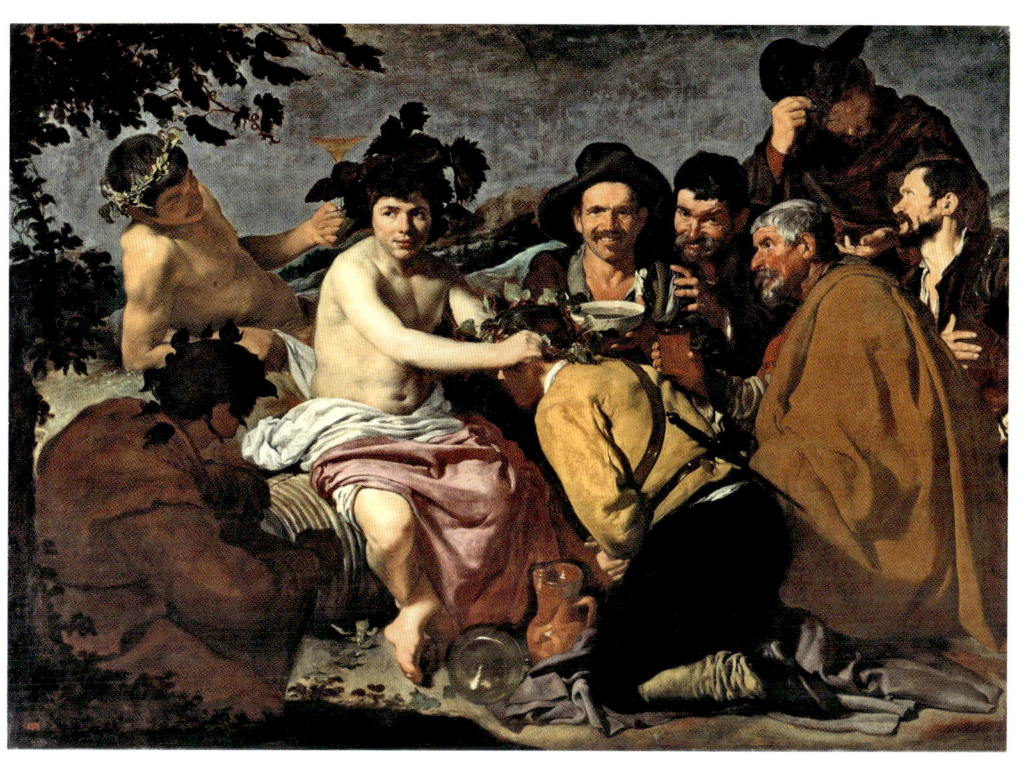

39 *The Triumph of Bacchus, 1628–29*

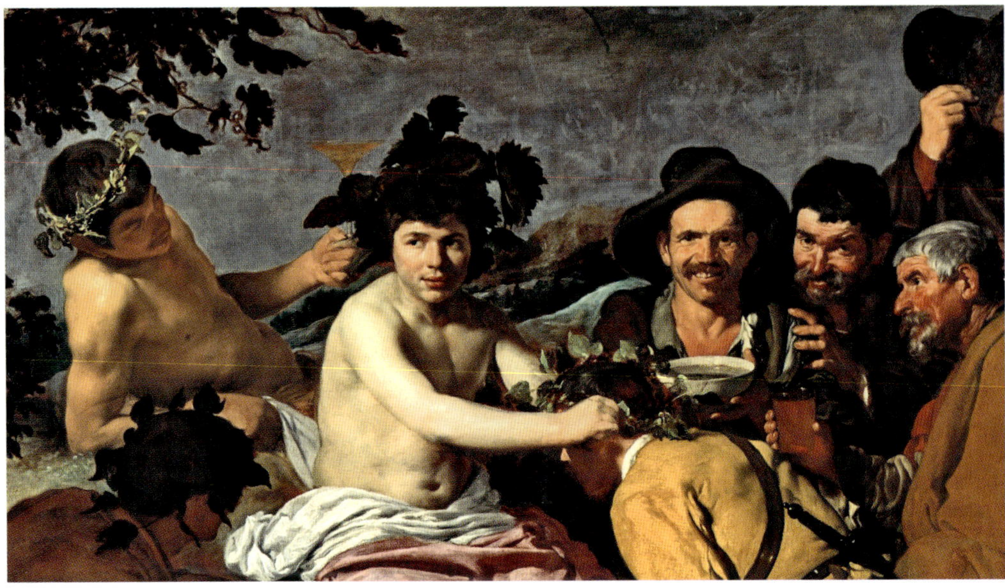

40 ABOVE *The Triumph of Bacchus*, 1628–29, detail
41, 42 OPPOSITE Peter Paul Rubens, *The Adoration of the Magi*, 1609/1628–29

of the King and letters of recommendation from the latter, the painter sailed from Barcelona on 10 August. Accompanying him on the journey was the Genoese general Ambrogio Spinola, recently engaged in leading the Spanish army in the war in the Netherlands. (Unknown to Velázquez at the time, this meeting was to prove propitious some five years later, when the King would commission him to depict Spinola's victory over the Dutch at Breda in 1625.) Disembarking in Venice, the painter stayed with the Spanish ambassador and immersed himself in the study of the great works of art by Titian, Veronese and Tintoretto to be seen there. He was particularly impressed by the magnificent cycle of paintings by Tintoretto in the Scuola di San Rocco and made many drawings after them, particularly *The Crucifixion*.

Upon leaving Venice, Velázquez went to Ferrara, where he stayed with the governor, Cardinal Giulio Sacchetti, who had been papal nuncio in Spain in the mid-1620s. From there he visited Cento, where it is tempting to imagine that he might have met the resident Italian painter Guercino, and proceeded to Rome, where he was to spend a year. He could hardly have chosen a better one, for Rome in 1630 was the very centre of the art world. The presiding genius was the sculptor and architect Gianlorenzo Bernini but there was also a galaxy of brilliant

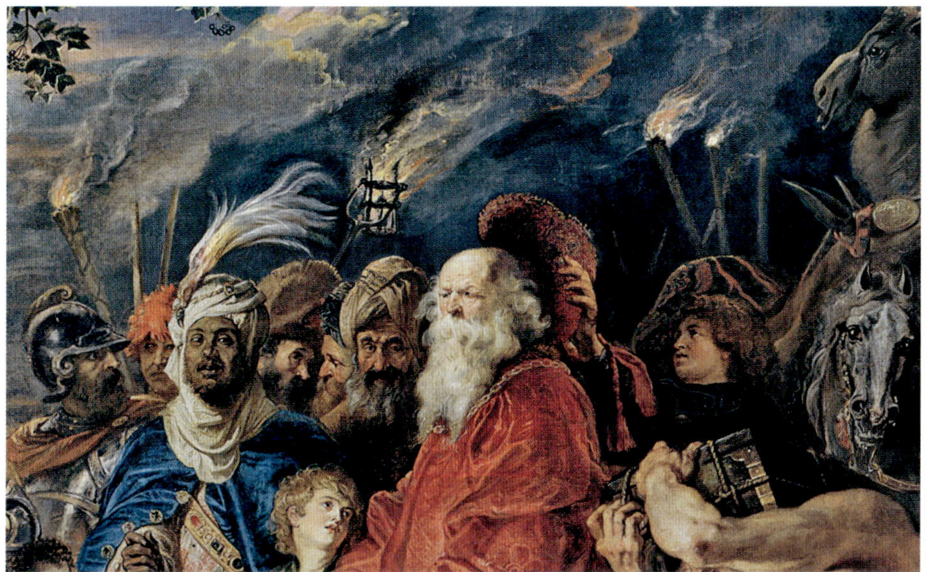

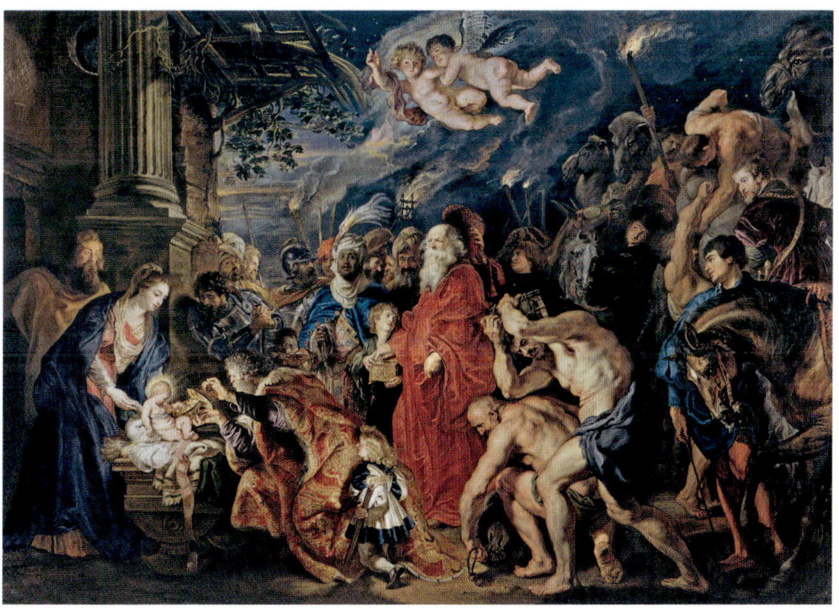

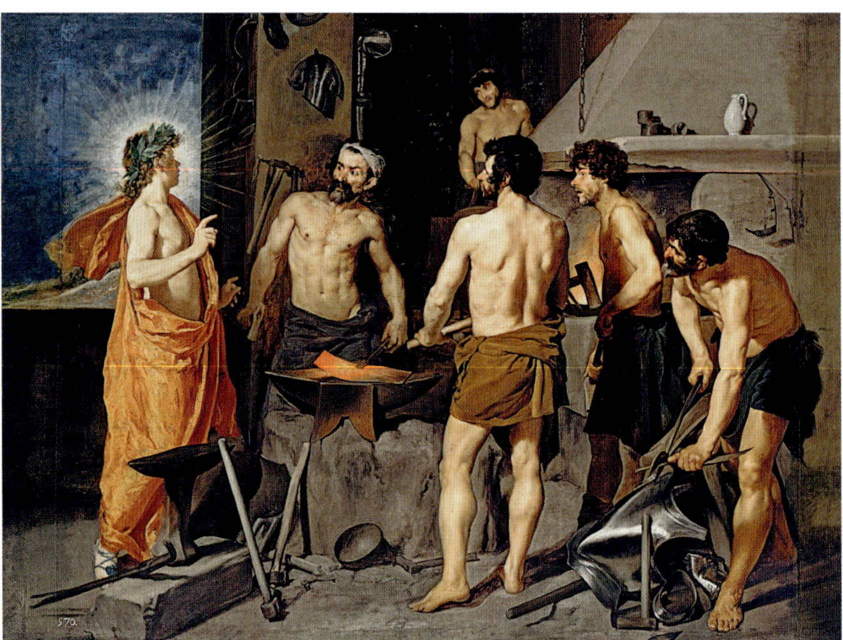

43 *The Forge of Vulcan,* 1630

young painters resident there, among them Pietro da Cortona,
Andrea Sacchi, Nicolas Poussin and Claude Lorrain. Given
the length of Velázquez's stay in the city he is certain to have
encountered all or some of them, but no proof remains of this.
What is known, however, is that he moved in favoured artistic
circles, including that of Cardinal Francesco Barberini, nephew
of the reigning pope Urban VIII and patron of many of the most
celebrated artists of the day, including Cortona and Poussin.
Barberini, who had visited Spain on a diplomatic mission in 1626,
when he is likely to have first made acquaintance with Velázquez,
gave orders that the latter be lodged in the Vatican Palace, giving
him keys to certain of its rooms. The artist studied the great
fresco cycles by Raphael and Michelangelo to be seen there and,
according to Pacheco and Palomino, made many drawings after
them, none of which survive.

The cumulative effect of these exercises and experiences on
Velázquez's own art was decisive and is made manifest in the
two chief canvases he painted on this trip, *The Forge of Vulcan*
and *Joseph's Bloody Coat Brought to Jacob*, which he took back
with him to Madrid and soon after sold to the King. Although
they were originally nearly the same size and are often regarded
as pendants, the *Forge* was enlarged on both sides in the

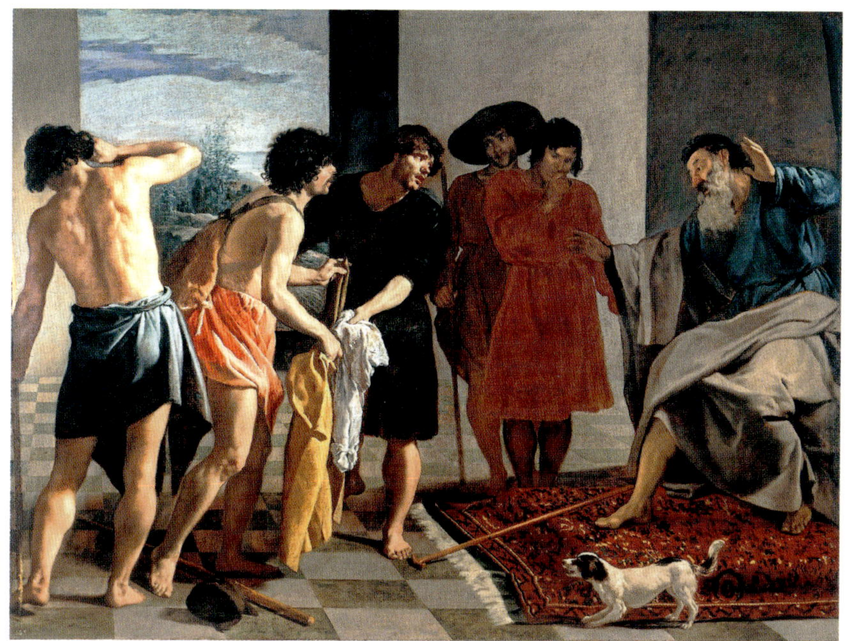

44 *Joseph's Bloody Coat Brought to Jacob,* 1630

eighteenth century, and the two canvases may best be seen as both complementary – and revolutionary. For they represent a radical departure in Velázquez's art from anything that had come before them.

First there are their subjects, one from Ovidian mythology and the other from the Old Testament, two sources that were entirely new to Velázquez's art. Yet they are loosely connected, for both are scenes of confrontation and revelation. In the *Forge*, Apollo appears to Vulcan, the husband of Venus, working with the Cyclopes at his forge, to announce that his wife Venus has committed adultery with Mars (Ovid, *Metamorphoses*, Book IV, 171–76). In the companion picture Joseph's brothers present their father Jacob with a bloodied cloak in a deceptive attempt to prove to him that his favoured son, Joseph, has been killed (Genesis 37:31–36). Thus, they are Velázquez's first true narrative pictures, each telling a story and relying on the viewer's knowledge of it to interpret the actions of the figures. Never before, then, have pose, gesture and expression mattered so much in the master's art.

In addition to their correspondence in theme, there are also their similarities in setting and conception. Both take place in a spacious interior with a large doorway or window on the left, the spatial recession convincingly marked, especially in *Joseph's Bloody Coat*, by the receding tiles on the floor. Both include full-length figures, in one case nude and in the other largely clothed, and unashamedly display the young artist's mastery of pose and anatomy. In both works, too, Velázquez seems to have relied upon the study of life models, as he had done throughout his early years, despite the fact that he was here depicting historical themes.

In *The Forge of Vulcan* Apollo bursts into Vulcan's workshop – an ethereal presence cloaked in flowing orange garments with a wreath and aureole crowning his head. Although his lithe torso and limbs befit his supernatural status, an oil study for his head suggests that Velázquez posed him from life, altering and elaborating upon the wreath and (of course) adding the aureole. X-rays of the picture also reveal that Vulcan was initially very different too, with his head tilted to the left rather than the right, his arms by his side and minus his beard or headscarf. In his revised pose, Velázquez ingeniously reveals not only that Vulcan is surprised and provoked by Apollo's announcement but also that he is lame, having been thrown down to earth from Olympus by Jupiter in a fit of anger. Although there were fewer alterations to his accomplices, all of these figures were clearly studied from life – indeed, Velázquez looks as though he had modelled them all on members of the same family – and the intervals and interactions of their poses and limb positions appear infallible, especially when counterpointed with the still-life objects of the foundry. These in turn reveal Velázquez's growing mastery of inanimate nature since his Sevillian years, especially the molten flame of metal emanating from the forge. Not only are these details stunning in their own right, but they also help to unify the scene. Thus, x-rays also reveal that Apollo was originally standing isolated on the left without the forge we now see in front of him, his unearthly presence perhaps separating him out too much from the rest of the picture.

Joseph's Bloody Coat is a somewhat less coherent composition, which has been cut down on both sides, making the strained and incongruous pose of the brother on the left seem even more obtrusive. It is as though Velázquez here wished to flaunt the lessons he had learned from studying the heroic nudes in the Sistine ceiling. Indeed the entire picture is testimony to the artistic advances he had made during his Italian visit. To begin with there is the tiled floor, which charts the deep and logical spatial recession into the back of the picture. Then there is the lighter and brighter tonality, subtler shading and much thinner and more fluid application of paint.

This is evident throughout, but especially in the two brothers lurking together in the half-shadow of the middle distance. Finally, there is the much wider range of colours, pinks, yellows, blues and greys replacing the predominantly earthy and brownish hues of the artist's early years. Coupled with this is the greatest innovation of all: Velázquez's impressionism. The small oriental carpet beneath Jacob is decorated with a design made up of touches and daubs of yellow, black and grey which shimmer as the light catches them but reveal nothing more because that is all that even the most observant eye would see from a distance.

This is not only the case with the carpet but also the view out of doors. If one compares it with the view in the portrait of Suárez de Ribera of ten years earlier, the gap is immense and the benefits of the Italian visit obvious. For one, it taught Velázquez's landscape to breathe. In the portrait the silhouetted and schematically shaped trees appear stuck on to the surface of the canvas and untouched by air, wind or breeze. Much the same may be said for the meagre and perfunctory clouds. In short, it is a notional landscape rather than a believable one. But in *Joseph's Bloody Coat* voluminous cloud formations fill the sky, trees bend in the breeze and their delicate fronds of foliage nearly dissolve as a result of their distance from us and the ambient air.

In the summer of 1630 Velázquez changed residence in Rome, moving to the Villa Medici on the Pincian Hill to escape the heat below. There he remained for two months and painted the only two landscapes of his career, pendant views of the gardens of the villa, which break entirely new ground not merely in his art but in art itself. Both were painted outdoors, a practice almost unknown at the time. They were also both painted under different conditions of light and atmosphere and are totally unprepossessing views. In one, two men meet and greet one another before an archway in the gardens containing a cast of the *Sleeping Ariadne*. Dappled light playing through the trees throws a motley range of shadows and half-shadows over the architecture of the pavilion, some of them painted onto it and others painted so thinly as to reveal the underlying canvas weave. Indeed, so light, fluid and spontaneous is the brushwork that the figures of the two men themselves may be seen through to reveal the lines of the architecture itself. In the companion picture, the façade of the Grotto-Loggia is to be seen, again centrally placed, as in the other landscape, the artist's only concession to the conventions of the classical tradition. The façade is boarded up, with restoration works apparently going on, and on the balustrade above it, laundry has been hung out

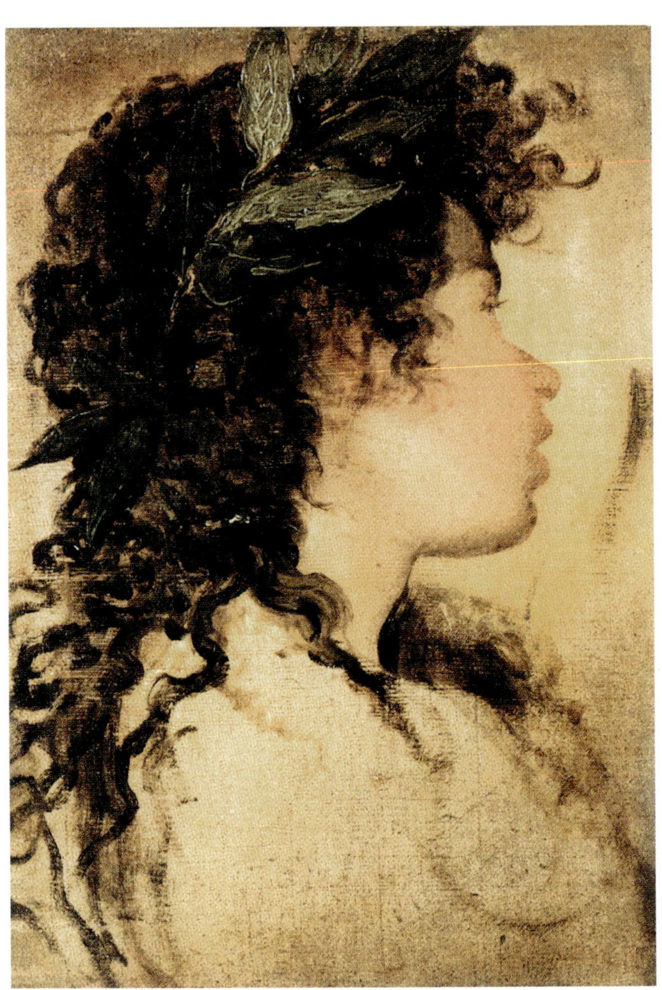

45 ABOVE *Head of Apollo,* 1630
46 OPPOSITE *The Forge of Vulcan,* 1630, detail

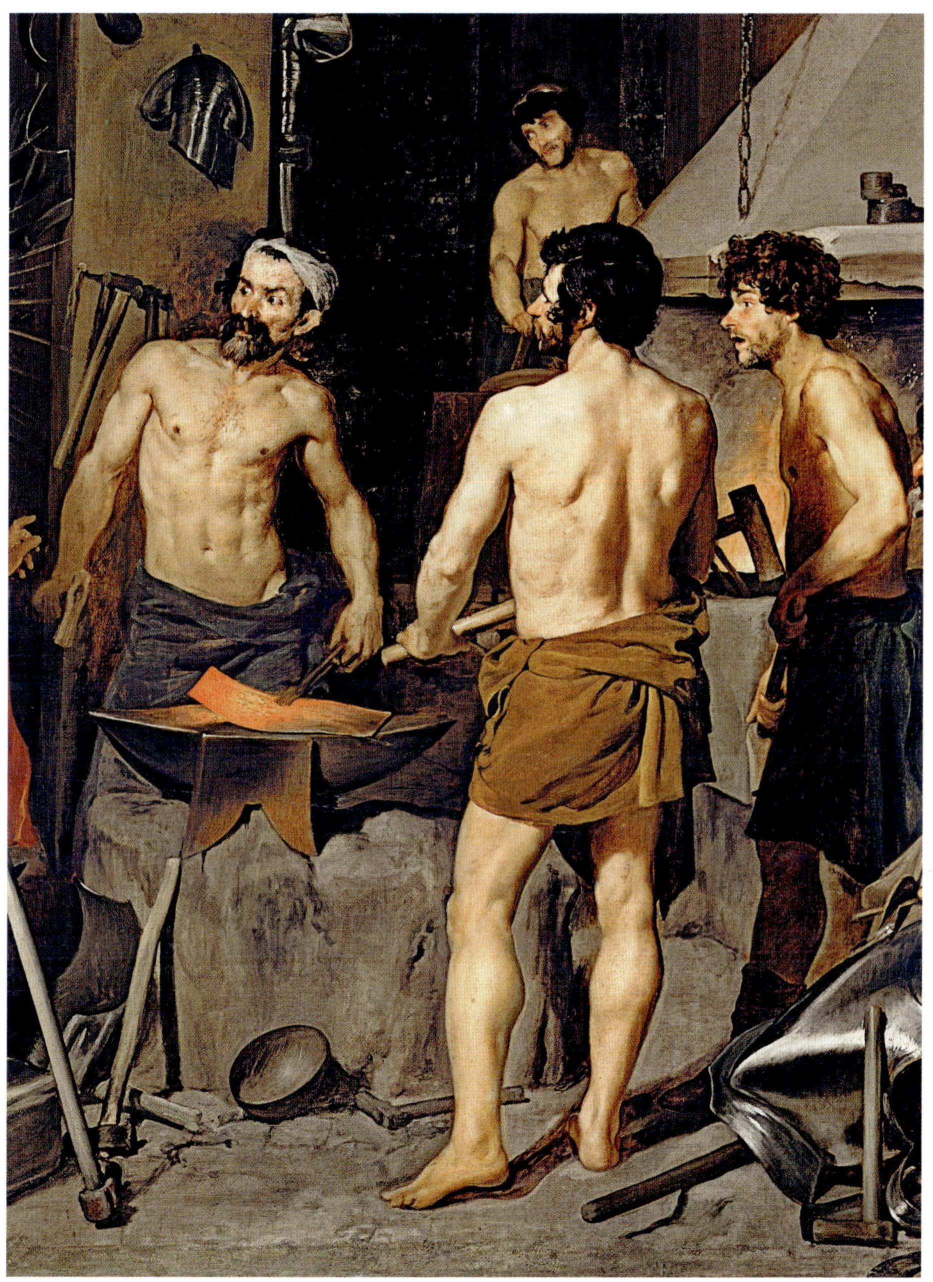

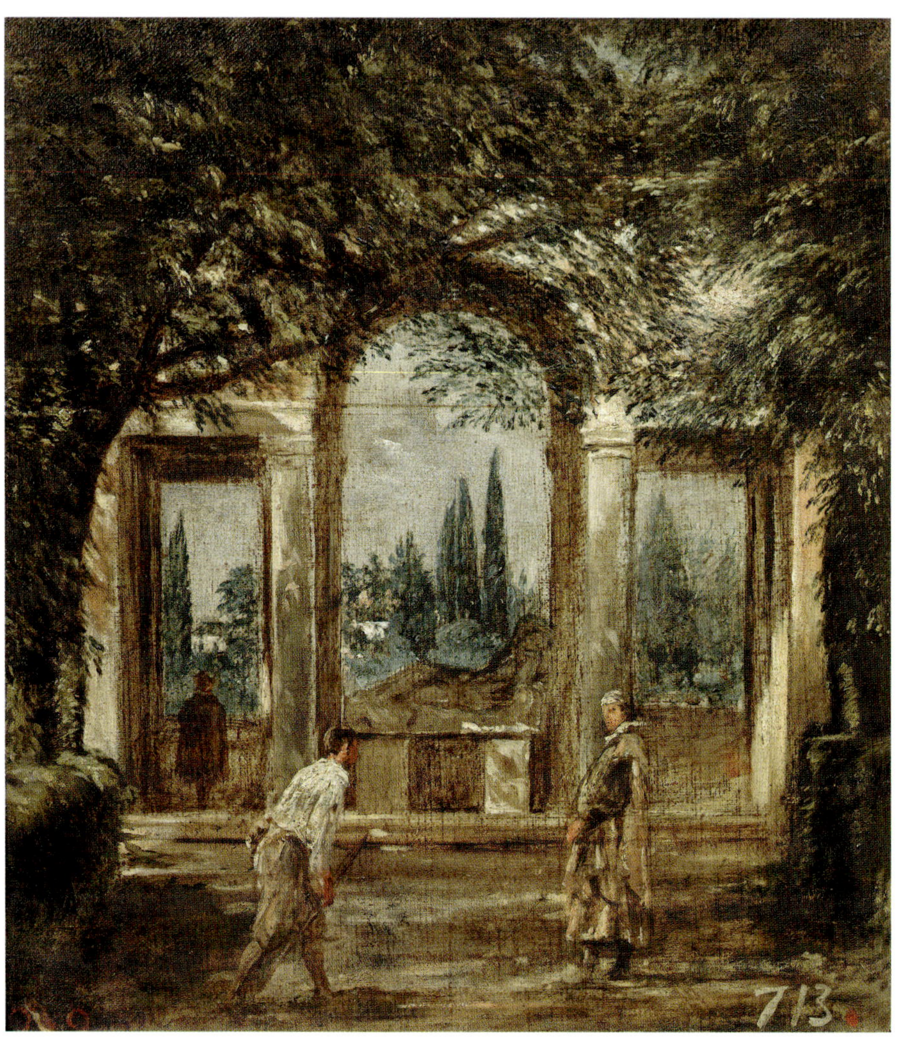

47 ABOVE *View of the Gardens of the Villa Medici, Rome, with a Statue of Ariadne*, 1630
48 OPPOSITE *View of the Gardens of the Villa Medici, Rome*, 1630

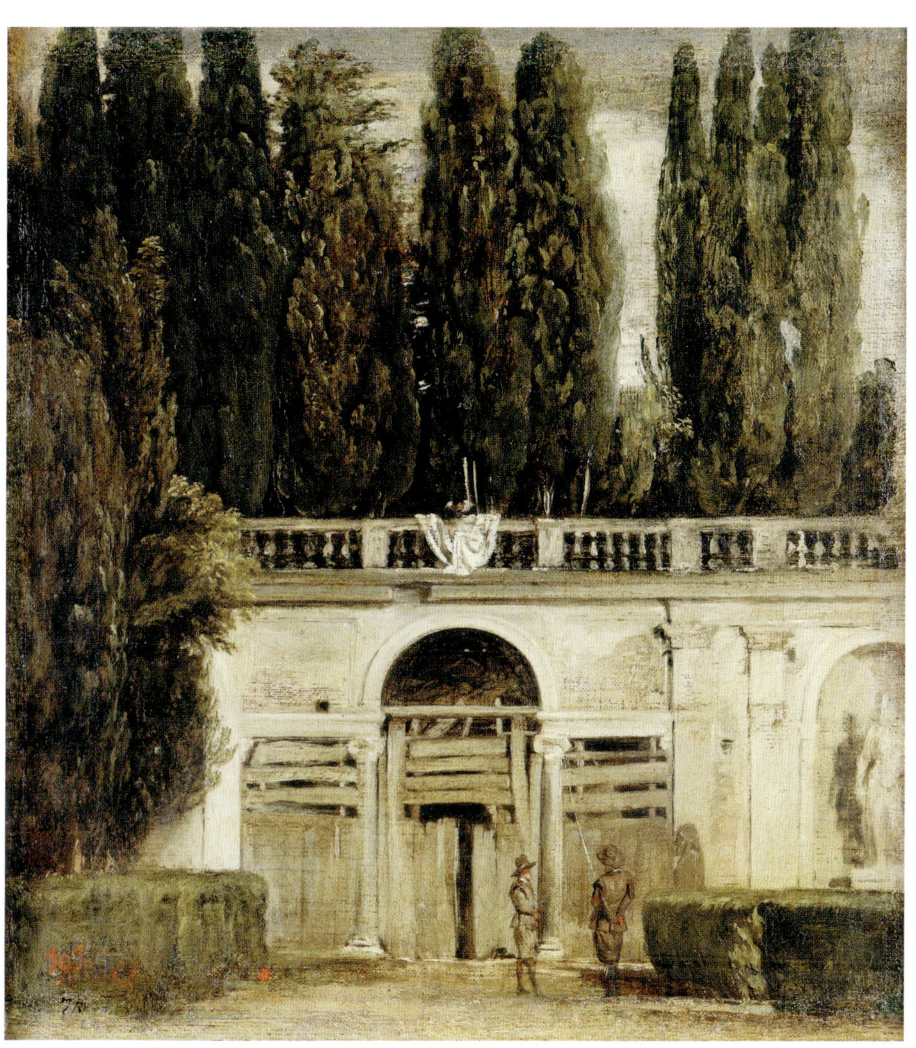

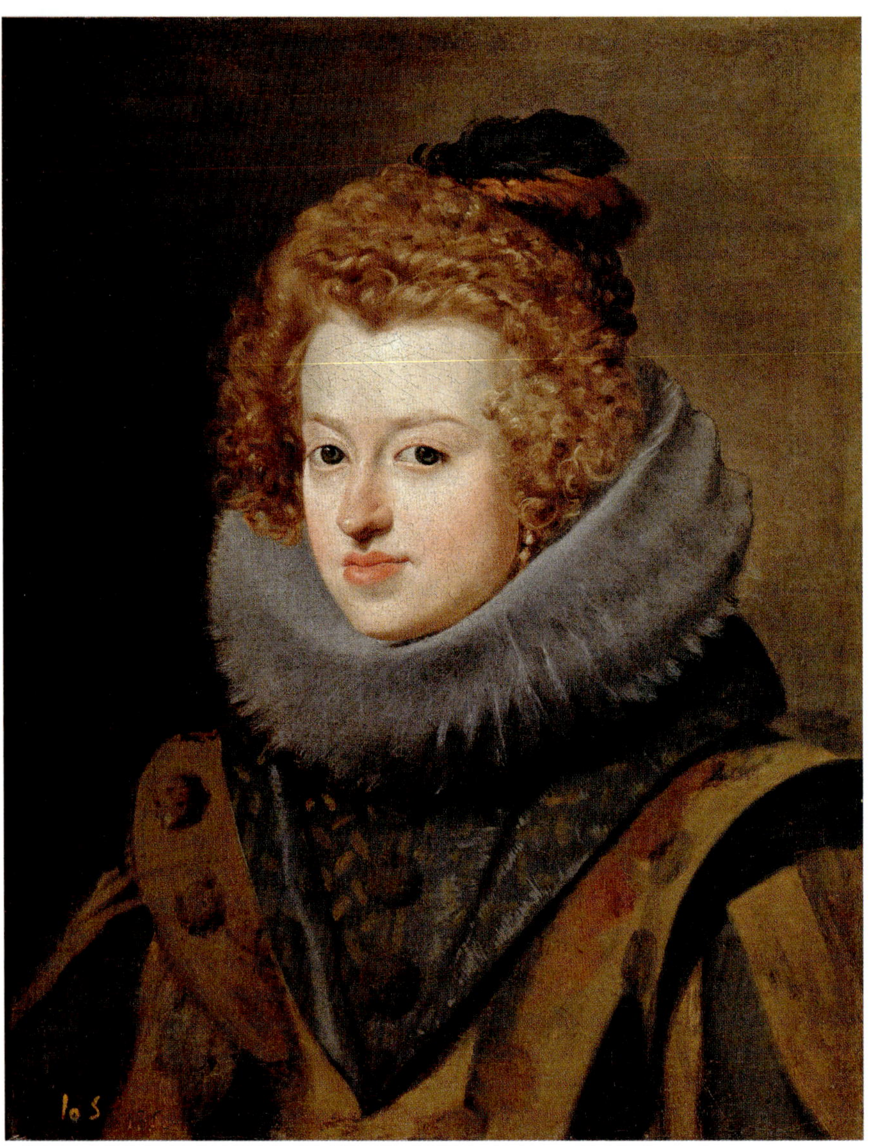

49 *Portrait of Doña Maria, Queen of Hungary, c. 1630*

to dry. Wooden scaffolding and washed clothes or bedding –
these do not belong to the concerns of high art. Making the
scene even more vernacular is the artist's rough and ready
technique, especially in the depiction of the grotto, where
seemingly random deposits of pigment are combined with
the scraped areas of canvas to describe the decaying plaster
of the grotto and the hidden brickwork beneath.

49   Late in 1630, Velázquez decided to return to Spain after a stay
in Italy of one and a half years. He travelled via Naples, where
he met and painted the King's sister, Maria, en route to join her
husband Ferdinand III, King of Hungary. A bust-length portrait
of her, which may be the one in question, reveals a warm and
winning personality, and its striking harmony of silvery greys,
blacks and russet browns testifies to the artist's newfound gifts
as a colourist. The portrait eventually found its way into the
royal collection in Madrid, where Velázquez himself arrived
early in 1631. Ahead of him was the busiest decade of his career.

Chapter 3
A New Prince and a New Palace

Prince Balthasar Carlos, heir to the Spanish throne, was born on 17 October 1629, an event greeted with much jubilation at court since it ensured the continuation of the dynasty. According to Pacheco, the King delayed having the prince's portrait painted until Velázquez could execute it, which he did shortly after returning from Italy. Considering the transformative effect that his exposure to Italian art had had upon his own style, it is not surprising that the resulting canvas is the most resplendently coloured work we have so far encountered in the artist's career. The young prince stands stiffly in the centre of the picture, one hand holding his baton of command and the other resting on the hilt of his sword. Together with his armoured collar or 'gorget' and the red sash across his chest, these are the attributes of a captain-general and foretell the military role he will assume when King. He wears an elaborately embroidered costume and on the cushion beside him rests his black hat, lavishly decorated with white plumes. Accompanying him is a court 'dwarf' who turns deferentially towards the prince. Although the sex of this figure has been much disputed, both the aproned dress and bead necklace suggest that it is probably a girl. She holds a rattle and apple, traditional childhood playthings which may here also allude to the orb and sceptre, attributes of royalty. Though the execution of the costumes is very precise and deliberate, the carpet and ceremonial drapery are more loosely brushed and the entire setting appears drenched in a rich crimson – in itself a fanfare of colour to celebrate the arrival of the young prince.

About two years later, when Balthasar Carlos was around four, the artist painted a similar portrait of him identically posed though now alone. As befits his age, the prince appears more confidently in control as he clutches his sword and grips

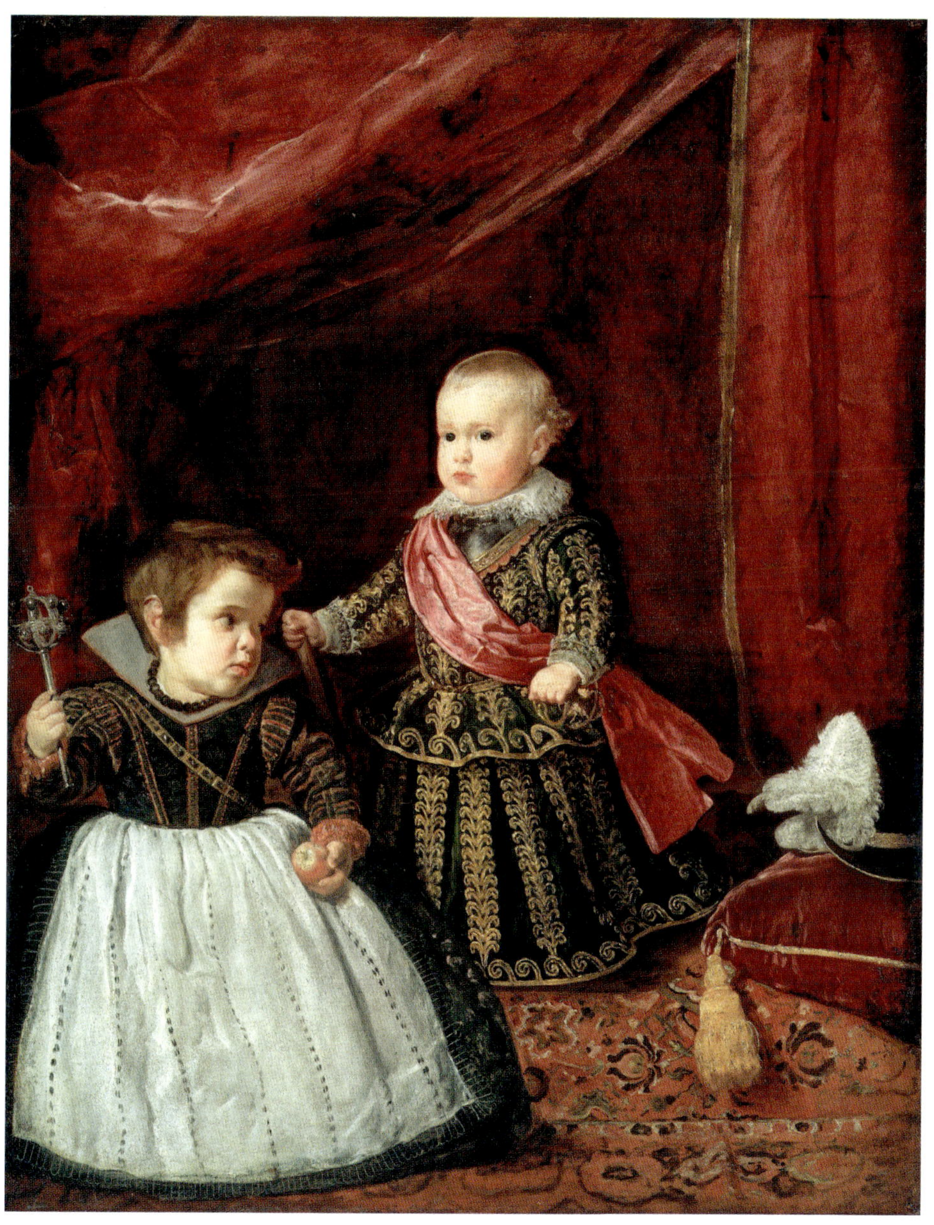

50 *Prince Balthasar Carlos with a Dwarf, 1631*

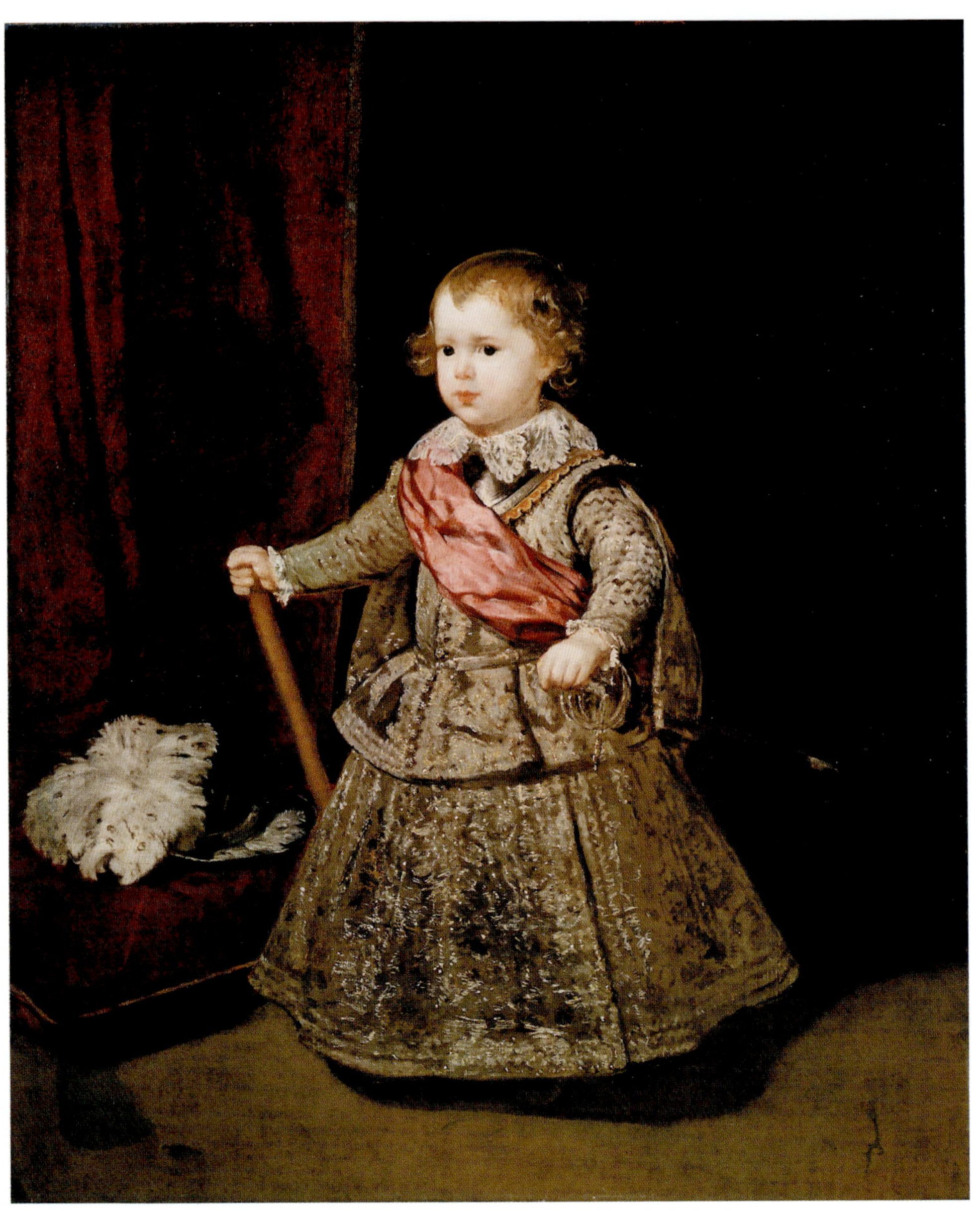

51 *Portrait of the Prince Balthasar Carlos, 1633*

his baton. His face has lost its baby fat and his hair has grown longer and acquired a full set of curls. As he has advanced in age so, too, has Velázquez's technique. In the mere two or so years since his last portrait of the prince, it has progressed from definition to abbreviation. The silver threads decorating Balthasar Carlos's costume now sparkle and shimmer with pinpoints of colour where the light catches them. Nothing is delineated or defined; instead, a seemingly random medley of dots and dashes of paint record the artist's sensations. Velázquez's own technical revolution – unmatched by even the greatest artists in his own century – has begun. Increasingly, from now on, his brushwork would be guided by suggestion rather than description.

A contemporary full-length portrait of the King himself shows this technique in embryonic form. *Philip IV in Brown and Silver* poses the monarch in the now familiar view facing three-quarters to our right and here dressed in an unusually ornate costume embroidered with silver thread. He wears a sleeveless jacket, his arms covered by a silver undergarment decorated with dark thread. Over his neck hangs the chain of the Order of the Golden Fleece. Clad in white hose and soft shoes, he holds a petition addressed to him which is signed with the artist's name, indicating both his allegiance and indebtedness to the King. On the wooden table beside him rests his ornately plumed hat and in the background on the left is a rich red drape.

Two features of this portrait are revolutionary, both connected and neither belonging to 1631–32, the likely date of the picture. The first is the rendering of the King's costume. In a supremely formal portrait, what could be less formal or official than this? An intricate brocade has been reduced to a filigree of strokes from which one can scarcely decipher the pattern of the decoration. As the light catches them, some outlines emerge and others recede, but all appear in flux. Our eyes may now have grown accustomed to such suggestion thanks to the legacy of the Impressionists, but this dates from 250 years before them and seems totally ahead of its time.

This leads inevitably to the other most innovative aspect of Velázquez's portrait, which is only indirectly of the artist's own making. This is the painting's title. Earlier known as *The Silver Philip*, it is now universally entitled *Philip IV in Brown and Silver*. To designate a picture by its colour chord is familiar enough in the works of Whistler, Matisse or Mondrian, but not before. To do so in the case of a painting by Velázquez is tacitly to acknowledge that the manner is as important as the matter – style as important as subject.

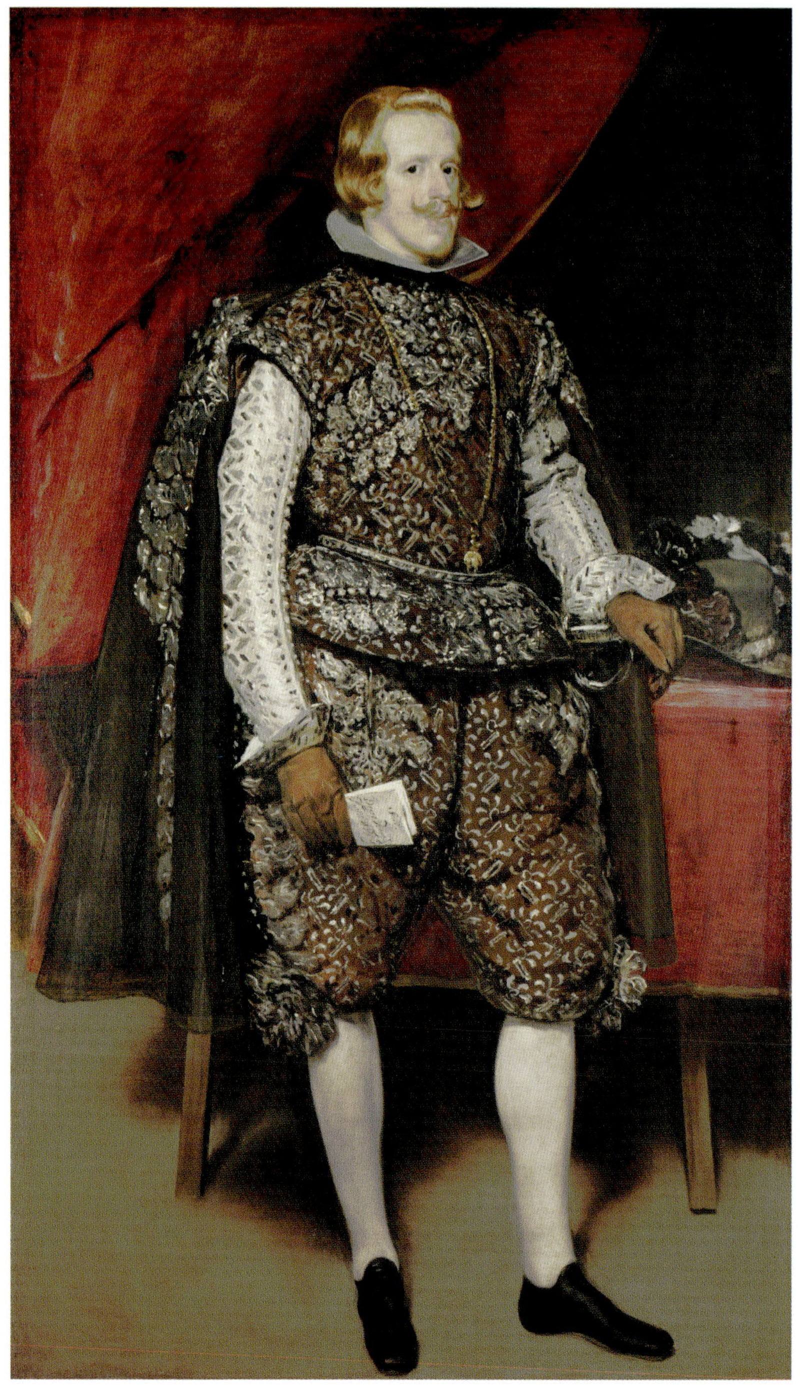

52 *Philip IV in Brown and Silver, 1631–32*

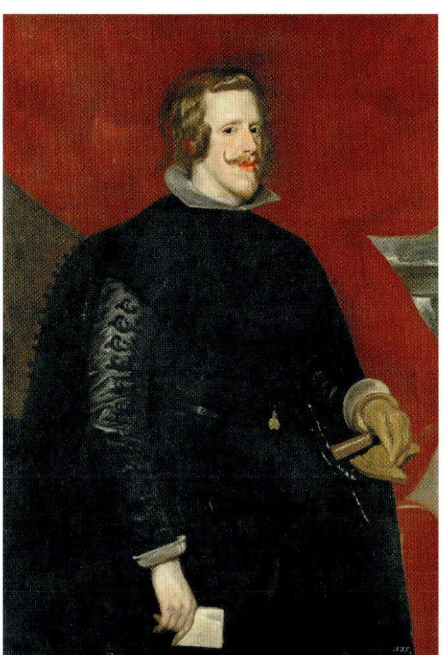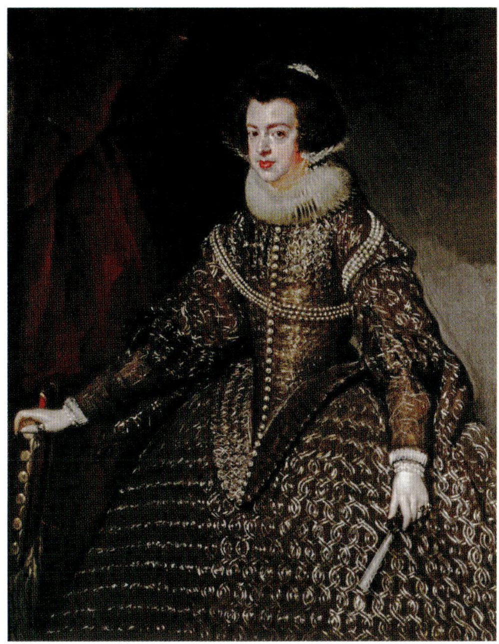

53 ABOVE LEFT · *Philip IV, c.* 1632
54 ABOVE RIGHT · *Isabella of Bourbon, c.* 1632

Nothing is known of the later history of *Philip IV in Brown and Silver* until it was taken from a royal palace in Madrid by Joseph Bonaparte in 1810 and eventually made its way into English collections. But images of the Spanish king and members of his family were widely disseminated to courts around Europe at the time as souvenirs, diplomatic gifts and (not least) a means of arranging royal marriages. Velázquez, a notoriously slow worker, could not possibly meet all of these demands unaided and, throughout his career, it is clear that he relied increasingly upon workshop assistants, sometimes to paint entire pictures and, at others, to collaborate with him in doing so. An early instance of this are the portraits of the King and his wife, Queen Isabella of Bourbon, of around 1632, which are probably identical to those sent to the Habsburg Emperor in Austria in that year. While the King's head is likely to be by Velázquez himself – and is nearly identical to that of the *Silver Philip* – the strident and amorphous red drapery that frames him and reveals a portion of a loggia beyond is both too crudely executed and too jarring in colour to be by the master himself. In the portrait of the Queen, the elaborately patterned embroidery on her dress is a passable simulation of the spontaneity of Velázquez but not

53, 54

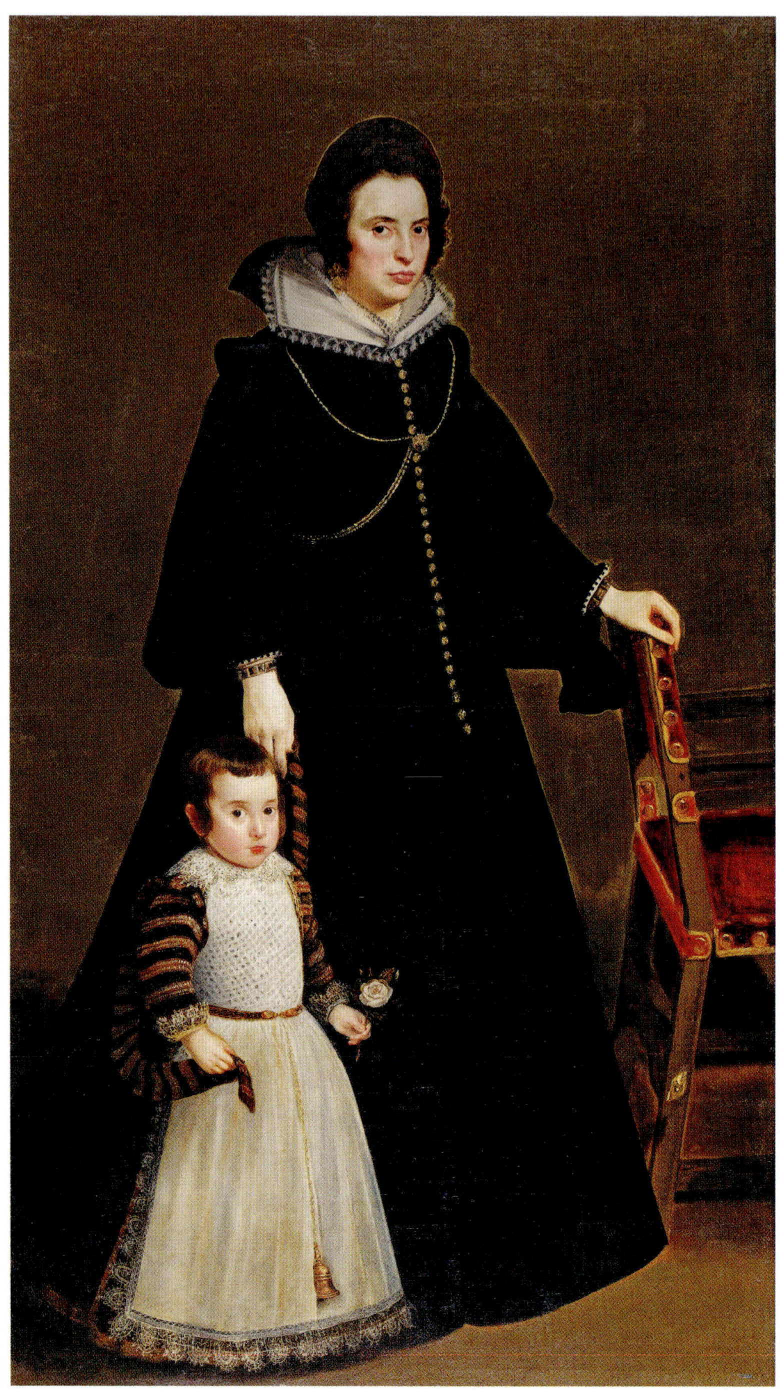

55 ABOVE *Doña Antonia de Ipeñarrieta y Galdós and Her Son Don Luis*, 1631–32
56 OPPOSITE *Don Diego del Corral y Arellano*, 1631–32

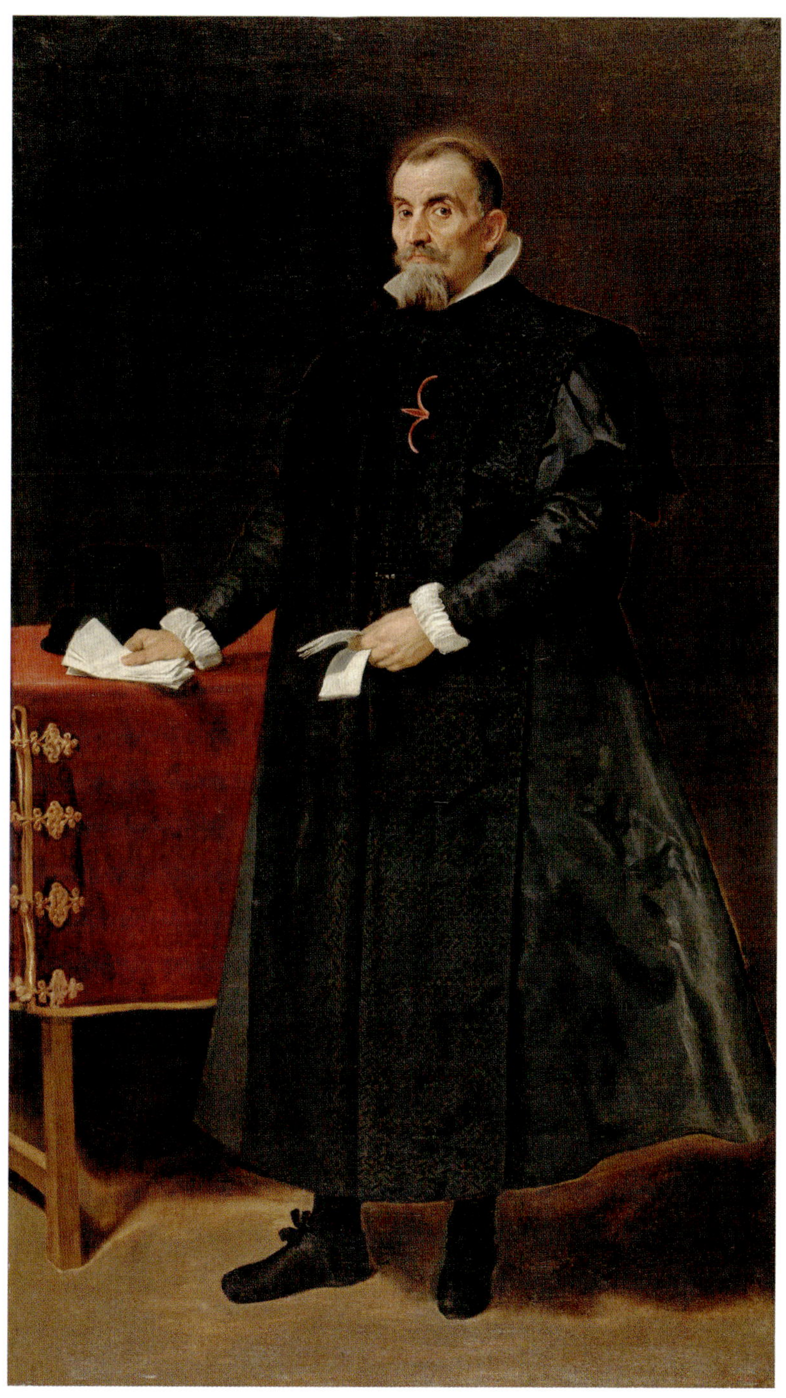

the real thing. Put simply, it relies on too much repetition. On the left are neatly spaced rows of orderly dabs of the brush, which reduce themselves to flatness rather than form; on the right, the parallel curves of the design weave up and down and are too pedantically painted to be by the artist.

Inevitably, it is in his non-royal portraits that Velázquez enjoyed greater freedom and probably less pressure, protocol, assistants, imitators and copyists being rarely of concern. Two of his finest of these years are the companion portraits of Don Diego del Corral and his wife Doña Antonia de Ipeñarrieta with their son Don Luis. The former was a noted jurist at the Council of Castile, a professor at the University of Salamanca and a distinguished intellectual. His wife was governess to Prince Balthasar Carlos and had commissioned three paintings from Velázquez in 1624, one of the King, another of Olivares and the third of her first husband, who died in that year. She married Don Diego three years later and, although her first marriage was without offspring, her second yielded six children.

It would be difficult to imagine two more dignified and austere portraits. Don Diego stands at his juror's table, his hands clutching official papers and his hat resting on the table. His broad robes part slightly to reveal the embroidered cross of the Order of Santiago and he gazes out with an alert and penetrating gaze that conveys both great wisdom and integrity. The painting of his robes is remarkable, for never can so many different blacks have seemed so luminous and colourful. To add to the gravity and authority of the portrait, the faintest aureole of light encircles his head, separating him from his surroundings.

A comparable radiance surrounds the head of his wife, who appears in every regard his moral and emotional equal. Dressed in black – perhaps in mourning for her first husband – she wears an open-sleeved garment, part of which is held in her hand and the tail end in that of the boy. Gazing sternly and formidably out at the viewer, she cannot have acted as a lenient governess to the young prince, whose youthful antics she is bound to have held in check. Her own young son appears timid, flat and less lifelike, but how long can we imagine that he would have been willing to pose for the artist? Resting her left hand on the back of a chair and filling the picture space, Doña Antonia nearly rivals Jerónima de la Fuente as the most formidable female sitter thus far encountered in Velázquez's career.

We will never know whose decision it was for Velázquez to depict Don Pedro de Barberana y Aparregui against a neutral background during these same years, that of the sitter or of

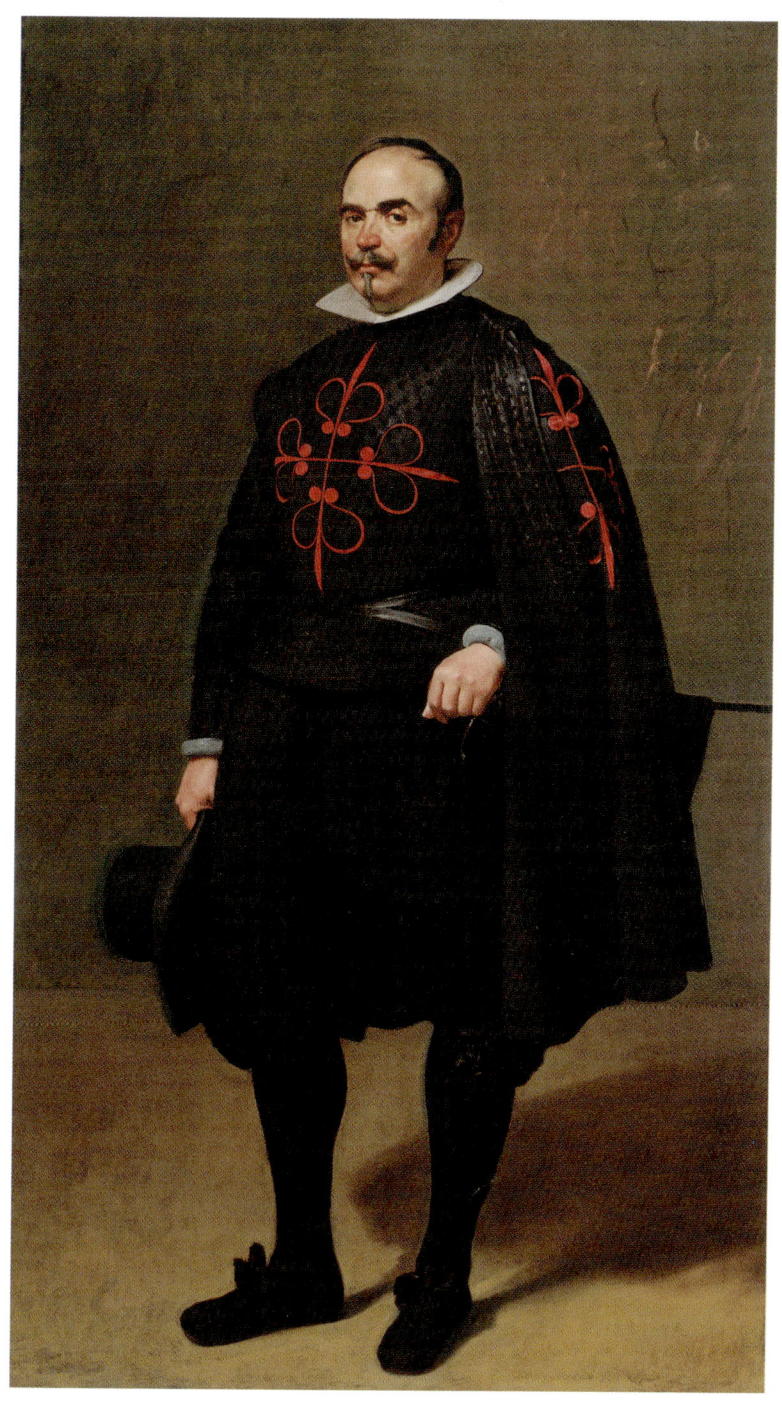

57 *Don Pedro de Barberana y Aparregui, c. 1631–32*

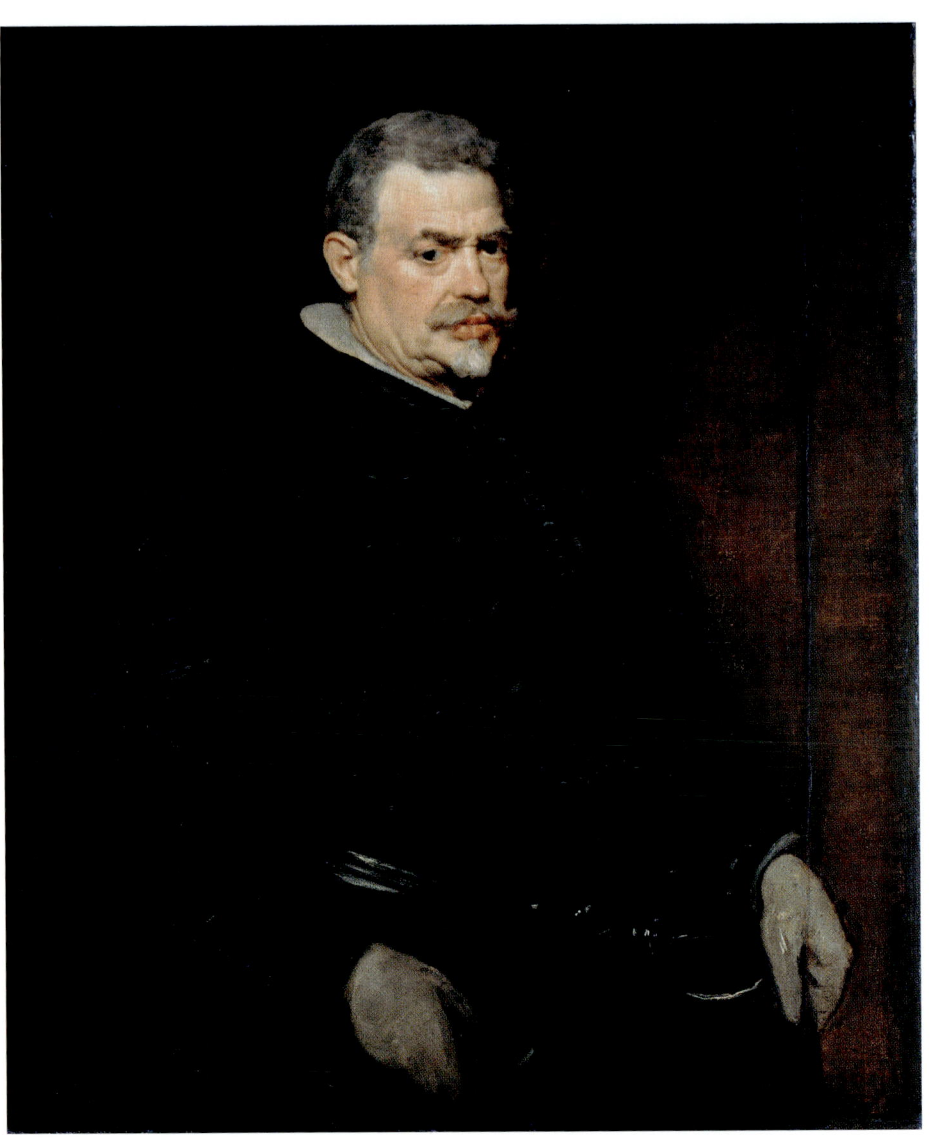

58 *Don Juan Mateos*, c. 1634

the artist himself. But the decision adds to the boldness and immediacy of the portrayal and proved to be the harbinger of at least one later portrait, which would be even more daring. Barberana was warden of the castle of Briones and served Philip IV as auditor of his accounts. Admitted to the Order of Calatrava in October 1630, with its cross emblazoned across his chest, he stands boldly before us dressed in black, with his feet firmly planted on the ground, a notable advance by Velázquez from the *Silver Philip*, where the King's right leg has yet to balance his weight. Although the sitter's pose is conventional, the treatment is anything but. With the floor line barely indicated and tonal gradations in the setting subtly modulated, the artist succeeds in evoking an assertive presence in ambient air. With the sittings concluded, Velázquez repeatedly wiped his brush on the upper right, as if to acknowledge a job well done.

58   One member of the household who sat for the artist in the early 1630s was Juan Mateos, master of the royal hunt. Mateos was responsible for organizing hunting expeditions for the court, such as that featured in the *Tela Real*, to which we shall return, and was also the author of an important treatise on hunting published in 1634. He appears again in Velázquez's art alongside Olivares in the so-called *Riding School*, but he is here seen three-quarter length against a neutral background, his worn and pensive features suggesting less a man of action than one of reflection. His burly figure fills the canvas despite the fact that the artist reduced its right contour somewhat, an alteration that now shows through. The hands are unfinished, the position of the right one explained by the fact that it was eventually intended to hold a pistol. That accounts for its position and would of course have been appropriate to Mateos's role. But one does not mourn its absence given the inward-looking nature of the rest of the portrait.

While portraiture dominated Velázquez's art of the early 1630s, he also painted a handful of important religious pictures during these years. One work that effectively combines the two

59   is his *Sibyl*, for which a life model clearly posed as one of the Old Testament prophetesses who had foretold the coming of Christ. She is here shown in strict profile gazing into the future, as befits a seer. Holding a blank tablet on which to record her prophecies, she wears beige drapery which blends with the muted and tawny colour scheme.

Velázquez was certainly familiar with the many sibyls painted by Italian artists both of the past and of his own time, among them those on the Sistine ceiling. But the gap between his own and theirs is irreconcilable, even if (as some have surmised) he painted this picture in Italy. A *Sibyl* by

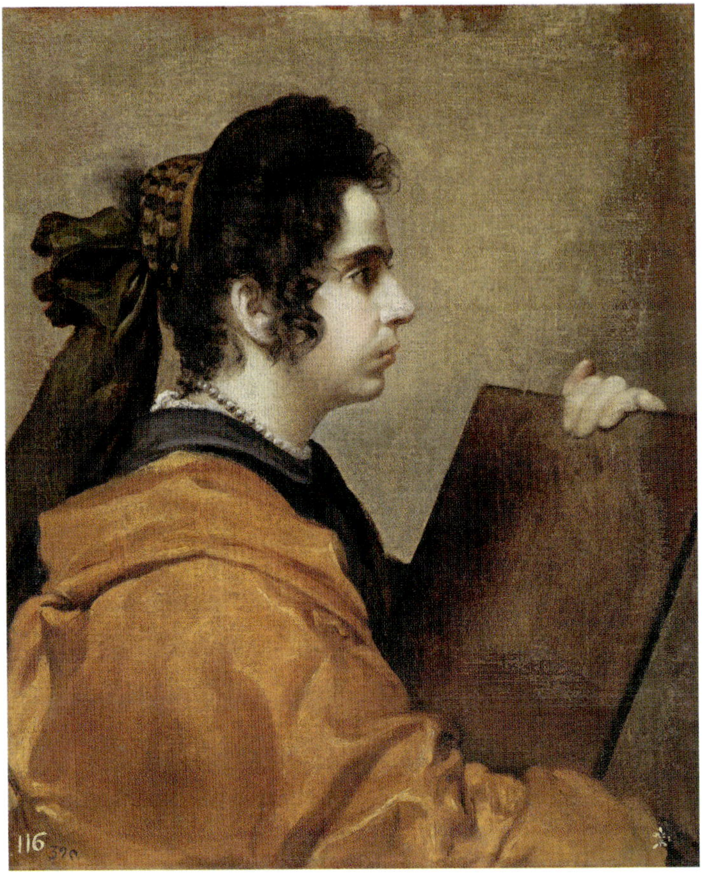

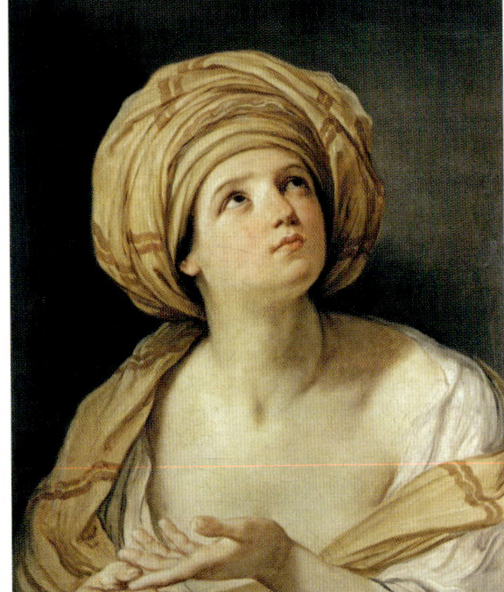

59 ABOVE *A Sibyl*, c. 1632
60 RIGHT Guido Reni, *Sibyl*, 1635–36
61 OPPOSITE *St Rufina*, 1632–34

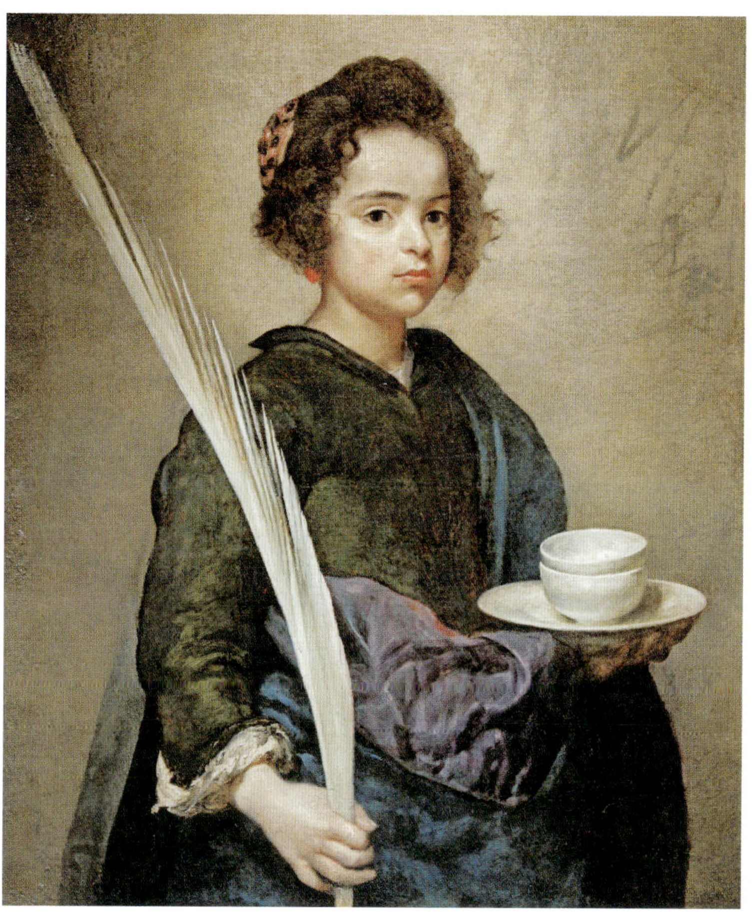

Guido Reni is roughly contemporary with it but belongs to a
different world. No one need to have posed for her bland and
idealized features as she gazes heavenwards, enumerating with
her fingers the prophecies she will relate. Wearing an exotic
oriental turban which trails down her neck and across her
breast, she is coloured with sweet, pastel tones, not the earthy
hues of Velázquez. His sybil wears a pearl necklace and boasts
frizzy black hair and a relatively modest headdress, making her
more a creature of her own time than one of the biblical past.

The plain and sober style of this *Sibyl* is also seen in a
recently discovered *St Rufina* attributed to Velázquez which
is likewise datable to the early 1630s. First recorded in the
collection of Gaspar Méndez de Haro, great nephew of Olivares,
this picture again reveals the artist relying on the close study

of a life model, here an adolescent girl. Along with her sister, St Justa, Rufina was a potter and both became patron saints of Seville, martyred for their refusal to allow their ceramic vessels to be used as cult objects in the worship of a pagan god.

Velázquez depicts Rufina holding a cup and saucer and a martyr's palm and wearing a billowing dress. Although her steady and expressionless gaze befits her saintly persona, her curly hair and puckered lips reveal the young model enacting this role. Velázquez, too, has left his own idiosyncratic signature on the painting. St Rufina is posed against a light greyish background through which one can plainly see the altered outline of her costume on the left and zigzagging lines along the upper right where the artist has scored the canvas while wiping his brush.

Velázquez's most ambitious religious painting of the 1630s is *The Temptation of St Thomas Aquinas*, a work whose origins are shrouded in mystery. In 1633 a painting of this subject was delivered to the College of St Dominic at Orihuela in the Kingdom of Valencia in eastern Spain. No artist was named, and the present painting remained there, unpublished, until 1906. Since that time it has aroused continual controversy, not least over the question of why Velázquez would accept a commission from such a remote destination and of who might have instigated it. The most likely candidate here is Fray Antonio de Sotomayor, Inquisitor General and Philip IV's confessor, who was the most important Dominican at court and was named protector of Orihuela's Dominican college in 1631.

The subject of the picture was unusual and bizarre enough to challenge any painter. When Thomas Aquinas decided to join a mendicant order, his parents strongly objected. Soon after he took the habit, his brothers abducted him and confined him in the hope that he would renounce the religious life, sending a woman to his quarters to tempt him. At the sight of her Thomas took a lit log from the fire, drew a cross on a nearby wall and fell into a deep trance. Two angels then appeared to succour him, one bearing a girdle to put around his waist and preserve his chastity.

Unlike his great contemporaries, Rubens and Rembrandt, Velázquez was not a born storyteller and was rarely called upon by his patrons to be so. But here he faced a complex sequence of events with many different focuses: the saint, the angels, the temptress, the smouldering log, the fireplace and the cross on the wall. Even the ambitious history pictures of his Italian years, *The Forge of Vulcan* and *Joseph's Bloody Coat*, had not involved so many centres of interest. The picture that resulted artfully incorporates them all. A kneeling angel supports the sleeping

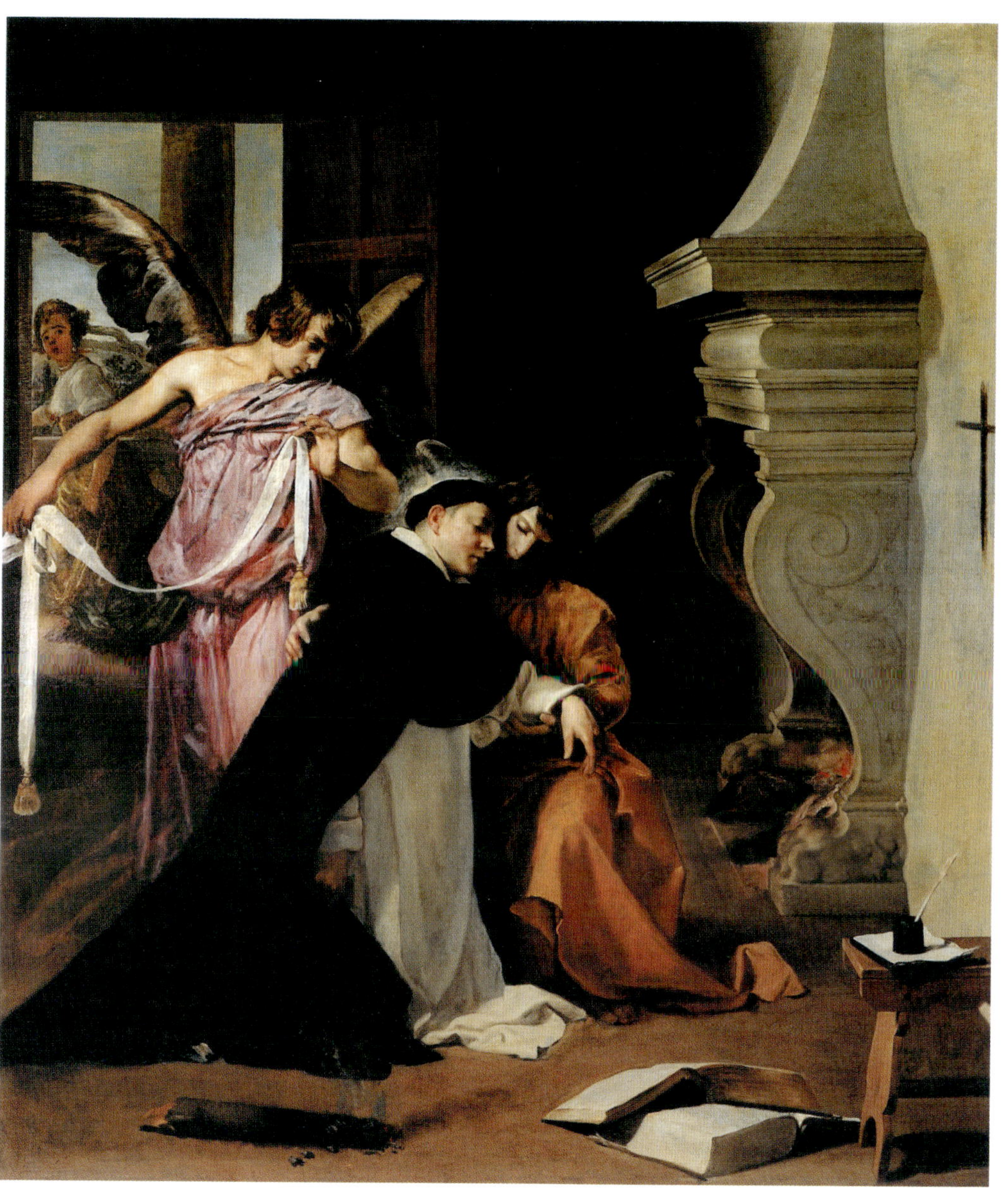

62 *The Temptation of St Thomas Aquinas, 1631–33*

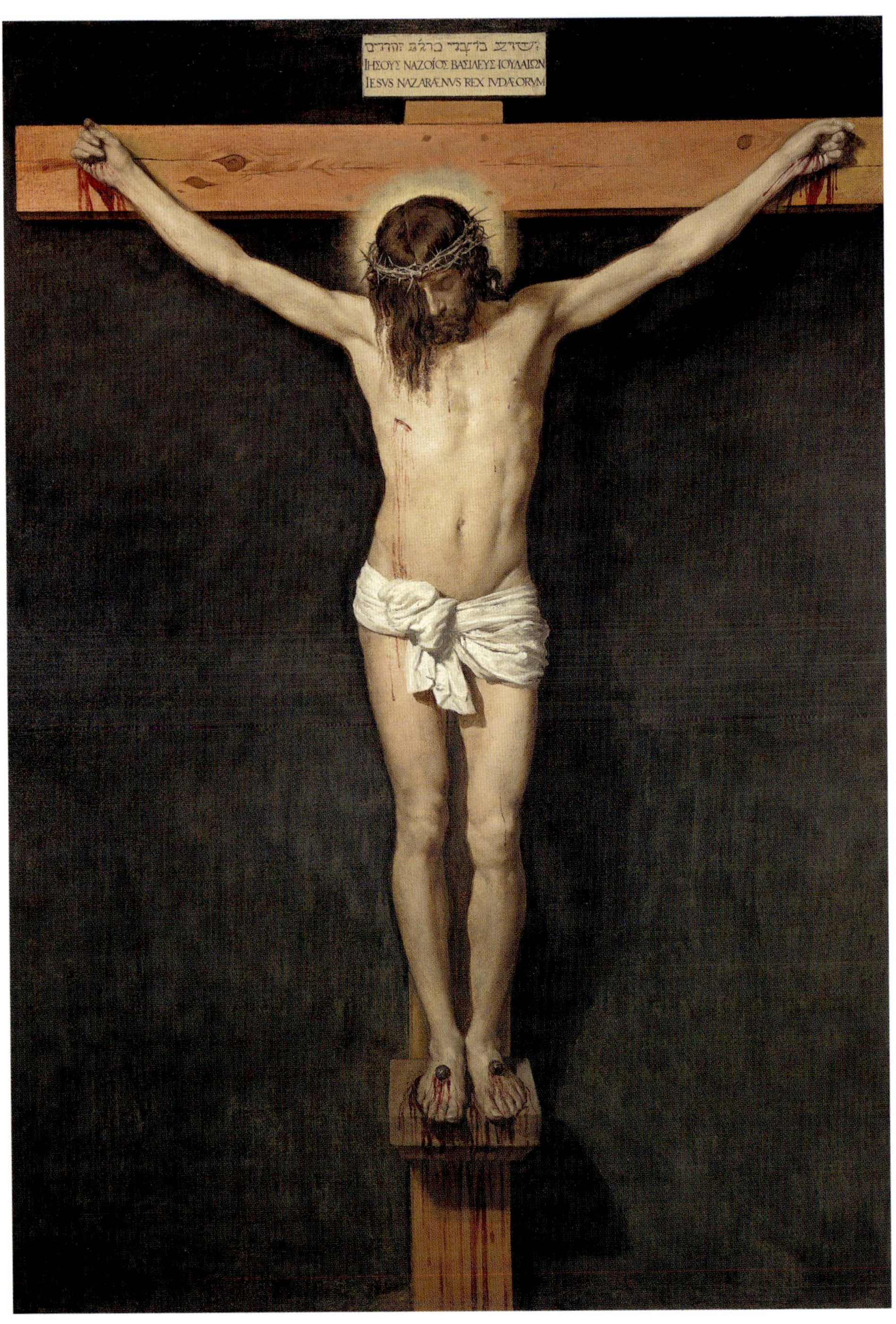

63 ABOVE *Christ on the Cross*, c. 1632
64 OPPOSITE Francisco de Zurbarán, *The Crucifixion*, 1627

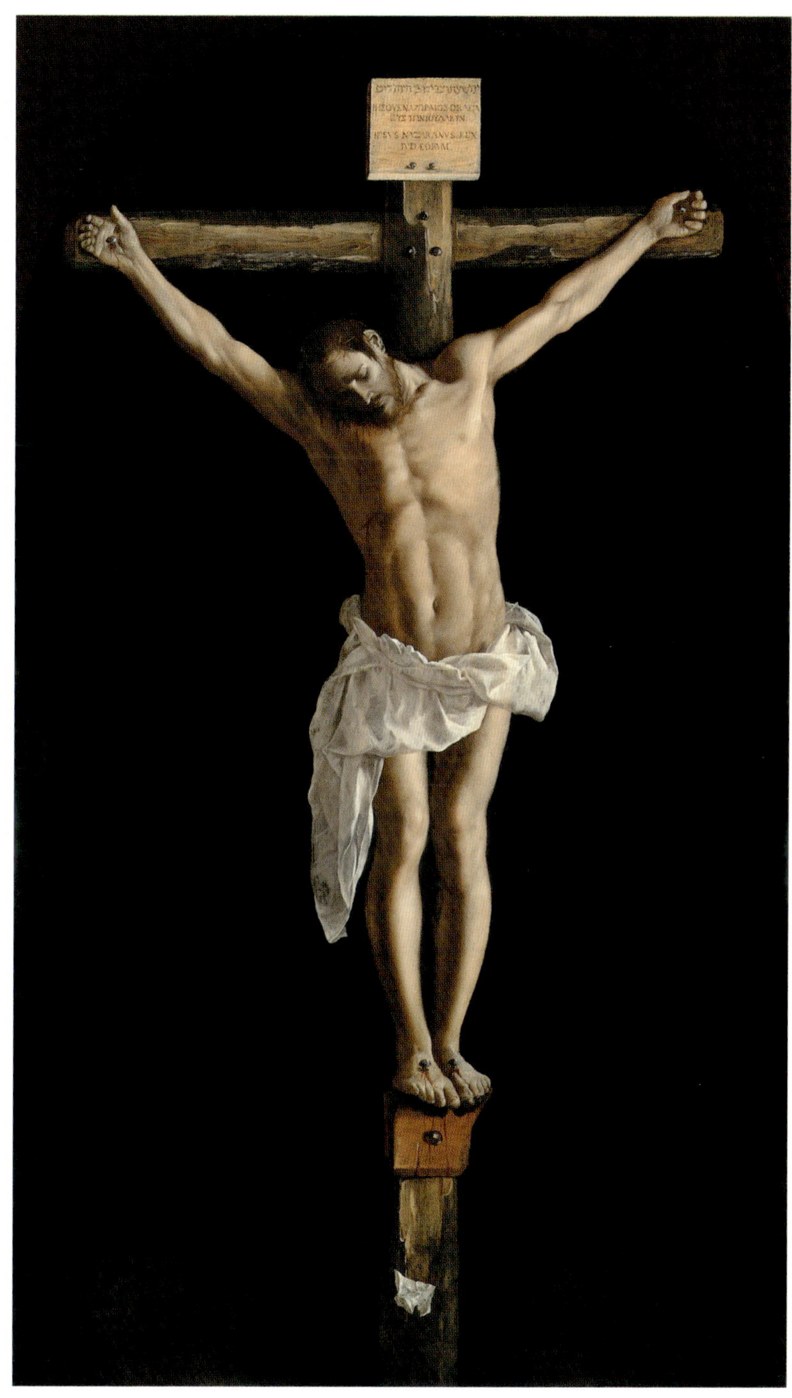

saint as another prepares to tie his waist with the girdle. On the floor before him lies the burning log, on the wall in front the inscribed cross and in the background the fleeing temptress.

The lithe limbs, flowing locks and freely painted draperies of the angels in this picture bear obvious similarities with those of Apollo in *The Forge of Vulcan*, and the visible removal of the flowing robes around the feet of the standing angel is wholly consistent with the master's practice of revising his thoughts in the course of painting. More surprising is the attention the artist has lavished on the architecture of the room and particularly the ornate fireplace, although the palatial setting clearly underscores the worldly pleasures that the saint is renouncing through the inscribed cross on the wall and his subsequent trance.

About 1632 Velázquez also executed his immensely moving *Christ on the Cross* for the Church of San Plácido in Madrid. Although multifigure depictions of the Crucifixion are common throughout the history of art, images of Christ alone on the cross only became popular from the late sixteenth century. El Greco and Rubens specialized in them, but their Christs are invariably still alive and gazing upwards, imploring the heavens for deliverance. Velázquez follows his father-in-law Pacheco's treatment of the subject in depicting Christ as already dead, his lean and decidedly unheroic body stretched on the cross, his nailed hands and feet and pierced side streaming blood. Though Christ has a halo and his cross is surmounted by the traditional superscription, the artist introduces a number of elements into the work that intensify its rawness and realism. The wood of the cross is pitted with knots, as wounded as Christ himself; the loincloth pulls tightly around his waist and is no more than is absolutely necessary; the lighting is natural and matter-of-fact, devoid of any sense of spirituality; and – the greatest master-stroke of all – Christ's head has fallen forward with his hair now concealing half of his face. 'And he bowed his head, and gave up the ghost.' (John 19:30). The veiling of Christ's face signifies the ultimate degradation and sacrifice.

Contrast this with an equally great *Crucifixion* by Velázquez's exact contemporary Francisco de Zurbarán, painted in 1627 for the Monastery of San Pablo el Real in Seville. Zurbarán's *Crucifixion* is virtually bloodless, his Christ more muscular and heroic and his loincloth draped with a generous flourish. Although Zurbarán's Christ is also dead, his head rests comfortably on his shoulder rather than falling forward, as in Velázquez's painting. Above all, the searing light that reveals him is not of this earth, but beyond it, bestowing a visionary quality on the image that Velázquez's singularly lacks.

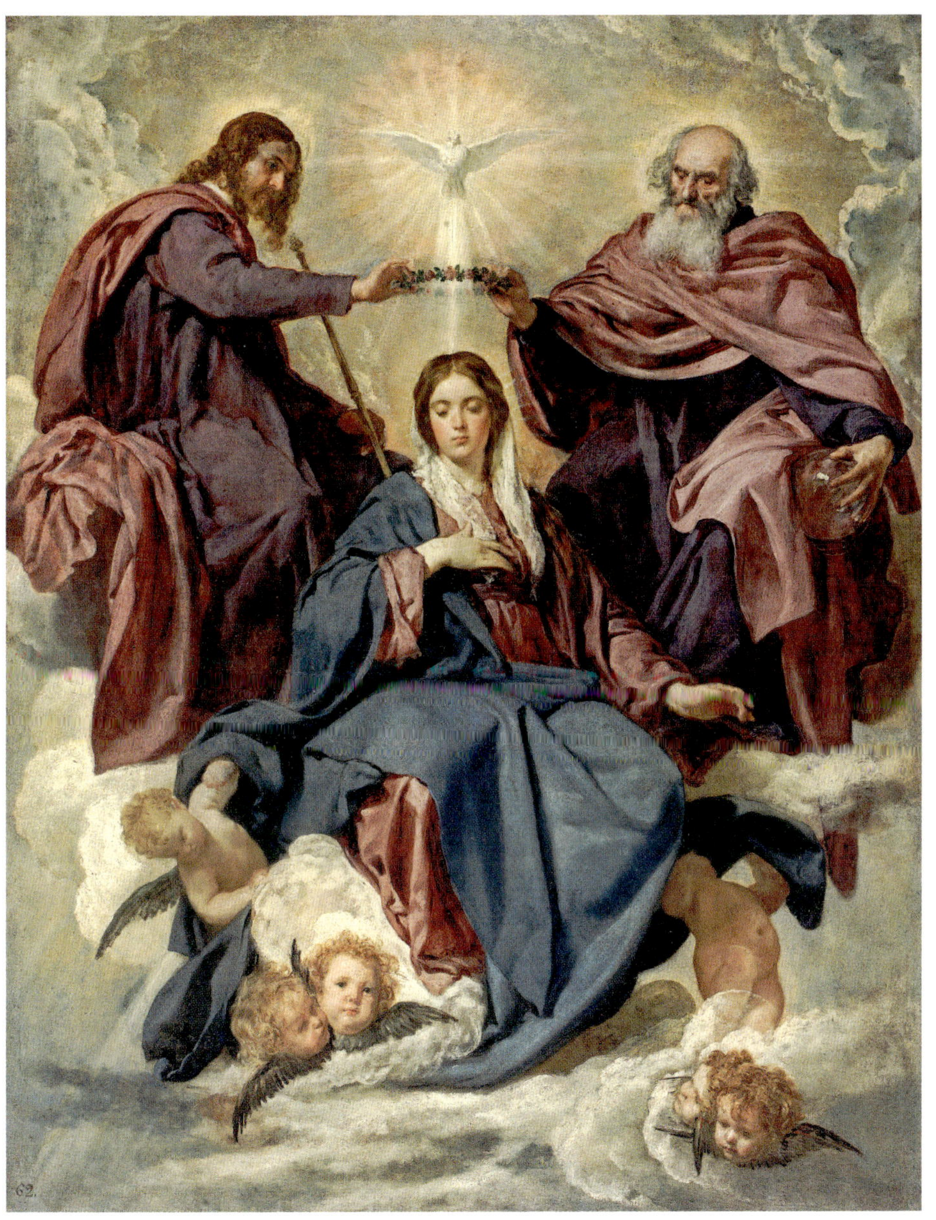

65 *The Coronation of the Virgin, 1635–36*

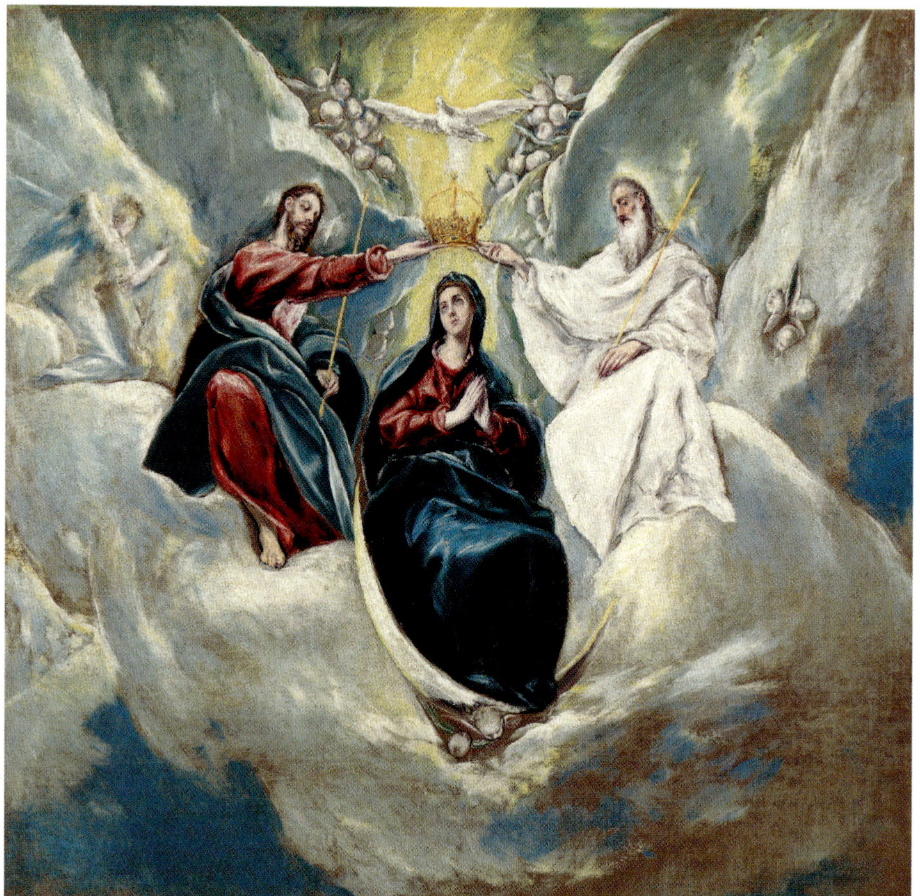

66 El Greco, *The Coronation of the Virgin*, c. 1590

This may explain the absence of a halo on Zurbarán's Christ, whose radiance emanates from within.

The *Coronation of the Virgin* is Velázquez's last religious picture and one of the best preserved of all his works, its sparkle and luminosity appearing as fresh today as they were when it left the artist's studio. It has an intriguing and fortunate history. In 1635, Cardinal Gaspar de Borja y Velasco (to whom we shall return), who had spent a long time in Rome, returned to Madrid. He had earlier sent Queen Isabella a present of nine paintings of the Feasts of the Virgin by an unnamed Italian artist recently identified as Alessandro Turchi, a master from Verona, and it was decided that these should be displayed in her oratory in the Alcázar along with

a tenth canvas by Velázquez, which would need to conform
with them in style and dimensions. The conservatism of
Turchi's style probably accounts for the fact that the *Coronation*
is Velázquez's most classically conceived composition. Strictly
symmetrical in arrangement and balanced in colour, it depicts
Christ and God the Father crowning the Virgin, with the dove
of the Holy Spirit hovering above and putti below. Father and
Son are clad in purple and rose and the Virgin wears a white
veil and rose garment over which is an expansive blue drape,
which anchors the design. Iconographically, the work is highly
orthodox, both male deities shown fully clothed to preserve
decorum, God the Father holding the globe in his left hand
and the Virgin serenely beautiful. Behind all the classicism and
orthodoxy, however, there can be little doubt that Velázquez
modelled the figures on real people, as was invariably his
preferred way. Moreover, his vision appears essentially
earthbound and unecstatic, especially when compared with a
Coronation of the Virgin by his greatest immediate predecessor,
El Greco. In the latter's picture of about 1590, the weightless
figures levitate, seemingly ascending into a realm of pure
spirituality. Velázquez's, by contrast, are solid and bound by
the laws of gravity. As in his *Immaculate Conception* of nearly
twenty years earlier, his only recourse to the divine is through
the human.

In the mid-1630s Velázquez's creative energies were almost
entirely dedicated to work for the King. The beginning of this
decade saw the gradual emergence of a new royal palace located
to the east of Madrid and incorporating the already existing
Monastery of San Jerónimo. A joint initiative by the King and
Olivares, the building was to function as a pleasure palace for
royal festivals and entertainments. It had spacious gardens
and eventually included a theatre, small hermitage chapels,
an artificial lake, a ballroom and an arena for bullfights and
tournaments. While the centre of government of the royal
household remained the Alcázar Palace nearby, the Buen
Retiro, as its name indicates, was a place of retreat from royal
duties where the monarchy could celebrate itself and delight
and revel in magnificent festivities and pageantry.

During the next years the Buen Retiro palace and its
surroundings increased in size until it was virtually half as
big as Madrid itself. Erected in record time and intended to
rival that great monument to the Spanish Habsburg dynasty
of Philip II, the Escorial, it was hardly its architectural equal
and the poor materials used in its construction – largely bricks
and wood – ensured that it would not survive intact for long.
But at the time it enriched and celebrated the achievements

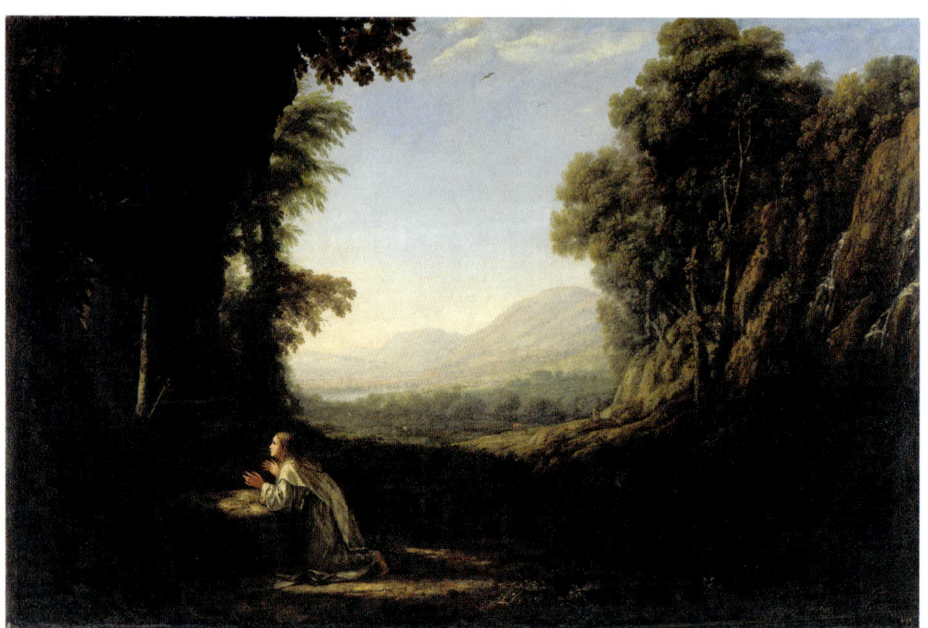

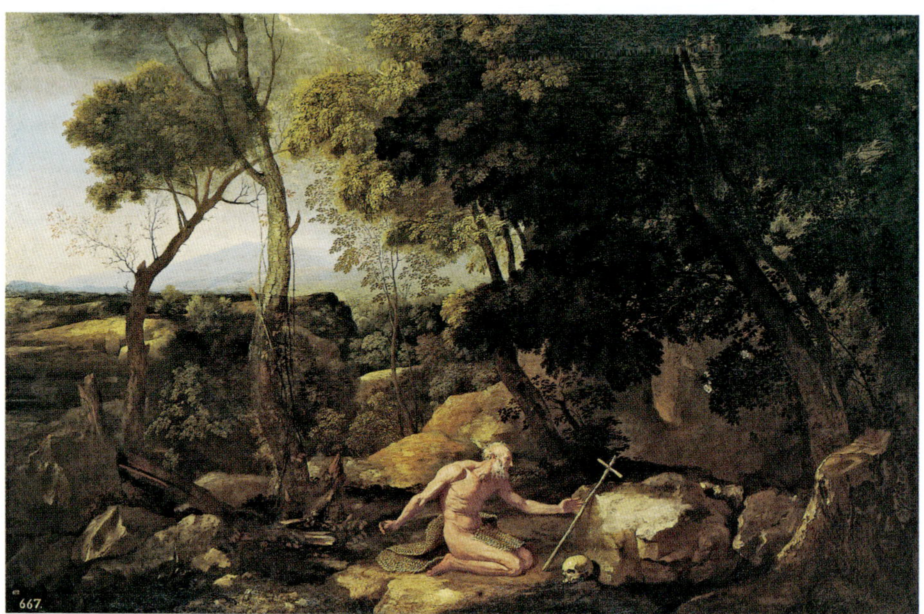

67 TOP Claude Lorrain, *Landscape with St Mary Magdalene*, 1637
68 ABOVE Nicolas Poussin, *Landscape with St Paul the Hermit*, 1637

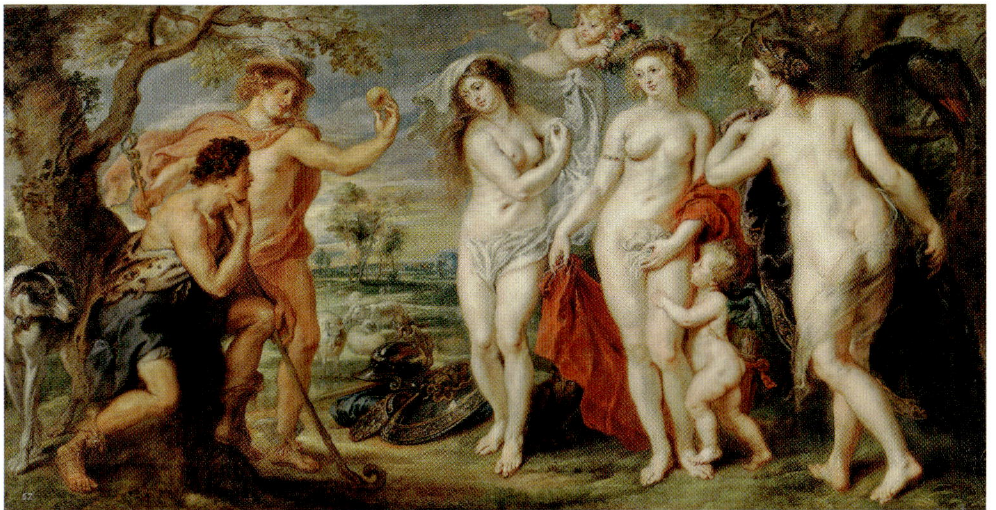

69 Peter Paul Rubens, *Judgment of Paris*, c. 1638

of the royal family, and nowhere more so than in the great
picture collection.

To decorate the vast gallery spaces of the palace,
Philip bought and commissioned a large number of paintings
from artists both native and foreign. Agents in Rome, Naples
and Flanders secured many of these for the King, not all of
them of the very highest quality. But many of them were
and may now be seen adorning the walls of the Prado in
Madrid. In 1633 and 1638 two big consignments of works
were sent to the capital by the Viceroy of Naples, which was
then under Spanish rule, including works by the majority of
notable artists then working in the city, among them Giovanni
Lanfranco, Massimo Stanzione and Artemisia Gentileschi. In
Rome a host of French and Dutch artists were commissioned
to supply anchorite subjects for the landscape gallery in the
Palace, Claude's exquisite *Landscape with St Mary Magdalene*
and Poussin's *Landscape with St Paul the Hermit* among
them. In Antwerp, Rubens and his workshop were repeatedly
pressed into service by requests from the King and his
courtiers, the majority of the pictures being executed by
members of the studio but a magnificent *Judgment of Paris*
by the master himself.

An even larger cohort of native artists contributed to the
decoration of the palace, from the most conservative and old
fashioned to the most radically innovative. If the results were
never to be homogeneous, they did provide a rich anthology

of the most diverse trends in much of European painting of
the period. The lion's share of the Spanish contribution was
allocated to the country's two greatest artists. Zurbarán was
summoned from his native Seville to paint eleven canvases for
the palace in Madrid, and Velázquez was to be responsible for
thirteen works, to which we shall shortly return. Even before
picking up his brushes for the new palace, however, he sold
eighteen works from his own collection to the King, including
two recent masterpieces he had painted, *The Forge of Vulcan*
and *Joseph's Bloody Coat.*

The most important room in the Retiro Palace was the
Hall of Realms, which was located in the centre of the north
wing. Previously used as a royal box when the palace served
as a theatre for fiestas, it was converted into a throne room
where the King could preside over court ceremonies and
entertainments. Measuring 34.6 metres long and 10 metres
wide, it bore a high ceiling flooded with light from twenty
windows above and was encircled by an iron balcony, making
it possible for courtiers to view the spectacle taking place
below. The vaults above the upper windows were decorated with
the escutcheons of the twenty-four kingdoms of the Spanish
monarchy, which gave the hall its name, and the ceiling itself
with elaborate gilt grotesques.

But the principal adornments of the room were the
twenty-seven paintings commissioned for it, which comprised
an apotheosis of the reign of Philip IV throughout the Spanish
kingdom. These consisted of twelve large battle paintings
displayed between the lower windows and commemorating
military victories of the Spanish armies around the world.
Above the windows were ten canvases depicting the labours
of Hercules, from whom the Spanish monarchy claimed direct
descent. (Although Hercules's legendary labours numbered
twelve and not ten, the number commissioned was determined
by the number of lower windows in the room.) Finally, on the
end walls were equestrian portraits of Philip IV and his Queen
Isabella of Bourbon and, above the door between them, another
of the heir to the throne, Balthasar Carlos. On the opposite end
wall were matching portraits of the King's parents, Philip III
and Margaret of Austria, on horseback.

All of these paintings were by native artists and represented
a cross-section of Spanish figure painting in the third decade
of the seventeenth century. Pride of place was deservedly given
to Velázquez and Zurbarán, although it must be conceded that
the latter was somewhat ill at ease with the labours of Hercules
commissioned from him. A master of monastic subjects of
solitude and stillness, he was not a natural choice to portray

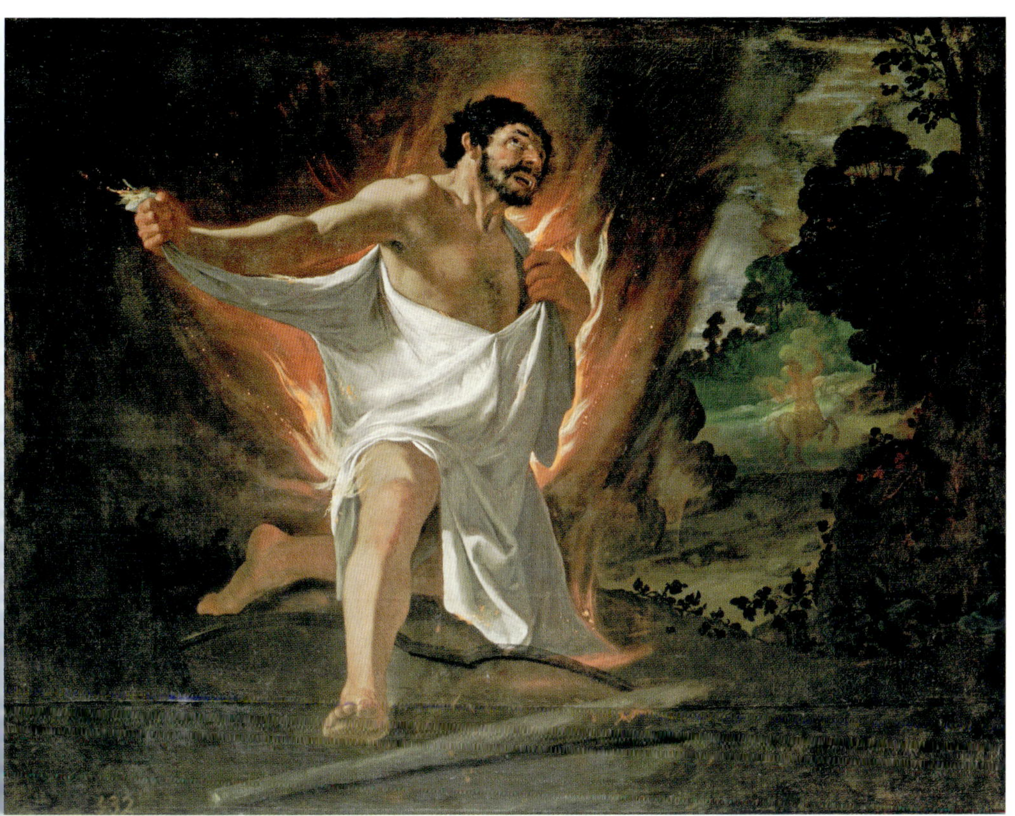

70 Francisco de Zurbarán, *Death of Hercules*, 1634

the strenuous efforts of a heroic male nude against multiple
adversaries, which may explain why the relative restraint
of the scene of his death in the burning robe is perhaps the
most convincing.

Velázquez was commissioned to paint six works for the hall,
the five equestrian portraits and one battle scene. Given that
these were all intended to be completed within a year for the
inauguration of the hall in the spring of 1635, he could not
fulfil so large a commitment without assistance.

This was certainly the case with the portraits of Philip III,
Margaret of Austria and Isabella of Bourbon, where the
meticulous and laboured handling of the sitters and their
mounts and the somewhat lifeless landscapes were clearly
executed by members of the artist's studio and then retouched
by the master himself in an attempt to breathe some life into
them. Understandably, this would have proved meddlesome

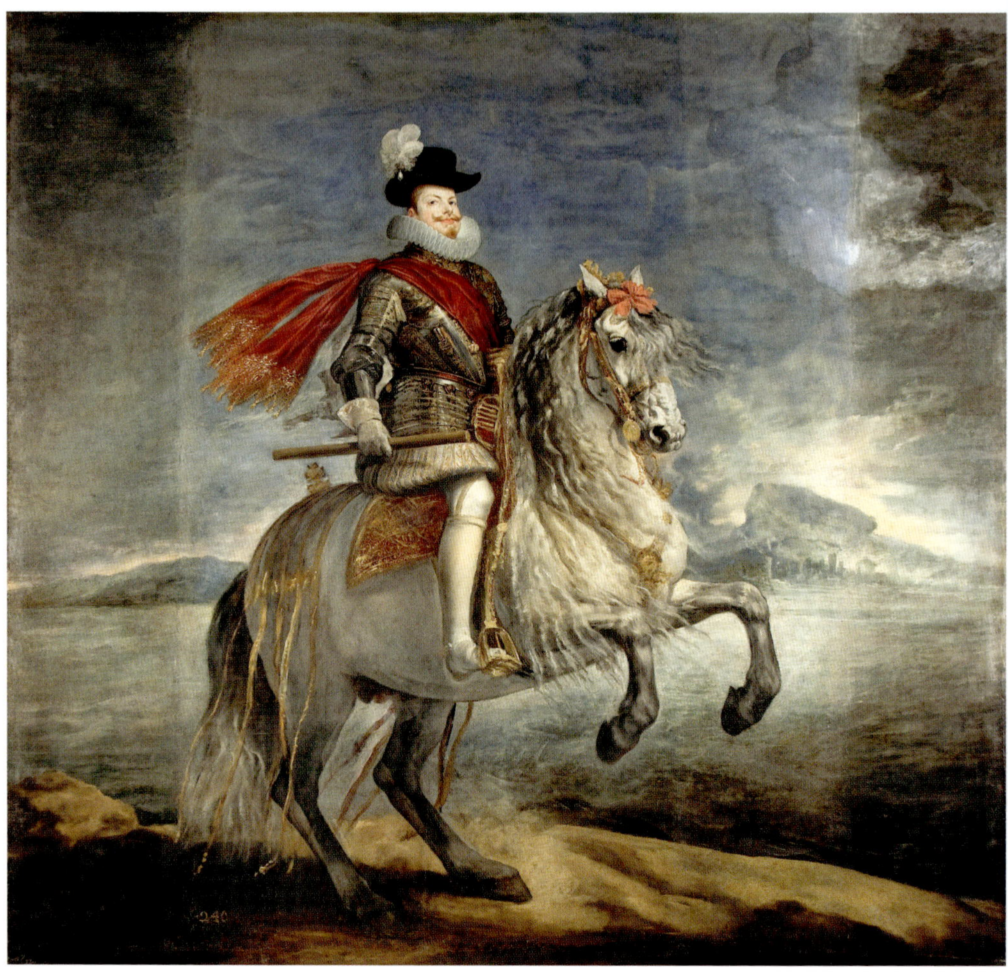

71 *Equestrian Portrait of Philip III, c.* 1635

with the royal personages themselves and was easier to achieve with the horses and settings. In the portrait of Philip III on a rearing horse, long, free-flowing strokes of the brush enliven the mane and girdle of the horse and reflect the dynamism of the pose. Although the companion picture of Margaret of Austria shows less intervention, it is here too that the horse's mane differs most noticeably from the pedestrian precision of the rest. This is certainly the case with Queen Isabella, where her head dutifully duplicates that already devised by the artist around 1632 but deft retouchings in the landscape and more daring ones to the head and mane of the horse betray

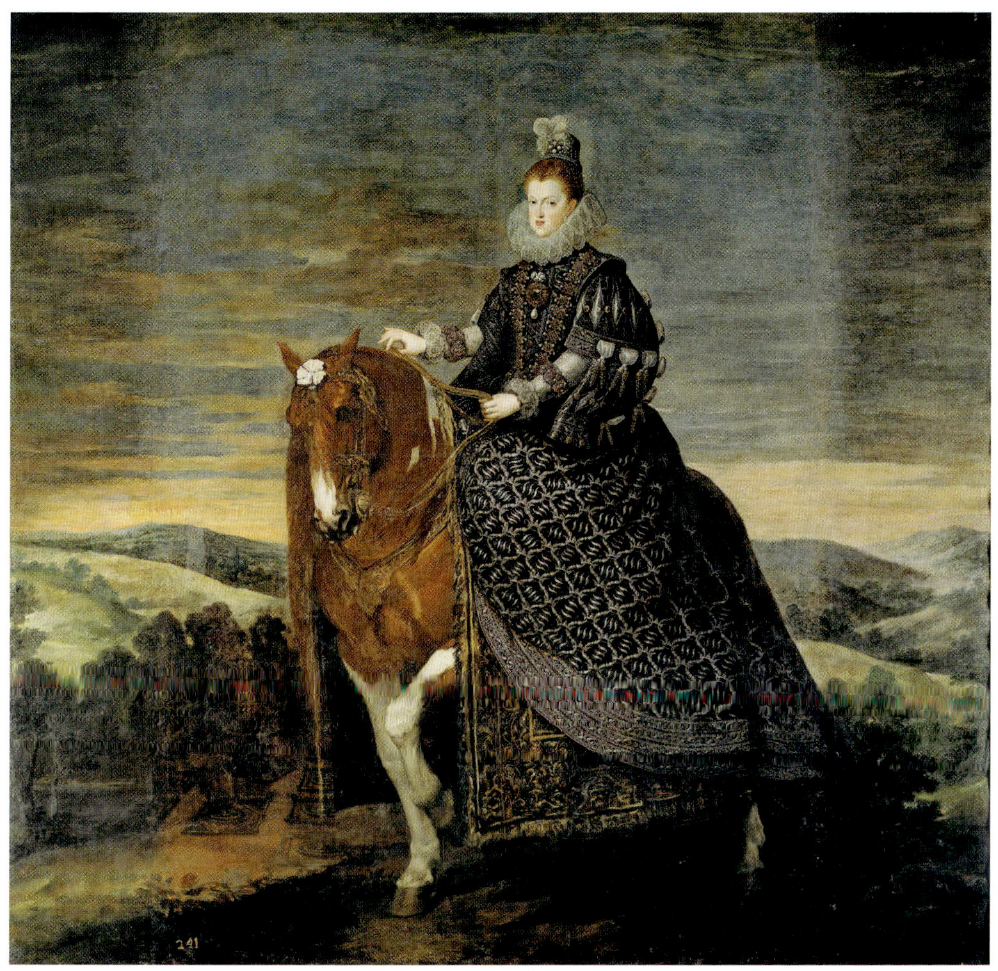

72 *Equestrian Portrait of Margaret of Austria*, c. 1635

Velázquez's own hand. It is worth noting, too, that all of the equestrian portraits were added to at a later date with strips of canvas on either side.

73   In contrast, the portrait of Philip IV is entirely by the artist and depicts the King in an heraldic profile pose, such as one might see on a commemorative medal. He is shown on a rearing horse performing the skilled exercise known as the *levade*, controlling his mount with only one hand on the girdle while the other holds his baton. He is dressed like a captain-general in the military, wearing armour and a flowing sash. Prominent pentimenti on the rear legs of the horse and

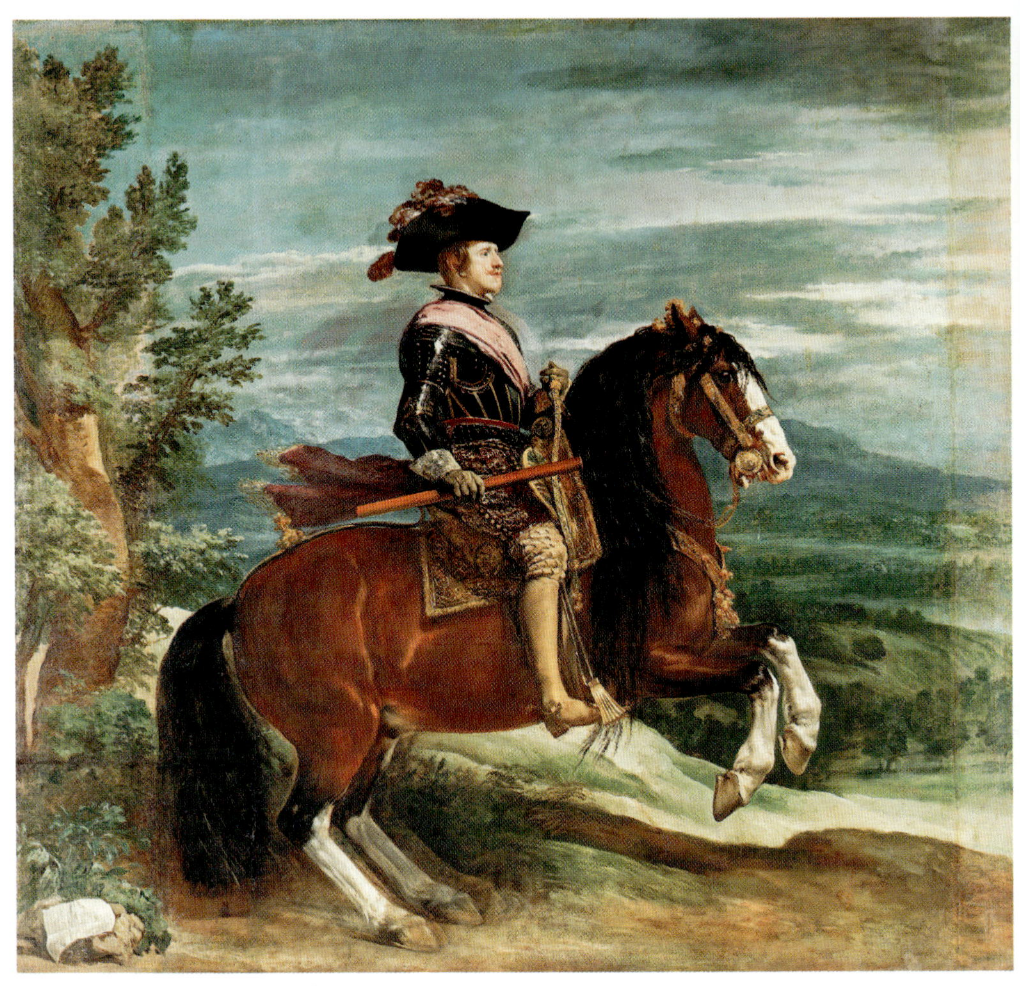

73 *Equestrian Portrait of Philip IV*, c. 1635

around the head and shoulders of the King testify yet again
to Velázquez's improvisatory methods of working, and the
variety of handling to his acute awareness of the appearance
of things. The gleaming highlights over damascened armour,
the insubstantiality of the plumes on a hat, the muscularity
of a horse's haunches and the flowing locks of its mane – all
are convincingly captured with a versatility and dexterity that
simply astound.

In between the equestrian portraits of the King and Queen
was that of the six-year-old Prince Balthasar Carlos. Riding a
rearing pony that appears to be leaping out of the picture, he

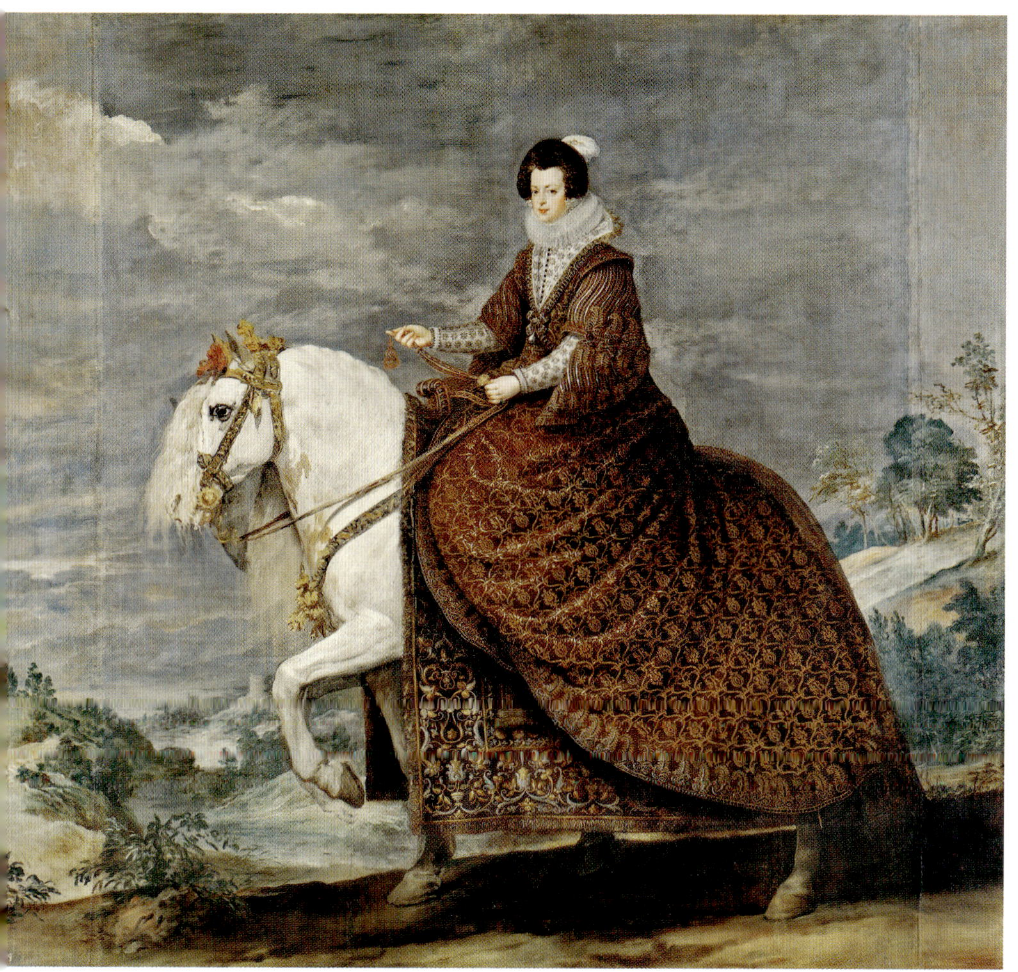

74 *Equestrian Portrait of Isabella of Bourbon, c. 1635*

brandishes his baton and seems in full command of his future
role. In the distance a blue-grey mist softens the contours of the
Guadarrama Mountains around Madrid, the land rising on one
side to counterbalance the rider on the other.

The barrel-chested appearance of the pony may here be
explained by the fact that the picture was intended to be viewed
from far below, and this may also account for the audacity of
the handling throughout, especially in the costume and face
of the prince. Thinly applied paint, which often permits the
canvas weave to show through, appears to be drizzled onto the
canvas and allowed to stand where it lands. Isolated strokes

and smears of pigment seemingly congeal over the surface, themselves infinitely suggestive but always promising so much more. But that is where our own creative faculties enter, able to fill in the gaps that the artist has deliberately left bare.

The Surrender of Breda is the largest painting of Velázquez's career and one of his greatest masterpieces. It was the artist's sole contribution to the series of battle paintings displayed along the long walls of the Hall of Realms, all of which commemorated victories by the Spanish army during the reign of the King. These were conducted under a range of great generals and their troops in all parts of the globe, from Cádiz and Genoa to the United Provinces and from Puerto Rico to Brazil. Although the paintings were intended to celebrate the valour and might of these great generals and their forces, behind them lay an even greater power – namely, that of the monarch himself and (not least) of his first minister, Olivares.

Five of the twelve victories commemorated in the hall had taken place in 1625, an *annus mirabilis* for the young king and his recently appointed count-duke. One of these was the routing of the English off the coastal city of Cádiz in Andalucía. Zurbarán painted this victory for the hall and his picture illustrates the form that the majority of these compositions took. Filling the foreground are the military leaders and, behind them, the enemy forces, besieged city and Spanish victors. Fernando Girón, the victorious general, was already old and ailing when this encounter took place and is here shown seated in a chair, raising his baton to order his deputy commander into battle. The picture thus combines both portraiture and history painting, although it is rarely the case that the portraits are accurate, as some of the generals were already dead when the pictures were painted.

Much more original than Zurbarán's painting is the moving *The Recapture of Bahía* by Juan Bautista Maíno, which is a scene of succour and mercy amongst ordinary people. The citizens of this Brazilian city had been driven from their homes by the Dutch when a combined Spanish–Portuguese fleet under the command of Don Fadrique de Toledo intervened. After a sustained battle, in which they suffered many casualties, the Iberian forces eventually triumphed over the enemy.

In Maíno's painting, the wounded and homeless fill the foreground of the picture and the battle takes place on the distant sea. In the right middle distance, the victorious general points to a banner depicting the true victor, Philip IV, being crowned with a laurel wreath by Minerva, goddess of war, and (in his own eyes at least) her male equal, the Count-Duke Olivares.

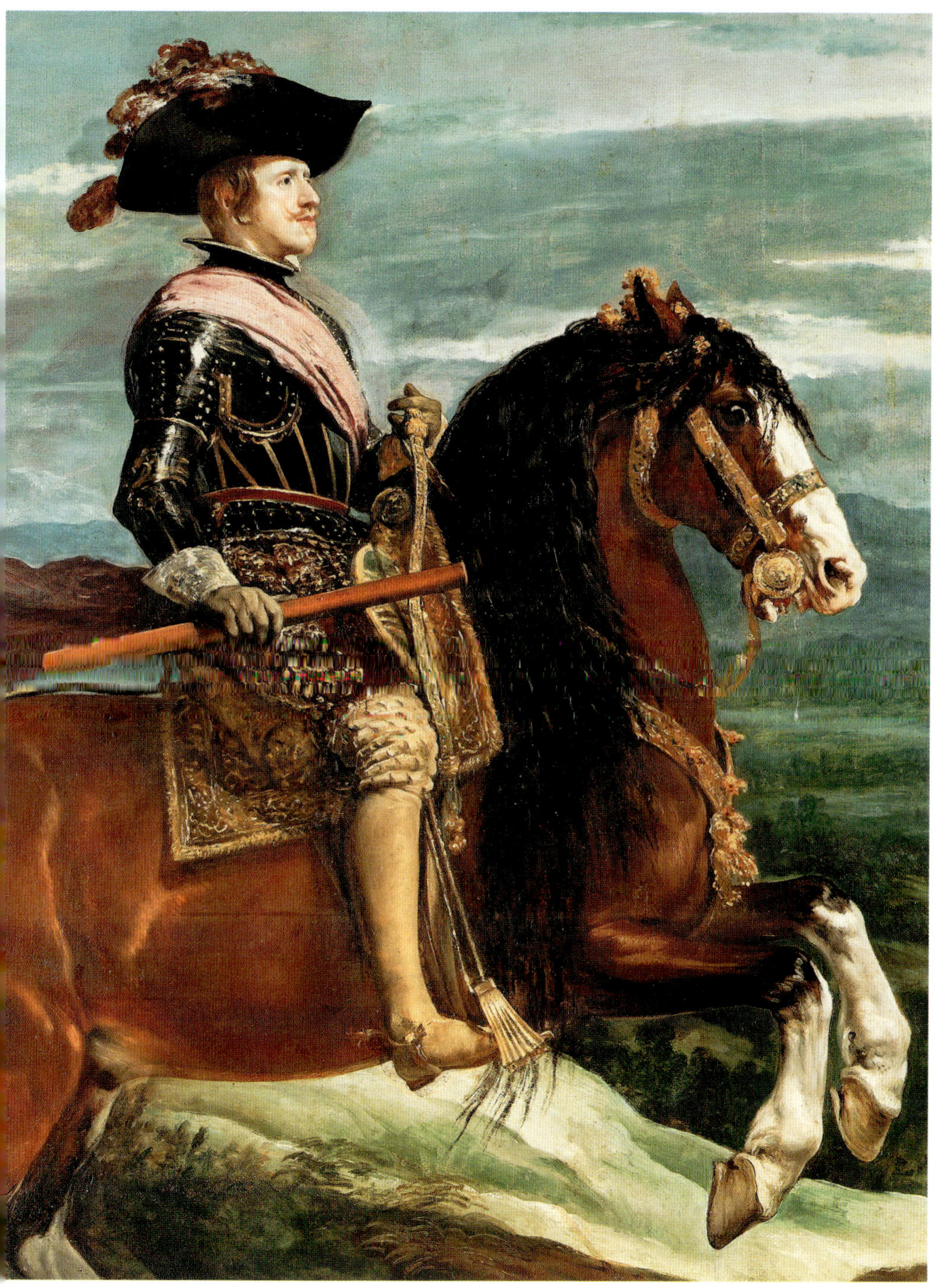

75 *Equestrian Portrait of Philip IV,* c. 1635, detail

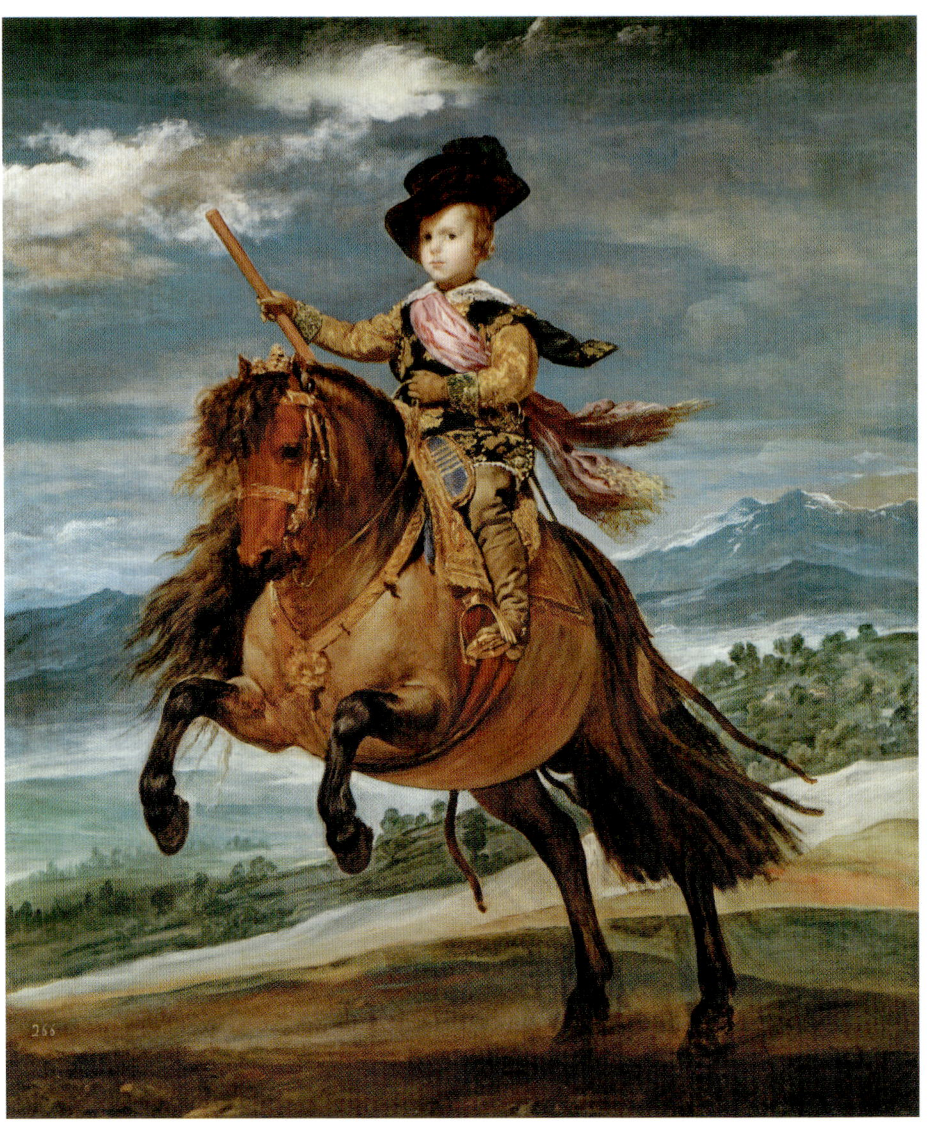

76 *Equestrian Portrait of Prince Balthasar Carlos, 1634–35*

The humanity of Maíno's picture was exceeded in the hall only by that of the *Surrender of Breda*, where it is bestowed upon the rival generals themselves. The event commemorated took place in June 1625 when, after a long siege at the heavily fortified Dutch town of Breda, Spanish forces commanded by Ambrogio Spinola defeated the native army, led by Justin of Nassau. Attended by their troops, the two men meet in the centre of the picture, with Justin handing over the keys to the city to the victorious general. In the middle distance, the defeated Dutch march past, exiting the city, and beyond lies the flat and misty terrain of the lowlands with its meandering waterways.

81

The striking originality of Velázquez's conception becomes immediately apparent if one compares it to another such surrender scene in the series. Jusepe Leonardo's *Surrender at Jülich* shows the same general, Spinola, receiving the keys to that city in the Lower Rhineland after a six-month siege in 1622. Still mounted on his horse, the victor reaches down to receive the keys from the defeated general, who is kneeling in submission below. In contrast, Velázquez's generals meet on an equal footing. Both have dismounted from their horses, which appear to either side. Justin is about to kneel when Spinola reaches out to restrain him. But it is not only the generals who are treated more equally; so, too, are their troops. In Leonardo's picture only the victors bear arms, whereas in *The Surrender of Breda* both sides do. But the Dutch bear fewer and less regimented arms than the victorious Spaniards, whose lances line up and reach to the top of the picture with military precision.

Contemporary accounts of the siege and surrender bear out Velázquez's interpretation, with the Irishman Gerat Barry noting in 1626: 'Spinola, holding them to be more wise who are more gentle in cruelty… judged it more expedient to prefer the majesty and clemency of his king (whose person he bore in this place) than either his own glory, or desire of revenge.' Although the artist is unlikely to have been aware of this testimony, he almost certainly knew the words given to Spinola on this occasion by the Spanish playwright Calderón de la Barca, whose *El sitio de Breda* (*The Siege of Breda*) was performed at the Spanish court within months of the arrival of the news of the surrender from Flanders. Offered the keys to the city on a salver by Justin of Nassau, Spinola exclaims: 'Justin, I receive them in full awareness of your valour; for the valour of the defeated confers fame upon the victor.'

Aided by such words though he may have been, Velázquez still had to realize them in paint. The picture testifies to

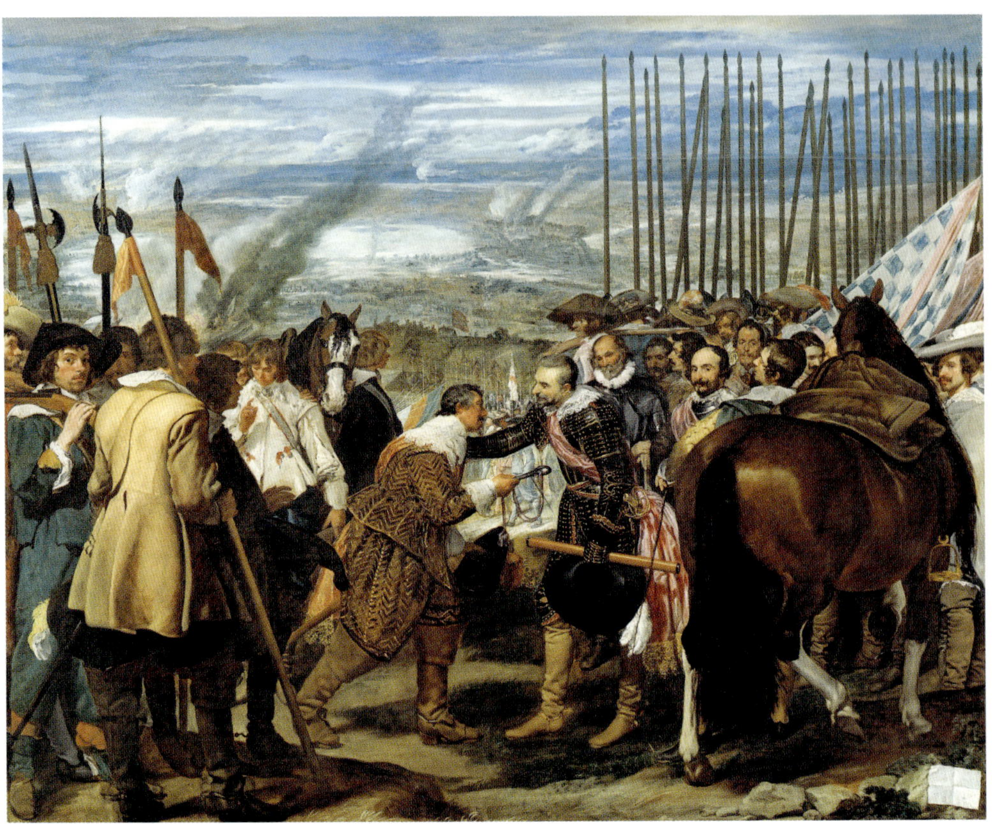

77 *The Surrender of Breda, c. 1635*

the ingenuity and imagination with which he achieved this,
especially since the ceremony of surrender that is the subject
of the work is nowhere recorded to have taken place.

The focus of the painting is the keys located in the very centre
of the composition and surrounded by an aureole of light. Then
there are the two generals, Justin bending lower down with his
face in shadow and Spinola standing higher, his benevolent
face and gesture bathed in light. If ever a human visage could
be beatified by natural light alone, it is here. But to understand
what happened moments before the one we are witnessing, we
must look to the horses.

The first thing to be noticed about them is that one reveals
exactly what the other does not. Justin's horse, already forming
part of the crowd, shows only its head, and Spinola's, everything
else. It is still shuffling into position to join its troop of soldiers
having suddenly found itself riderless, its sleek hindquarters

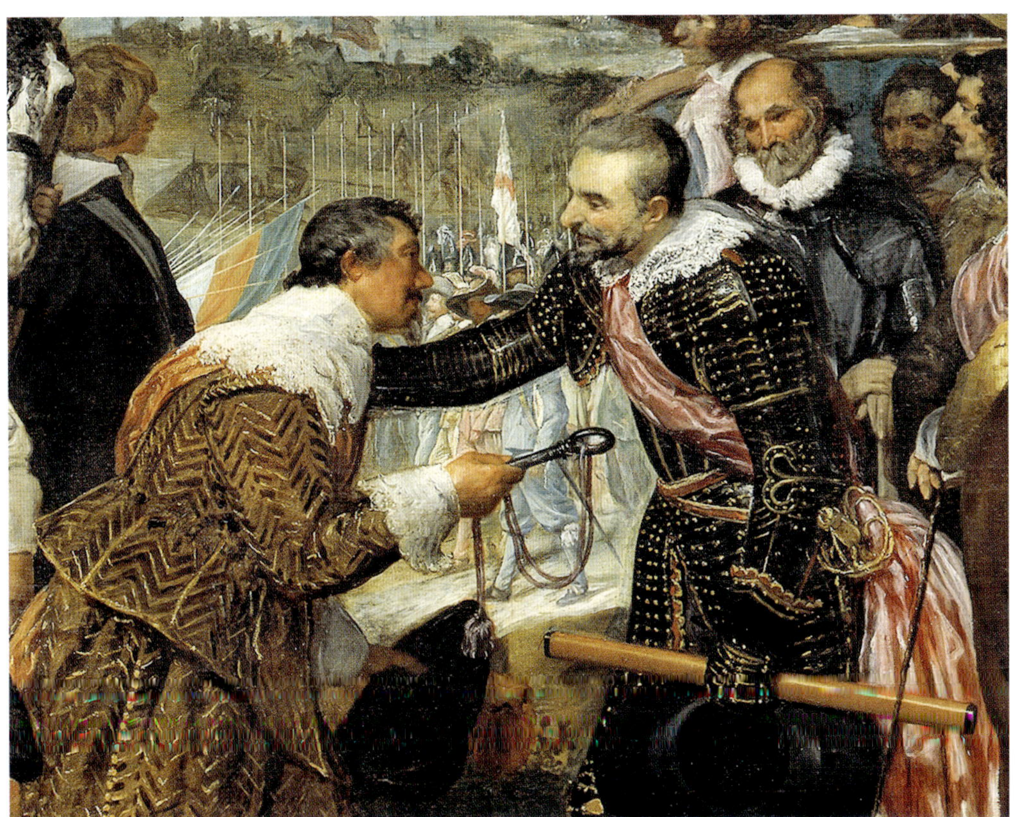

78   *The Surrender of Breda, c.* 1635, detail

brilliantly framing the right-hand side of the composition.
Thus, Justin must have dismounted first, preparing to kneel
before the mounted victor, when Spinola suddenly abandoned
his own horse to forestall this show of obeisance and reveal
his own clemency – and humanity.

Next there is the behaviour of the troops, who respond just
as any other cross-section of humanity would, some engaged,
others distracted and still others seemingly unaware. On the
left, where we enter the picture, a gallant young Dutchman
looks out, immediately attracting our attention. While some
of his cohorts focus on the ceremony, others converse, or gaze
into the distance, seemingly oblivious of the momentous event
taking place in their midst. The Spanish troops are scarcely
more engaged. Although one elderly soldier thoughtfully focuses
on the meeting of the generals, others appear diverted or just
there to be seen. One of these is the dapper hatted soldier on

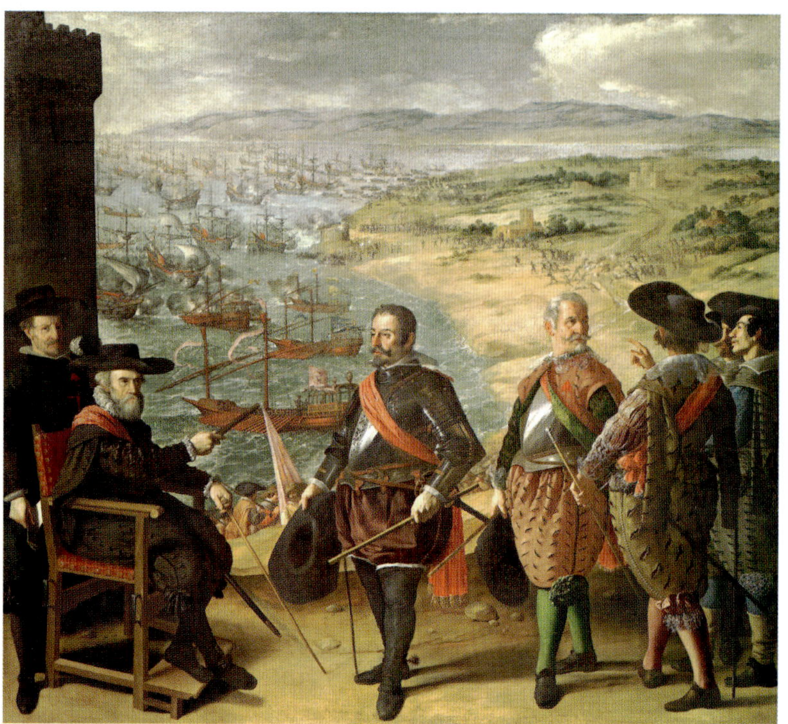

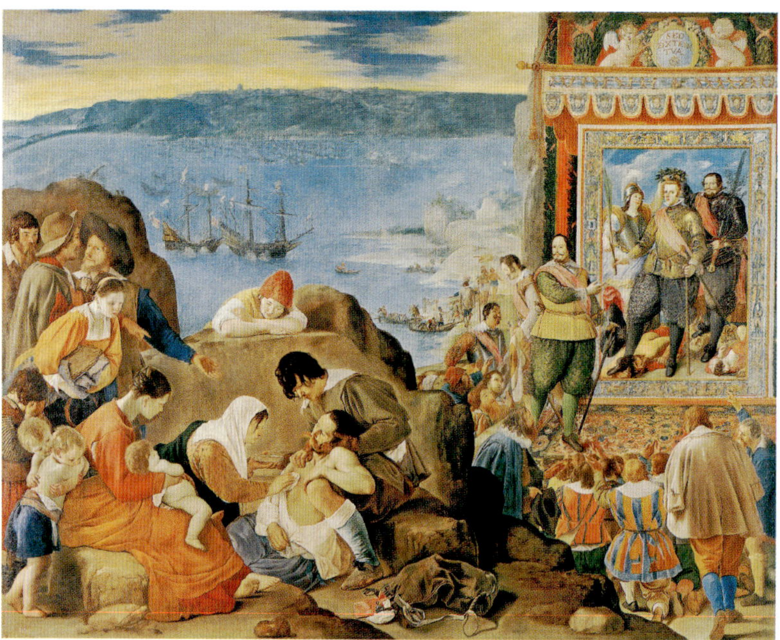

79 TOP Francisco de Zurbarán, *The Defence of Cádiz*, 1634–35
80 ABOVE Juan Bautista Maíno, *The Recapture of Bahía*, 1634–35
81 OPPOSITE Jusepe Leonardo, *The Surrender at Jülich*, 1634–35

the right-hand margin, who may be a self-portrait of the artist.
In the midst of all this, flags get in the way, some soldiers
already appear to be departing and others are just caught up
in the fray. No ceremony of surrender could ever have been so
unceremonial, or so true to life. Reminding us that this is a
picture, however, is a piece of folded paper attached to a rock
at the bottom right. It is blank, but may have been intended to
bear the artist's signature. Painted so illusionistically that we
are tempted to try to remove it, it testifies to the realism of the
rest of the scene.

For all its seemingly improvisatory nature, the composition
of this picture was carefully devised. Two drawings exist
for it, and they are among the very few such works that are
universally accepted as by the artist. Executed in black chalk on
a double-sided sheet, one depicts the back of a soldier bearing
a weapon, with another soldier very faintly drawn on the right.
It corresponds somewhat to the Spanish soldier in the painting
looking over his shoulder behind Spinola's horse. On the other
side of the sheet is a lightly drawn sketch for Spinola himself,
reaching out to Justin though not yet holding his baton and hat.
The signatures of the artist on both sides are later additions.

X-rays reveal that Velázquez painted the work on a finely
woven canvas, applying his colours in thin fluid strokes that
allow the weave to show through. Although the brushstrokes are
otherwise very difficult to read, they do show that a number of
additional heads have been painted out and, most importantly,
that the height of the Spanish lances on the right was greatly

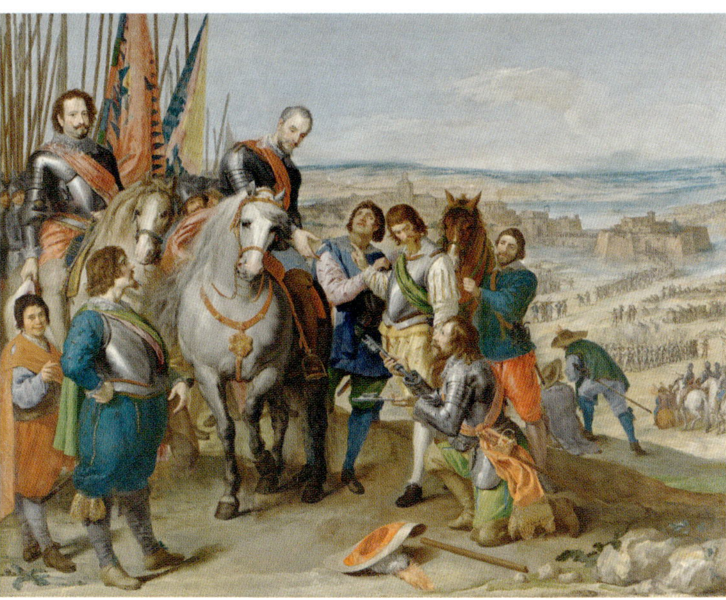

82 ABOVE LEFT   Study for the figure of Spinola in *The Surrender of Breda*, 1634–35
83 ABOVE RIGHT   Study for *The Surrender of Breda*, 1634–35

increased as the artist proceeded, reinforcing their message of impregnable might.

While the victory at Breda ultimately glorified the King, the reflected glory from it fell upon his military mastermind, Olivares. During these same years the latter also commissioned his own equestrian portrait from Velázquez and, predictably, it is a testament to his arrogance and ostentation. The largest of all the artist's single portraits, it depicts the Count-Duke on a rearing horse – like the King – raising his baton as he gallops forward and grips the bridle with the other hand, a demonstration of his prowess in horsemanship that mirrors that of the monarch, and has nothing to do with the facts. In reality, the obese and humpbacked Olivares could not mount a horse by this time and had never engaged in a military battle. He gazes over his left shoulder at the viewer, a pose that could be interpreted in two ways, only one of which the Count-Duke would have endorsed. Either it suggests that he is master of all he surveys, or that he is always on the lookout for enemies – of which he had plenty at the court by this time. In the distance under the horse's forelegs a battle skirmish rages.

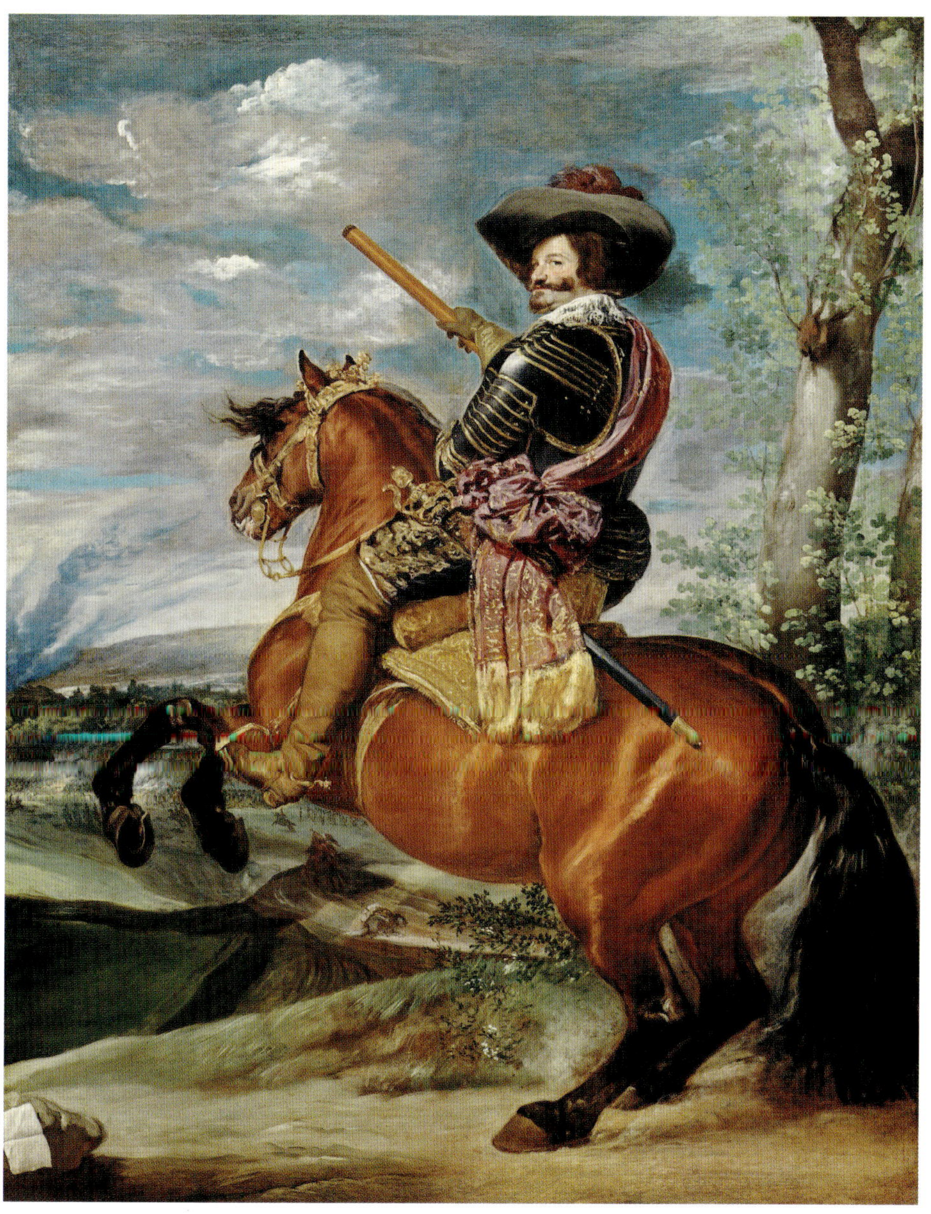

84 *Equestrian Portrait of the Count-Duke of Olivares, c. 1636*

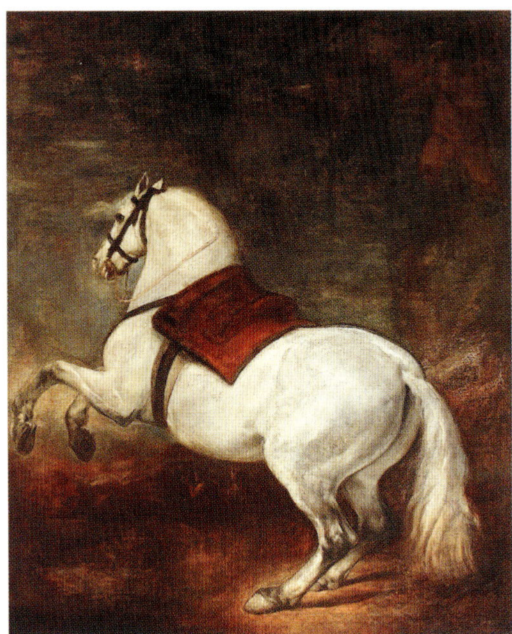

85 *White Horse*, 1634–38

Technically the picture is a masterpiece that, as the x-rays
reveal, underwent many changes, especially in the position
of the legs and rump of the horse, as well as in the figure of
Olivares, whose body shape was slightly reduced and whose
ruthless and suspicious glance was originally more frontal.
Velázquez may also have relied on a full-scale study of a leaping
white horse that is recorded in his studio at his death and is
identical in pose, although the sleek and sheened chestnut-
brown hide of the horse that the Count-Duke rides surpasses
even that. Finally, the artist adds his own signatures to this
tour de force of painting: a blank sheet of folded paper on the
bottom left and a cloud of dust kicked up by the horse's hind
legs. No need to sign one when he could paint the other.

Chapter 4
Entertaining the King

While Olivares was waging the King's wars (if only by proxy), Philip IV was indulging in his private pleasures and especially his passion for hunting. This had long been regarded as an ideal preparation for the rigours of the battlefield and, although the King was largely to be spared those, his pursuit of four-legged quarry was never-ending. To further it he commissioned the building of a hunting lodge about ten miles north of Madrid in 1635, the Torre de la Parada, or Tower of the Stopping-place. It was located in an area of forests and hills near the Prado Palace and intended to serve as an ideal resting place for the monarch and his retinue on their hunting expeditions. Around a sixteenth-century watch tower that still stood there was erected a two-storey building that was eventually to be lavishly decorated with paintings, thereby indulging another of the King's passions. In 1636, Rubens received a commission for over sixty canvases depicting scenes from Ovidian mythology destined for the Torre and about the same number of hunting and animal paintings was ordered from the Flemish master of these subjects, Frans Snyders. Although the vast majority of these were to be executed by members of their workshops, Rubens's oil sketches for the Ovidian series survive in large numbers and are among the most spirited and spontaneous works of his career. In addition, Velázquez was commissioned to paint a number of pictures for the building, including some for the Galería del Rey, which was dedicated to celebrating the King's skills as a huntsman. Included among these were three portraits of the King, his youngest brother and prince Balthasar Carlos in hunting costume, which rank among the artist's masterpieces of understatement. Only the identities of the sitters themselves qualify them to be regarded as royal portraits. Otherwise they are just two well dressed men and a young boy enjoying country pursuits.

All three portraits adopt the same format, the sitter standing holding his gun in the centre, framed by a tree to one side and a view of landscape on the other. That of the King underwent the most complex gestation. Philip IV is shown wearing a hat and amber gloves with a black-faced mastiff seated by his side. He is plainly attired in a brown jacket and dark breeches. Clearly visible under the landscape by his side is evidence of a major alteration to his pose made in the course of painting. His left hand and leg were positioned differently, the gun barrel was longer and he was originally depicted holding his hat. Since at least one copy of the picture exists showing it in this earlier state, it must have undergone a prolonged evolution – whether in the artist's studio or elsewhere – before these changes were made.

The King displays a proud and dignified demeanour, his face turned as usual three-quarters to our right. Only the Flemish lace collar and embroidered sleeves single him out as a person of wealth or distinction, and the refinement and restraint of the portrait is enhanced by the exquisite colour scheme. Browns, greens and greys of a seemingly unlimited range of nuance and variation create a ravishing colour harmony over the entire picture. No mere trappings of office could have added greater distinction to the monarch.

The portrait of the King's brother, Don Fernando, is more conventional in pose and shows fewer pentimenti, although Velázquez slightly altered the outlines of the figure and daringly darkened the colour of the sky at the upper left to contrast with the head of the sitter. Don Fernando, who was four years younger than the King, was made a cardinal in 1619 and became governor of the Spanish Netherlands in 1634. He left Madrid for good in 1632 and this portrait may be based on an earlier likeness, depending upon its precise date, which is uncertain. By the time the portrait was painted, however, he wore his hair longer and had grown a moustache. In contrast to the portrait of the King, who holds his gun in a casual and nonchalant manner, Don Fernando appears more formally posed, as is his hunting dog. The artist also introduces a subtle colouristic distinction between the two works. In place of the brown and green harmony of the first is the blue green colour chord of this picture. This ensured that they would look well together but also slightly differ.

Thematically connected to these two portraits is Velázquez's sole surviving animal painting, *Head of a Stag*. Nothing is known of the date and circumstances of its commissioning,

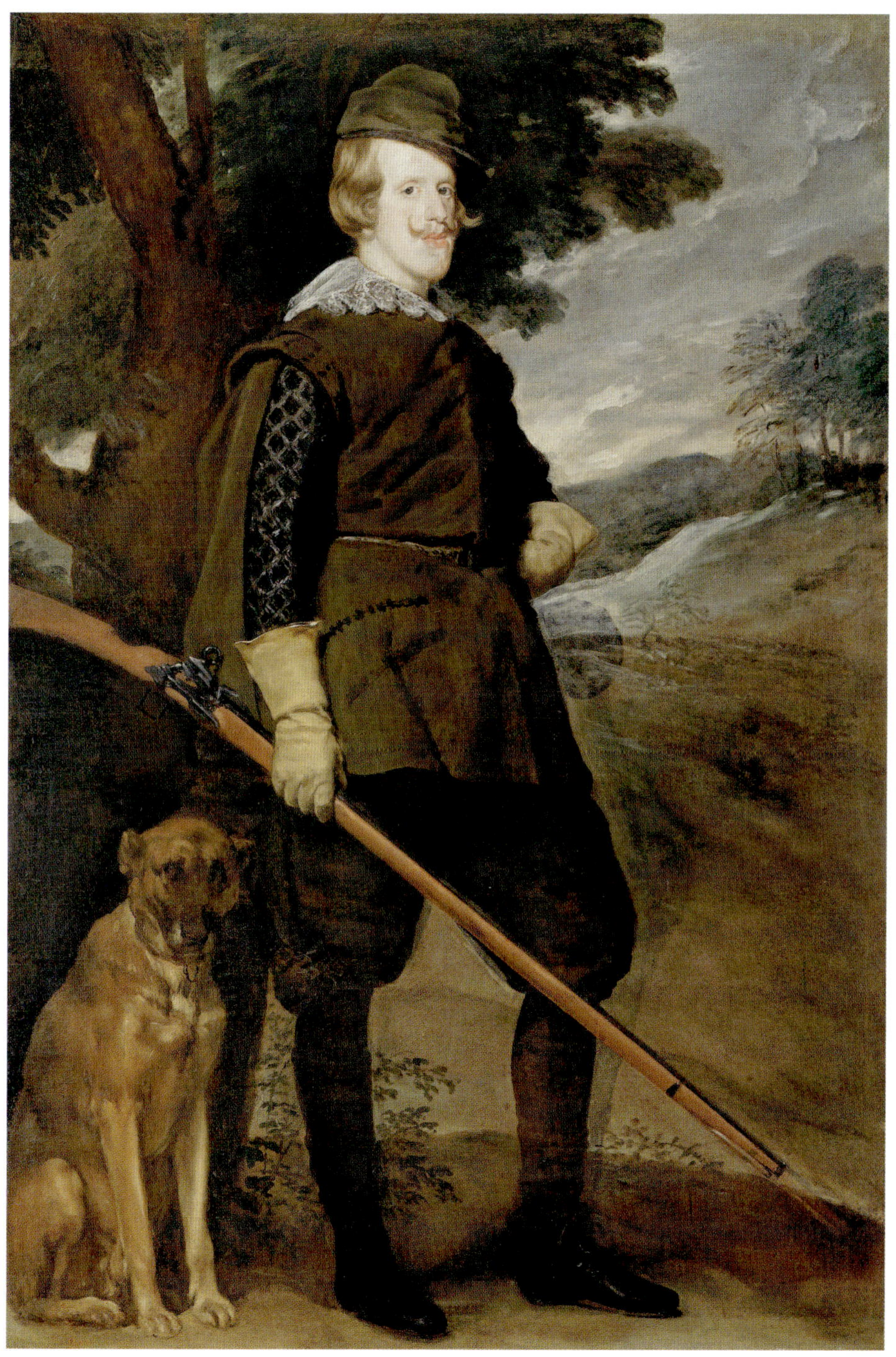

86 *Philip IV as a Hunter, 1632–34*

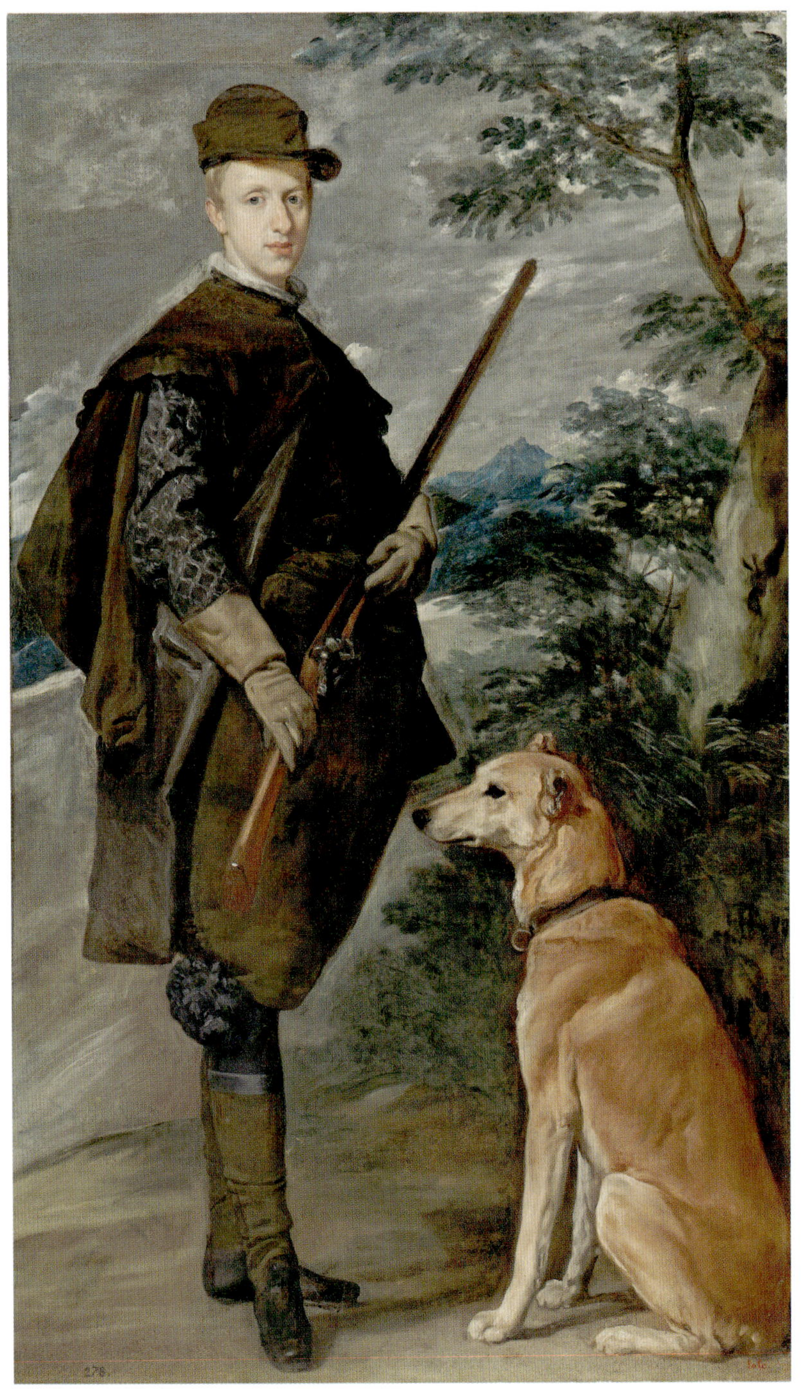

87 ABOVE *Cardinal Infante Don Fernando as a Hunter, 1632–34*
88 OPPOSITE *Head of a Stag, 1626–28*

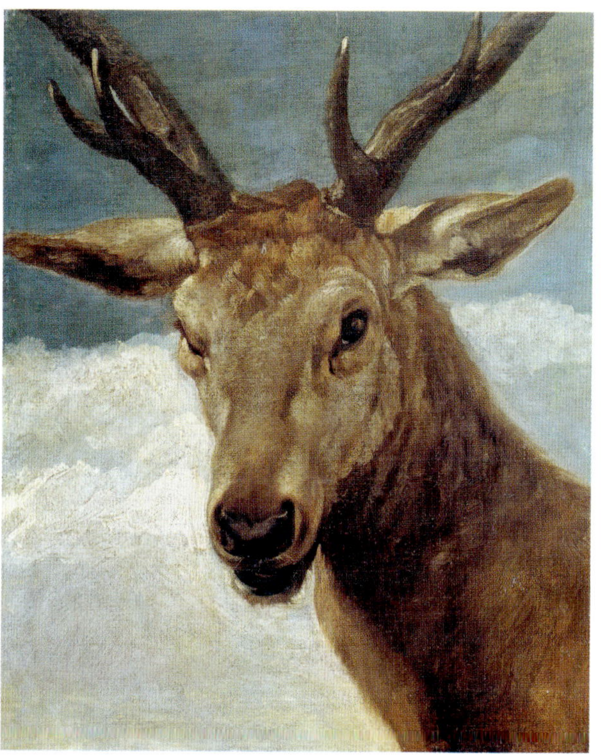

but it may depict one of the King's prize hunting trophies captured in the moments before the kill. If so, then the intelligence and tenderness that the artist invests in this creature might in themselves have persuaded even the most hard-hearted marksman to desist.

Inevitably the most engaging of the hunting portraits is that of the young prince, Balthasar Carlos. According to an inscription at the bottom left, it depicts him at the age of six. Technical analysis and existing copies of the picture show it has been cut down on both sides, most especially on the right, where there was originally another greyhound sitting. The young prince stands proudly and self-assuredly gripping the barrel of his gun, a white and brown pointer asleep by his feet. He is dressed similarly to his father, the King, his peaked brown cap playfully mimicking the blue-grey summits of the Guadarrama Mountains beyond. In his treatise of 1634, *Origin y dignidad de la caza* (*Origin and dignity of the chase*), the master of the hunt, Juan Mateos, remarks that the young prince had successfully hunted wild boar since his early childhood, so the

89

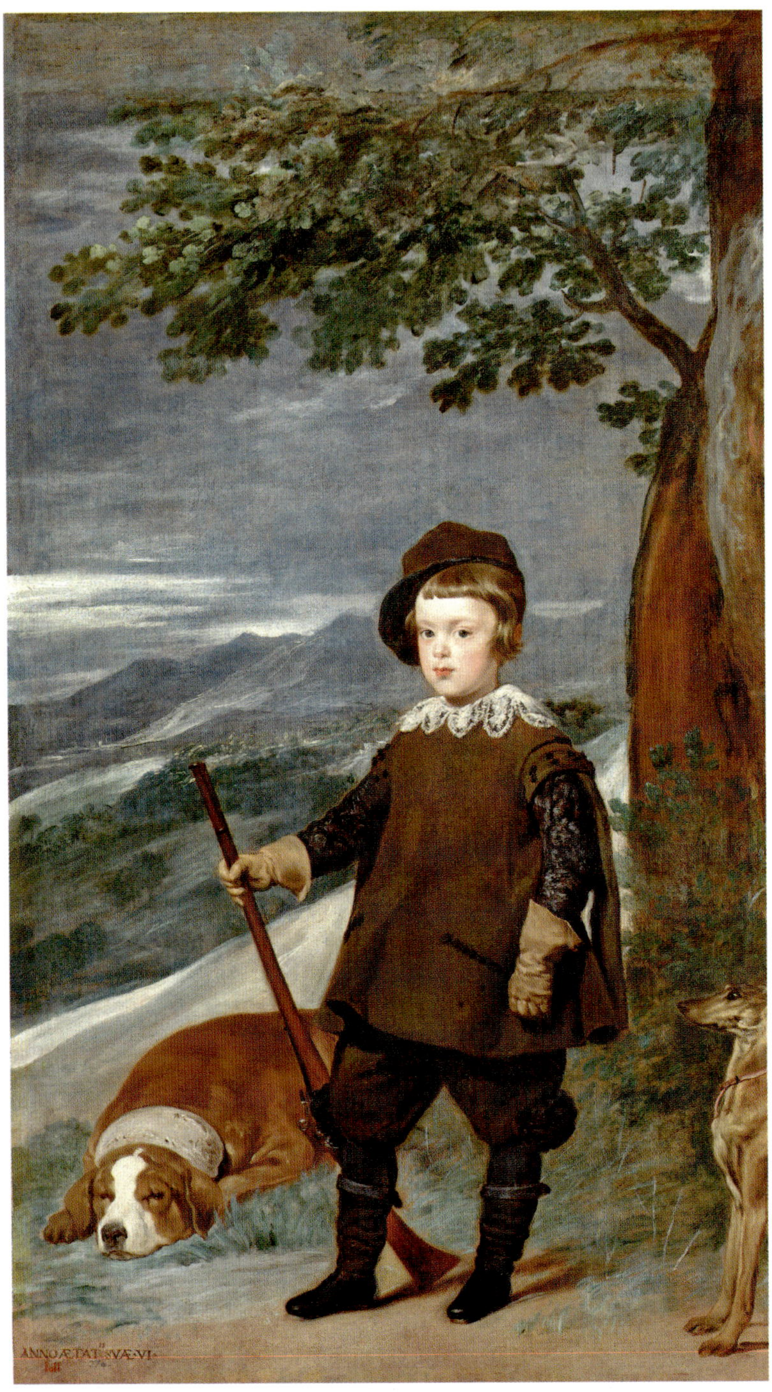

89 *Prince Balthasar Carlos as a Hunter, 1635–36*

self-confidence he exhibits here was well merited. Although there are minor pentimenti around the outlines of the figure, the picture exhibits no major changes, Velázquez's assurance matching that of the young prince. Particularly spontaneous are the filigreed leaves of the overhanging tree and the apparently carefree strokes of paint that spring up as blades of grass around the prince's feet.

Hand in hand with Balthasar Carlos's youthful prowess as a huntsman went his skills in horse riding. These form the subject of one of the most intriguing and controversial works attributed to the artist, *Balthasar Carlos on Horseback* or *Prince Balthasar Carlos in the Riding School*. In the foreground the prince is seen performing a curvet, holding a leaping horse with just one rein. In the right middle distance, Olivares – who was entrusted with the prince's training – accepts a lance from an aide to the prince to guide the latter round the ring. Standing next to them is the master of the hunt, Juan Mateos. Behind is a wing of the Buen Retiro palace containing the prince's living quarters, and looking on at the scene from its balcony are the King and Queen accompanied by their retinue. Finally, at the extreme left, a royal dwarf points to the prince as though in recognition of his skill.

Three scenes are kaleidoscoped together to become a cross-section of the royal household: the King and Queen, the heir-apparent and their ministers, masters and minions. As has often been noted, this offers a foretaste of the artist's greatest masterpiece, *Las Meninas*. But here there are three isolated incidents stitched together by the same setting and story: the royal couple observe their young son practising his horsemanship under the guidance of his royal masters. Moreover, the composition is overweighted on the left in its balancing of masses. These weaknesses have led some critics to attribute it not to the master but to his pupil and son-in-law, Juan Bautista Martínez del Mazo. This dispute will doubtless rage on, but the conception is so ingenious – if ill-digested – that it is more likely to have originated with Velázquez himself than with a pupil.

In 1635 the court summoned the great Sevillian sculptor Martínez Montañés to Madrid to make a model bust of Philip IV in wax or clay to be sent to the Florentine sculptor Pietro Tacca, as the basis for an equestrian monument of the King to be erected in the gardens of the Buen Retiro palace. Montañés arrived in the capital in June of that year and departed the following January and, during his stay, Velázquez painted a portrait of him at work on his bust. As fellow Sevillians it is conceivable that the two had met

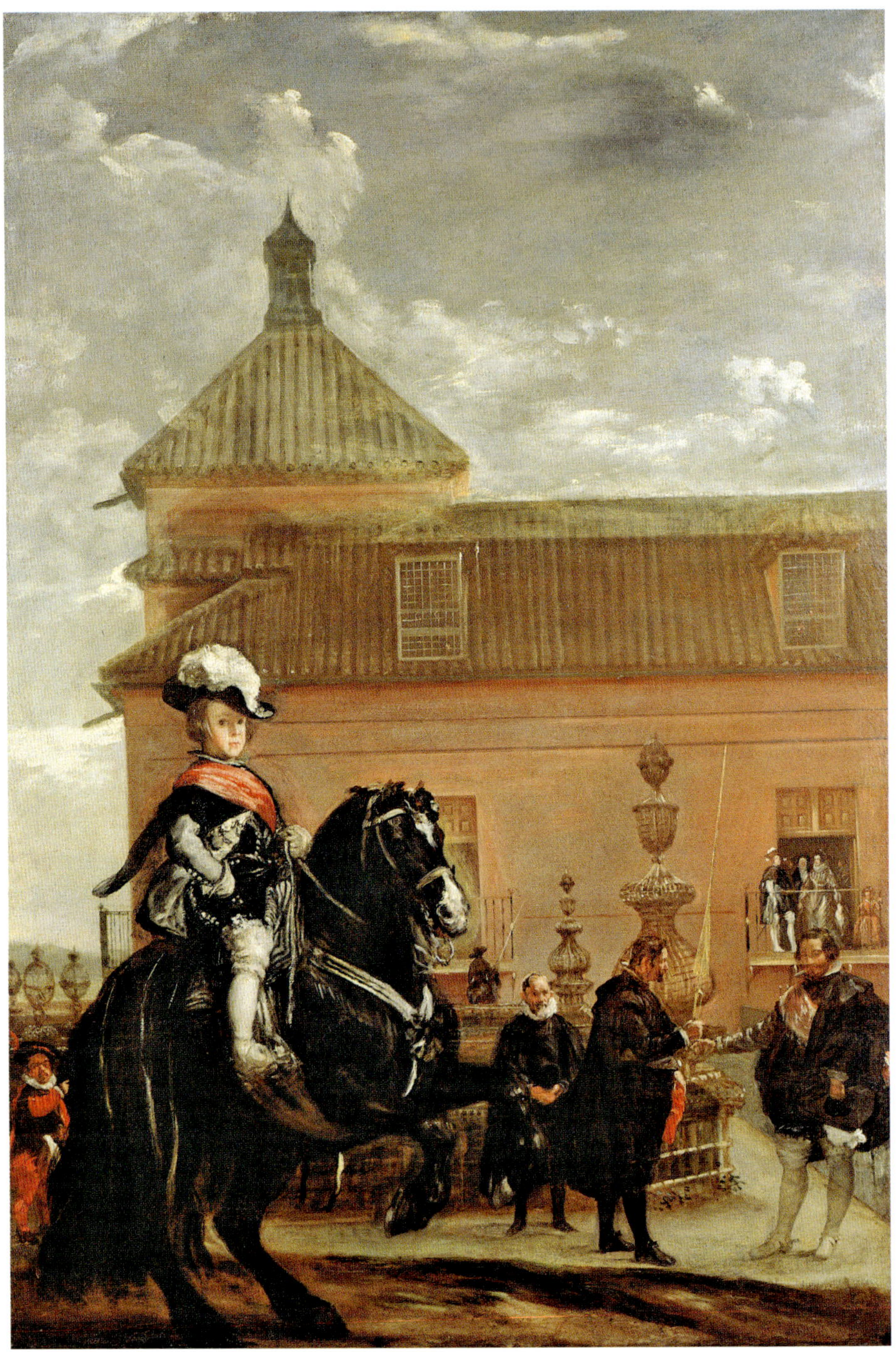

90 *Prince Balthasar Carlos in the Riding School,* c. 1636

before but, whether that is the case or not, as fellow artists they shared much in common and the resulting portrait anticipates that of himself at work that Velázquez would introduce into *Las Meninas* twenty years later. Montañés, who was 67 at the time, holds his modelling tool and looks out of the picture, wearing a serious and thoughtful expression. Casting his head into relief is the dark background behind it, which turns lighter at the lower right to reveal the larger-than-life bust of the King, which is immediately recognizable from its hairstyle. It looks clearly unfinished but, for once in considering an unfinished painting by the artist, we face an unusual dilemma: is this because Montañés's bust is unfinished or Velázquez's painting? More likely the former, for what better way to depict the modelling of a bust in the making?

Montañés's bust was eventually dispatched to Florence by Olivares along with an equestrian portrait of the King on a rearing horse. Tacca completed his bronze sculpture in 1640 and it now stands on the Plaza de Oriente in front of the Royal Palace in Madrid.

In September 1638 Queen Isabella gave birth to a daughter, Maria Theresa, who would eventually marry Louis XIV of France and lived until 1683. This happy event brought another distinguished visitor to the city when the King invited Francesco d'Este, duke of Modena, to serve as godfather to the royal baby. The duke arrived almost immediately and stayed in Madrid for nearly six weeks. During that time he was lavishly hosted by the court and Velázquez painted his portrait. A small bust-length picture, it shows the duke wearing the insignia of the Order of the Golden Fleece, to which he was only admitted on 24 October 1638. Since he left Madrid ten days later, the notoriously slow-working Velázquez had only a short time in which to paint him. This may account for this portrait's small size and sketchy nature although it lacks nothing in penetrating the duke's character. His torso directed to one side, he turns his head to face the viewer with a haughty and disdainful air guaranteed to silence any courtier.

Palomino tells us that 'the Duke honoured Velázquez greatly, praising his rare genius, and since he had portrayed him much to his liking, he rewarded him most liberally, especially with a precious gold chain that Velázquez sometimes would wear around his neck, as was the custom on festive occasions at the Palace'.

Even more penetrating is the masterly *Portrait of a Man* from these same years, which may depict José Nieto, the palace marshal who (as shall be seen) also appears framed by the doorway at the back of *Las Meninas*. Dressed in black

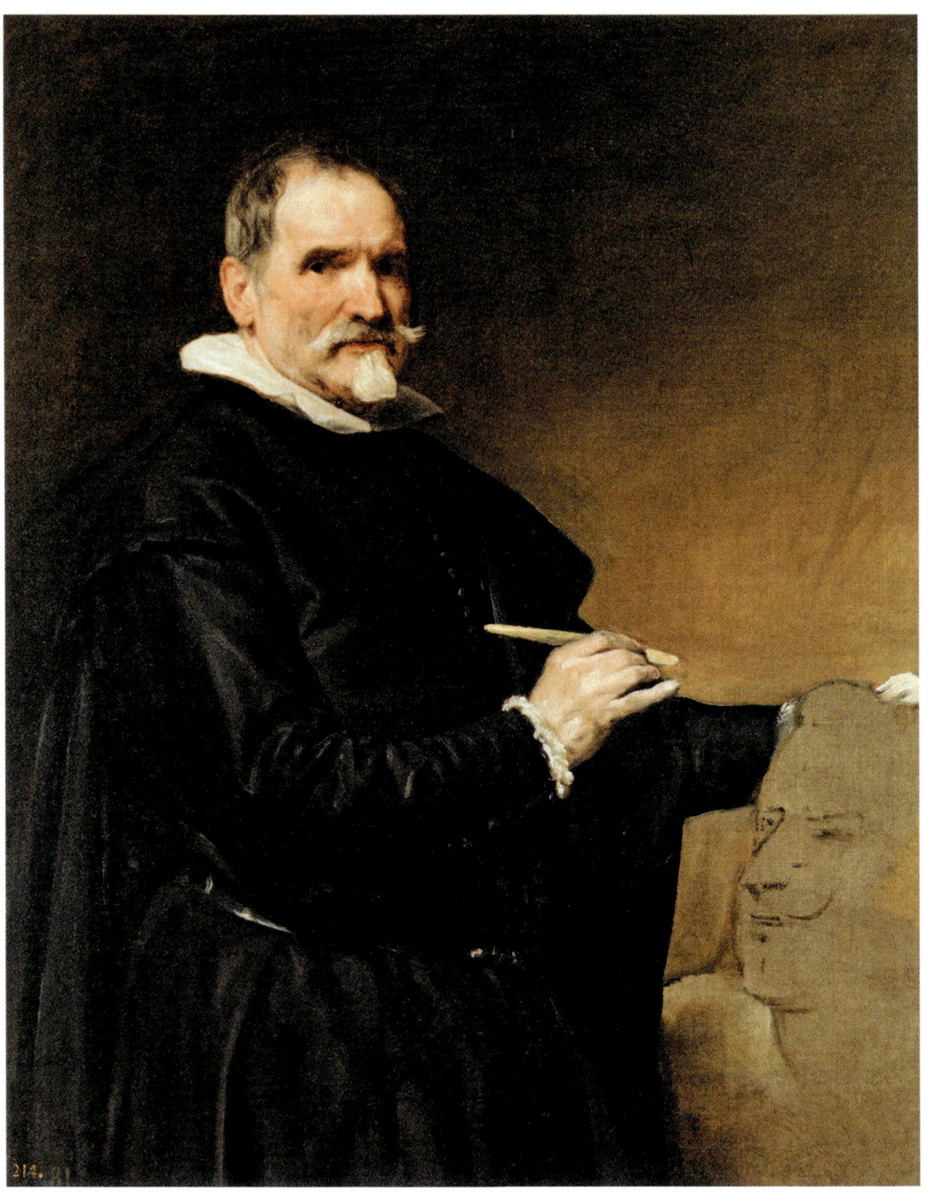

91 ABOVE *Portrait of Juan Martínez Montañés*, 1635
92 OPPOSITE Pietro Tacca, *Equestrian Bronze of Philip IV*, 1634–40

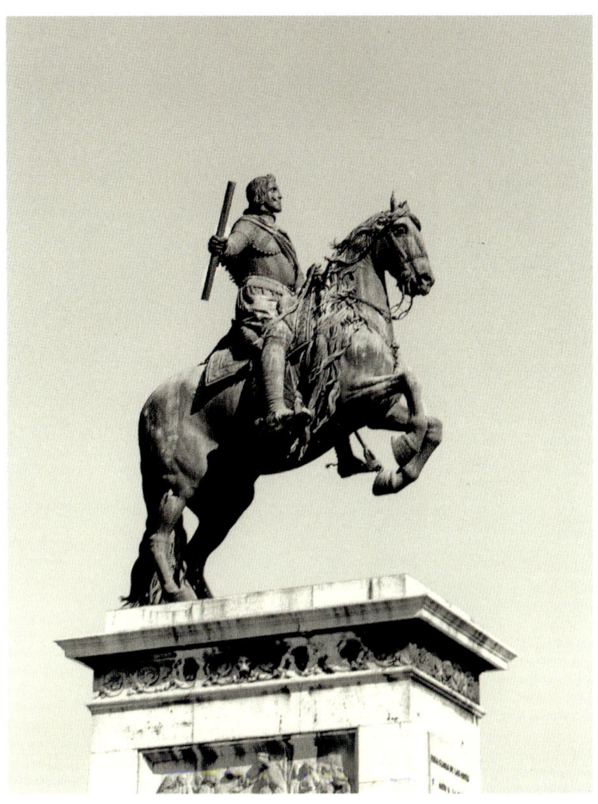

and shown against a light brown background, the picture is
a marvel of economy, wisps of hair around the sitter's head
dissolving into the surroundings, his moustache eliding
with the shadow on his cheekbone, and a mere blob of
white paint followed by a sliver of the same comprising his
collar. Although the sitter's pose is similar to that of the
Duke of Modena, the piercing gaze of this man conveys not
arrogance but unease. It is hard for the viewer not to feel
that they have just interrupted him.

In the late 1630s Velázquez also painted his most arresting
female portrait, *The Lady with a Fan*. The sitter's identity is
unknown although there has been speculation that she was
the artist's daughter, Francisca, but this is unproven. Wearing
a brown, low-cut dress and white gloves, she holds a fan in her
right hand and raises her left to clasp the edge of her mantilla,
revealing a rosary around her wrist below which is a blue
ribbon holding a medal. Touches of red next to them set this
whole passage of the picture alight. Her attractive face, with

95

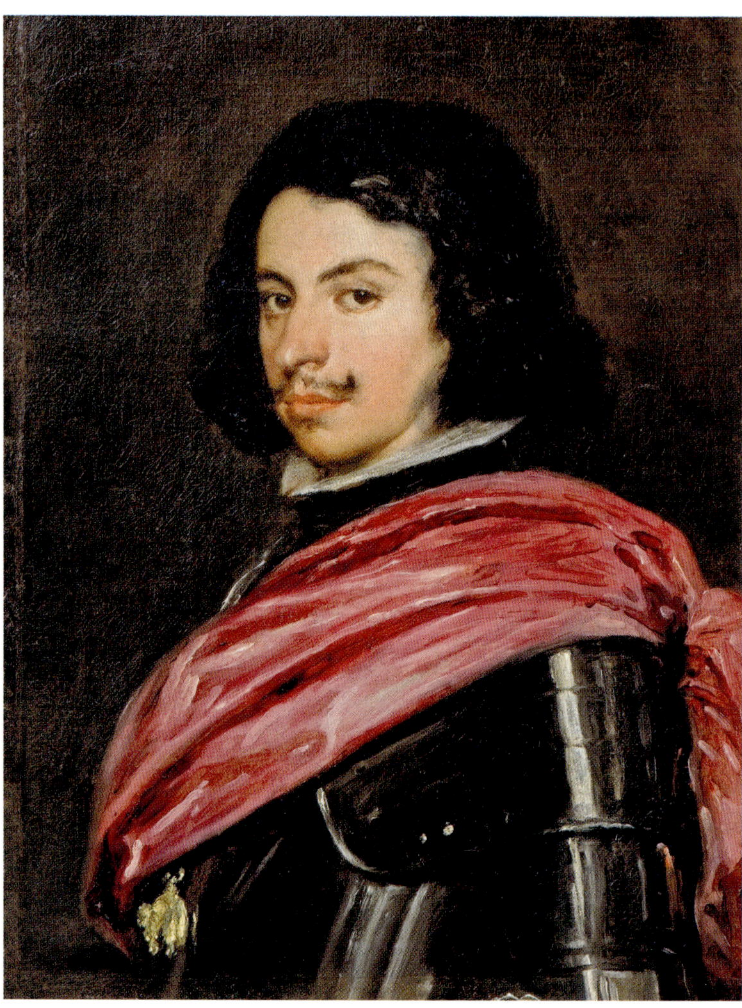

93 *Francesco d'Este,* 1638

its large brown eyes and sensuous lips, gazes out at the viewer impassively. The allure of the portrayal is enhanced by the daring decolletage – so much so that in April 1639 a royal decree stipulated that such low-cut dresses were prohibited to be worn by all women except prostitutes.

A second glance at this captivating portrait also reveals how cunningly it is conceived, for this is no stationary pose but a fleeting encounter between sitter and viewer. The woman is placed off centre and stands as though just striding into the picture. Adjusting her veil, she flicks open her fan, as if preparing to move on. Close inspection of the lower edge of the fan reveals that Velázquez originally painted it fully opened and then changed his mind. A slight alteration perhaps but one that transformed a fixed moment in time into one in motion.

In the early 1630s Velázquez embarked upon another branch of court portraiture which was to result in some of his most audacious and moving works. This focused on what may loosely be defined as figures for royal amusement: jesters, buffoons, dwarfs and mock-heroic depictions of figures from ancient history or mythology. All of these works are full length and relatively large in scale and were intended to line the walls of the Buen Retiro in order to induce mirth or mockery in the eyes of their royal viewers.

96   Don Juan of Austria was a court jester in the King's service between 1624 and 1654 who was amusingly named after the illegitimate son of Charles V, one of the heroes of the Battle of Lepanto fought by the Holy League against the Turks in 1571. He stands here in an unsteady pose borne by spindly legs, holding his commander's baton and wearing pantaloons. His quizzical expression is framed by a large moustache and outsized hat tipped at a rakish angle as though it is about to fall off. Strewn at his feet are the weapons of war, cannon balls, a musket and assorted pieces of armour. No less incongruous is the tiled floor, which flouts Renaissance perspective by adopting differing viewing angles as it moves back in the picture and by disappearing altogether before it arrives there. Crowning the picture's pretence is the naval battle raging on the sea seen through the door. Here thinly diluted strokes of colour seemingly breathed over the weave of the canvas evoke a violent clash of arms that belongs not to this preposterous jester but to his earlier namesake. J. M. W. Turner can never have viewed this pyrotechnic display by Velázquez, but it awaited his arrival two centuries later to paint anything to match it.

97   Don Cristóbal de Castañeda y Pernia was known as Barbarroja or 'Red Beard', a name given to an Algerian pirate of the sixteenth century known for his boasts as a soldier and bullfighter. This jester served at the court between 1633 and 1649 and was notable for his ill-tempered nature. Velázquez's portrait of him shows him dressed in red from head to toe and brandishing his baton and sword. But could he ever wield them? Gazing out of the picture, he fills the frame, a light grey cloak draped over his shoulder.

The picture was left unfinished by Velázquez, the cloak being completed by a much later hand, and a comparison between it and the rest of the painting is a lesson in the

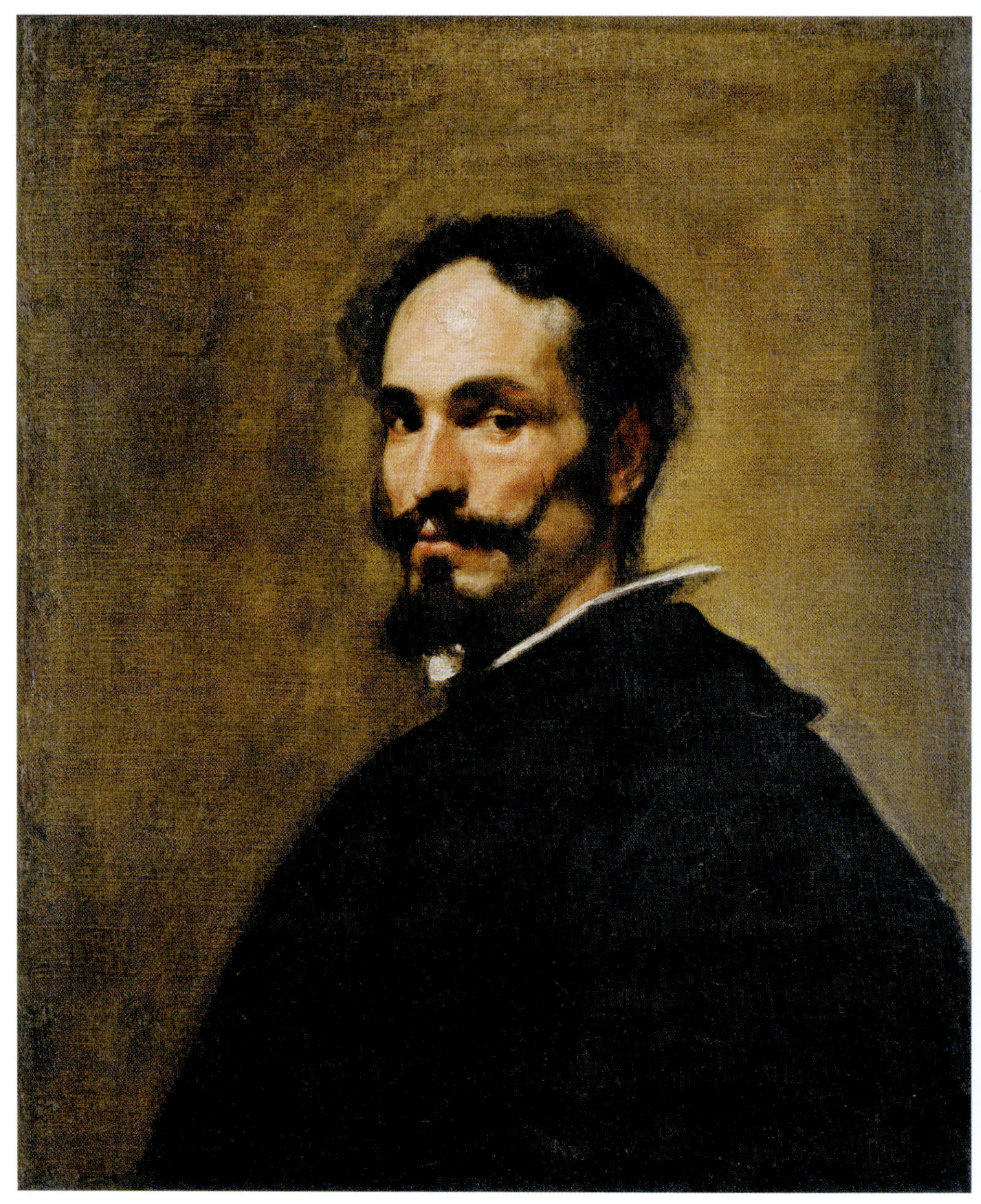

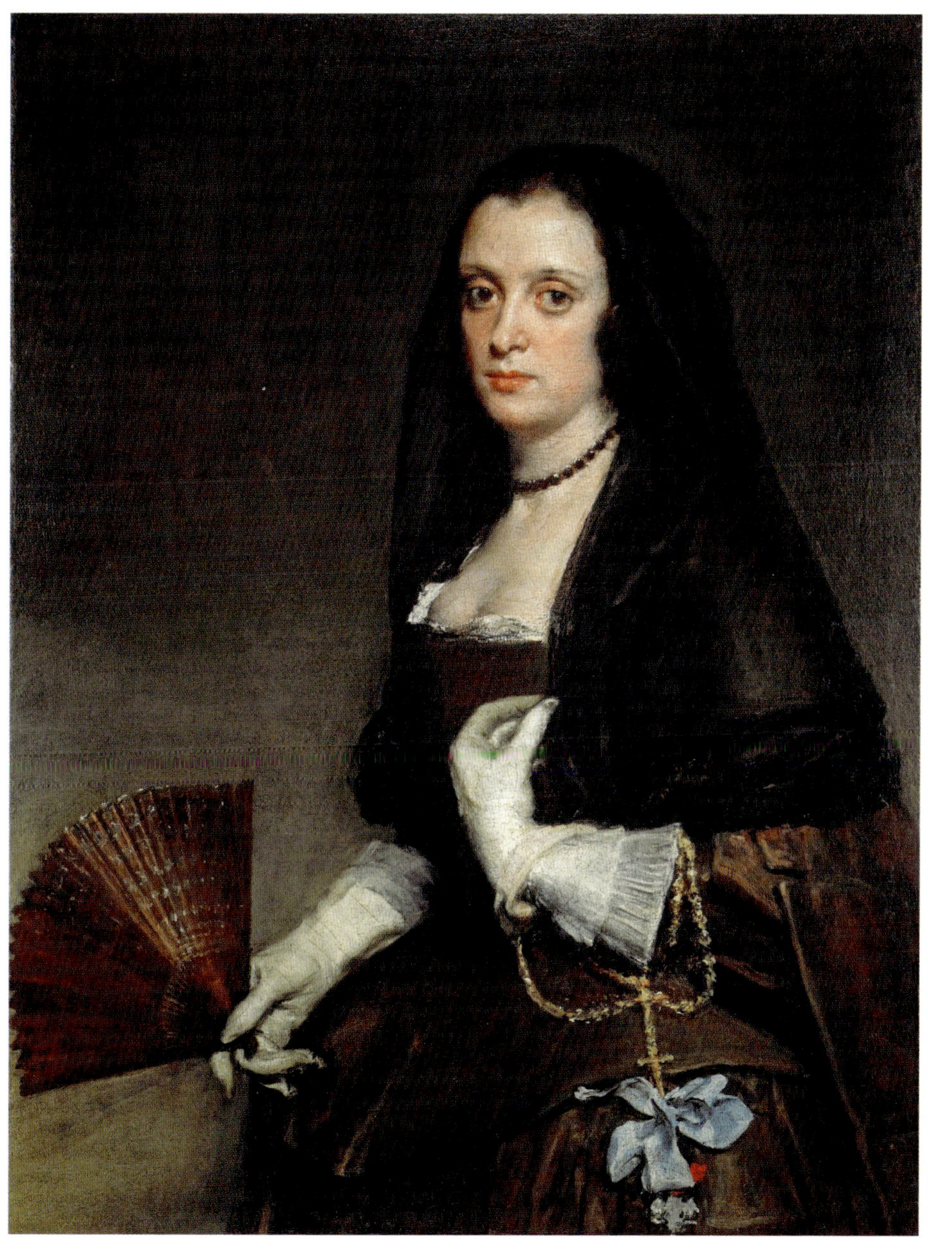

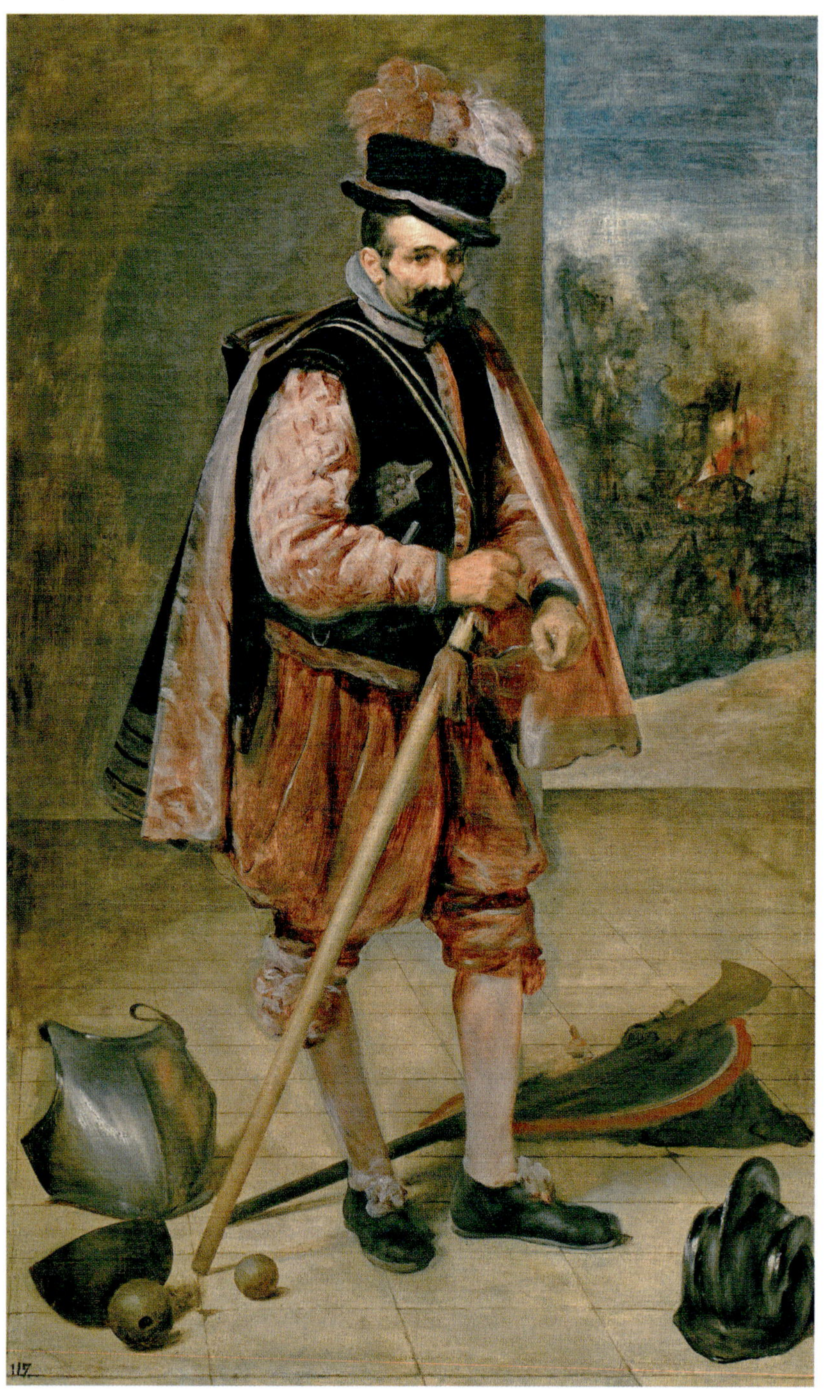

96 ABOVE *The Jester Named Don Juan of Austria, c. 1632–33*
97 OPPOSITE *The Jester Barbarroja or Don Cristóbal de Castañeda y Pernia, c. 1637–40*

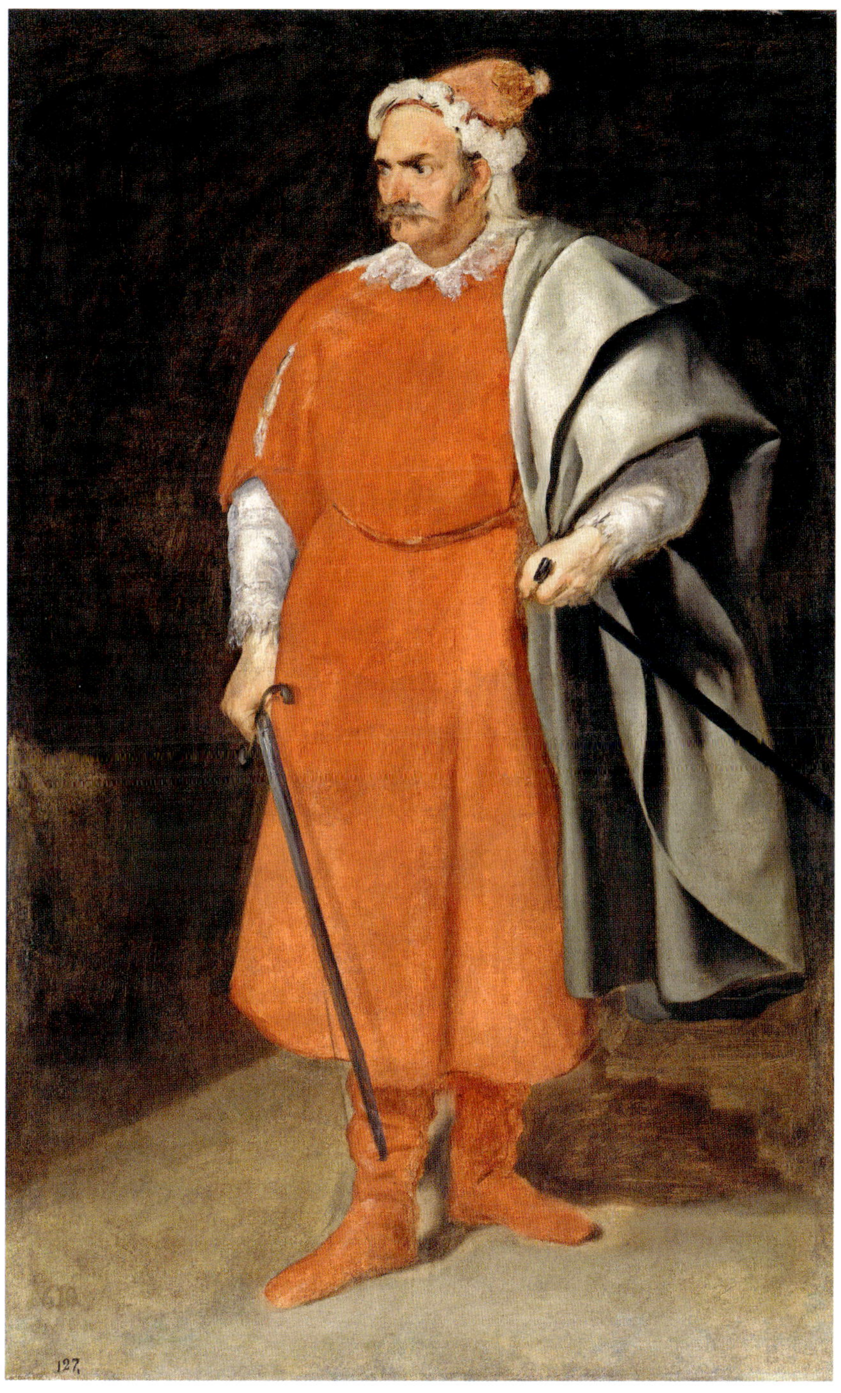

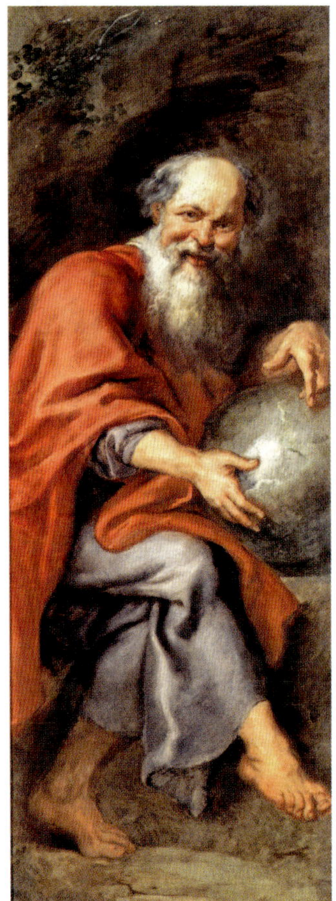
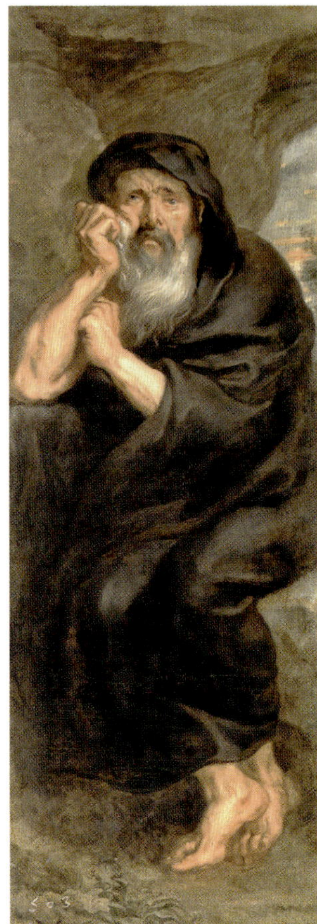

special nature of the master's pictorial world. Nothing in
Velázquez's mature art is as solidly modelled, sharply defined
or tangible as this, and the artist would never have completed
the picture in this way. The sculpturesque handling of this
cloak invites a tactile response in the viewer, much as the
ceramic vessels in the early *bodegones* had. But the later art
of Velázquez exists in a more fluid and intangible realm –
one of pure visuality. Rather than urging us to reach out
and touch, it beckons us simply to behold.

In the spring of 1638 Philip IV took delivery of a vast
consignment of paintings by Rubens and his workshop
destined for the Torre de la Parada. Included in it were two
98, 99   canvases by the master himself representing Democritus
and Heraclitus, the laughing and weeping philosophers of

ancient Greece. Pouring scorn on the world for its folly and vanity, the former is depicted pointing to a globe to direct his contempt, much as Velázquez himself had depicted him in the late 1620s. Perhaps spurred by the sight of these works by the great Flemish master, Velázquez painted two other ancient philosophers in these same years, also destined for the Torre de la Parada.

His pictures depict Aesop and Menippus – an unprecedented pairing – the former a fifth-century BC Greek writer celebrated for his fables and the latter an obscure Greek philosopher of two centuries later renowned for his avarice, none of whose works survive. Both were noted cynics, given to castigating mankind for its excesses and to shunning civilization in favour of the simpler virtues of the common man.

Velázquez depicts them as beggar-philosophers dressed in ragged clothes, disillusioned and unkempt. Aesop faces the viewer holding a tattered book, his coarse and bloated features and slouched stance declaring his disengagement from life. Around his feet lie the things of this world, a bucket draped with a cloth among other still life objects. Everything about the picture conveys a sense of lassitude and ennui. Some critics have seen this as humorous, but it is hard to agree. This Aesop has been battered by life and appears to desire it no more.

Velázquez's Menippus goes even further, turning his back on life (and us) as he draws his cloak over himself, a sly and contemptuous backward glance bidding goodbye to the world. An upright pitcher and several books lie at his feet, but now only to fill a space, being no longer of use.

The startling originality of these works cannot be overestimated, even when compared with those by Rubens. The latter belong to a type and hold few secrets. Democritus and Heraclitus are a universal pairing and they are here doing exactly what is expected of them, seated facing forward and addressing the viewer, either laughing or crying. But they are not the uncouth creatures of everyday life, only those of art. Velázquez's, on the other hand, have no artistic pedigree, just that of raw life, in all its wretchedness and misery.

Mars, god of war, is the subject of another picture by the artist destined for the Torre de la Parada and, since it is virtually the same size as *Aesop* and *Menippus*, it may have been intended to hang with them. But this Mars is not doing battle. Instead, he is seated, slumped and dejected, at the edge of a bed, limply holding his baton and with the paraphernalia of war strewn at his feet. Wearing a blue loincloth and seated on a pinkish-red drape, he is the very picture of lassitude, his brawny frame relaxed and slightly sagging and his magnificent helmet almost too large for his head. Adding to the droll nature of

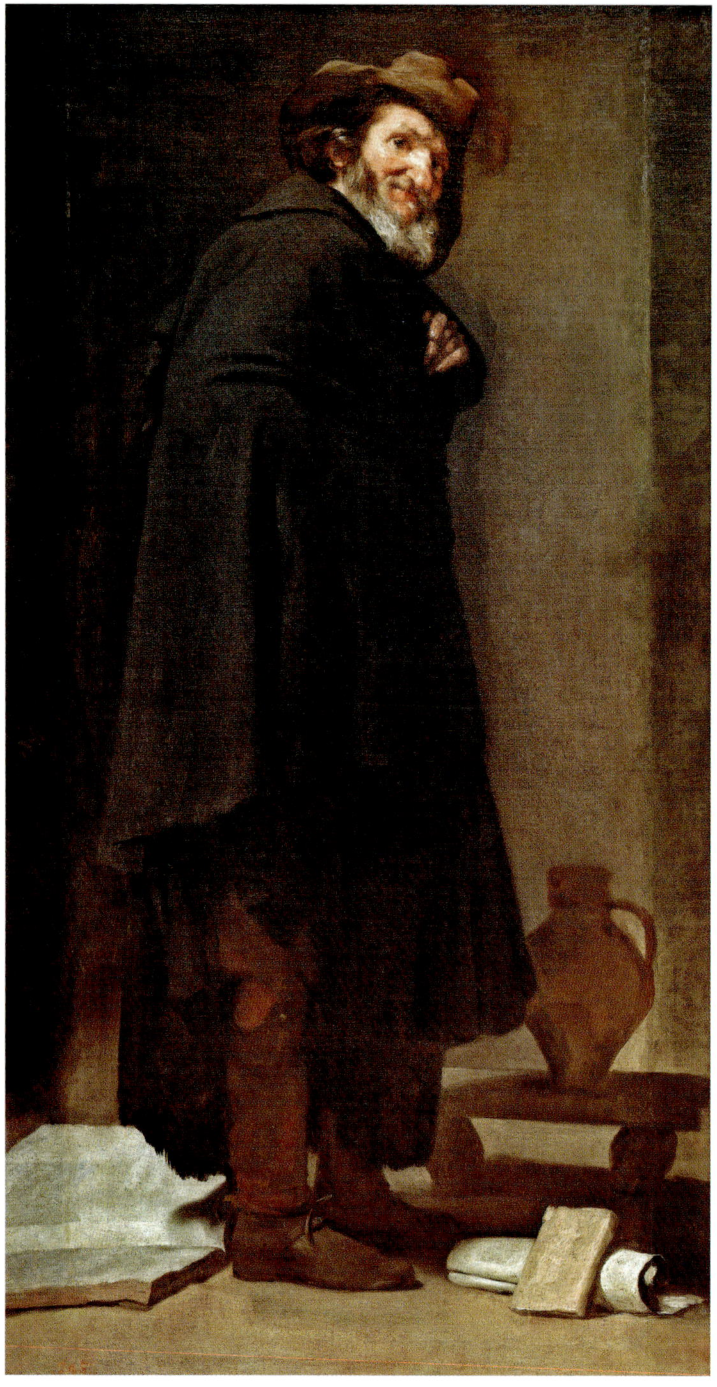

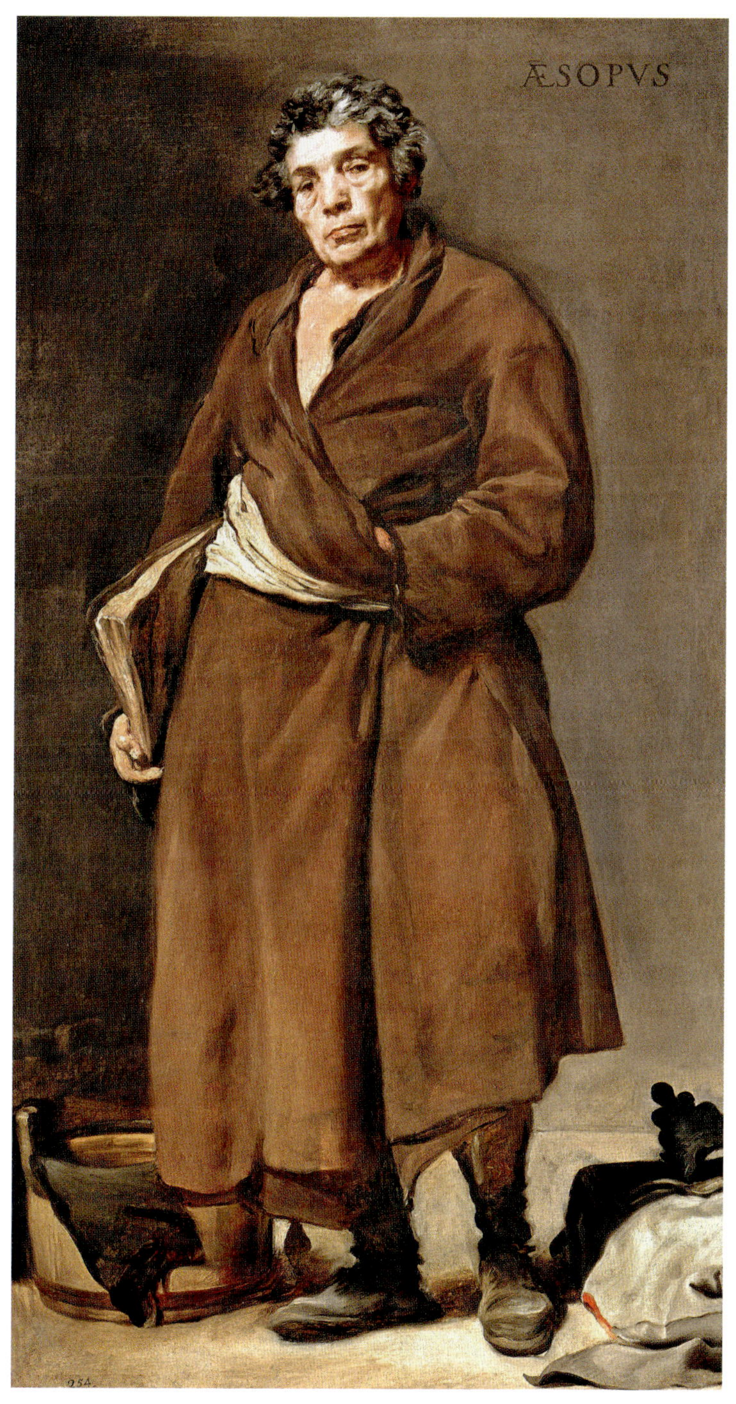

101 *Aesop, c. 1638*

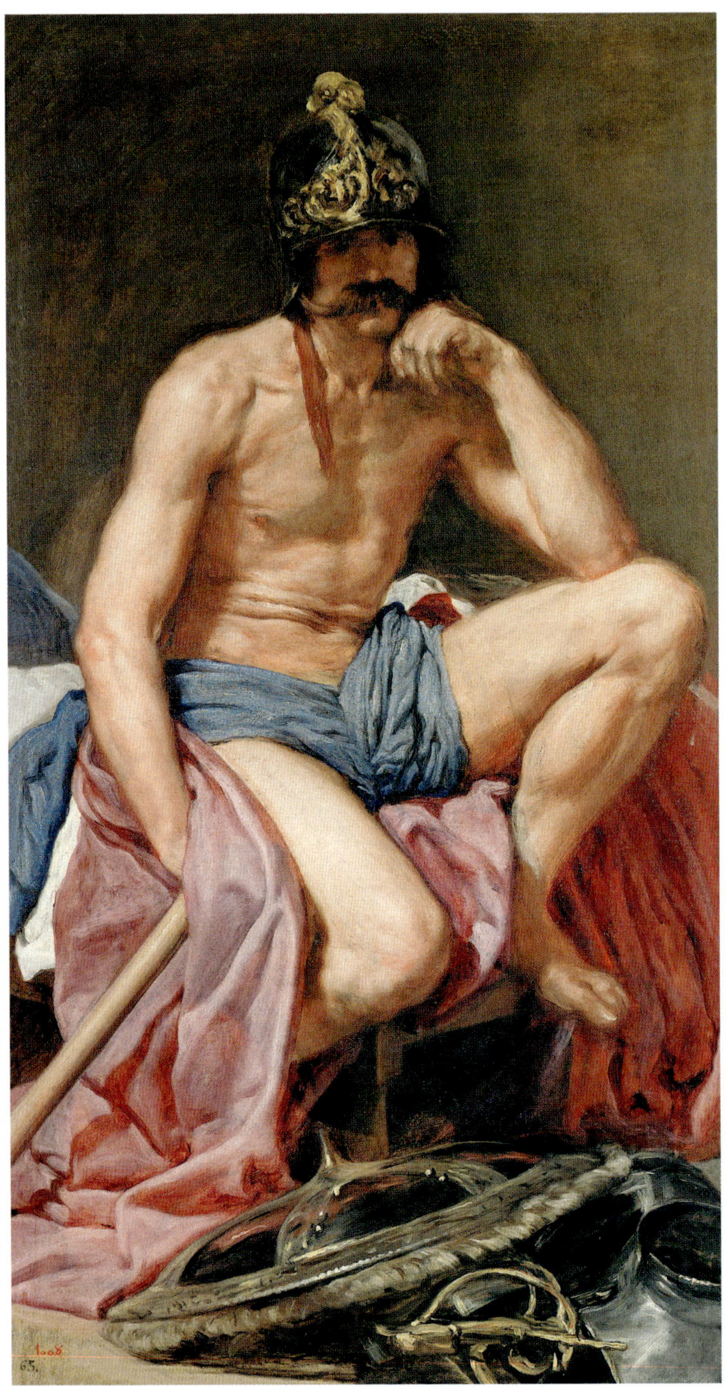

102 *Mars Resting, c. 1638*

the characterization is his absurdly lengthy moustache and the
no less oversized left hand that props up his chin. All of these
bespeak a Mars unfit for duty, even at the height of the Thirty
Years War. But how can Velázquez have meant the picture
to be read?

The most plausible explanation is that it be seen as a sequel
to *The Forge of Vulcan*. After Venus had cuckolded her husband
Vulcan with Mars, the former trapped and ensnared them in
their bed. Then exposed to the mockery of the gods, they were
eventually released and abandoned each other. Hence the
dejected Mars of Velázquez's picture and the empty bed and
dishevelled bedding on which he sits.

But there is another perspective through which to interpret
Velázquez's picture and that is through his lifelong approach
to mythological subjects. *The Triumph of Bacchus* and *The
Forge of Vulcan*, together (as we will see) with the artist's later
mythologies, could hardly be more earthbound or rooted in
reality. Something of the same may be said for his religious
pictures. If Velázquez's creative intelligence is missing
anything, it is that he cannot believe in what he cannot see.
But this omission also accounts for the unwavering truth and
sincerity of his art.

However accustomed one may be to Velázquez's daring
originality as a painter, his portrait of Pablo de Valladolid
will still come as a revelation. Looming into view from out
of nowhere, this court jester seems to breach the boundaries
between painting and performance, whether just having
made his grand entry onto the stage or now courting his final
applause. Dressed in black with his cloak thrown over his left
shoulder, Pablo is recorded in the King's service between 1632
and his death in 1648. His animated and commanding pose
appears to have been established with only minor pentimenti
throughout, especially visible still around his right leg. An even
more remarkable feature of the picture is its convincing illusion
of space and solidity without any of the usual aids. There are
no receding tiles, no floor line, nor any setting or surrounding
objects. Pablo creates his own space by putting one foot in
front of the other and by the shadow these cast on the ground.
A halo of light around his head and a darker passage of tone at
the upper right project him forward; then there are the myriad
blacks with which the artist models the figure, darker around
his limbs and lighter around his belly.

Minus the distractions of traditional painting, *Pablo de
Valladolid* possesses an astonishing immediacy. It also displays
an innate sense of pictorial style, evident in the distribution
of interest within the picture. On the left, Pablo's right hand

103

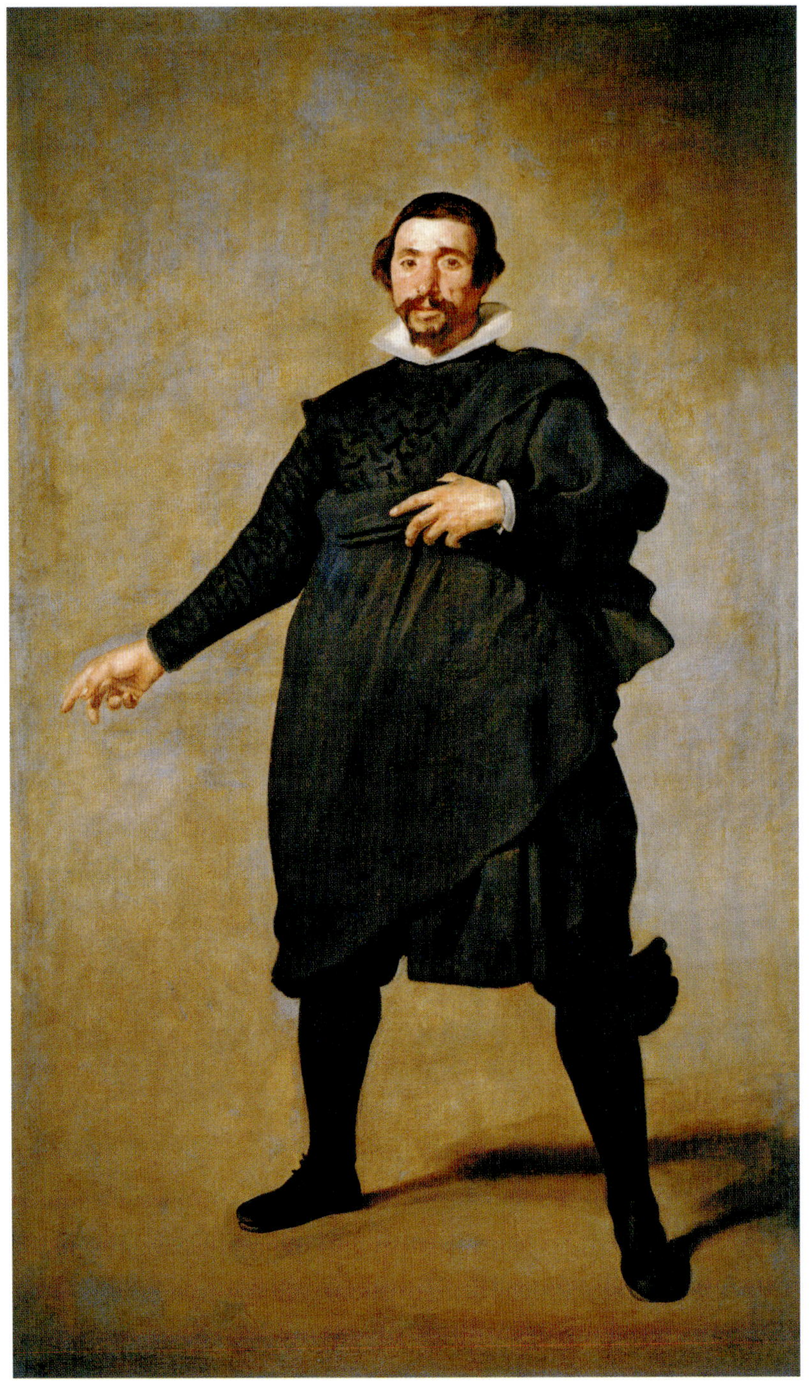

103 *Portrait of Pablo de Valladolid, c. 1636–37*

reaches out, commanding our attention. But counterbalancing this on the right is the scalloped silhouette of his cloak, itself reaching out into thin air.

Pablo de Valladolid was one of six paintings of court jesters by the artist destined for the Buen Retiro palace and executed in the mid-1630s. Also painted for the hermitage chapel of San Pablo in this palace was one religious picture by Velázquez, *St Anthony Abbot Visits St Paul the Hermit*, which is an exceptional work in the artist's career. It is his most ambitious landscape, one of the most fluidly executed of all his pictures, and derives its inspiration from earlier Northern art. As befits a hermitage retreat, it is a theme of monastic existence, based on *The Golden Legend*. Anthony Abbot has gone in search of St Paul, the first Christian hermit, and is seated alongside him in the foreground. Both are aged men, Anthony Abbot 90 years old and St Paul 113. Living a long life of solitude in the wilderness, the latter is daily visited by a raven bringing him a ration of bread. Obligingly, the bird here descends with two portions to feed both men. Other scenes in the picture enlarge upon the story. In the far distance on the left St Anthony asks directions from a centaur. Further forward he encounters a satyr who informs him where to find St Paul's cave. In the right background he knocks on its door. After their meeting, St Anthony departs, only to receive a vision on his homeward journey of St Paul's soul being transported to heaven. Returning to the scene, he sees the body of his friend laid out for burial and kneels to pray before it while two lions dig St Paul's grave. This episode is depicted in the lower left.

Velázquez found inspiration for the principal group in a woodcut of the same subject by Albrecht Dürer of about 1503. But this depicts St Paul greeting the raven rather than giving prayerful thanks for the ration. It also omits any of the other episodes in the story. Velázquez's inclusion of these follows the practice of fifteenth-century Flemish painters, who were well represented in the Spanish royal collection. The fantastic rocky landscapes of Joachim Patinir, among others, also provide the most obvious prototype for Velázquez's setting, with its mountains and valleys and precipitous rock arches. It is worth noting, too, that the painting originally had an arched top, like an altarpiece, and was only converted into a rectangular format in the eighteenth century.

Technically the picture's most remarkable feature is its lightness of touch, its sheer luminosity. The distinguished Velázquez scholar Jonathan Brown has plausibly suggested that this effect may be inspired by the many landscapes in

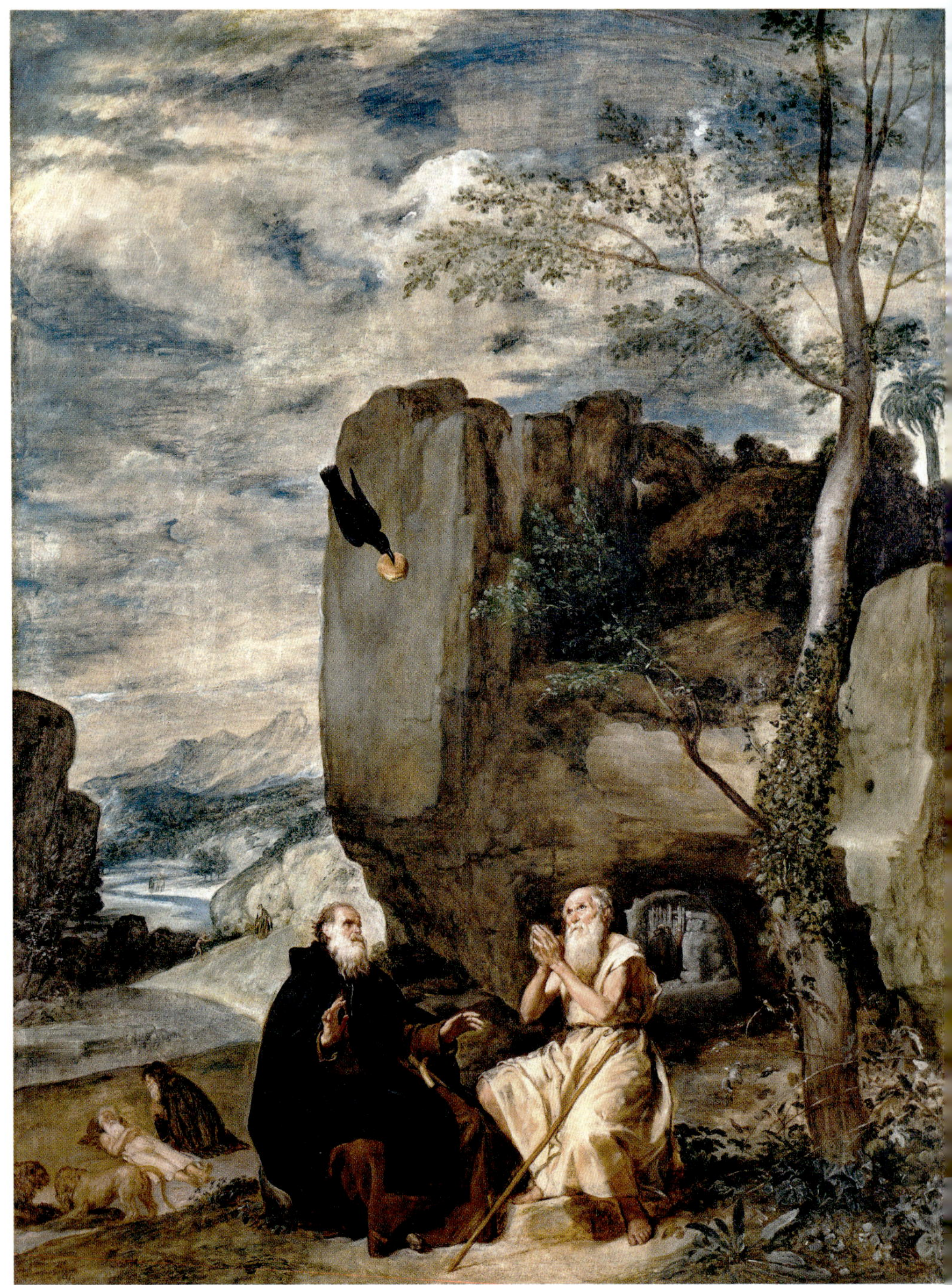

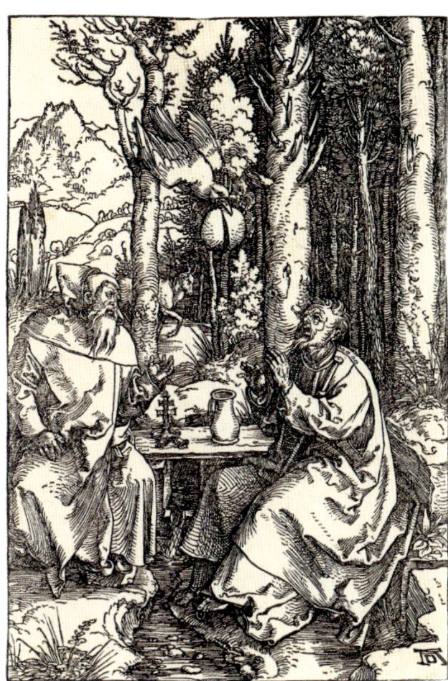

104 OPPOSITE *St Anthony Abbot Visits St Paul the Hermit, c. 1634*
105 RIGHT Albrecht Dürer, *The Hermits St Anthony and St Paul, c. 1503*

fresco that Velázquez could have studied on his trip to Italy
a few years earlier and it certainly emulates their translucency.
The background scenes especially are so thinly painted that
the fine weave of the canvas readily shows through them.
Although the x-ray of the picture is very difficult to read,
the principal forms appear to have been established both
quickly and decisively. This degree of spontaneity – even for
Velázquez – may have been prompted by the picture's chosen
setting and by the fact that so much of it is landscape. But,
whatever the explanation, as the great Carl Justi observed, 'the
colours... seem blown on to the canvas, the drawing quivers as
if seen in the distance through a thin gauze veil'.

Although commissions for the Buen Retiro palace consumed
the majority of Velázquez's creative energies throughout the
1630s, he also found time for other works, all of them portraits.
The most modest and affecting of these is the small, unfinished
Head of a Young Girl. The sitter's identity is unknown, but it
seems unlikely that she had court connections. Confining
himself entirely to a limited range of browns and blacks, the
artist has fully modelled the young girl's pertly smiling face
but left her costume and torso barely sketched in. Nonetheless
this little portrait is prophetic of the challenges to come in
the painter's career. Limiting the colour chord of a picture
while widening its tonal range will increasingly become a

106

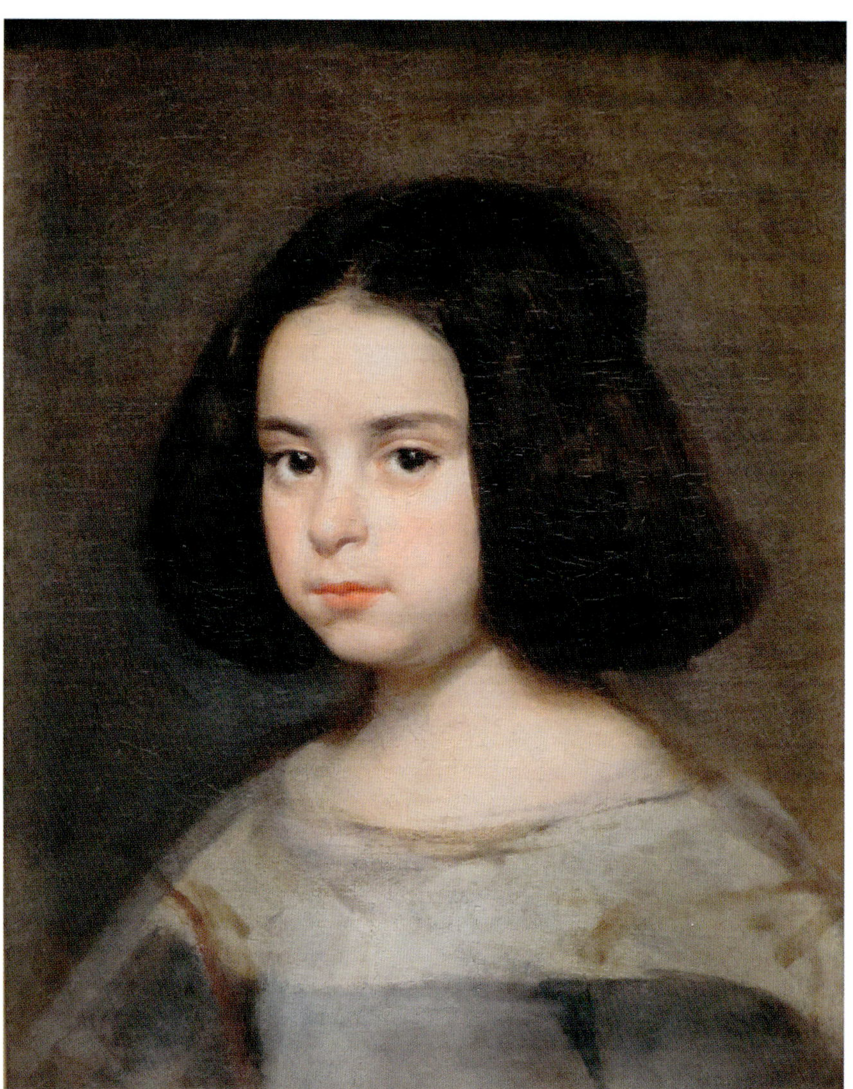

106 ABOVE *Head of a Young Girl, c. 1638–42*
107 OPPOSITE *The Prince Balthasar Carlos, 1638–39*

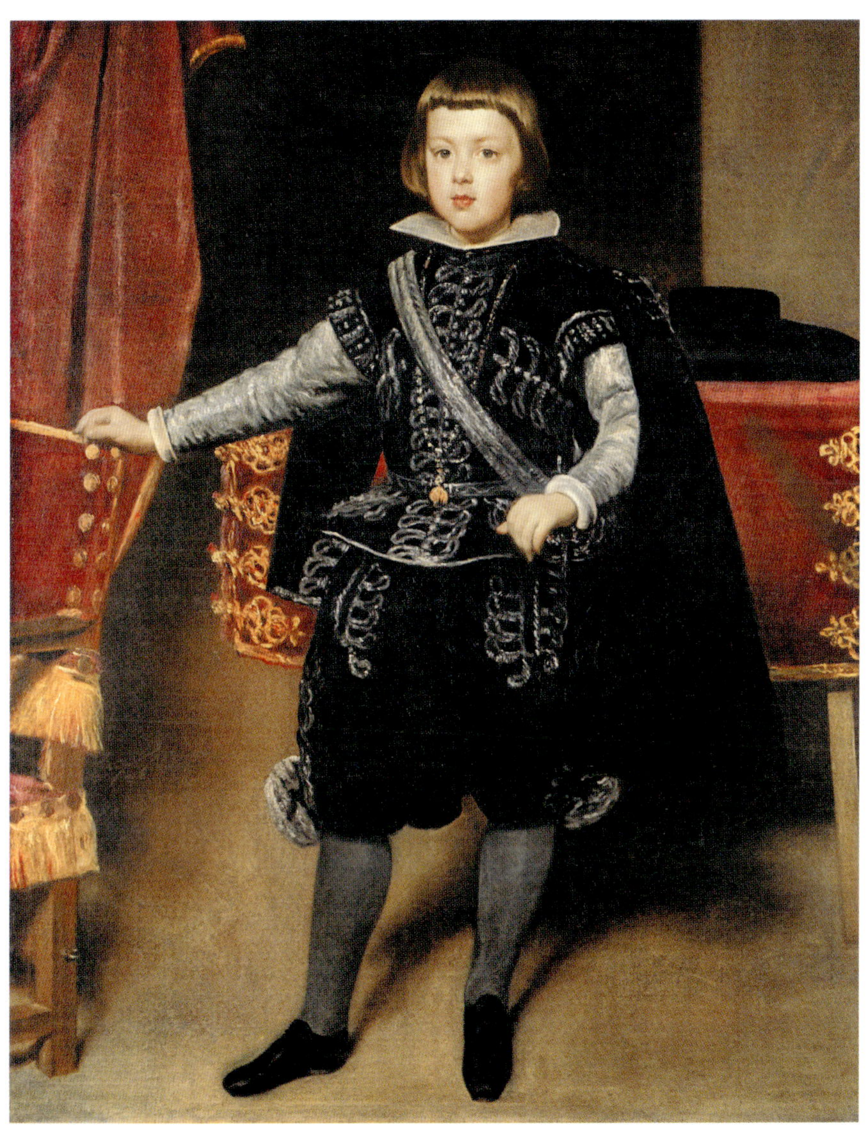

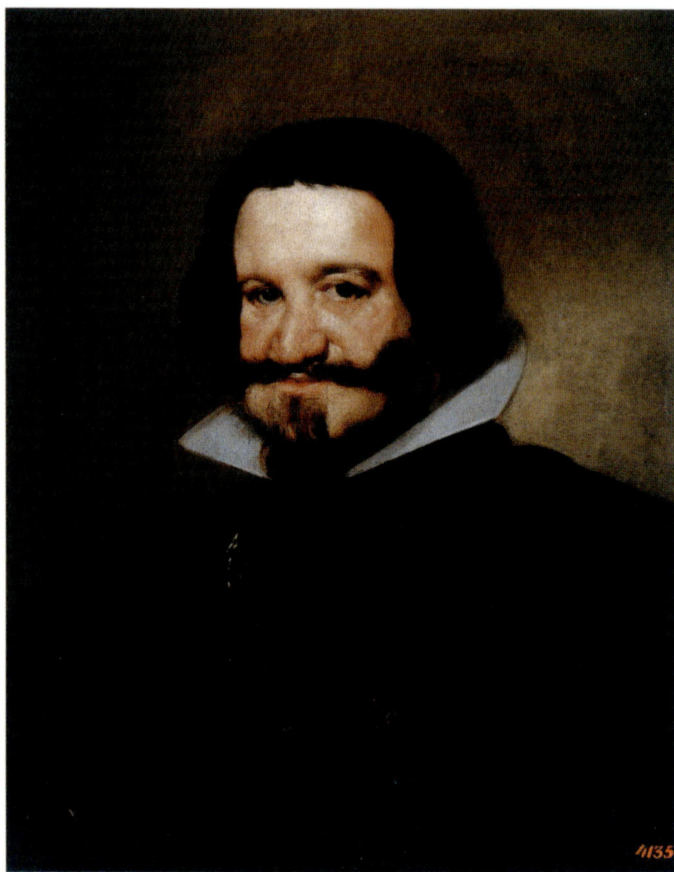

108 *Portrait of the Count-Duke of Olivares, c. 1638*

characteristic of his later works, and choosing to paint a young
girl (of which this is his first) initiated him into what would
become one the central concerns of his last years.

107 Velázquez's last portrait of Balthasar Carlos dates from the
end of the 1630s, when the prince was aged almost ten. Standing
proudly, with one hand gripping his sword and the other
holding the back of a chair, his fresh, beaming countenance
and pursed lips amply convey his youthful vigour and
amiability. Although Velázquez probably designed and outlined
the whole composition of this picture, he only painted the head
of the prince and the rest was completed by his workshop. This
accounts for the flat and lifeless treatment of the red drapery
throughout, the somewhat fussy and overworked embroidery
on both the prince's costume and the tablecloth and – not
least – the total absence of pentimenti visible to the naked

eye, especially around the legs. Had Velázquez executed the entire picture he might have had second thoughts about their awkward and unsteady positions.

The two portraits just considered – one unfinished by the artist and the other finished by another – suggest a certain casualness and even indifference on Velázquez's part regarding both the completion of a work of art and its wholly autograph nature. After all, unfinished works abound among his pictures, as do collaborations. The two most obvious explanations for this are the pressure of time and the artist's notoriously phlegmatic nature. Both factors undoubtedly played their part, with Palomino admitting that Velázquez was so burdened with other duties that he was not allowed enough freedom to practise his profession. Thus his royal honours and employment became 'the sort of reward that seems to wear the disguise of punishment'.

But another facet of Velázquez's creative personality and practice may also have contributed, and this was that he found painting a great strain because he refused to evolve a formula or routine for doing it. The absence of preparatory drawings by him and the large number of pentimenti to be found in his works indicates that the progress of an individual picture was more of a journey of discovery than a question of following the rules. This is because he was essentially an instinctual artist who preferred to find his way with a subject rather than plot his course in advance. As a result we are left with far fewer pictures by Velázquez, for instance, than we are by Van Dyck, despite the fact that the latter died twenty years earlier than him. But whereas Van Dyck's paintings can often appear formulaic, those by Velázquez are all unique creations, even in those instances where they depict the same sitter.

The artist's last portrait of Olivares dates from no later than 1638 since it provided the source for an engraving of the Count-Duke dated to that year. It is tempting to conclude that its bust-length format and small size reflect not only its suitability for replication but also Olivares's declining mental and physical health and his gradual fall from grace at court. Long given to diverting the King from the affairs of state with lavish and costly pageants, palaces and plays – above all the Buen Retiro palace itself – Olivares's own grip on power was ending in disaster. By 1642, Portugal and Catalonia were rebelling against the crown, the King had suffered defeat in Aragon, and Spain was increasingly being eclipsed by France as the leading European power. There was mounting pressure on the King by his courtiers to dismiss his favourite Count-Duke and, on 17 January 1643, Philip IV finally yielded, sending Olivares permission to retire. He died two years later at Foro, having by then gone mad.

In this much darkened portrait Olivares wears his usual duplicitous gaze and machinating grin but his eyes are less piercing than in earlier years and his cheeks more puffy and sagging. Intriguingly, painted copies and several engravings after this work depict the Count-Duke wearing the cross of Alcántara, but not Velázquez's original.

Throughout the 1630s not only was Velázquez busily painting but he was also reaping the rewards both financially and in his steadily rising position within the royal household. In the mid-1630s he was granted the use of a new house in Madrid valued at 500 ducats a year, and in 1636 he was appointed Assistant in the Wardrobe of the palace. By 1640 his annual salary had also increased to 1,550 ducats a year plus free medical care and an additional 500 ducats annually for all pictures painted for the King. The latter also gave him an extraordinary grant of 2,000 ducats in 1643. According to Palomino, 'he [the King] honoured him as well with the key to his bedchamber, something that many Knights of the Orders would like. And continuing on his advancement, Velázquez came to hold the post of Gentleman of the Bedchamber, although he could not exercise it until the year 1643.' The oath of office ceremony admitting him to this position was held on 6 January 1643 and administered by the Count-Duke Olivares, one of the last official duties he performed before his dismissal by the King eleven days later.

Chapter 5
Consolidating his Style

In February 1644 Philip IV left Madrid for Aragon, where, following a rebellion in Catalonia, the French army had invaded the region and taken the city of Lérida. Accompanying the King was a royal entourage of around five hundred, including Velázquez in his capacity as Gentleman of the Bedchamber and also to document the anticipated victory of the King. Following several stops along the way, the royal party settled in Fraga, which was to serve as its headquarters during the siege of Lérida. According to Palomino, the city of Lérida, which had been overpowered by the French armies, surrendered at the appearance of its King and natural lord on Sunday 31 July of that year and His Majesty entered it to sovereign applause on Sunday 7 August. During the siege, Velázquez painted the King's portrait as he had entered Lérida in full military dress. But before this could be done a portable makeshift studio for the sittings had to be constructed.

In May 1644 the King requested a carpenter to make an easel for the artist and ordered that two windows be cut into the wall of his lodgings. Next the room in the royal dwelling was restored because its walls were collapsing and the floors were unpaved. Eventually, the King sat for the artist on three occasions, after which Velázquez presumably returned to his own quarters to work further on the painting. The result, which is colloquially known as the *Fraga Philip*, could equally be titled *Philip IV in Red and Silver* and is the artist's most felicitous portrait of the King.

Unusually, Philip stands posed to our left, his head turned in the opposite direction to that we have grown used to. Holding his military baton in one hand and a black hat with crimson feathers in the other, he wears a rose-coloured

109

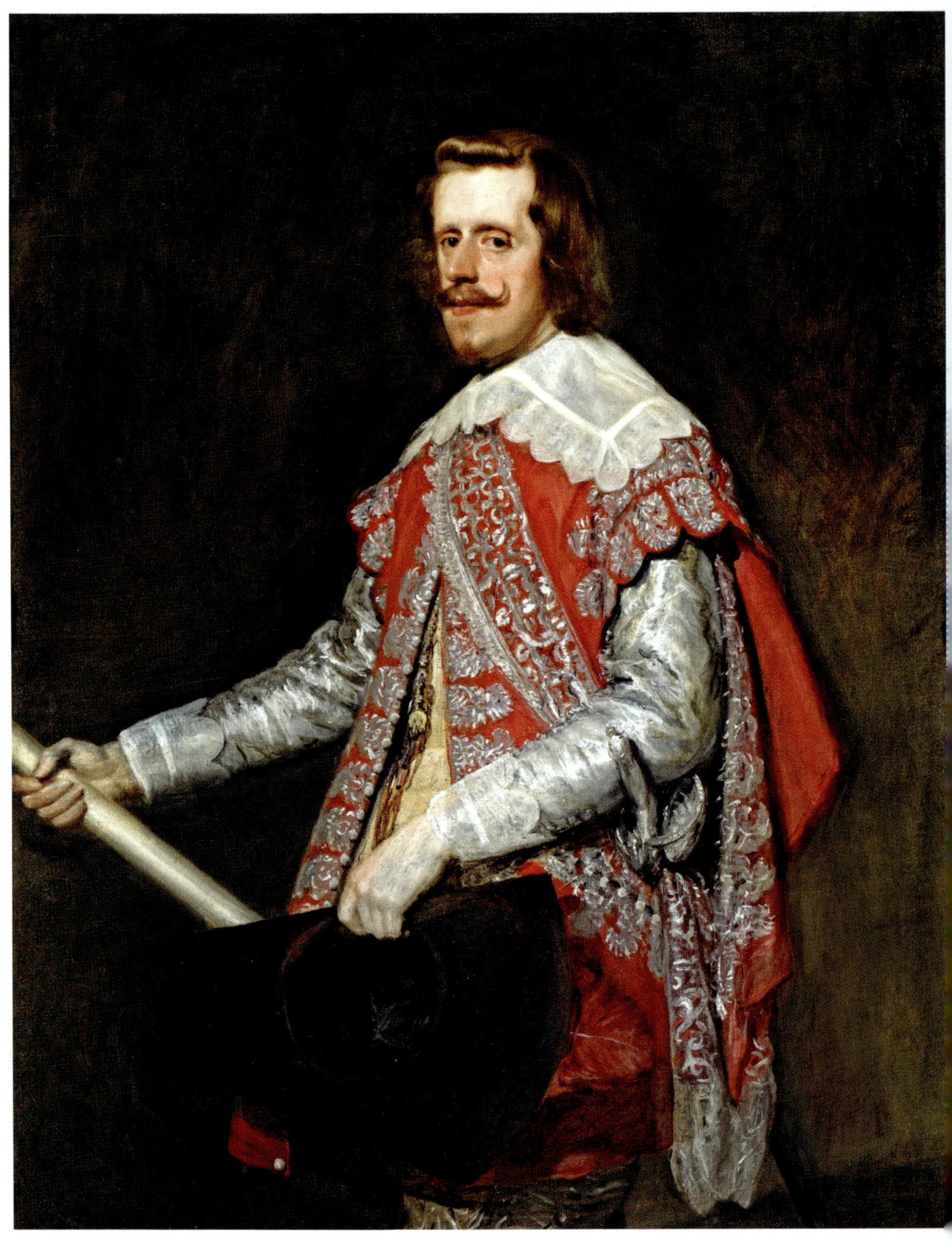

109 ABOVE *Portrait of Philip IV at Fraga*, 1644
110 OPPOSITE Anthony van Dyck, *Cardinal Infante Ferdinand of Austria*, 1634

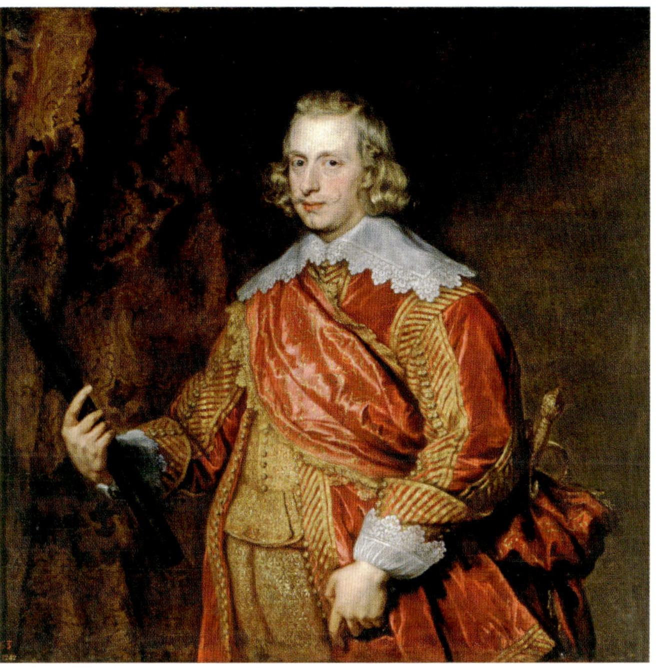

cloak and baldric, a falling Flemish collar and silver sleeves.
Velázquez seems to have based both the general pose and the
costume on a portrait of the King's youngest brother Cardinal
Infante Ferdinand of 1634 by Van Dyck, which had arrived in
Madrid in 1636 from Flanders, where Ferdinand was serving as
governor. Holding his baton up to celebrate his victory against
the Swedes at the Battle of Nördlingen, he is dressed in red
and gold rather than silver like his brother, but there are also
much more fundamental differences between the two works,
which reveal a crucial disparity between two of the seventeenth
century's greatest portraitists.

The Cardinal Infante Ferdinand strides forward, wielding
his baton of victory as though to celebrate his success and to
impress his authority upon the viewer. Velázquez's Philip IV,
on the other hand, stands fixed and frozen before us, his
arms aligned exactly parallel to each other and his baton in
counterpoise to them. He greets no one, but simply invites
scrutiny – and submission. When you do look closer, what do
you see? Perhaps the best way of answering this is to compare
Velázquez's technique in this picture with that of another great
magician of the brush among his contemporaries, the Haarlem
portraitist Frans Hals.

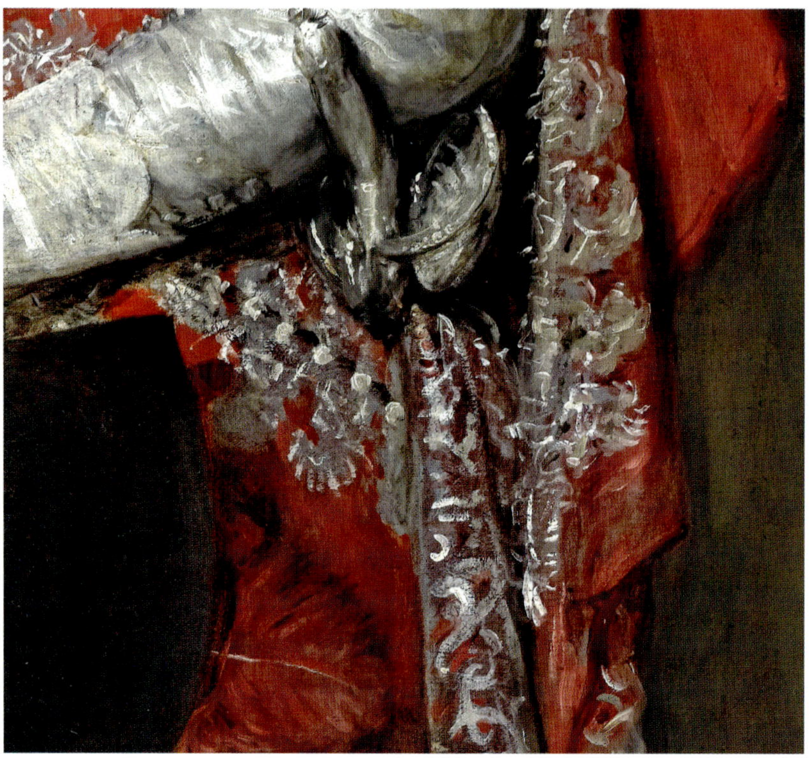

Hals's portrait of Jasper Schade of 1645 depicts the 22-year-old son of an aristocratic Utrecht family who was to go on to hold a number of high offices but (one suspects) always remain something of a dandy. In the very year that Hals painted him he is reported to have spent 300 francs on a suit of clothes in Paris, and one could hardly imagine him more flamboyantly dressed than here. But how has Hals's technique achieved this?

Jasper Schade's vest and sleeve dazzle with light and energy, but the brushstrokes that create them can be reduced to a scheme – in short, a pictorial handwriting. Whether straight, angled or zigzagging, they are all essentially linear and, ultimately, much the same.

Now compare these with the costume of Philip IV, which utterly defies analysis. Squiggles, strokes, stains, blobs, painterly deposits – call them what you will, these no longer resemble pictorial handwriting, more a form of mark-making with a brush. Neither planned nor predictable, this imbroglio of brushstrokes appears to have been willed onto the canvas by a conjurer rather than a painter.

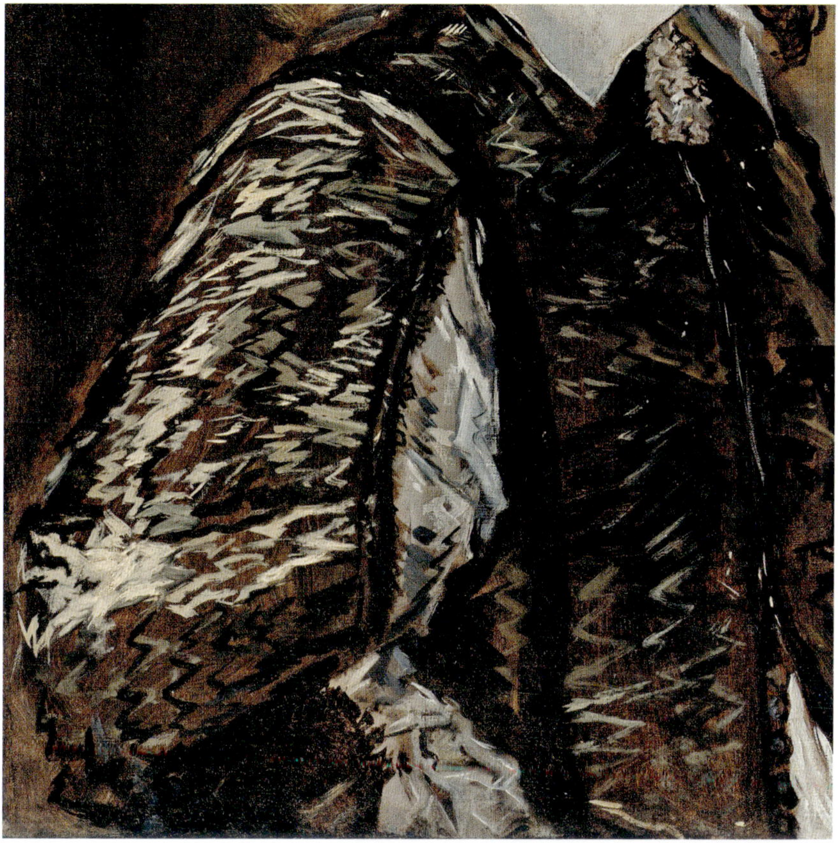

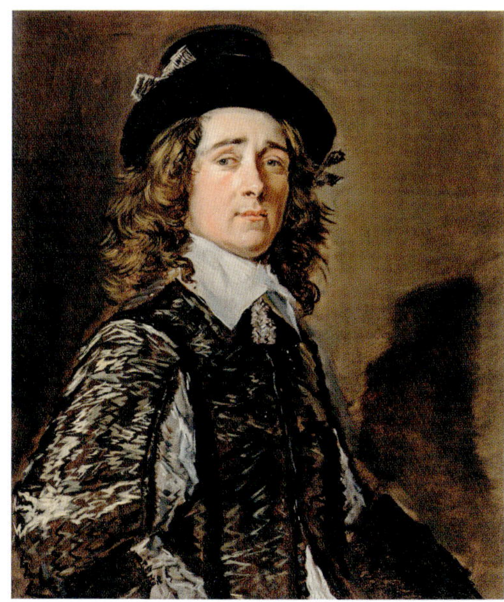

111 OPPOSITE *Portrait of Philip IV at Fraga*, 1644, detail
112, 113 ABOVE (DETAIL) AND RIGHT Frans Hals, *Jasper Schade van Westrum*, 1645

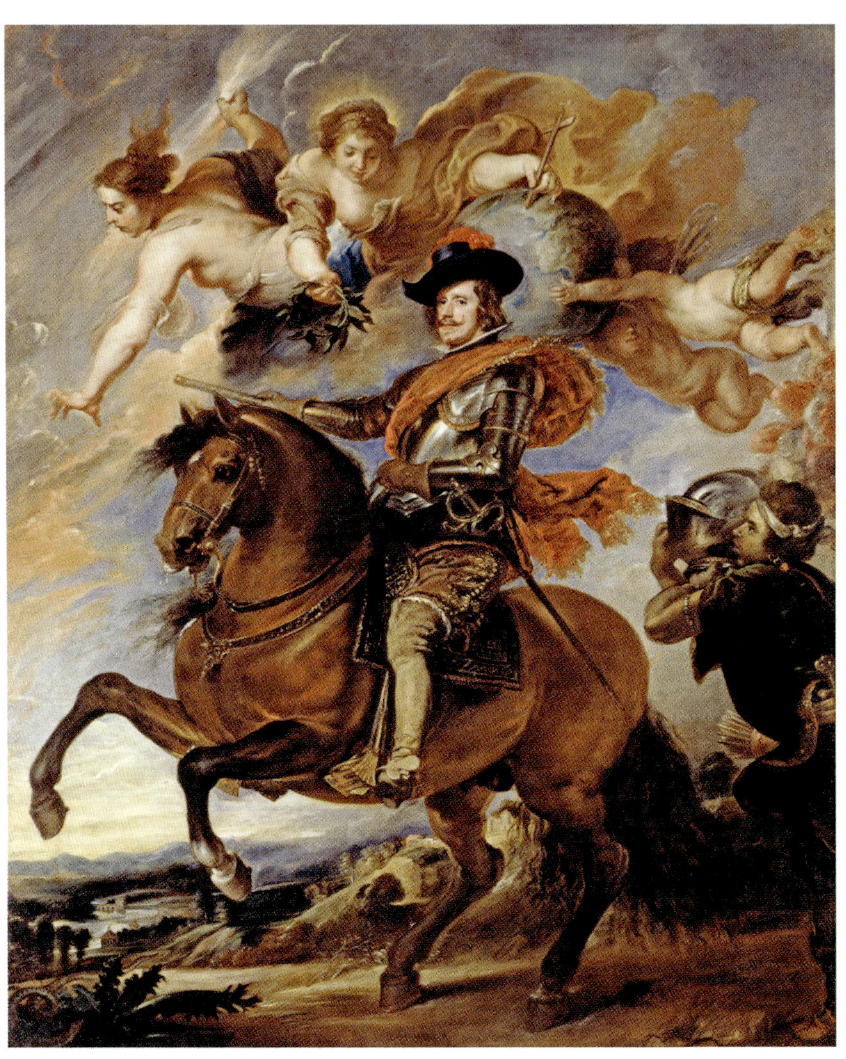

114 Workshop of Peter Paul Rubens, *Philip IV on Horseback* (copy), c. 1645

Virtually identical to the head of the King in the *Fraga Philip* is that of an equestrian portrait of him after Rubens datable to about 1645 which exists only in a copy. The original, which is now lost, was painted by Rubens during his visit to Madrid in 1628–29 to replace the equestrian portrait of Philip painted by Velázquez in the early 1620s, which had won much admiration at court and is now also lost. According to an inventory of the Marquis of Heliche's collection, the head of the King in the copy after Rubens was painted by Velázquez, but whatever the truth of this evidence, the portrait itself belongs to a different world from that of the Spanish master. Philip is shown riding a leaping horse and wearing a hat identical to the one that he holds in the Fraga portrait. Striding behind him a young black attendant holds his helmet, and above him putti accompany two female figures of Divine Justice and Religion, the former hurling a thunderbolt and the latter holding a crucifix and the laurel wreath of victory. As they wield their weapons the tumultuous skies surrounding them recede to encircle the King in clear blue.

For all their mutual admiration, Rubens speaks a very different pictorial language from Velázquez, enlisting allegory and symbolism to enlarge upon the victories and virtues of the King. This brings with it the advantage of embellishing his picture with a greater variety of figures, including women, children and people of different races. In contrast, Velázquez pares down his portrait to essentials, avoiding embellishments of any kind. He will not embrace a world of fantasy and the imagination, believing only in the world that he knows. In this sense, Velázquez's is an art of ineloquence.

Also attending the King at Fraga was Don Diego de Acedo, nicknamed 'El Primo' (The Cousin), likewise to be painted by Velázquez on this occasion. El Primo served as a member of the royal bureaucracy and was attached to the secretariat office of the Stamp, responsible for safeguarding a facsimile signature of the King that could then be applied to royal orders and decrees. Such supernumeraries were commonplace throughout the courts of Europe, and nowhere more so than in Spain, where jesters, buffoons, fools and dwarfs frequently formed part of royal life as diversions, entertainers or minor functionaries of the King. Their ultimate function, in truth, was to magnify the monarch's glory through their stark contrast to it. Often, too, they served to provide a corrective to a royal deficiency. Thus, Philip IV was only 15 years old when he ascended to the throne, as one critic noted, 'more a boy than a man'. Very early in his reign, however, Villandrando chose to depict him alongside a favourite dwarf, El Soplillo, as a way of

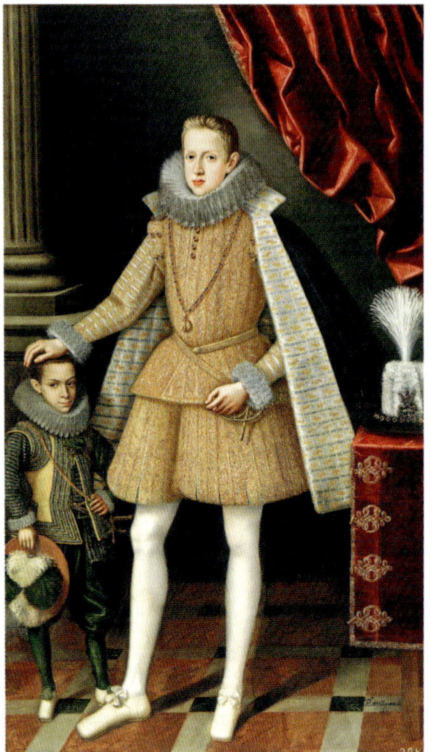
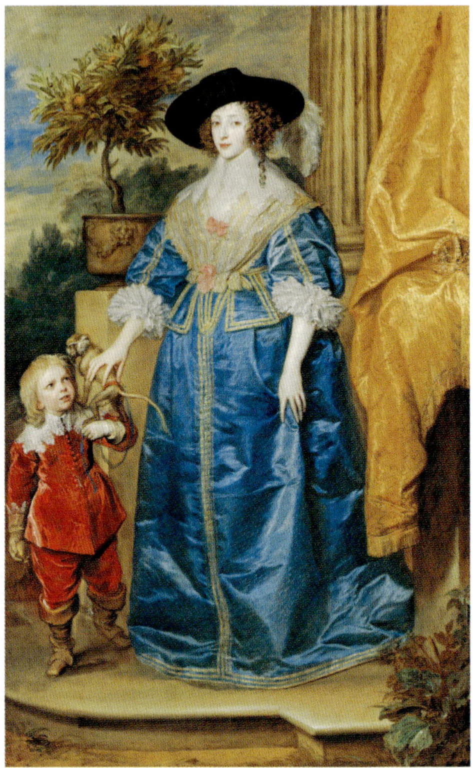

115 ABOVE LEFT Rodrigo de Villandrando, *Prince Philip and the Dwarf, Miguel Soplillo*, c. 1620
116 ABOVE RIGHT Anthony van Dyck, *Queen Henrietta Maria with Sir Jeffrey Hudson*, 1633

avowing his maturity and eligibility for the role. At the opposite end of Europe, at the court of Charles I, his queen Henrietta Maria was notoriously short in stature. How better, therefore, to make her appear taller than to set her beside the dwarf, Jeffrey Hudson, as in Van Dyck's great portrait of about 1633?

In the late 1630s Velázquez painted the first of what would become a set of four portraits of royal subordinates, one a buffoon of average stature and the other three dwarfs. All of these pictures are roughly the same size and usually hung together in the Prado today but there is no proof that they were intended as a series – except in one way. In all four the sitters are seated and thus subservient to the viewer, ostensibly to be looked down upon by us. This distinguishes them from other portraits of palace entertainers such as the standing-length figures of Don Juan of Austria or Pablo de Valladolid, who in their stance at least confront the viewer on equal terms. Instead, these four members of the royal household are made to accept their lowly status, literally below us, but refuse to relinquish their innate human dignity; as a result, they emerge as amongst the most searching and compassionate of all the artist's portraits.

Juan de Calabazas was in the King's service from 1632 until his death in 1639. His real name is not known but his given name means 'gourd' or 'bonehead' in Spanish, and he is depicted by the artist seated on a low wooden stool in the corner of a room and flanked by two gourds, one of which (on the right) was painted over an upright pitcher, a change still visible to the naked eye. Everything about this portrait is unsettling. The spatial recession is unclear, receding on the right by way of a door and then fading into obscurity. Calabazas sits in a foetal position, his legs crossed and drawn up to his body and his hands nervously clasped on one knee. Dressed in a deep green costume with black sleeves and an elaborate lace collar, he stares vacantly into space, his small sunken eyes and forced smile speaking of a simple and unhinged inner world. Adding to his helpless and pathetic nature is the viewpoint: we are made to look down upon him in more than one way. Then there is the thin, fluid and fluctuating handling of paint. Executed on a canvas of a thin weave, which constantly shows through, the brushstrokes seem at times not to know

where to go. This is especially marked – and moving – around the lace collar, where they appear to hover in mid-air in search of the neck.

Don Sebastián de Morra was the sitter for Velázquez's most confrontational portrait of a dwarf. Originally in the service of the Cardinal Infante Ferdinand in Flanders, who died in 1641, he then entered that of Prince Balthasar Carlos and remained at court until his own death in 1649. Little is known about him but, judging from Velázquez's portrait, he was evidently very much a man of his own mind. Seated on the floor and defiantly posed, he is dressed in a red cloak and green doublet and hose, a complementary colour combination that immediately alerts one to stand up and take notice. Then there are the strict parallelisms of the pose, from the fall of the cloak to the ball-like fists and protruding soles. The picture itself is central and symmetrical, but it was not originally so. A strip of canvas was removed from the right, probably in the eighteenth century, when the picture was framed in an oval, the pressure marks of which may still be seen around the edges. But the original format depicted Don Sebastian off-centre to the left with a standing pitcher by his side, as known from an early copy of the painting. This would have made it conform more closely with the still life included in the Calabazas portrait and

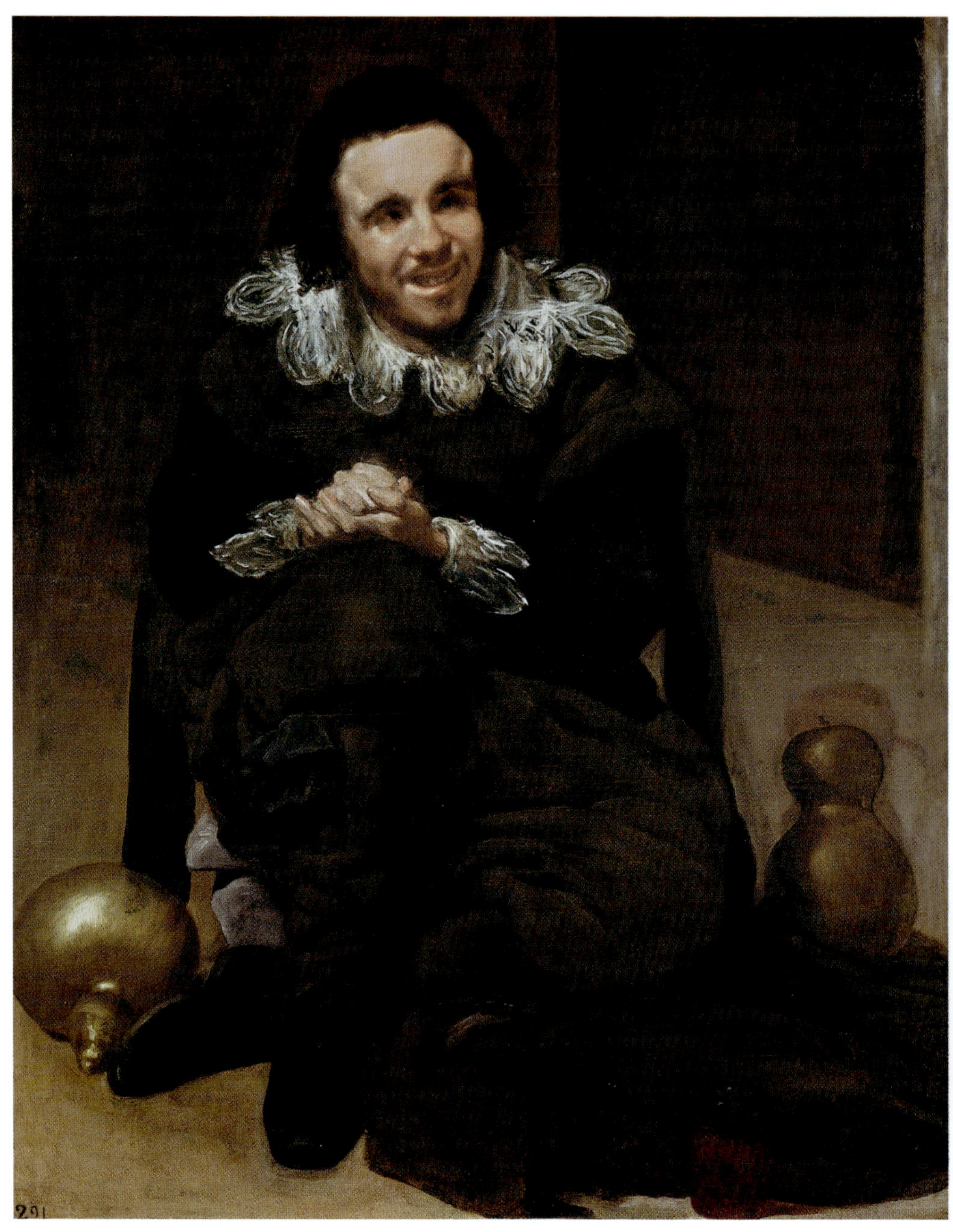

117 ABOVE *The Jester Calabazas,* 1635–39
118 OPPOSITE *Portrait of Sebastián de Morra,* c. 1645

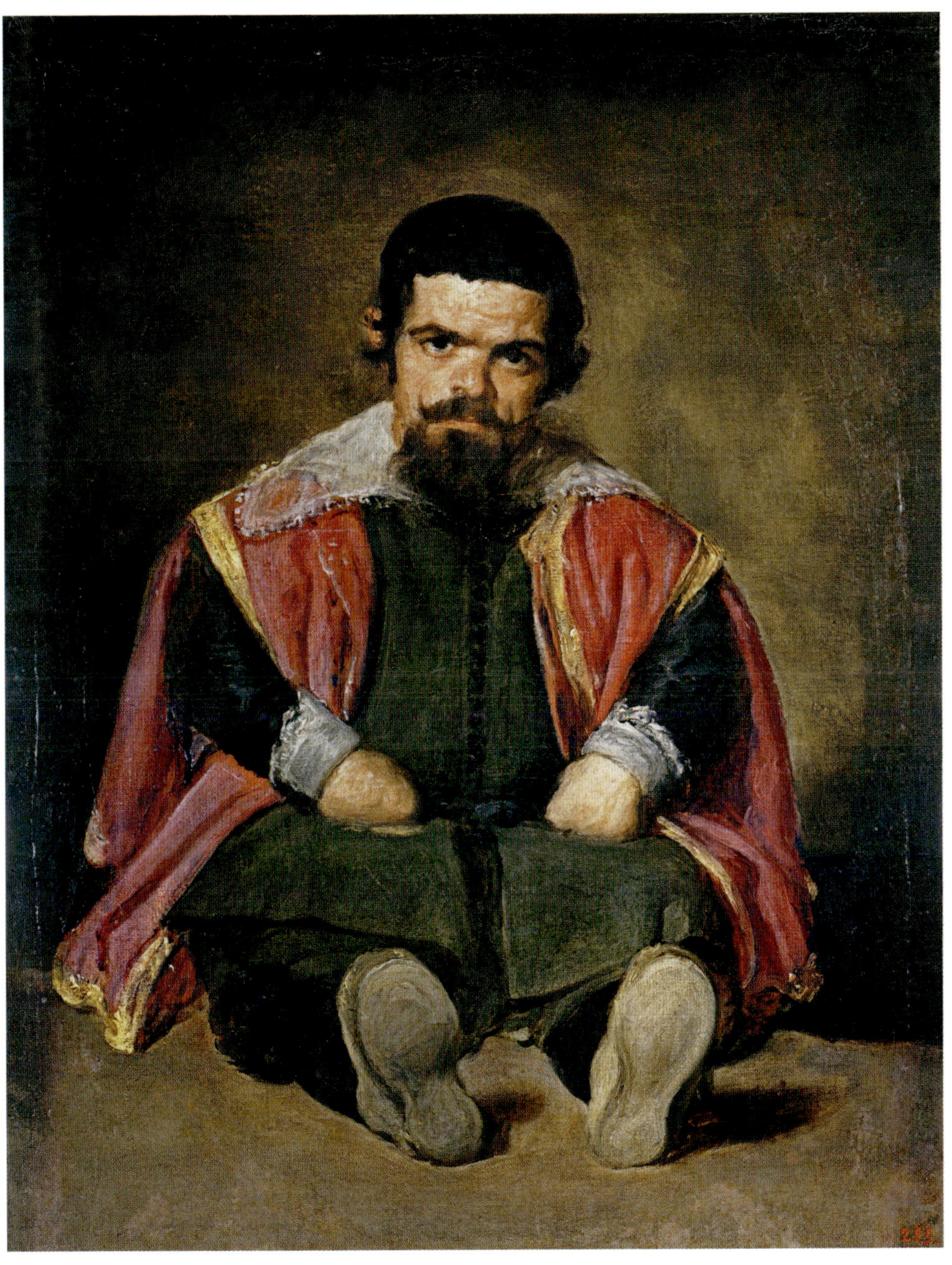

the two portraits in this group yet to be discussed, both of which include other elements in the composition.

As for de Morra's defiant pose and threatening demeanour, no one characterized these better than the great Velázquez scholar Carl Justi: 'You feel that, if you venture to stand and look at him you will be received with a volume of abusive language. An inquisitorial judge could scarcely overawe a wealthy... apostate with a more terribly piercing glance.'

If Don Sebastián de Morra's steady gaze is fixed on his audience, that of Francisco Lezcano barely seems to register that one is even there. Seated on a rocky escarpment and mechanically fingering a pack of cards, Lezcano exudes an air of disequilibrium, with unfocused eyes, head thrown back and legs dangling precariously into space. Adding to the sense of instability is the loose and filmy nature of Velázquez's technique and the low viewpoint – both of which suggest that the picture may originally have been intended to be displayed above a window or door. Two other features of the portrait are especially noteworthy. One is its subtly subdued but ravishing colour harmony, the pine greens and frosty creams of the sitter's costume blending naturally with the landscape beyond. The other is its candour. Faced with a sitter who could so readily have invited condescension or mockery, Velázquez evinces neither. The wayward and uncoordinated pose suffices to convey the disorientated state of Lezcano's being. Beyond that, however, we are confronted above all by the picture's unremitting honesty.

The aforementioned portrait of Don Diego de Acedo or 'El Primo' shows him wearing a wide-brimmed hat and fingering a large tome that rests on his legs. Seated before a landscape, he casts a firm and serious gaze out of the picture and is accompanied by the tools of his trade, a pot of glue or ink, ledgers and books. X-rays reveal that the picture underwent many changes in the course of painting, El Primo originally wearing a large collar that fell down his shoulders instead of the present *golilla*. His hat was also placed much further back on his head, revealing more of his forehead, and evidence of the free and easy way in which the artist adjusted the contours of it and the sitter's body are still visible to the naked eye. More surprising – and revelatory – still are the many vertical streaks of paint plainly visible in the landscape and sky. These presumably arose when the artist was testing his colours or wiping his brush. But why did Velázquez not cover them up? Moreover, why did the King not complain? These questions will never, of course, be answered, but we can consider what we gain by what we see. Those seemingly random strokes belong to the genesis and gradual gestation of the picture and document its very making. Covered up, they would render the picture more conventionally finished but less of a living thing. Velázquez is an artist who makes the very process of painting part of the finished result.

Cardinal Borja, whose gift of paintings to the Queen provided the impetus to the creation of Velázquez's *Coronation of the Virgin* in the mid-1630s also became the sitter for a later portrait by the artist. Born in 1582, he served as Archbishop of Toledo from 1643 until his death in 1645, and the portrait dates from this period. The original canvas no longer survives but is known through copies and variants and (by the happiest of coincidences) a chalk drawing unanimously attributed to the master and his most important surviving work in this form. Although it is evident that Velázquez made few drawings after his Sevillian years, the Borja study reveals that this was not through any lack of skill. The bust-length study set in an oval surround reveals a sensitive handling of the chalk both in defining the contours of the face and in modelling it. Particularly impressive is the graduated use of shading over the left-hand side of the face to define both the underlying bone structure and the play of light. Moreover, the scrutinizing gaze, warily looking to one side with his mouth tightly pursed, anticipates that of another ecclesiastical sitter soon to come before the artist, namely Pope Innocent X.

Wearing a similar but less penetrating gaze is an unidentified *Knight of the Order of Santiago* of the late 1640s. A sensitive and restrained portrayal of a somewhat world-weary gentleman sporting an elaborate moustache and goatee, this modest portrait provided Velázquez with few technical challenges. But there was at least one. Who else but this master could conjure forth an ear seen through strands of silken hair as skilfully as has been done here?

With the exception of the *Fraga Philip*, the 1640s are noticeably free of royal portraits compared with the previous decade. However, that was soon to change with the sad loss of the heir to the throne. In 1646, Prince Balthasar Carlos was betrothed to Mariana, daughter of Emperor Ferdinand III. On a visit to Saragossa in the same year the 16-year-old prince caught a cold and died. About two years after this, Velázquez and his workshop embarked upon a series of bust-length portraits of the King's daughter, Maria Theresa, doubtless intended for prospective royal suitors throughout Europe. All are relatively modest and hardly allowed the master to deploy his skills to the full. What is probably the earliest of them depicts her aged about ten (she was born in 1638) and is clearly unfinished, only

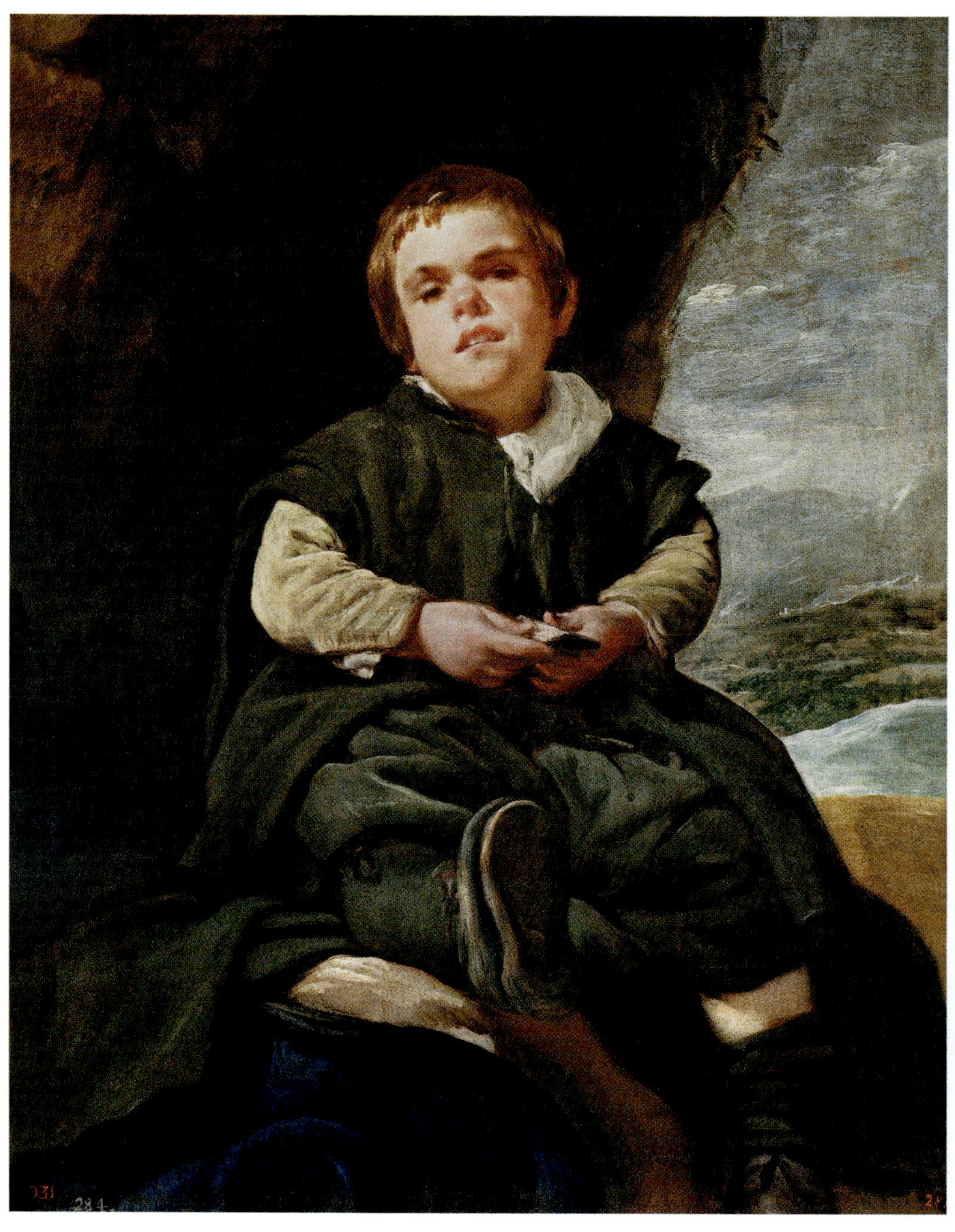

119 ABOVE *Portrait of Francisco Lezcano*, c. 1645
120 OPPOSITE *The Jester Don Diego de Acedo or 'El Primo'*, c. 1645

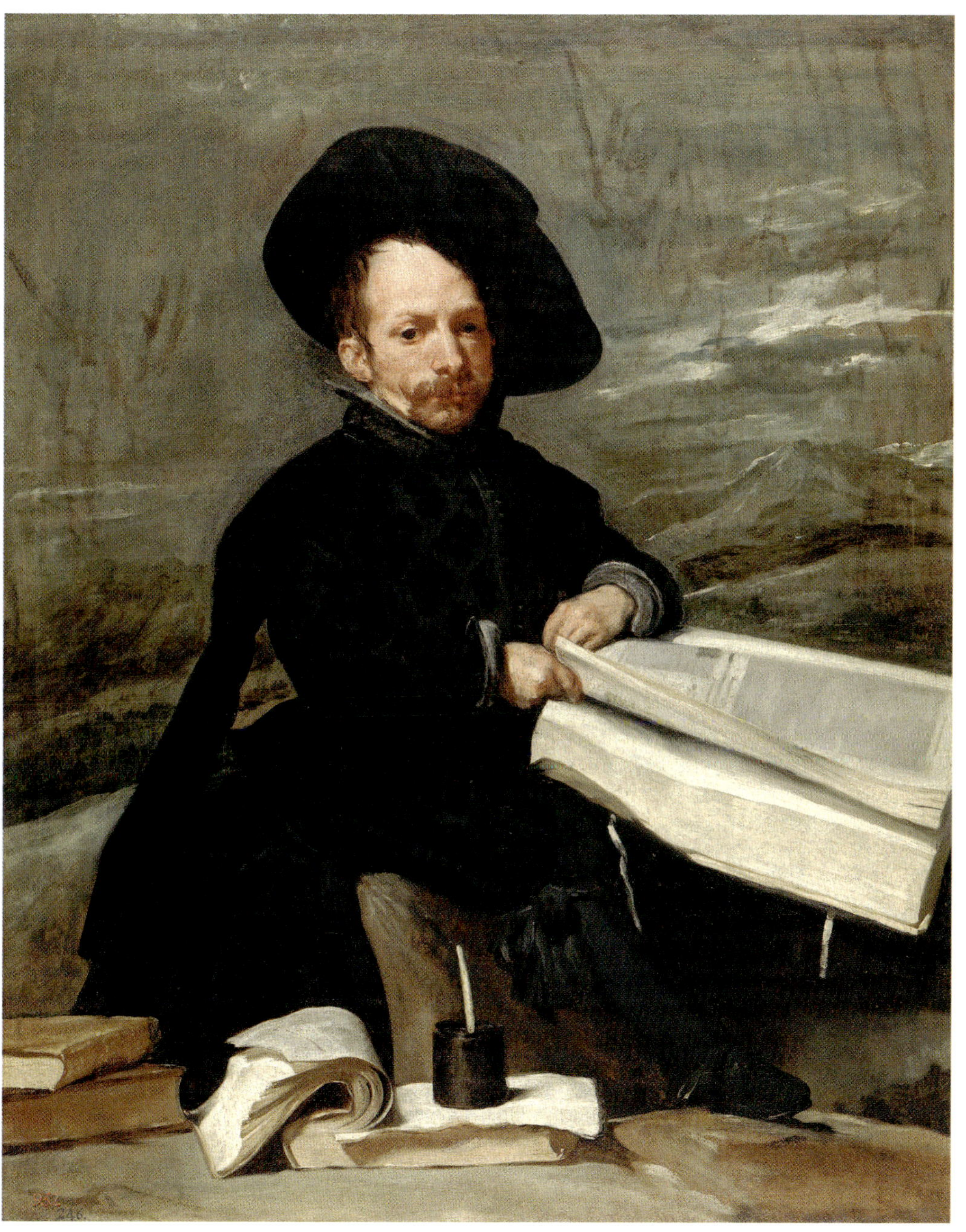

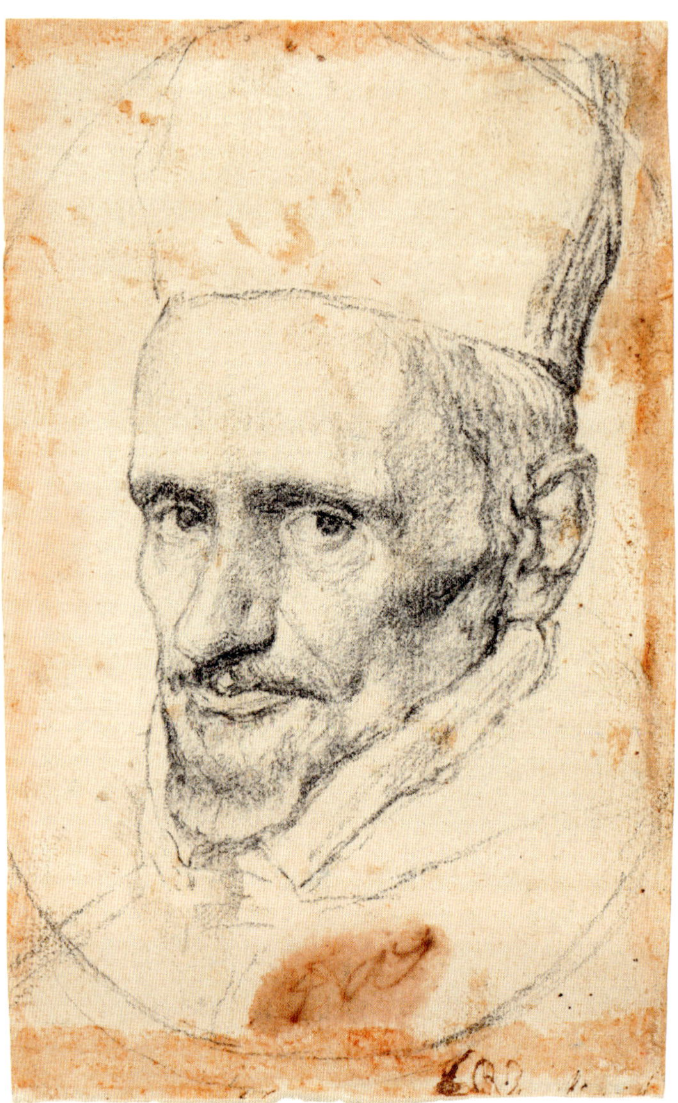

121 ABOVE *Portrait of Cardinal Gaspar de Borja y Velasco*, 1643–45
122 OPPOSITE *Knight of the Order of Santiago*, 1645–50

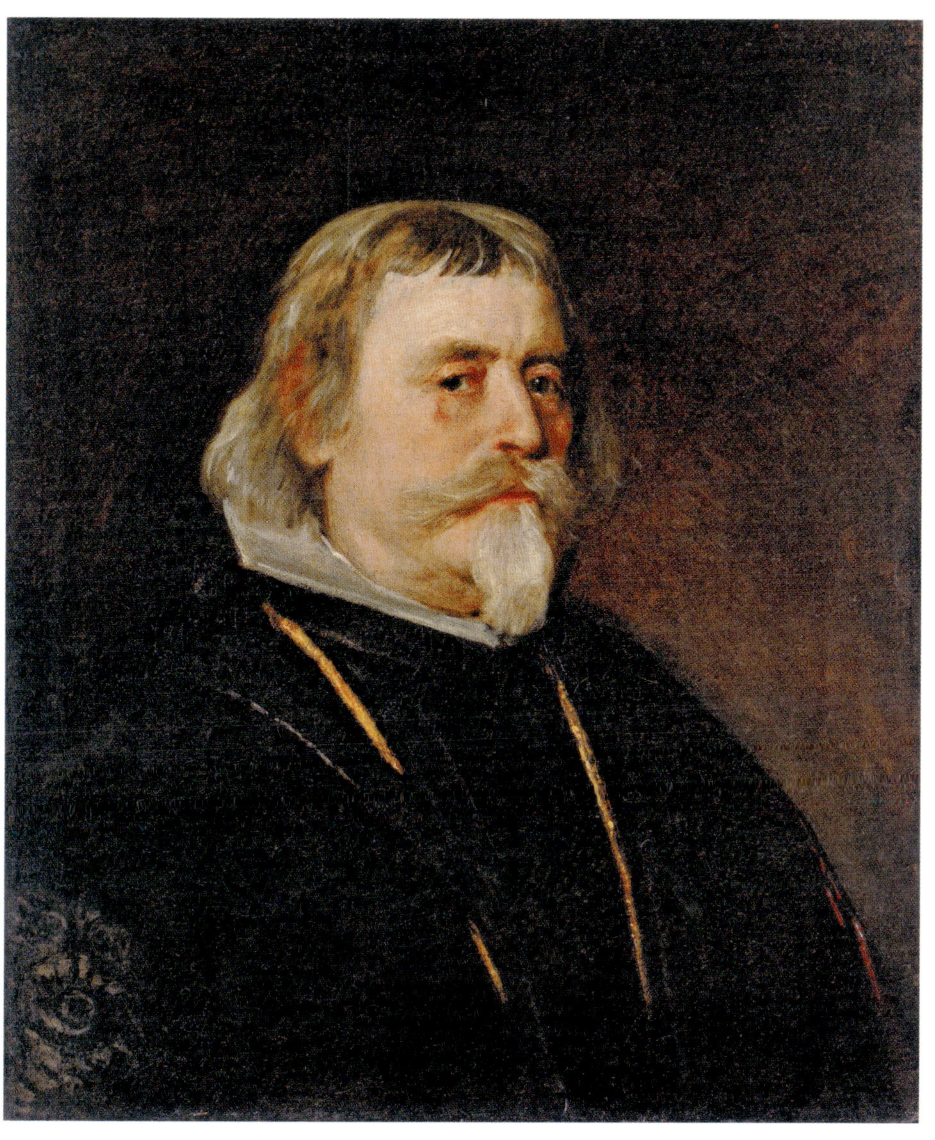

the princess's face being fully described, with its fashionably
rouged cheeks and chalky white skin. Her upper garment,
elaborately decorated with pearls, is only seen in embryo, but
the ornate, perhaps floral decoration worn in her hair is a little
miracle of brushstrokes, whatever it is intended to describe.

Doubtless due to the nature of the commission, Velázquez's
brushwork appears relatively tightly constrained in the
portrait of Maria Theresa. But the same may not be said of
another female likeness of these years, sometimes known
as a *Sibyl* but probably best considered a *Female Figure*. An
attractive young woman seen in profile and clad in a loosely
fitted chemise with her arms bared holds a tablet to which she
points with her finger. With her casually gathered hair and
absence of adornments she strikes a different note from the
artist's classically posed and regally attired *Sibyl* of about 1630,
despite the inclusion of the tablet. Given Velázquez's apparent
indifference to the boundaries between subject matter, it
is entirely conceivable that this spirited young woman was
handed this studio prop by the artist and asked to point to it
while he rapidly sketched her, unconcerned with what posterity
would wish to read into it. Along with his *Needlewoman* of the

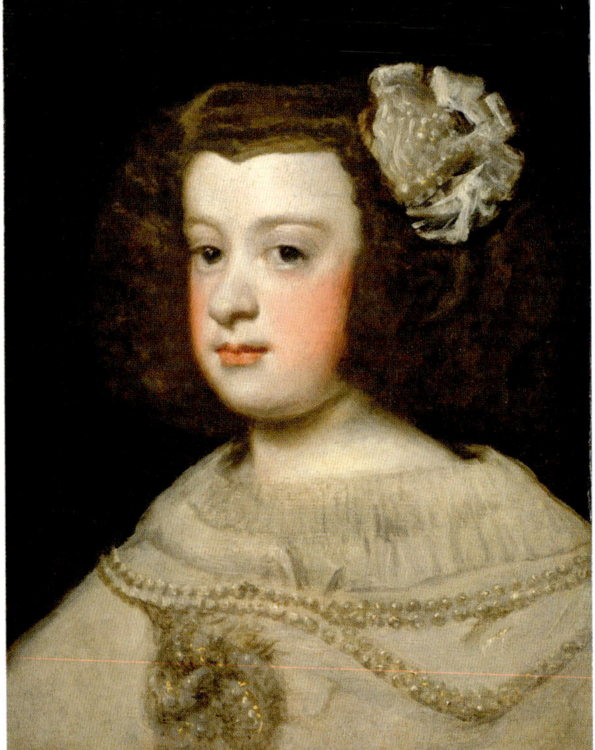

123 LEFT *Maria Theresa, Infanta
of Spain, c. 1648*
124 OPPOSITE *Female Figure
(Sibyl with Tabula Rasa), c. 1648*

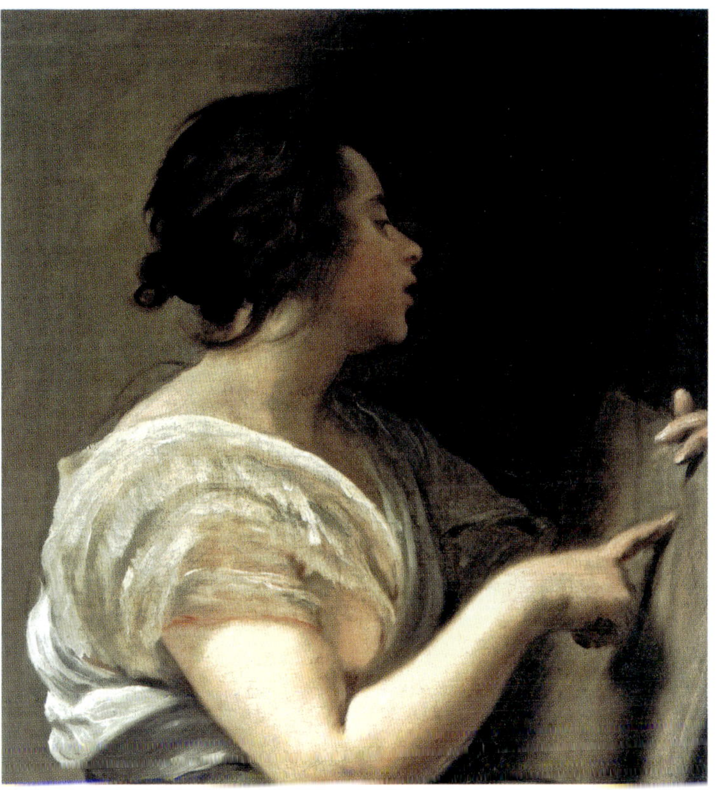

same period, the picture remains the only true genre scene of the artist's maturity.

The liquid technique and freely flowing brushstrokes of the *Female Figure* also characterize one of the greatest masterpieces of the artist's career, *The Toilet of Venus (The Rokeby Venus)* which also dates from the late 1640s and depicts the goddess of love gazing at her reflection in a mirror held up by her son, Cupid. Unusually for the artist at this stage of his career, it was not a royal commission and is first recorded in the collection of a Madrid-based painter and art dealer from whose estate it was sold in 1652 to the great nephew of the Count-Duke of Olivares, Gaspar de Haro y Guzmán, Marquis of Heliche. But neither of these individuals is likely to have commissioned the picture and that question will probably forever remain unresolved.

What we do know is that when Haro owned the painting he hung it next to a canvas of *Venus reclining in a landscape* by an anonymous Italian sixteenth-century master to which it provided the ideal complement: one a frontal view of a nude

125

128

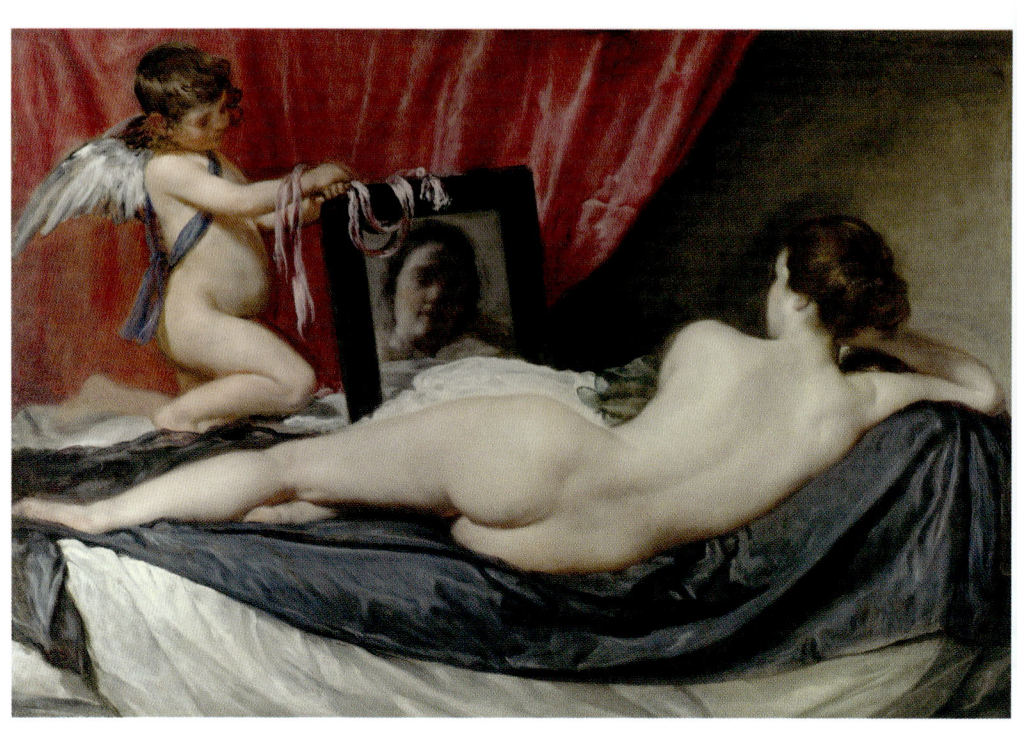

125 *The Toilet of Venus (The Rokeby Venus)*, c. 1647–51

in a landscape, the other a back view of one in an interior. But there was another equally big difference between the two: one was from Italy, where the subject of the reclining nude had long been established, and the other from Spain, where it was completely unknown.

Haro's Italian *Venus* can trace its ancestry to the first painting of the subject in Western art, Giorgione's *Sleeping Venus* of about 1510, which depicts the goddess serenely asleep in an idyllic landscape. Her accomplice, Cupid, was originally seated at her feet, but has been painted out because of damage. Nearly thirty years later, Giorgione's pupil Titian transported this figure to an indoor setting in his celebrated *Venus of Urbino* of 1538. His Venus is now awake and bejewelled, reclining on a bed in a palatial setting, a lap dog asleep at her feet and maidservants attending to her wardrobe at the rear of the room. Although Titian retains the red–green contrast surrounding the Venus of Giorgione's picture, his is an even more sumptuous image, from Venus's seductive and all-knowing glance to her luxuriant golden tresses and the cluster of roses in her hand.

Velázquez was certainly aware of this tradition when he embarked on *The Rokeby Venus*, not least because another, later reclining Venus by Titian was already in the Spanish royal collection by then. But it was yet another matter when such a subject was painted by a Spanish artist. Although mythological subjects involving nudity were much admired and collected by the native aristocracy, the religious authorities regarded these as a threat to and even offence against morality. As a result they were almost entirely avoided by Spanish painters, the only other female nude known from this period in Spain being the figure of Eve in Alonso Cano's *Christ's Descent into Limbo* of 1645–50, exactly the period of Velázquez's picture. Perhaps it is no mere coincidence that she, too, is seen from the back in a concession to prudery and in a standing pose that is otherwise virtually identical to that of *The Rokeby Venus*.

Velázquez was not the first artist to depict Venus gazing at her image in a mirror. Titian preceded him in this in a canvas of about 1555. But where his reflection tells us nothing that we cannot already see in the painting, Velázquez's does, and his mirror image occupies the very centre of the scene. Such use of a mirror to reveal something otherwise hidden in a picture is, however, to be seen in Van Eyck's *Arnolfini Portrait* of 1434, where the figure of the artist painting the newly wedded couple is visible in the mirror at the back. Velázquez may have been aware of this precedent – at least by reputation – since this picture had been in the possession of the sister of Philip IV, Mary of Hungary, earlier in the century.

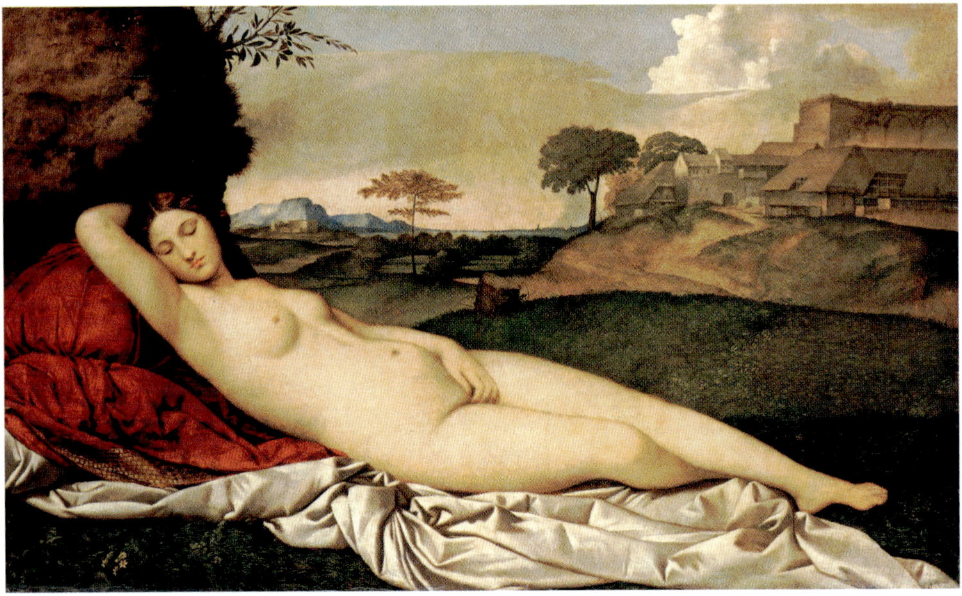

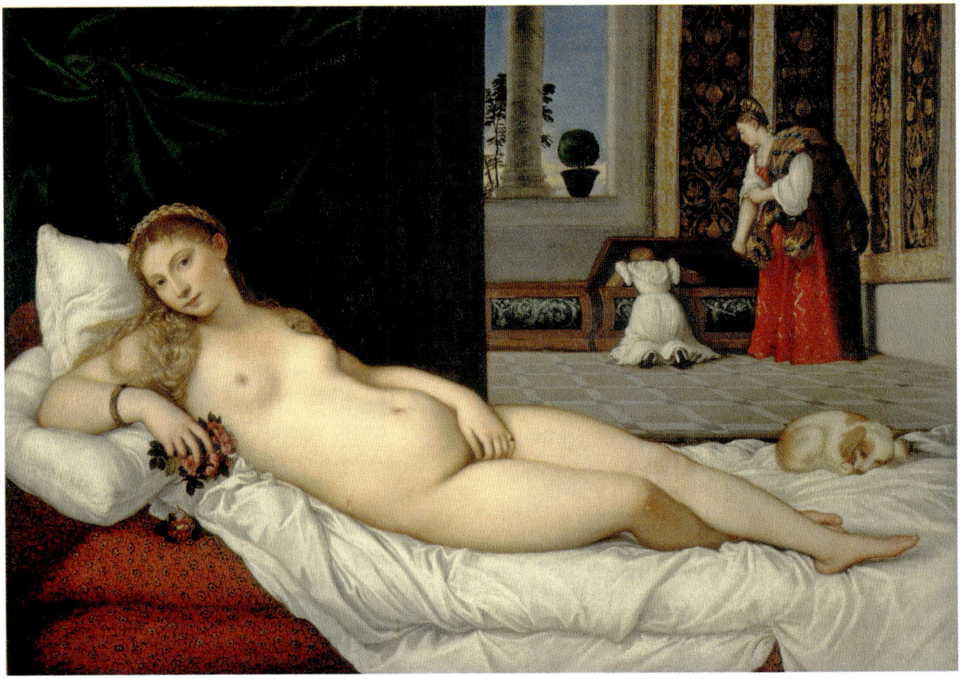

126 TOP Giorgione, *Sleeping Venus*, c. 1510
127 ABOVE Titian, *Venus of Urbino*, 1538

Among the many reasons why *The Rokeby Venus* sticks in the mind, and is many people's favourite Velázquez, are its harmony and simplicity. The painting is bound by curves, beginning with the lapping contours of Venus's body, which are counterpointed by the sweeping slate-grey drapery that supports her from below. Then there are the curves of Cupid's limbs and wings, those of the curtain in the background, of the white bedding that follows Venus's hips and – not least – of the looping curves of the ribbon draped over the mirror.

Even more striking perhaps than the picture's formal harmony is its harmony of colour. Adopting the term of a later admirer of Velázquez – Whistler – *The Rokeby Venus* is a symphony in mauve, grey and white. These modulate towards blue in Cupid's body band and a touch of dull green around Venus's breast but otherwise they dominate the picture – and nowhere more strikingly than in the flesh tones of Venus herself. Rather than the more traditional warm and glowing creams of other Old Master nudes, Velázquez's Venus is comprised of a cool pink and white with a prominent admixture of grey. This is entirely in keeping with the aloof stance of the entire picture. Here is a Venus who tempts one not to reach out and touch but, rather, simply to behold.

100 *Venus Reclining in a Landscape*, Italian, 16th century

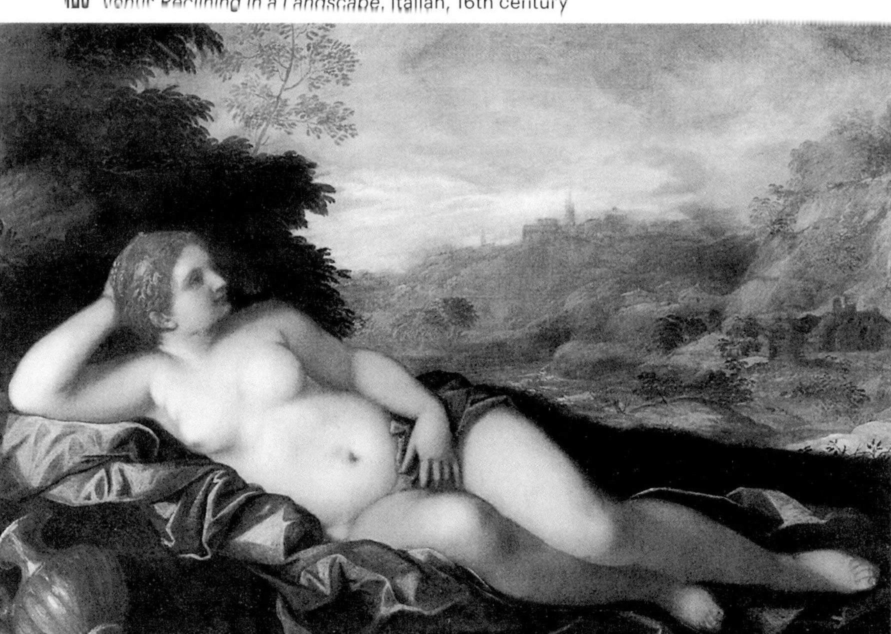

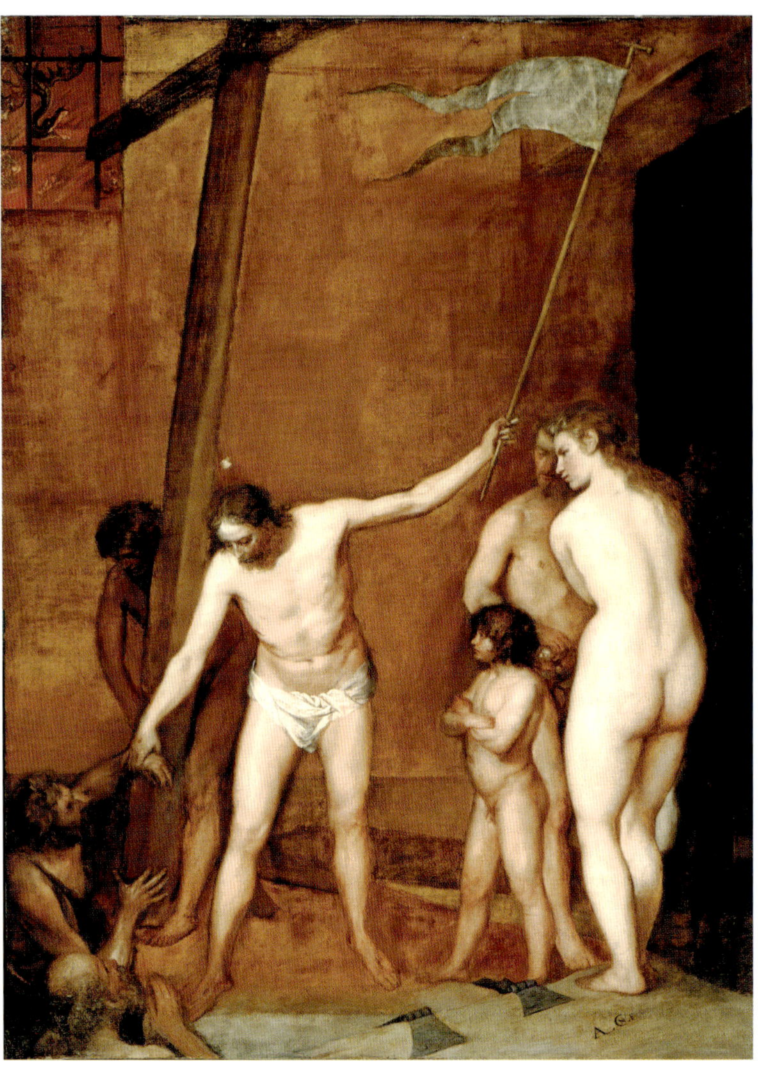

129 ABOVE Alonso Cano, *Christ's Descent into Limbo*, 1645–50
130 OPPOSITE ABOVE Titian, *Venus with a Mirror, c.* 1555
131 OPPOSITE BELOW Jan van Eyck, *Arnolfini Portrait*, 1434

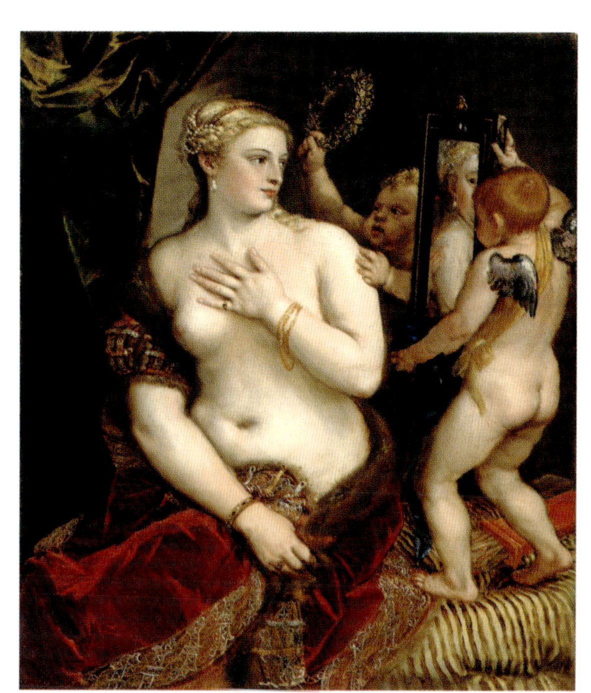

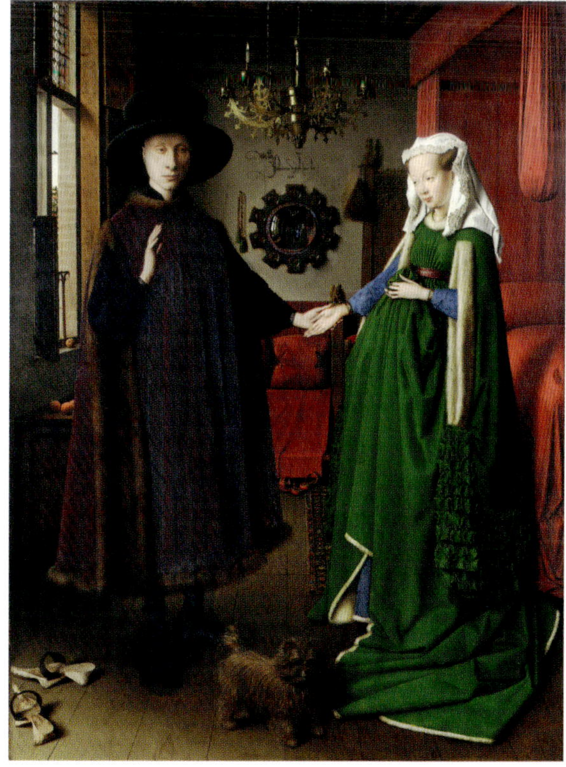

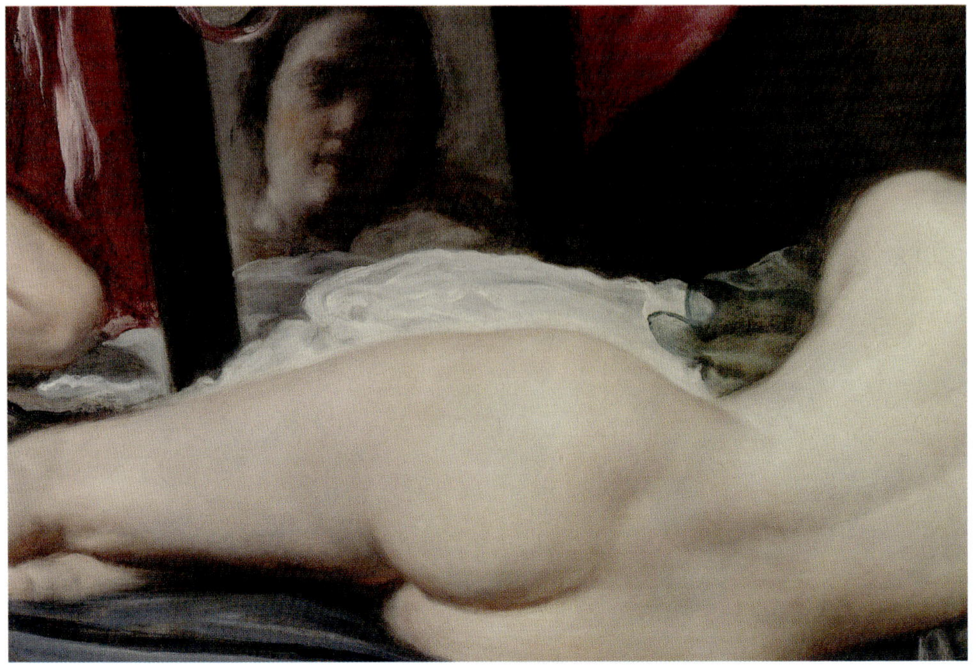

132 *The Toilet of Venus (The Rokeby Venus)*, c. 1647–51, detail

Further aiding the picture's harmony is its utter simplicity and total lack of fussiness. Even when comparing it to the handful of illustrations included here, notice how plain it is. No distractions, no landscape, lap dogs, maidservants or palatial interiors – in fact, hardly anything that one could call much of a setting. And added to these 'omissions' is its astonishing unity of vision.

The most sharply defined passage in the entire picture is Venus's left hip, situated at the very centre of the composition. To either side of this everything is slightly blurred, gradually fading out to her right elbow and her feet, which are reduced to flesh-coloured smudges. This is not the way Old Master pictures normally look. We have grown used to everything in them vying for equal attention, providing that it is in the same position in space, with more distant objects merely getting smaller and less distinct. But that is one reason why so many works of art are so demanding, because they do not replicate human vision, which focuses on one thing at a time through pinpoint vision, around which all else appears to swim in a haze, even if it is in the same spatial plane. Velázquez was the first artist to acknowledge this – and to paint in the way that we see.

Chapter 6
Serving the Court and Painting the Pope

Writers on Velázquez often remark on the relatively small number of paintings to survive by the artist, and with good reason. After all, in a working life of more than forty years – most of these spent in the service of the Spanish King and, therefore, financially secure – an output of about one hundred and twenty paintings and fewer than five drawings hardly qualifies as prolific. Compare it, for instance, with that of the equal working lives of two of the artist's greatest contemporaries, Poussin and Rembrandt, themselves artistic opposites but neither financially secure. In a career spanning just over forty years the French classical master produced over two hundred paintings and nearly four hundred drawings and the Dutch genius more than three hundred canvases and a veritable torrent of drawings and etchings. Moreover, whereas the vast majority of Velázquez's works are limited to single figures, that cannot be claimed for his more prolific contemporaries, both of whom excelled in multifigure compositions.

The most obvious explanation for Velázquez's small remaining output is the number of his paintings that have been lost. According to the accounts of his early biographers or reliable documents from other sources, this number is about thirty, which, added together with the extant canvases, constitutes roughly one fifth of his life's work. Many of these perished in the aforementioned fire that engulfed the Alcázar Palace in 1734, among them the *Expulsion of the Moriscos* – certainly his most ambitious multifigure composition of the 1620s – and the three overdoors of mythological subjects he also painted for the Hall of Mirrors in the same palace at the very end of his career, which will be discussed later. But others are simply unaccounted for by any means, including his equestrian portrait of Philip IV of about 1623, which aroused such an enthusiastic response when it

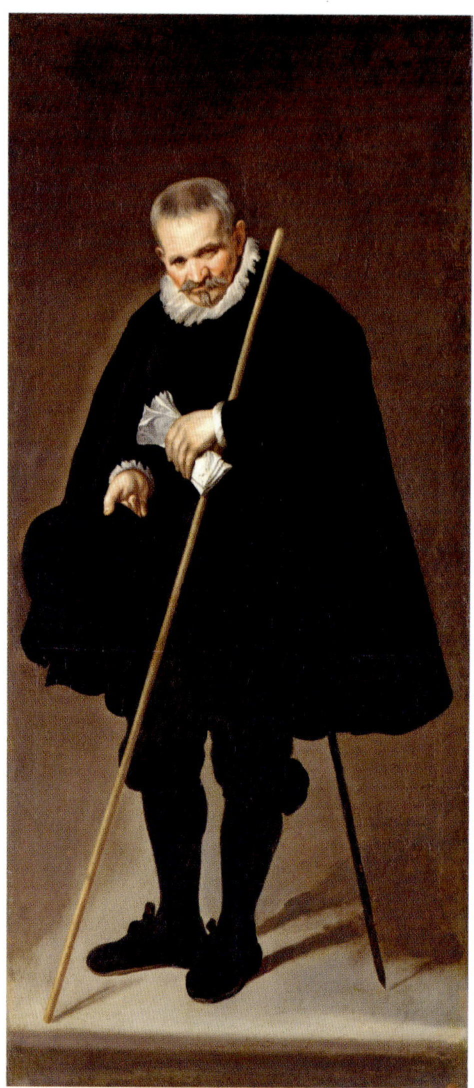

133 LEFT After Velázquez, *Francisco de Ocáriz y Ochoa*
134 OPPOSITE After Velázquez, *Portrait of Francisco de Quevedo,* mid-17th century

was subsequently displayed for the King's subjects, and is now lost from view.

Happily, a handful of Velázquez's lost works do survive either through copies or from fragments of the original pictures. An example is a portrait of one of the King's court jesters listed in a Buen Retiro inventory of 1701 as 'Ochoa, the gatekeeper, holding some petitions'. A jester of this name referred to as 'the little old man' is recorded in the service of the royal household in

1636 and, although Velázquez's original picture of him now no longer exists, a copy of it is known which fits this description. With his bent and submissive stance, this old man provides a striking contrast to the expansive and bravura pose of *Pablo de Valladolid*. But at least one feature of the copy is atypical of the artist: namely, the ledge on which Ochoa stands. While this may not be enough to discount its status, it may make one question its accuracy.

Palomino records another such lost work when he notes that the artist 'painted Quevedo with spectacles', the sitter being the renowned poet and satirist Francisco de Quevedo y Villegas (1580–1645), who praised Velázquez in his poem 'El pincel' ('The paintbrush') as an artist who 'brings flesh to life / using isolated strokes / which achieve truth rather than likeness' and was also the author of a political and moral epistle to the Count-Duke of Olivares. Velázquez's original portrait is here too lost, but three

copies of what may be it survive. One of them is inscribed with Quevedo's name and it and one other show him wearing the cross of Santiago, of which order we know he was a member. But perhaps the most certain evidence that these copies record the artist's original are the sitter's cynical expression and his scraggly and unkempt hair. Velázquez recognized an artistic type when he saw one.

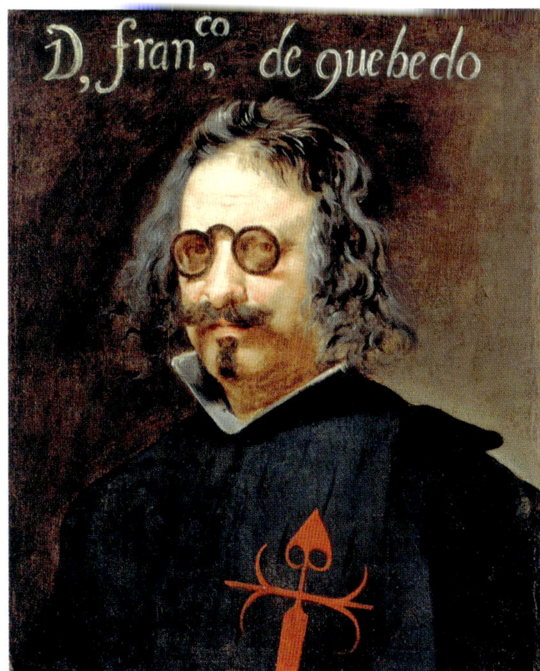

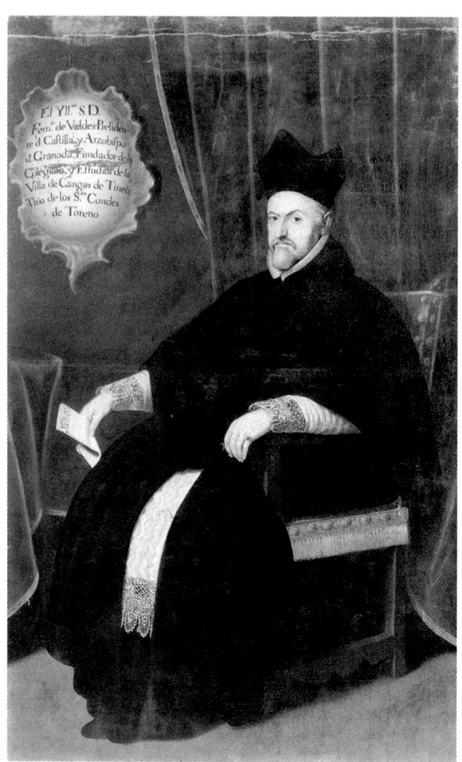

135 LEFT After Velázquez, *Archbishop Fernando de Valdés*
136 OPPOSITE ABOVE Attributed to Velázquez, *Portrait of Archbishop Fernando de Valdés*, 1640–45
137 OPPOSITE BELOW Fragment of a hand, c. 1630

An even more complex problem is posed by a portrait of Archbishop Fernando de Valdés, which he commissioned from the artist when he was resident in Madrid in the 1630s. A copy of this survives showing him seated full length and holding a
135 piece of paper bearing Velázquez's signature with an elaborate escutcheon hanging above bearing details of the sitter. The whole obviously comprised one of the artist's most important non-royal portraits of the 1630s.

137 A fragment of the original survives showing the right hand of the ecclesiastic holding the inscribed piece of paper. It is executed with the free and liquid brushwork one identifies with the artist and is widely accepted to be part of the missing
136 original. A bust-length portrait of the Archbishop also exists which many maintain is part of the original and is of high quality but not the same style. Its brushwork is flatter and more constrained and lacking in any of the vigour of the hand fragment. While it is obviously welcome to have preserved two fragments connected with the lost canvas, it is very difficult to agree that they are by the same artist. The hand holding the

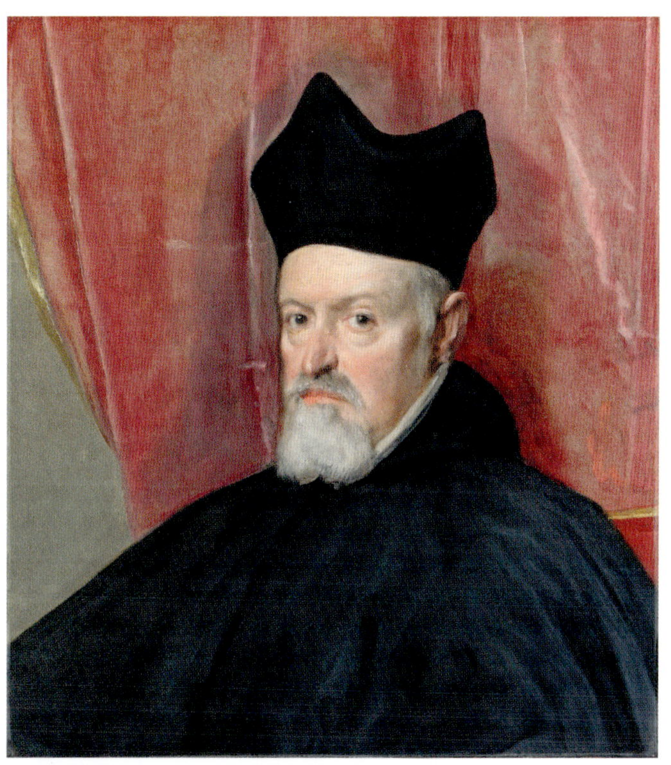

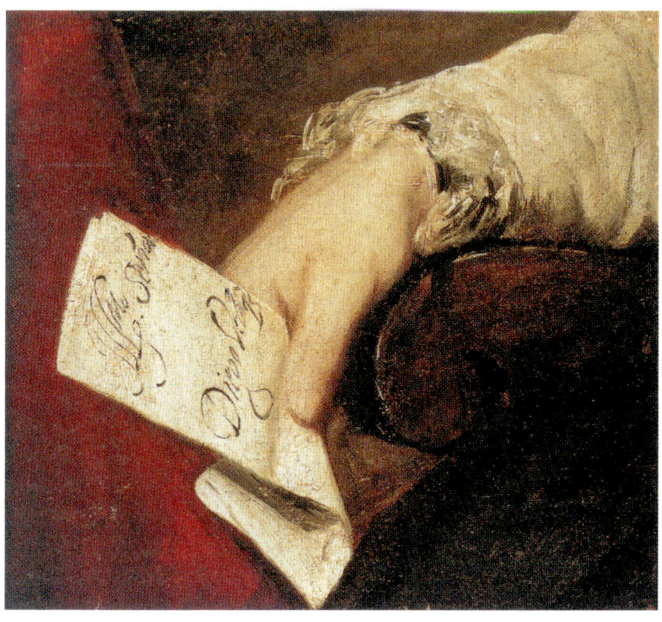

original paper seems convincingly by Velázquez but the bust-length head probably does not.

In addition to the substantial number of lost works by the artist that have reduced his existing oeuvre there are also many problem pictures to contend with. These are works that have good claims to be by Velázquez but about which scholars and critics cannot agree. Only two of these may occupy us here, with the reader being warned in advance that no firm decision will be reached in either case. Rather the purpose is to indicate the nature of the problems posed by such works.

Certain of the artist's early *bodegones* exist in variant versions which some consider to be autograph. One of these is *Three Men at a Table* of about 1617, a version of which replaces the laughing youth in the centre of the table with a young girl pouring wine and alters the pose of the young man on the right so that his gaze is now directed across the table at the old man. Other changes have also been introduced: the format is now horizontal, the wall hanging has been removed, some still life objects have been changed and the old man's right hand now reaches out to receive the glass of wine being poured by the girl.

138 **BELOW** Attributed to Velázquez, *Tavern Scene with Two Men and a Girl*, c. 1618–19
139 **OPPOSITE** *Head of a Young Man*, c. 1618–19

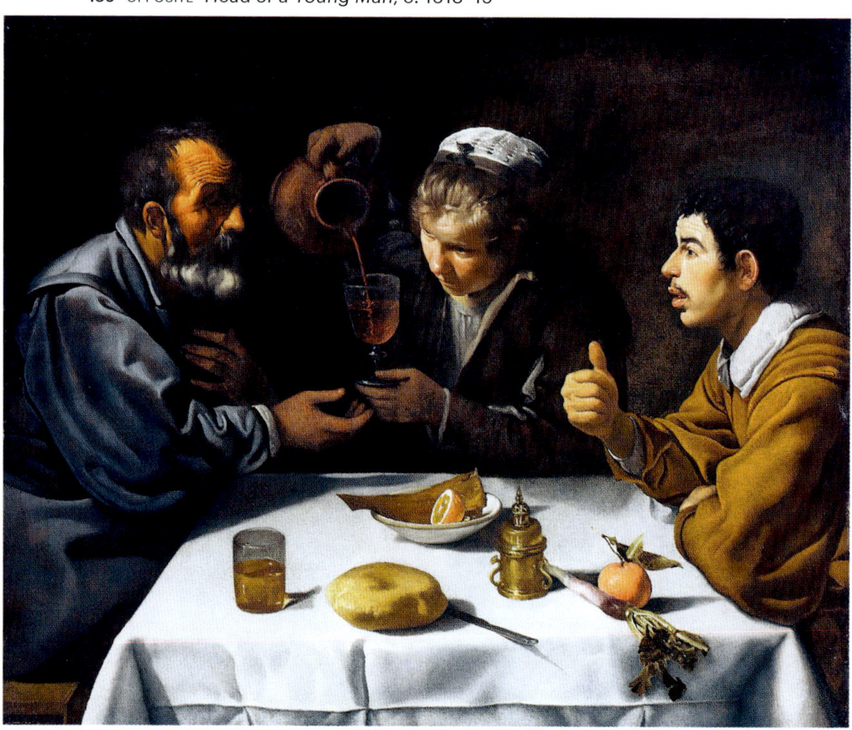

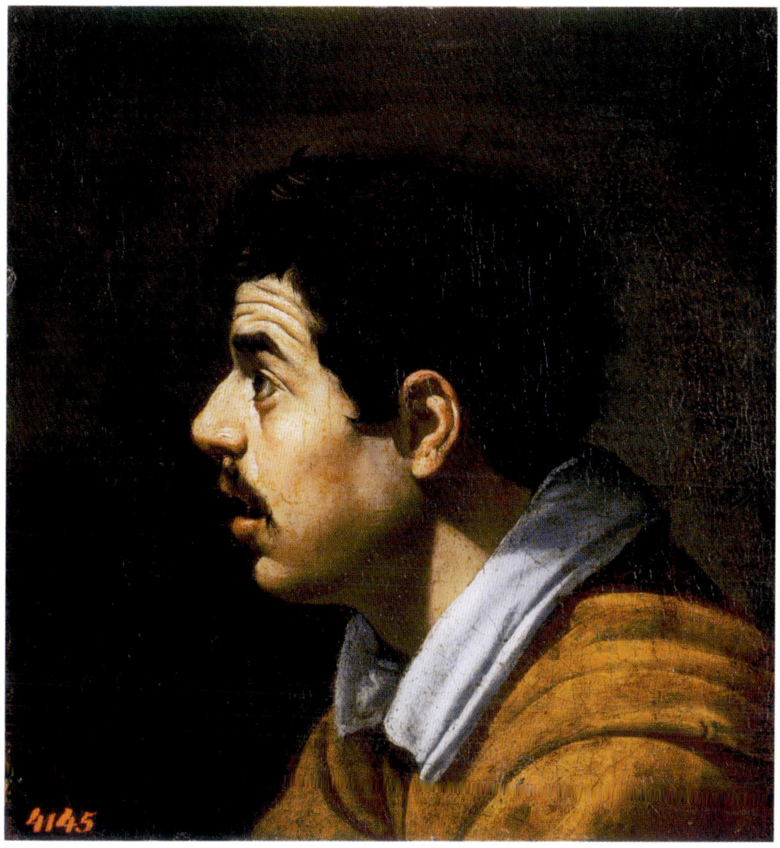

Aspects of the picture are of very high quality, notably the head of the girl, the still life objects and the gesturing young man on the right, for which a painted life study exists of the type occasionally encountered in Velázquez's career, such as for the head of Apollo in *The Forge of Vulcan*. This, too, is undoubtedly impressive and readily explicable when one considers the significant changes made to this figure from one version to the next.

But other features of this second version are noticeably weaker, especially the gesture of the girl pouring wine, the harsh modelling of the old man's head and the metallic folds of his sleeve. Even more perfunctory are the overhanging folds of the tablecloth and the still life on the table from which all the intricacies and irregularities of the original have been simplified or 'smoothed over'. So wide are the disparities of quality and style within the picture that it is difficult to

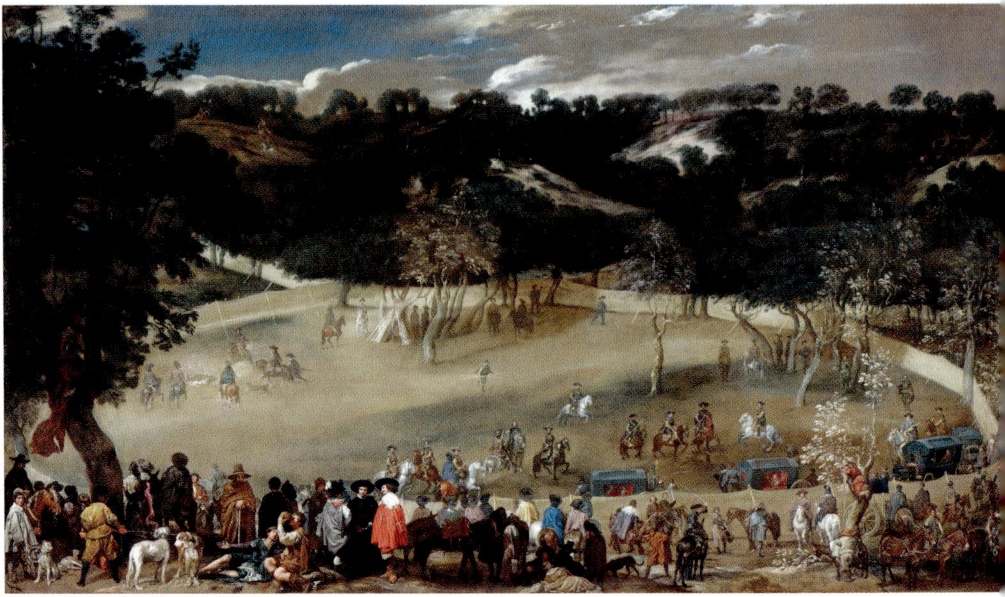

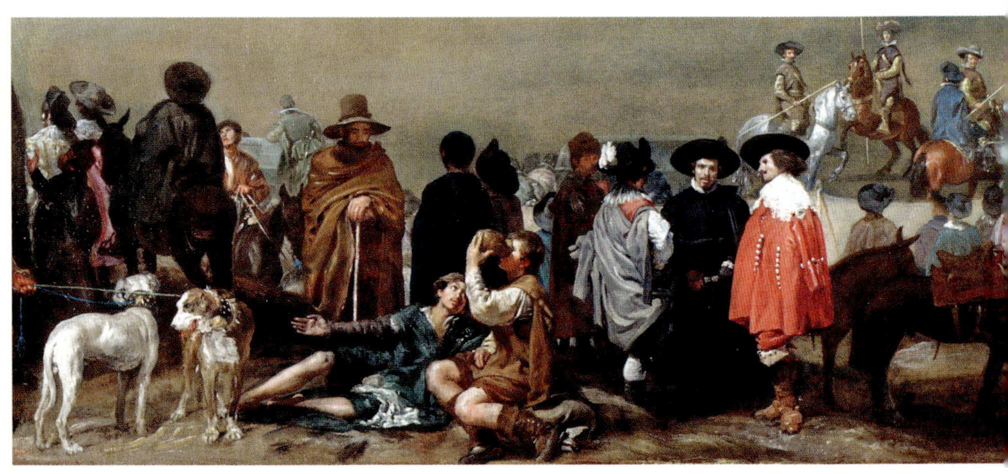

140, 141 *Philip IV Hunting Wild Boar (La Tela Real)*, probably 1632–37

accept that it is all by one artist. We know that Velázquez attracted imitators and followers already in his years in Seville. But did he agree to collaborate with one of them on a single picture? It is certainly not impossible.

Philip IV Hunting Wild Boar, also known as *La Tela Real (The Royal Enclosure)*, is the only painting of its kind ascribed to Velázquez and, along with *Balthasar Carlos at the Riding School*, the only one to depict an event in court life. That the King was fond of hunting has already been seen, and one of his favourite types of pursuits was boar-baiting, as takes place here. In this costly endeavour, boar were driven into a specially constructed enclosure to be pursued and eventually dispatched by the royal party and their hunting dogs, watched from a safe distance by spectators.

Velázquez's picture was one of four such hunt scenes painted for the Torre de la Parada in the mid-1630s and is extensively damaged and restored, compounding any problems of attribution. A vast panoramic landscape seen from a bird's eye view, it depicts the King and his accomplices on horseback left of centre, watched by the Queen and other members of the royal party in carriages at the edge of the enclosure. Velázquez must surely have witnessed such events, although there is no reason to suppose that he commemorates a specific one here. But the alien nature of the subject clearly tested his powers to the limit. His only other landscapes – the two little Villa Medici views – had been painted out of doors, but the *Tela Real* could not be. However restored its landscape may be, it is here treated with such bland uniformity as to indicate that this artist could not reinvent nature from the confines of his studio, as his French contemporary Claude could. But the audience in the foreground – tending their dogs, guzzling their drink or simply conversing with each other – are a different matter. True, they are better preserved but, as such, they reveal a dexterity of handling and ingenuity of invention that could only be the work of a master. Perhaps it is most sensible to regard the *Tela Real* as a ruined picture by Velázquez that, given the nature and limitations of his genius, was also a somewhat thankless commission from the King.

Nor, it could be argued, was it the only such commission; for increasingly from the 1640s onwards, Velázquez's duties as court painter were diverted towards other services for the royal household, which deprived him of the opportunity for painting. One of these was a visit to Valladolid in 1640 to find pictures to replace those that had been in a fire in the Buen Retiro. Then, between 1645 and 1648 the artist was heavily involved in the remodelling and renovation of portions of the Alcázar Palace.

This entailed the extensive redisplaying of the royal collections of painting and sculpture – a task for which Velázquez may have been ideally suited, but one that still prevented him from pursuing his own painting career.

In addition to assisting in the decoration of the royal residences, the artist faced an even larger task where the King's artistic tastes were concerned: namely, that of adding to them. Although a weak ruler, Philip IV was (like his English counterpart, Charles I) a passionate lover of art, who from the 1630s began to add to the royal collection an array of masterpieces for which any visitors to the Prado can only be grateful today. These included the two great bacchanals by Titian, *The Andrians* and *The Feast of Venus*, and soon after began a host of commissions for the King's favourite painter, Rubens, which amounted to nearly one hundred works, many of them painted by the Flemish master's assistants and destined for the Torre de la Parada. In addition to these the King acquired more than 50 paintings from the posthumous sales of Charles I's collection, including masterpieces by Mantegna, Raphael, Correggio, Titian and Van Dyck.

While there is scant evidence of Velázquez's role in aiding and advising the King on his collecting, Palomino does provide an informative account of the role the artist played when ordered by the King to take 41 paintings recently acquired from Charles I's collection among others to the Escorial:

'Diego Velázquez made a description and report to show to his Majesty, in which he gives information about their quality, subjects and authorship and the places where they are hung. This was done with such elegance and aptness that it gave proof of his erudition and great knowledge of art, for these works are so excellent that only from him could they receive the praise they deserved.'

In October 1644, Queen Isabella died, and with the death of Balthasar Carlos two years later, the King turned his attentions increasingly to enlarging his art collection. With this in mind he requested Velázquez to pay another visit to Italy in 1648, both as a special emissary to the Pope, who was about to celebrate his jubilee year in 1650, and to purchase works of art for the royal collection.

Velázquez sailed from Málaga late in January 1649 in the company of the Duke of Nájera, who had been sent to escort the King's new queen (who was his own niece) Mariana of Austria, to Spain. The party disembarked at Genoa in early March, whereupon Velázquez left the group and travelled to Venice via stops in Milan and Padua. According to Palomino he purchased

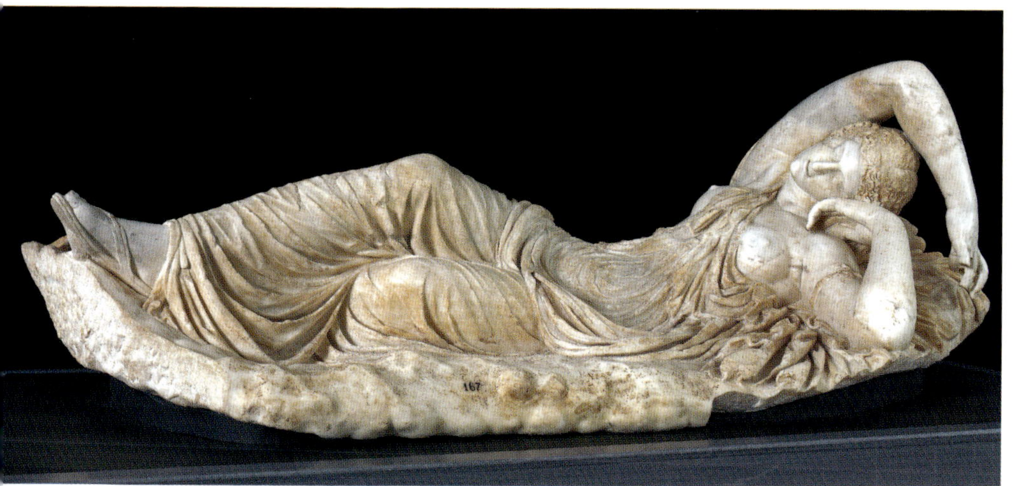

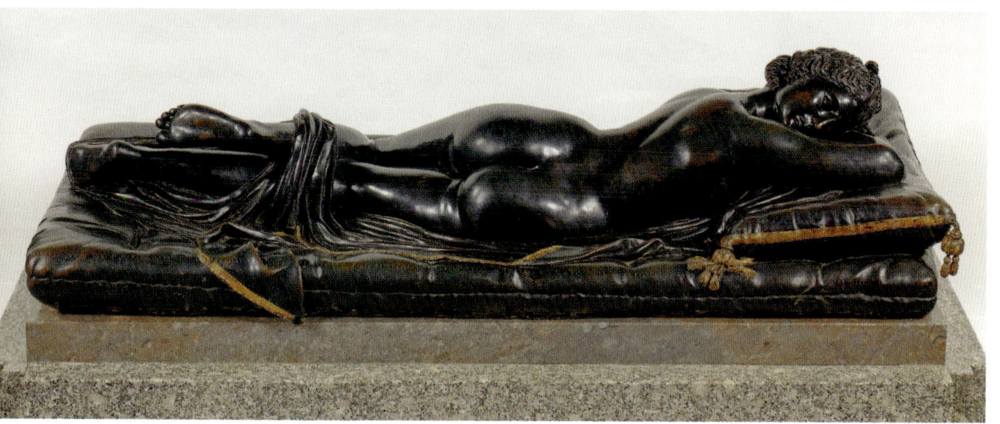

142 TOP *Sleeping Ariadne*, Roman version of a 2nd-century BC Greek sculpture, 150–75 AD
143 ABOVE Matteo Bonarelli (after the Antique), *Sleeping Hermaphrodite*, 1652

several works by Tintoretto in Venice, but he was to make his most important acquisitions there at the end of his Italian stay in 1651. He then visited Bologna, Parma, Florence and Modena before arriving in Rome in April 1649. No sooner had he arrived there than he was called away to Naples to collect money owed to him since 1643 and there he met Jusepe de Ribera, a fellow Spaniard who was the greatest painter resident in the city. Finally settled back in Rome, he began negotiations to acquire works for the King's collection and to acquaint himself with many of the eminent artists, princes and ecclesiastics of the city.

Rome in 1650 was a cauldron of creative genius divided between baroque and classical masters respectively led by Bernini and Poussin, both of whom were then at the height of their powers and, according to Palomino, befriended Velázquez. He also met Pietro da Cortona, Mattia Preti and Bernini's arch rival among sculptors, Alessandro Algardi. Unlike him, none of these masters specialized in painting portraits so it was not long before Velázquez's skills in this regard were much in demand in the Eternal City. But that appears to have been a sideline from his task of purchasing and ordering casts of many of the masterpieces of antique sculpture to be seen there. Palomino enumerates literally dozens of these, many of them still to be seen in the Prado today. They testify to Velázquez's wide-ranging knowledge and taste for the achievements of the classical past but – even more notably – to his own imperviousness to its influence upon his own art. Just occasionally, his own interests are reflected in his acquisitions for the King. Thus, having recently completed *The Rokeby Venus* it is perhaps no surprise to find him drawn to buying casts of two reclining female figures from ancient art: *Cleopatra* (now known as *Sleeping Ariadne*) and the *Sleeping Hermaphrodite*. He also purchased a large number of Roman portrait busts and a head of Moses after Michelangelo, based on the original sculpture in San Pietro in Vincoli. As Velázquez's own art was soon to demonstrate in his portrait of the reigning pope, the fierce intensity of this head of the Hebrew leader was not to be lost on him.

If Palomino is to be believed, Velázquez painted more than twice as many portraits in Rome as the five that still survive, another indication of the very high degree of losses amongst his works, which may only be explained by the fact that, since many of these pictures were of relatively minor individuals, their portraits would have most likely passed on to their families and relations and, eventually, especially if the sitter's identity was lost, been strewn to the winds. One sitter whose portrait escaped such a fate was Cardinal Camillo Astalli, adopted nephew of the pope, who was created a cardinal in

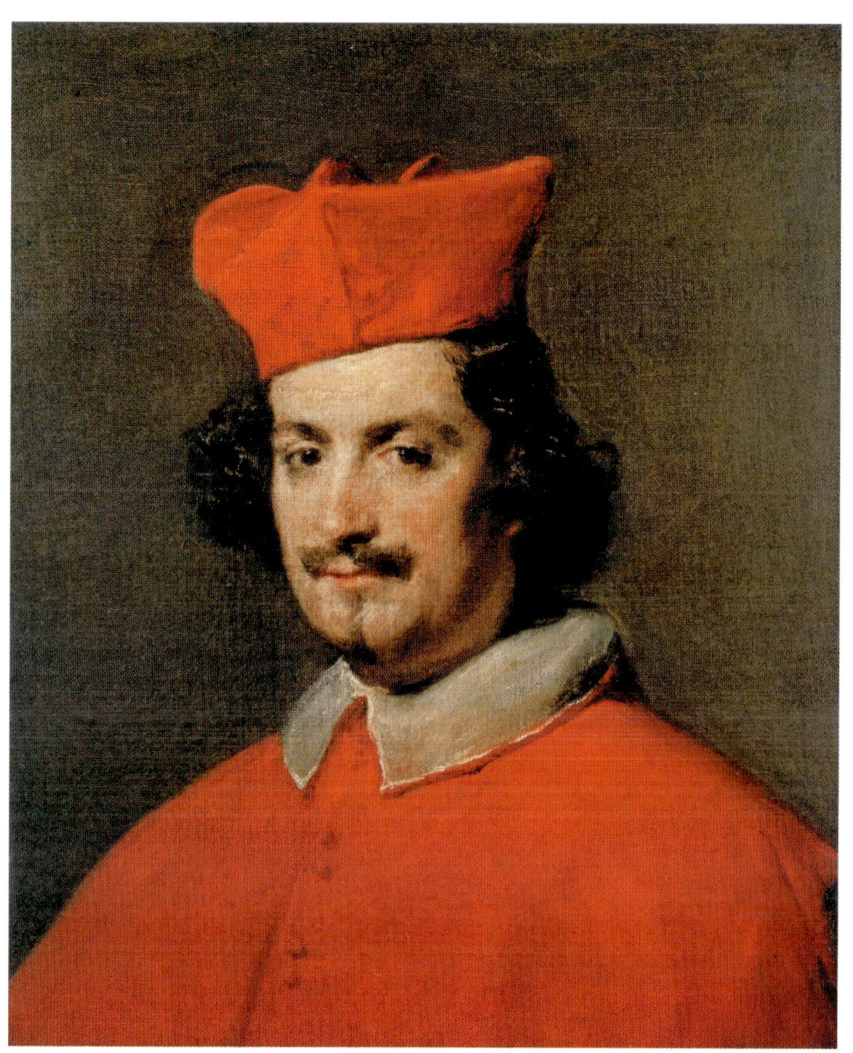

144 *Cardinal Astalli, 1650*

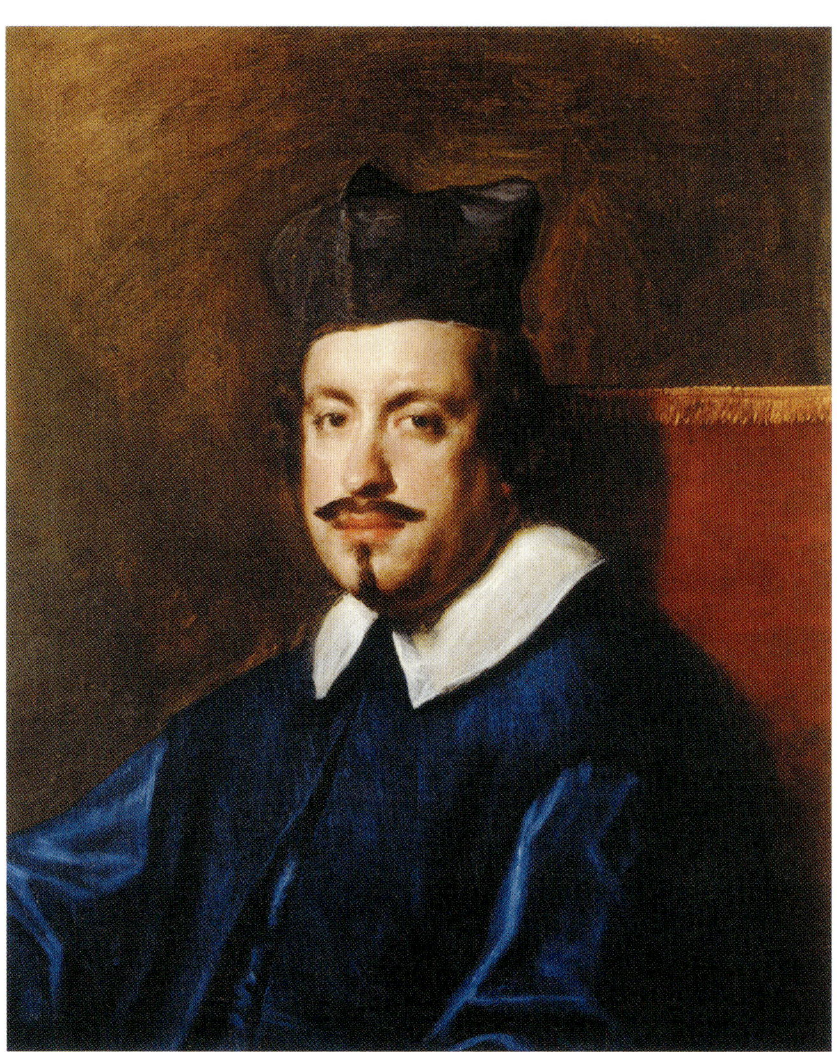

145 ABOVE *Camillo Massimi,* 1650
146 OPPOSITE *Ferdinando Brandani,* 1650

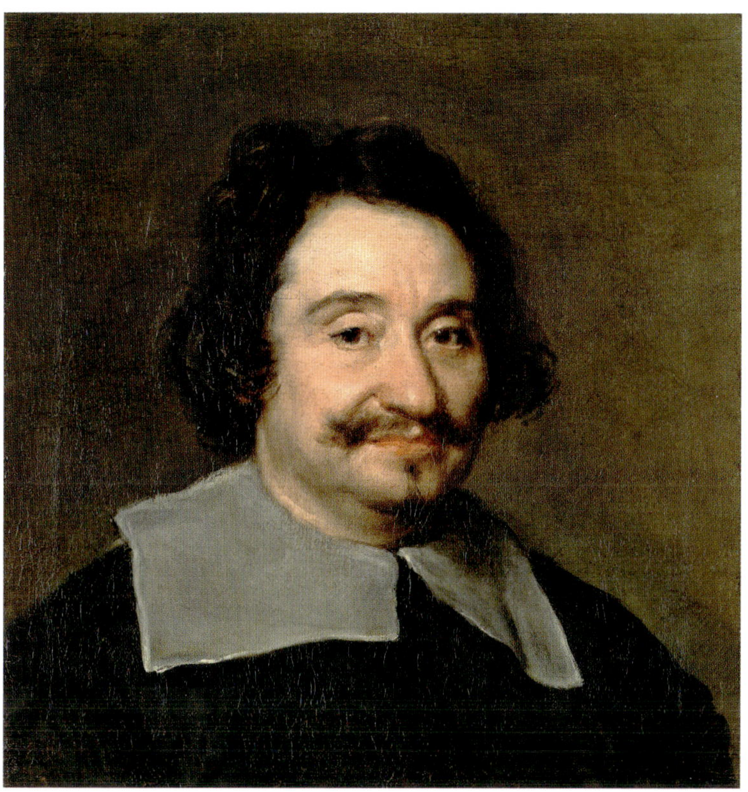

September 1650 and whose papal favour was revoked four years later, his incompetence in administering papal business having proved his undoing.

Velázquez's bust portrait of Astalli could not be more sparing. Thinly painted over a finely woven canvas, it shows visible signs of reworking around the biretta, which was originally set squarely on the sitter's forehead. This adds an undercurrent of tension and duplicity to Astalli, who gazes at the viewer out of the corner of his eyes with a slightly suspicious air. Most miraculous of all, however, is the painter's wizardly technique – how the contour of the nose somehow emerges from the sitter's right cheek or a tuft of brown hair springs loose from a nearly identically coloured background.

Camillo Massimi was a descendant of one of the most notable Roman families. A learned scholar and antiquarian, he was also an important art collector and the only one to commission works from the three greatest painters active in Rome in 1650: Claude, Poussin and Velázquez. He owned

no fewer than six works by the Spanish master, the majority
of them acquired during the mid-1650s when he was serving
as papal nuncio in Madrid and almost certainly witnessed the
artistic fruits of Velázquez's last years. But they also included
a portrait of Massimi commissioned in Rome in 1650 which is
a model of the artist's candour and understatement throughout
his career.

The sitter is depicted bust length and seated in a dark red
chair fringed with gold. He is dressed in the official costume of
the *camerino segreto* to which the Pope had appointed him in
1647, a rich peacock-blue that Velázquez has painted in the costly
pigment of ultramarine. Matching the richness of his costume
and office is the evident assurance of his gaze, his coarse and
fleshy features suggesting an inner contentment that was
borne as a natural right. Poussin is known to have admonished
Massimi for keeping too many servants, and Velázquez's portrait
of him reveals how pampered and self-satisfied he was.

The smallest of the artist's Roman portraits is also the most
endearing. Palomino lists a picture of Ferdinando Brandani,
chief officer of the Pope's Secretariat, among Velázquez's
commissions at this time and this portrait has been identified
as one recently acquired by the Prado. It depicts a genial and
slightly elderly man clad in ordinary dress and wearing a warm-
hearted smile that radiates humility. Thinly and seemingly
effortlessly painted, it is tempting to imagine that it was the
product of a single sitting in the life of a man unaccustomed to
posing for great painters but all too willing to serve others.

Soon after Velázquez arrived in Rome, he received the
opportunity of painting a portrait of the Pope. In a city notable
for its lack of distinguished native portrait painters, this was
hardly surprising and eventually it also led him to paint the
Pope's notorious sister-in-law, Donna Olimpia. To exercise his
brush before painting the pontiff, Velázquez (Palomino tells us)
chose first to depict an assistant of his who had accompanied
him on his journey and was himself a painter, Juan de Pareja,
who had joined the master's workshop in the early 1630s. With a
friend and colleague to portray, and no official protocol to obey,
the result inevitably turned out to be one of the most candid
and captivating of all his portraits. Pareja is depicted half-
length and left of centre, his torso thrown forward and his right
arm wrapped around his waist as if to assert his own presence.
The implied momentum of this stance and the empty space
left to be filled on the right suggest that he is in the process of
turning to greet the viewer. Matching the braggadocio of his
pose is his proud – even haughty – expression. Pareja's self-
portrait on the far left of his own *Calling of St Matthew* of 1661

wears a comparable expression, although he curiously seems not to have aged in the twelve years since Velázquez had depicted him.

Notwithstanding the bold presence of the sitter and the vigour of the characterization, the greatest miracle of Velázquez's portrait is the colour harmony. It is a symphony in greys, the cooler and deeper tones in the background and the warmer and richer ones comprising the sitter's costume and modulating into a near-black shot with grey on his sleeve. The handling throughout is free, sketchy and even somewhat impulsive, as befits a picture intended as a dry run for a more prestigious commission. In short, this may be seen as both Velázquez and Pareja caught off-guard – two cohorts engaged in a frank and intimate conversation.

Upon completion the portrait of Pareja was exhibited in the rotunda of the Pantheon in Rome, 'where it received such universal acclaim that in the opinion of all the painters of different nations everything else looked like painting, this alone like reality.' Palomino concludes his account of this picture by informing us that it also reaped the artist the ultimate reward: 'On the strength of this Velázquez was received as a Roman Academician in the year 1650.'

In painting the Pope, Velázquez was heir to a long and distinguished tradition. Raphael had established the prevailing form for such pictures in his portrait of Julius II of 1511–12. The Pope is shown seated three-quarter length in his chair of state and seen at an angle to the viewer's right with a ceremonial curtain behind him. He wears a red papal cap and short cape with a white surplice below, and his head is gently lowered as if he is lost in thought. Raphael complements the richness of his costume and the gold tassels of his chair with an equally vibrant green drape to frame the figure, thereby neutralizing the combination of colours while at the same time heightening their splendour. But when Titian adapted this same basic scheme for his portrait of Pope Paul III in 1543 he abandoned the contrasts of complementary colours and opted instead for a deep red cloak with the white surplice supplemented by the added reds of the chair and the purse held in his right hand. Yet the dark, neutral background and the muted and more variegated range of reds coupled with an extensive use of transparent glazes serve to distance the image from the viewer.

Velázquez makes no such concessions. His *Innocent X* is red, white and gold throughout, insistently ablaze with colour and offering no point of rest or escape for the eye. Where light falls on the Pope's mozzetta, it turns white to chime with his surplice and sleeves. Even his face is of a blotched

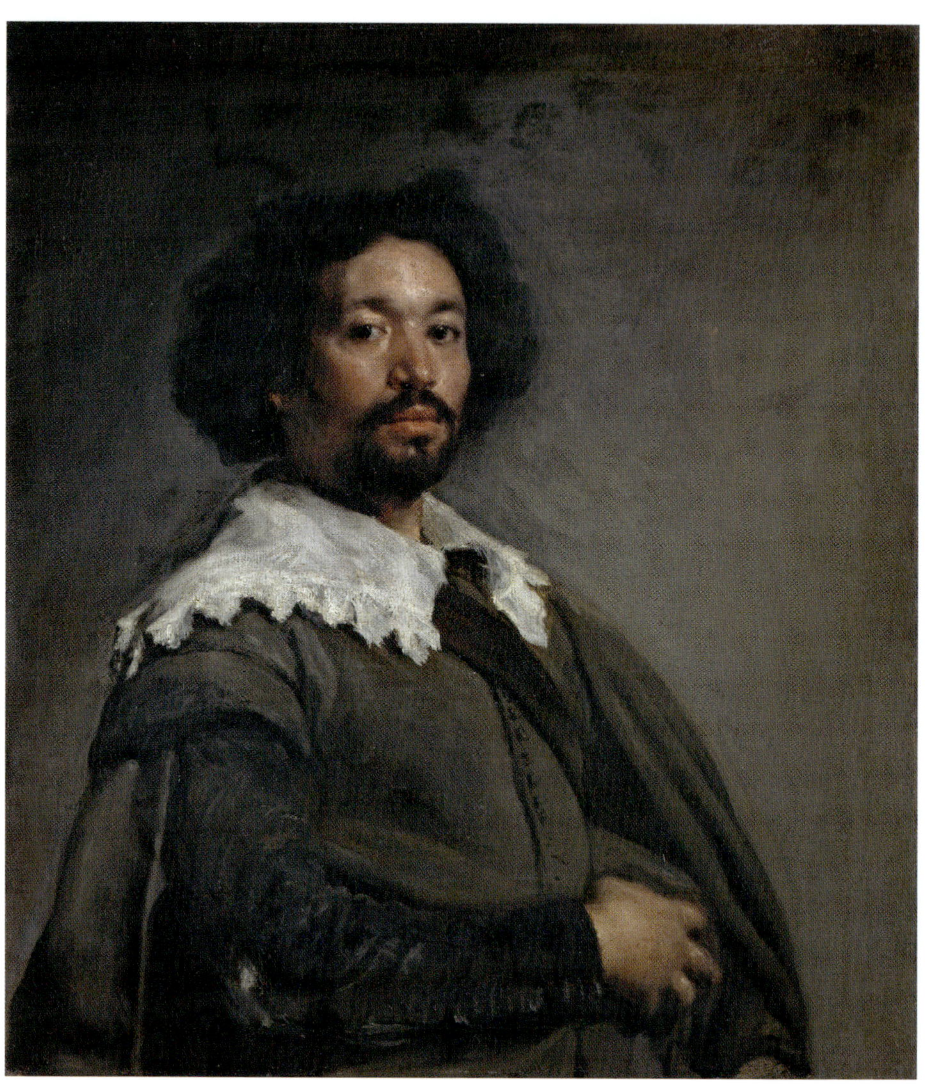

147 ABOVE *Portrait of Juan de Pareja*, 1649–50
148, 149 OPPOSITE Juan de Pareja, *The Calling of St Matthew*, 1661

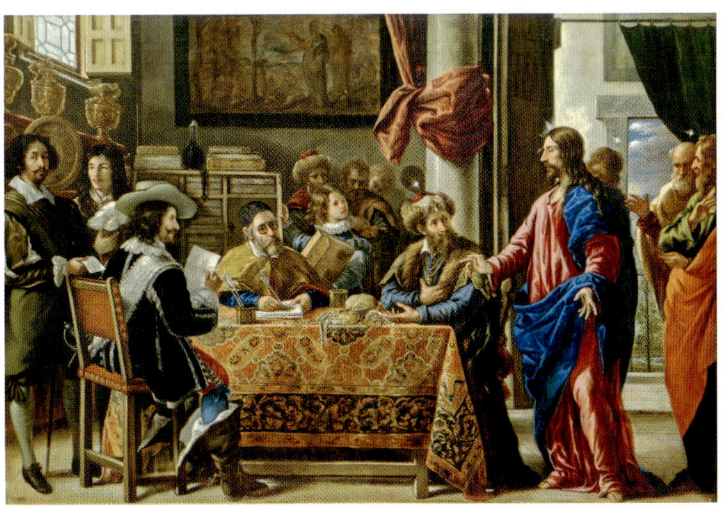

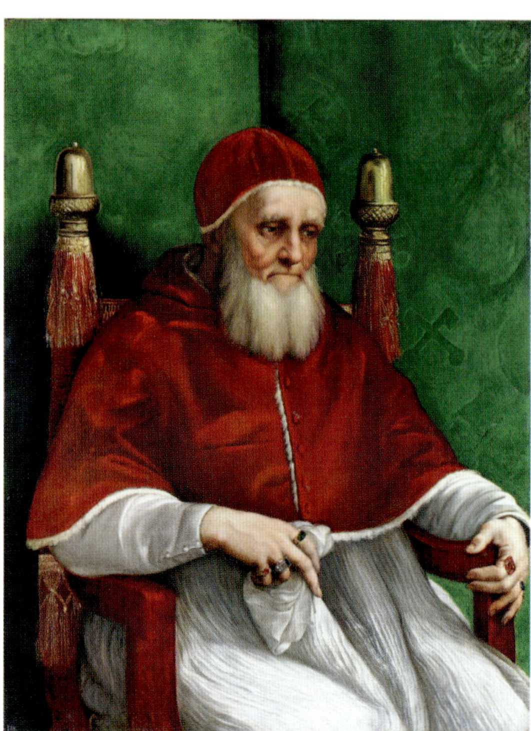

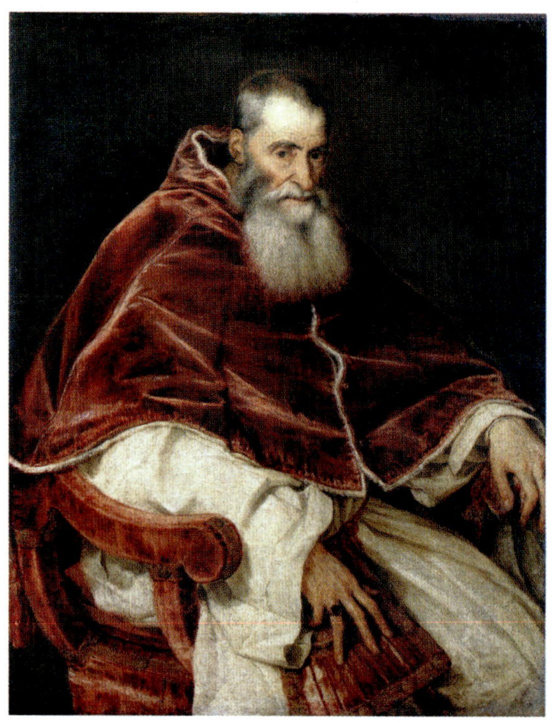

150 LEFT Raphael, *Portrait of Pope Julius II*, 1511–12
151 BELOW Titian, *Portrait of Pope Paul III*, 1543
152 OPPOSITE *Portrait of Innocent X*, 1650

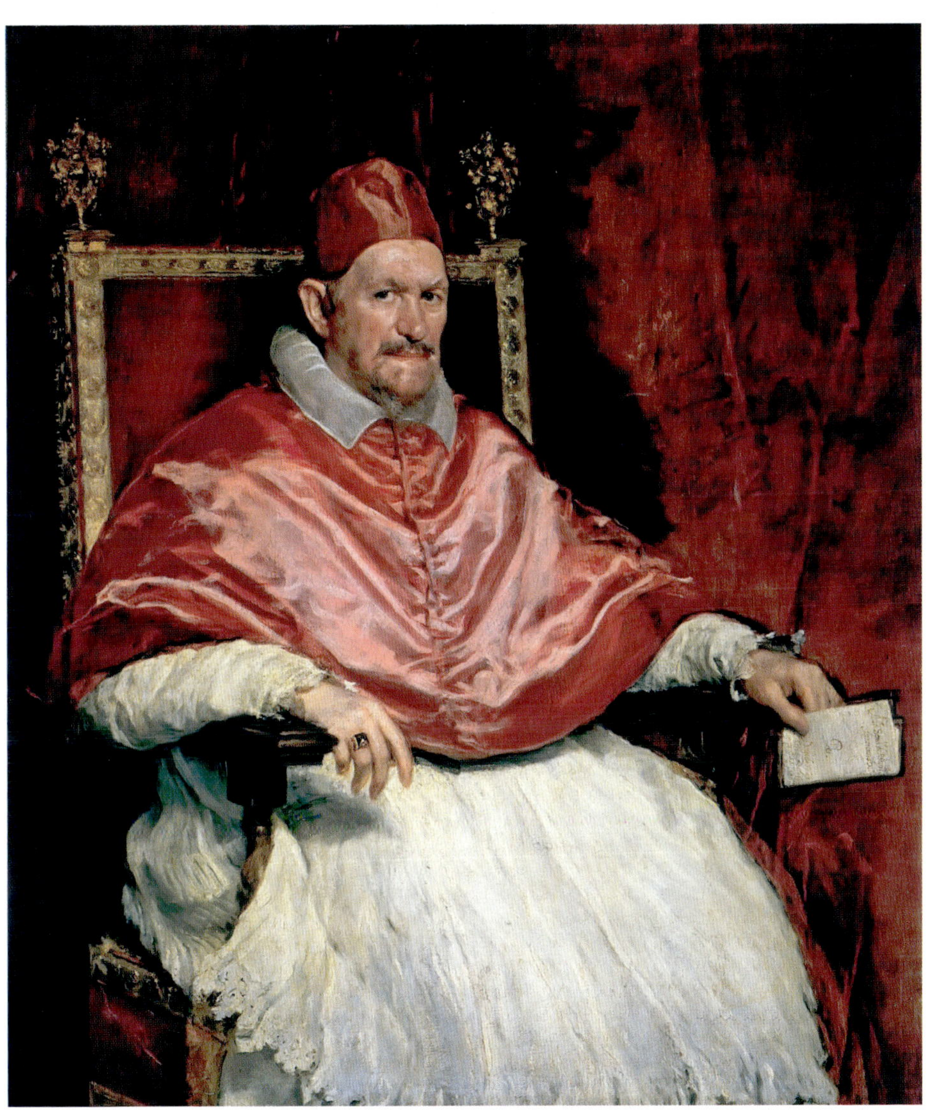

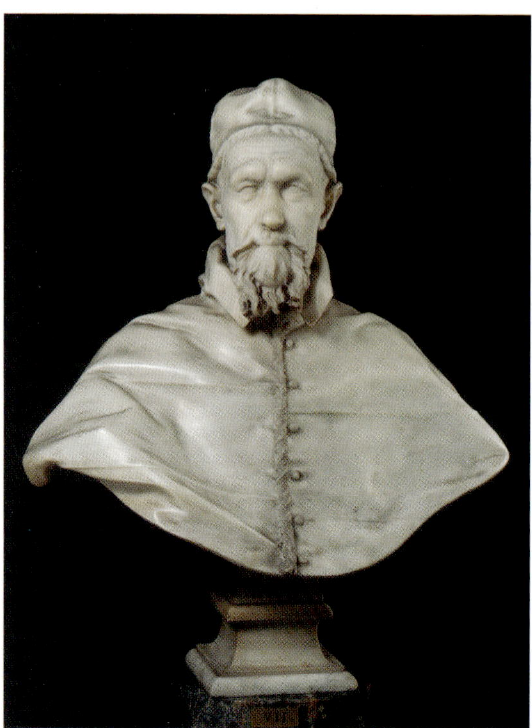

153 Gianlorenzo Bernini, *Bust of Pope Innocent X*, c. 1650

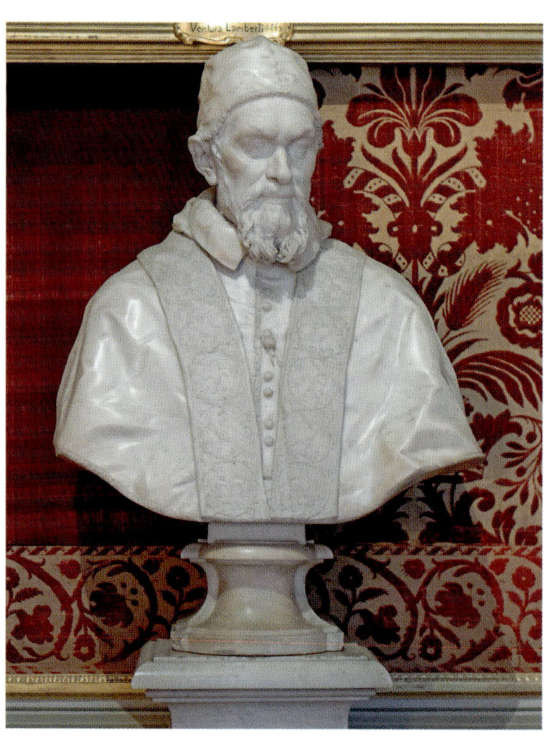

154 Alessandro Algardi, *Bust of Pope Innocent X*, 1647–48

and reddish complexion that does nothing to lower the temperature. Most intimidating of all, he looks straight out of the picture and out of the corners of his eyes with a wary and menacing glance.

Innocent X was 75 years old when this portrait was executed and was renowned for his robust physical health and stamina, as well as for his ugly appearance. Justi relates that 'in the Conclave of 1645 his satanic aspect was stated to have been urged as a disqualification for his election to the pontifical chair'. Possessed of a wide and heavy forehead, deep-set eyes, a coarsely featured nose and mouth, a thin beard and flushed and bloated skin, he sits here holding a piece of paper inscribed and signed by the artist. On the opposite armrest the fingers of his right hand dangle in the air, less at ease than in anticipation of their next move. Coupled with the penetrating and suspicious gaze of the pontiff's eyes, we get the impression that that hand may at any moment take grip of the armrest, allowing him to rise up and hurl us with abuse. It is an unsettling and nerve-racking encounter, not so much a privileged audience with the Pope as the onset of an interrogation.

153, 154 How different the two great portraits of the Pope from these same years by the rival sculptors Bernini and Algardi. The former depicts a lively, inquisitive and intelligent man, gaunt and thin-featured but hardly unsightly, and fully up to his papal role. Algardi's Innocent is more private and introspective, his eyes not turned to the world but, rather, inwards, towards his own thoughts and soul. Neither, however, is as searching and disquieting as Velázquez's, which becomes all the more remarkable when one remembers that, of the three artists, the Spaniard is likely to have had much more limited access to the Pope. Bernini was the leading Roman sculptor and an acknowledged master of portrait busts, although by the time he carved this one, his talents were so much in demand for some grander projects that it was to prove his last portrait bust. The classicist Algardi had by then supplanted Bernini in Innocent's favour and presumably had near-unlimited access to the pontiff. But the alien Spaniard? Who knows? Maybe only two or three sittings.

Upon completion of the portrait of the Pope, Innocent X presented the artist with a gold chain bearing a medal with a portrait of himself in relief. For an artist always eager to advance his social status, this is certain to have been welcomed, although in truth it was the Pope himself who had reaped the greater prize. Further proof of the painter's pride comes in an anecdote told of the Pope's payment to the artist: namely, that when the pontiff sent a chamberlain to offer this, Velázquez

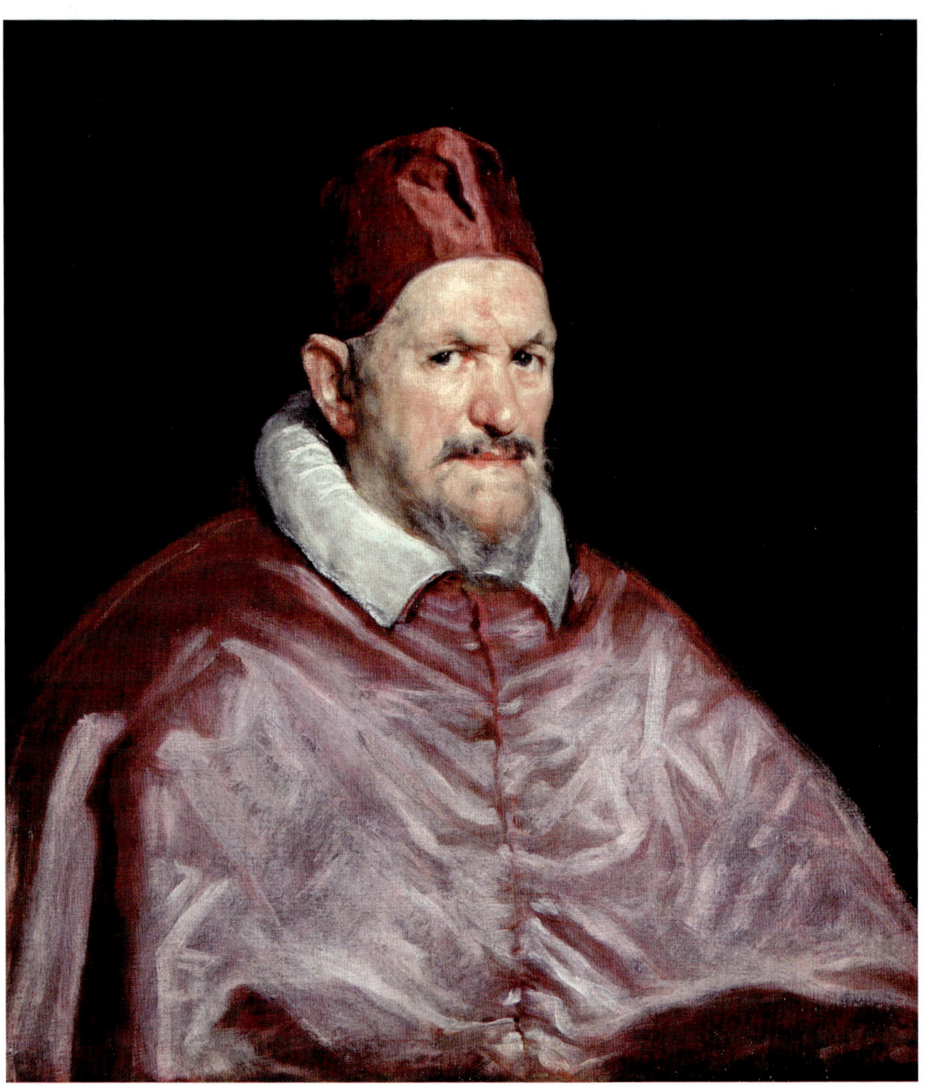

155 *Pope Innocent X*, 1650

refused it, saying that the King, his own master, always paid
him by his own hand.

Velázquez departed Rome in late November 1650, leaving
behind him a group of portrait masterpieces from which his
greatest Italian contemporaries and successors could learn.
If his first visit to Italy twenty years earlier had been for himself
to learn, his second (as Palomino remarked) was for him to
teach. From Rome he travelled to Modena and Venice and
sailed from Genoa in late May, arriving back in Madrid at the
end of June 1651.

Accompanying him on his journey was presumably Juan de
Pareja, bearing with him the astonishingly lifelike portrait his
master had painted of him. As if that would not be enough to
stun the court and painters of Madrid, Velázquez also bore
with him a bust-length replica of his portrait of the Pope to
show to the King. Although early sources describe it as a copy
of the painting in Rome, it is equally plausible that it was an
original study for it, but, in either case, it is simplified. The
papal chair has been omitted altogether and the background is
now nearly black. The folds of the Pope's mozzetta are painted
even more freely, with bold slashing strokes merely blocking it
in. (Viewed on their own these would not appear out of place
in an abstract expressionist painting of the twentieth century.)
Moreover, the mozzetta no longer reflects the glaring white
light of the original and its colour has been altered from a
brilliant crimson to a muted, medium pink. But the Pope's
head is unchanged and its piercing glance undiminished.
A fitting and maybe even unnerving souvenir for Philip IV
of an original that Sir Joshua Reynolds would later proclaim
to be 'the finest picture in Rome'.

155

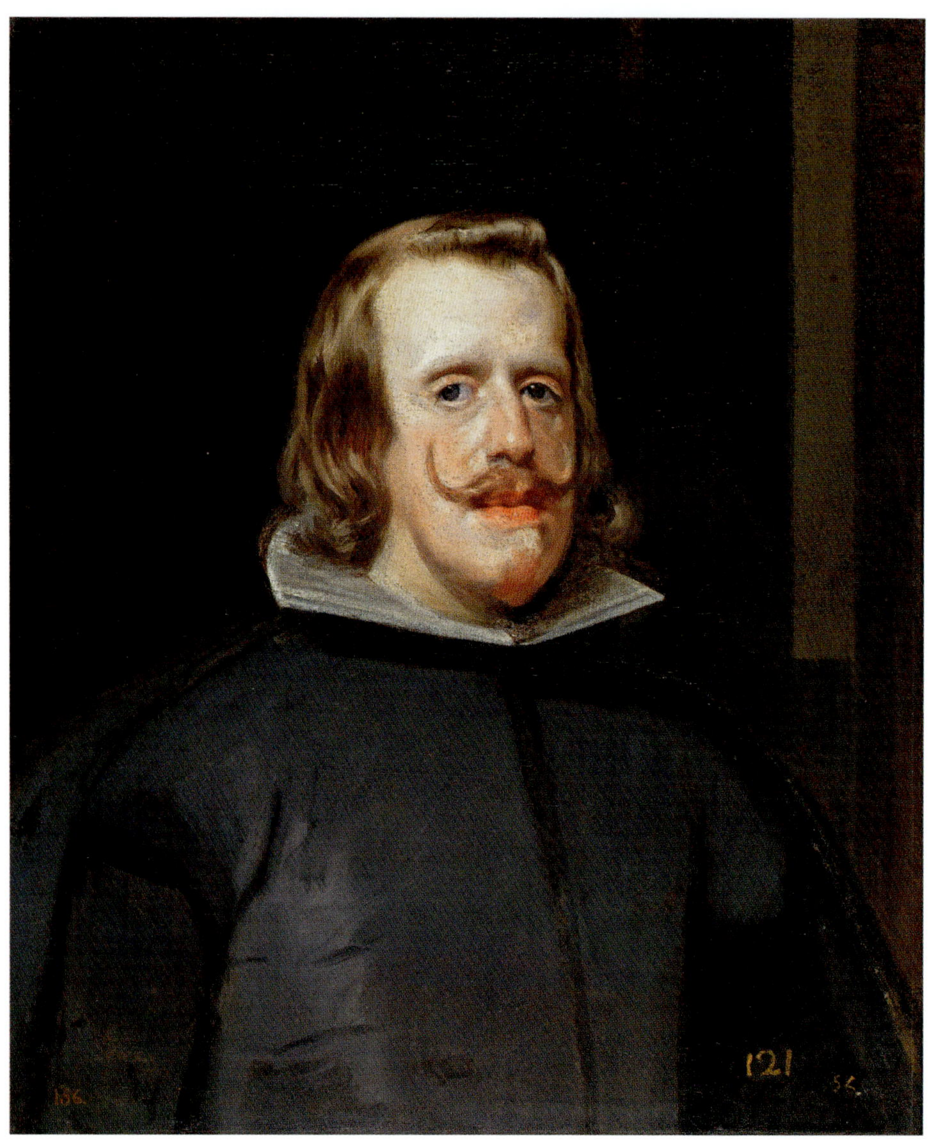

156 *Bust of Philip IV, c. 1653*

Chapter 7
'The Painter of Painters'

Back in the Spanish capital in the summer of 1651, Velázquez entered the last and most divided decade of his career. He was still to serve as first painter to the King, a role that would henceforth be dominated by painting portraits of the royal children to be sent to courts around Europe either as tokens of goodwill or as enticements to a royal marriage, or both. But in February 1652 he was also promoted to Chamberlain of the Royal Palace by the King, a post that was increasingly to divert him from his duties as a painter. This entailed arranging the King's travel lodgings, decorating and furnishing his apartments, responsibility for his bed linen and floor coverings as well as his works of art and the supervision of a host of palace servants. The financial rewards of this 'new position' were considerable, as was the enhancement of the artist's prestige, although one is inevitably led to wonder why one of the greatest of all painters would have consented to subject himself to such menial tasks. But the wisdom of hindsight can never supplant the motives of the moment, and it has to be conceded that Velázquez viewed social advancement as one of his life's great goals. Moreover, in the years immediately following his promotion it also bore legitimate creative fruits. One of his principal tasks then was to reinstall the royal art collection in the monastery of El Escorial, as he had previously done with the Alcázar. To be daily preoccupied with engaging and displaying one of the finest of all royal art collections, and one that was especially rich in works by both the King's – and the artist's – favourite painters, the Venetians, can hardly have seemed burdensome to Velázquez and was bound to nurture his own creative genius still further.

In the early 1650s, the only surviving child of the King and his first wife, Isabella of Bourbon, the Infanta Maria Theresa, reached marriageable age. This led to a rush in royal demands of Velázquez and his workshop for portraits of her to

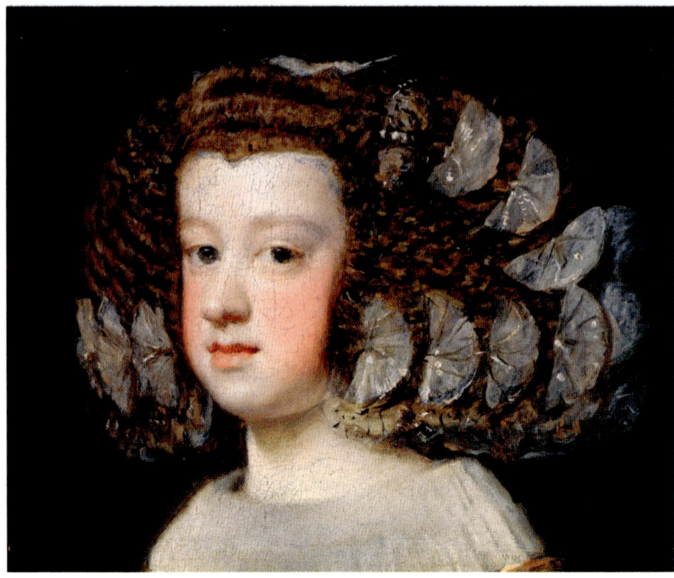

157   be sent to prospective royal suitors. One of these is a fragment of a larger picture showing the charming 15-year-old wearing an elaborate wig decorated with butterfly ribbons that seem spun onto the canvas by Velázquez's wizardry with a brush. Her heavily rouged face wears a winning smile but it was to confront almost insuperable diplomatic obstacles before it could engage its desired suitor. He was the future king of France, Louis XIV, a non-Habsburg and a ruler with whose country Spain was currently at war. Only when a peace treaty between the two nations was concluded in 1660 could the marriage take place. Until then, however, the Infanta was open to invitations, hence the spate of portraits of her that proliferated from the master's workshop.

158   The finest and most ambitious of these to survive by Velázquez himself is a three-quarter length showing her dressed in an elaborate silver crinoline, or *guardainfante*, decorated with two red ribbons bearing watches at the end. She is posed before a blueish-green background and wears an elaborate and heavily decorated wig matched in colour with her ornately pleated collar and patterned sleeves. In her left hand is a large white napkin which sets the artist the challenge of painting white against silver. Velázquez more than passes this test by painting one very thinly over the other, the brushwork only gradually thickening as the napkin reaches her hand. Two centuries later, Whistler would set himself similar challenges but he would arguably never match the artistry or economy of this.

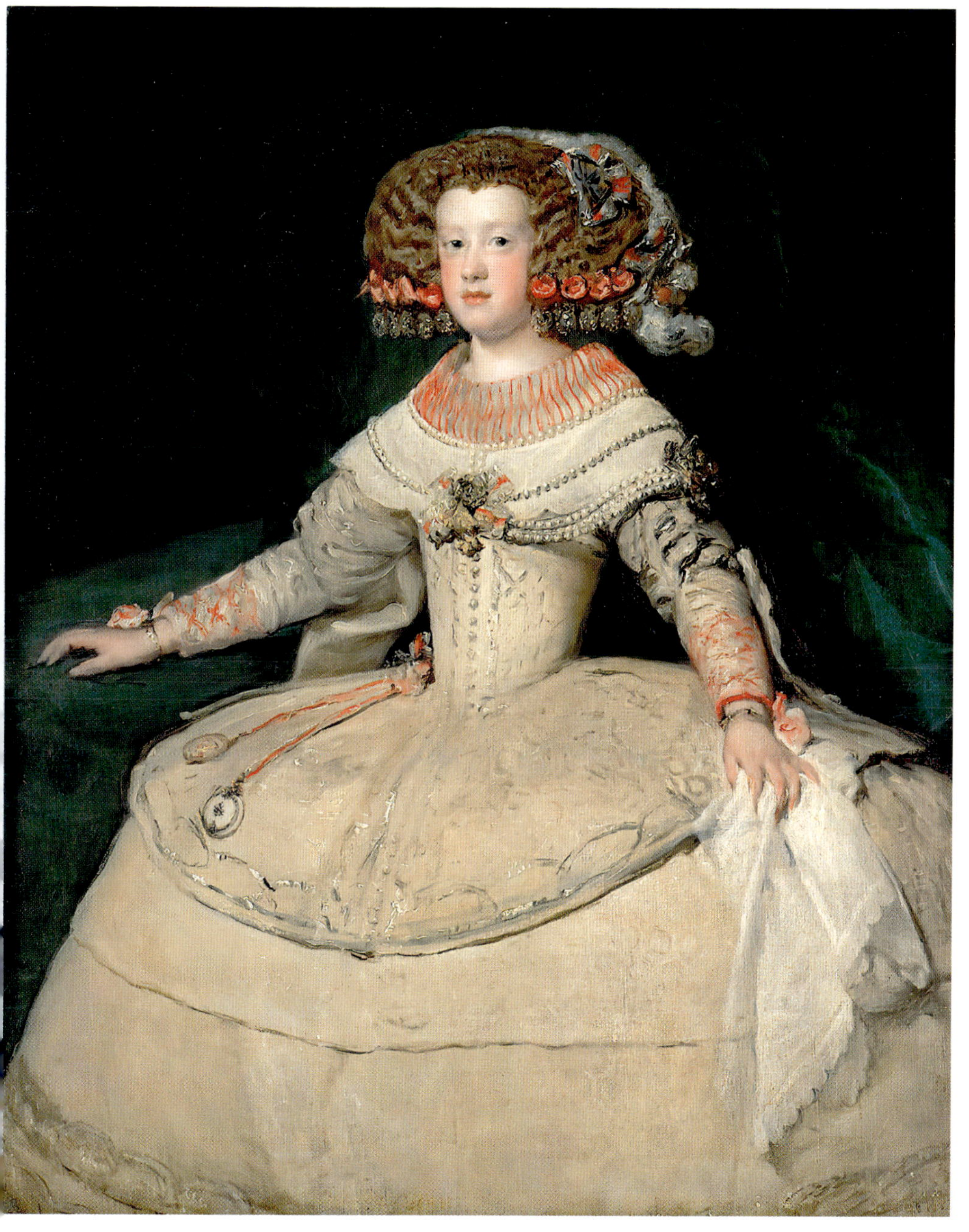

157 OPPOSITE *Maria Theresa, Infanta of Spain*, 1652–53
158 ABOVE *Portrait of the Infanta Maria Theresa of Spain*, c. 1652–53

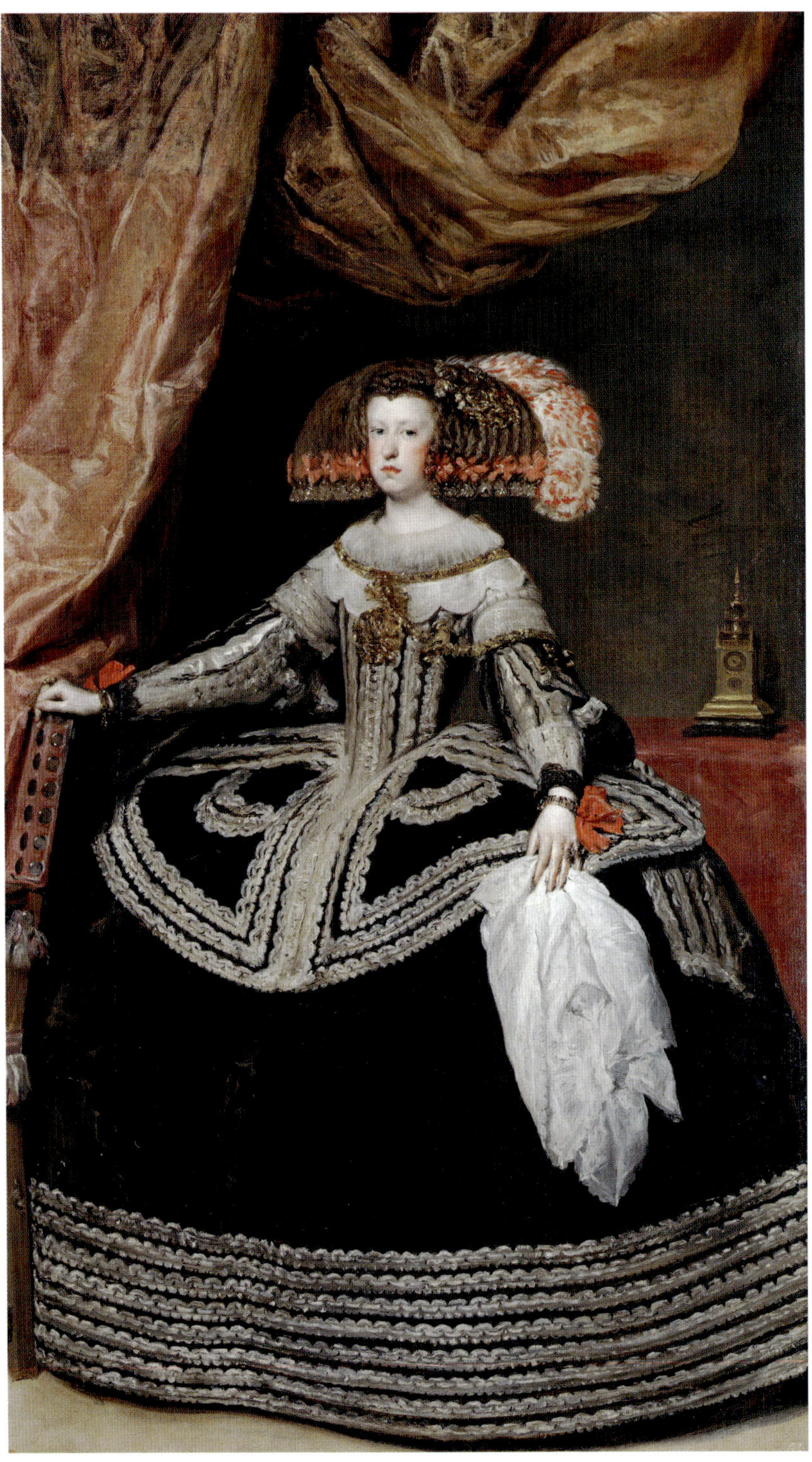

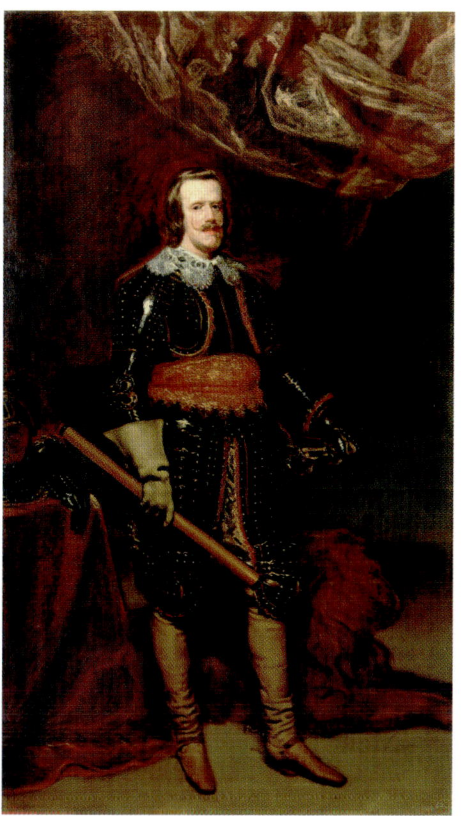

159 OPPOSITE *Portrait of Mariana of Austria, 1652–53*
160 RIGHT Workshop of Velázquez, *Philip IV in Armour, with a Lion at his Feet, c. 1653*

In July 1653 Philip IV wrote a letter in response to a request for a portrait of himself admitting that he had none available and had not had one painted for nine years – i.e., since the *Fraga Philip*. He also complained about Velázquez's phlegmatic manner of working and his own gradual ageing. Soon after, a bust-length portrait of him was painted by the master which subsequently served as a model for more ambitious full-length portraits by his workshop. It depicts the King in a plain silk costume which has been left only barely sketched in by the artist. He wears a sombre, even sorrowful, expression, his drooping eyelids, sagging features and increasingly pronounced Habsburg jaw all adding to the valedictory mood of the whole. But his grand moustache and fair, silken hair add a more uplifting note to the likeness, which is throughout a marvel of artistic reticence and restraint.

The simplicity of this portrait may partly be explained by the fact that Velázquez was also engaged at this time on his

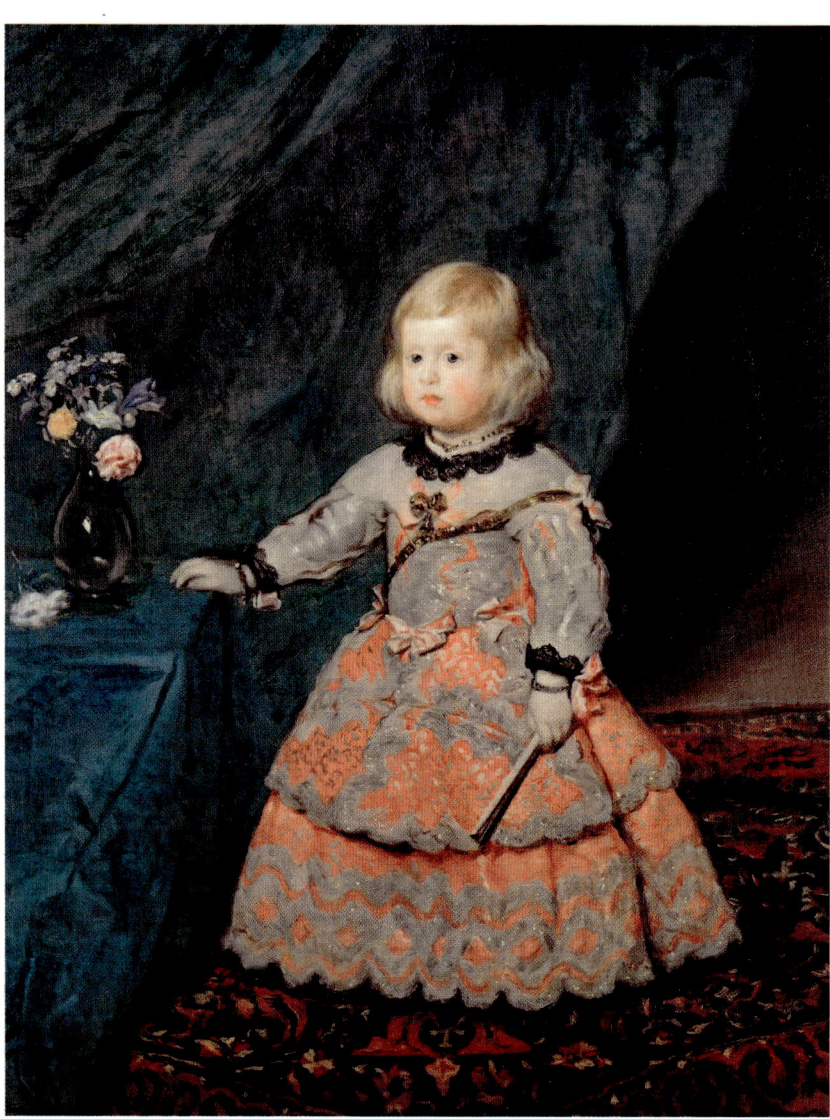

161 ABOVE *The Infanta Margarita*, 1653
162 OPPOSITE *The Infanta Margarita*, c. 1656

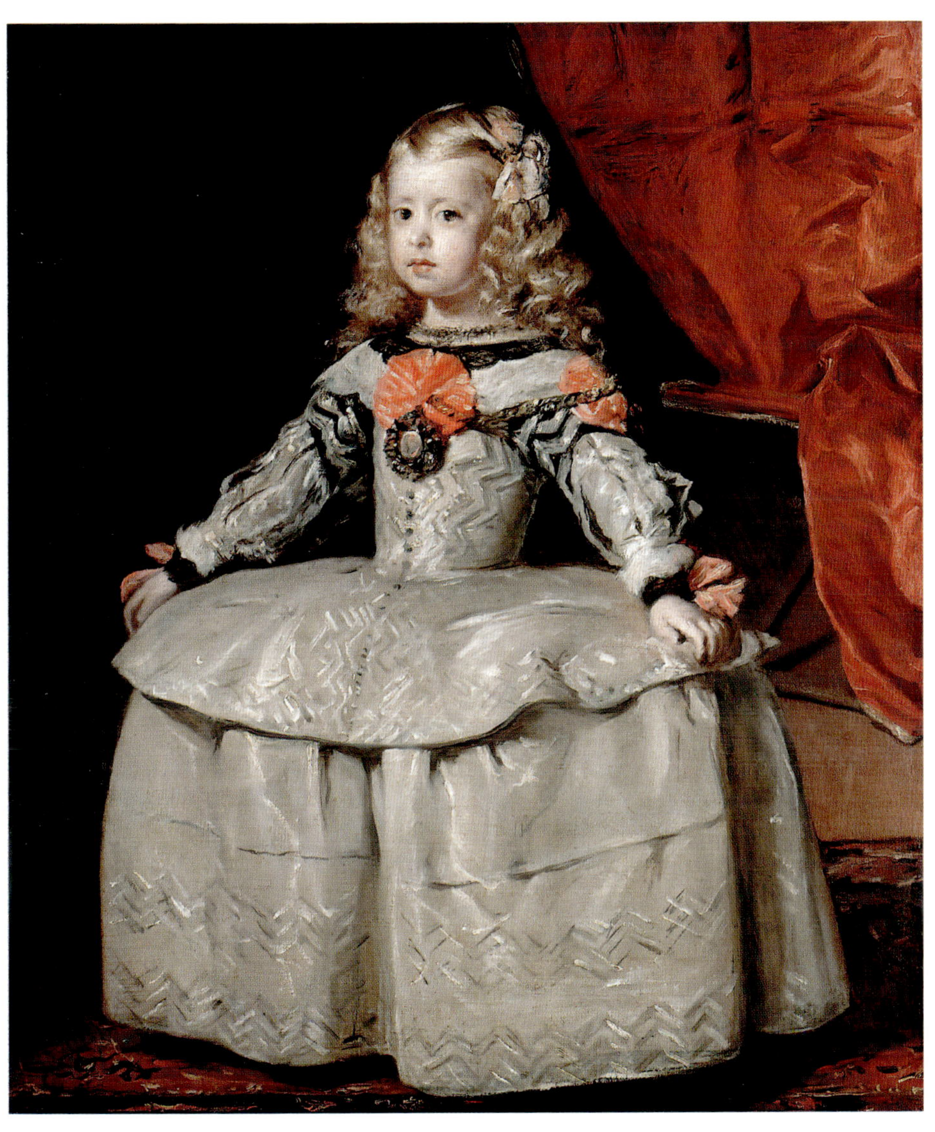

only full-length portrait of the new queen, Mariana. Daughter of the Emperor Ferdinand III and Philip's own sister, the Infanta Maria, Mariana was twenty-six years the King's junior and would live until 1696. In the magnificent portrait Velázquez painted of her she adopts an identical pose to that of the Maria Theresa portrait of these same years. Dressed in a capacious silver-braided black costume adorned with red ribbons, gold chains, bracelets and a large gold brooch, she gazes impassively out, her rouged face weighed down by a large and ornate headdress decorated with ribbons and plumes. In the background stands a table with a gold clock and above the Queen is a swathe of pinkish-red drapery. As is plainly visible even in reproduction, much of this has been added to the top of the picture, a seam across the canvas still showing through. In an already sumptuous portrait, this addition all but overwhelms the Queen. But it was done to make the picture match the size of a full-length portrait of the King with the Habsburg lion at his feet painted by the workshop and based on the bust of Philip just discussed. The cumbersome drapery above the armoured King and that added to the portrait of the Queen are so similar in style as to suggest that they are by the same hand – and one very far from Velázquez's own.

On 12 July 1651 Queen Mariana gave birth to her first child, the Infanta Margarita, who was destined to marry the Emperor Leopold I in 1666 and to die only seven years later. She became the subject of three entrancing portraits by Velázquez which chart her growth and increasing self-awareness and are among the most richly colourful of all the artist's works. In the first of these, of about 1653, she stands stiffly and obediently on a patterned oriental carpet wearing a salmon pink and silver dress trimmed with black and gold. A blue-green curtain is draped behind her and she rests one hand on a table clothed in a radiant deep blue. In her other she holds what appears to be a folded-up fan and on the table stands a vase of flowers. One rose has fallen from it and rests on the table, a naturalistic touch that adds a note of informality to the proceedings and would later become an artistic cliché at the hands of the Impressionist painters. In truth, the portrait as a whole is a visual bouquet, Velázquez countering the reticence of the little Infanta with the most ravishing and animated interchange of colours and patterns. Moreover, it is no longer a tactile but a purely visual world that the artist creates. One cannot clasp one's hands around the vase in this portrait as one could around the glass in the *Waterseller*.

A second portrait of the Infanta of about two or three years later shows her in a more spirited pose, as though playfully

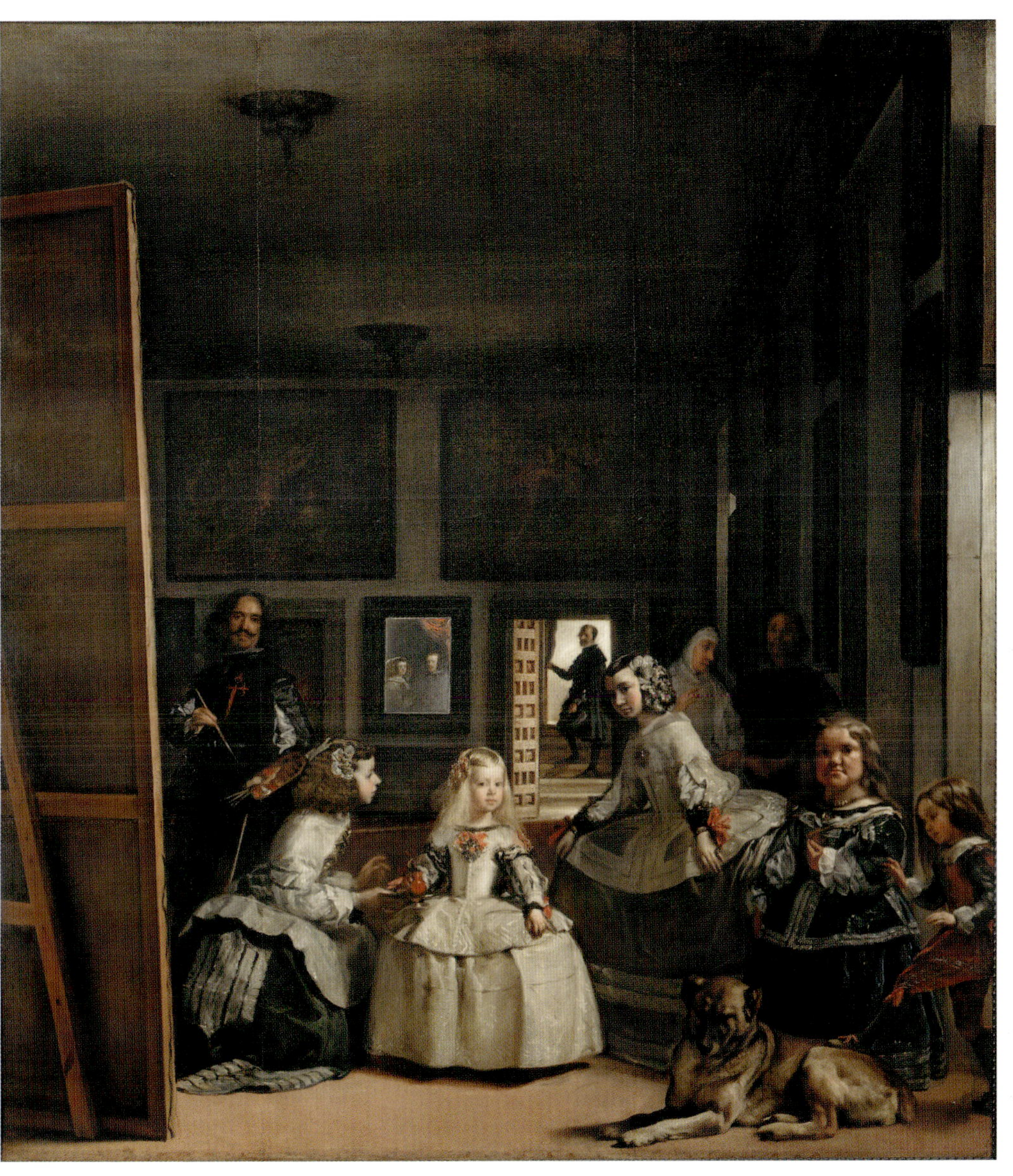

163 *Las Meninas*, 1656

bidding for the artist's attentions through the radiance
and liveliness of her stance. Framed now by only a plain
red drape, her blond hair has grown longer and her perky
personality emerged. There is no longer any need for tables
and vases of flowers, for the Infanta has herself learned how to
engage with the viewer. Small wonder that she was described
in these years by the visiting Marshal-Duke of Gramont from
France as 'a little angel' who was 'as sprightly and pretty
as possible'.

Wearing the same dress and an even more beguiling smile,
the Infanta Margarita takes pride of place in Velázquez's
greatest masterpiece and (many would argue) the greatest
masterpiece of Western painting, *Las Meninas*. Although
the *Mona Lisa* and the *Laughing Cavalier* may exert a firmer
grip on the public imagination, being single portraits with
enigmatic expressions, no other picture by any artist has
attracted greater admiration, controversy and imitation than
Las Meninas. Painted in 1656, it depicts a cross-section of the
royal household grouped around the Infanta in the manner of
an informal portrait. Palomino identifies them. To the left of
the princess is Doña Maria Sarmiento, offering the princess
water from a clay jug. Opposite her and about to curtsy is Doña
Isabel de Velasco. They are the maids of honour or *meninas*
that have given the picture its name. To the right are Mari
Bárbola, described by Palomino as 'a dwarf of formidable
aspect', staring out at the viewer, and next to her, Nicolasito
Pertusato, who playfully prods a large mastiff asleep at his
feet. Standing in the shadows behind them are Doña Marcela
de Ulloa – a Lady of Honour – and an unnamed escort to the
ladies-in-waiting. On the left is Velázquez himself, poised
with his brush and painting before a large easel. Reflected in
a mirror on the back wall are Philip IV and Queen Mariana,
and silhouetted in a doorway in the distance is José Nieto, the
Queen's chamberlain. The setting is not Velázquez's studio but
a large room in Prince Balthasar Carlos's former apartments in
the palace hung with painted copies by Mazo of two pictures
by Rubens that hung in the Torre de la Parada.

What exactly is taking place here? The most straightforward
scenario would probably run something like this: Velázquez
is painting a large portrait of the King and Queen when the
sitting is suddenly interrupted by the appearance of the
Infanta and her entourage, who have come to divert the
sitting and entertain the royal couple. This is the action
Palomino describes, noting that many members of the royal
household visited the artist while he was painting the picture,
'considering this a delightful treat and entertainment'.

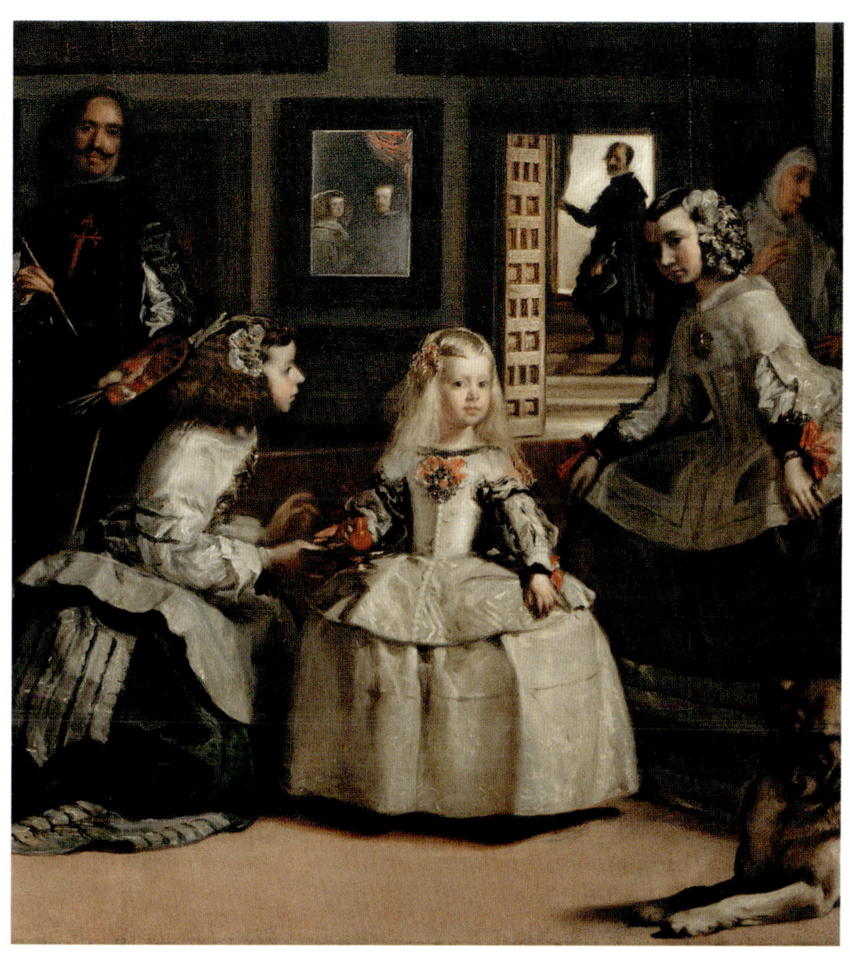

164 *Las Meninas,* 1656, detail

But this is unlikely to be correct for a number of reasons. Double portraits – as distinct from family portraits – do not exist in the Spanish tradition, although they are frequently encountered in the art of the Low Countries. Velázquez himself never painted one, and nor did Goya later. In addition to that, consider the height of the canvas upon which the artist is working in *Las Meninas*. This must be at least 10 feet. Compare it to the full-length portrait of Queen Mariana just considered, which has been added to at the top to make it nearly 8 feet high. The addition of two more feet on top of the royal couple, if that were what Velázquez was painting, would completely have swamped them, being nearly twice as high as the figures.

If it is not the King and Queen being painted, then it can only be the Infanta and her companions. Admittedly the artist is positioned behind them rather than in front, but one or more mirrors placed outside the picture space could have reflected the group back to him and the action would be reversed. By this reading it would be the figures in the foreground who are informally posing for the artist and the King and Queen who are witnessing the sitting. This would immediately make more sense of the height of the canvas upon which Velázquez is working, which appears to be the height of *Las Meninas* itself. When the presence of the King and Queen is also taken into account, the picture would then depict a cross-section of the royal household, literally from top to bottom: the monarch and his consort, their daughter, her attendants and handmaidens, a palace official, royal entertainers, a dog and, lastly, the court painter himself caught in the act of bestowing immortality on the group through the motions of his brush.

Admittedly, Velázquez had never painted anything like this before and it cannot be classified as an orthodox royal portrait. Rather it is a hybrid creation which combines elements of a group portrait and a genre scene and is a curious forerunner of the English conversation piece of the eighteenth century. But it does have something of an ancestry in Velázquez's own career, beginning with the double portrait of *Balthasar Carlos with a Dwarf* of 1631, where the twin poles of human existence come together, one upright and proud and the other submissive. An even more obvious precedent for *Las Meninas* is the so-called *Riding School* of the 1630s, an equestrian portrait of Balthasar Carlos overseen by the King and Queen, Olivares and other members of the royal household. This, too, is a cross between a dynastic portrait of the monarch and his heir and a scene from everyday palace life. In the end, however, it breaks up into three separate scenes located in three planes in space which are scarcely related to one another. In *Las Meninas*, however, the

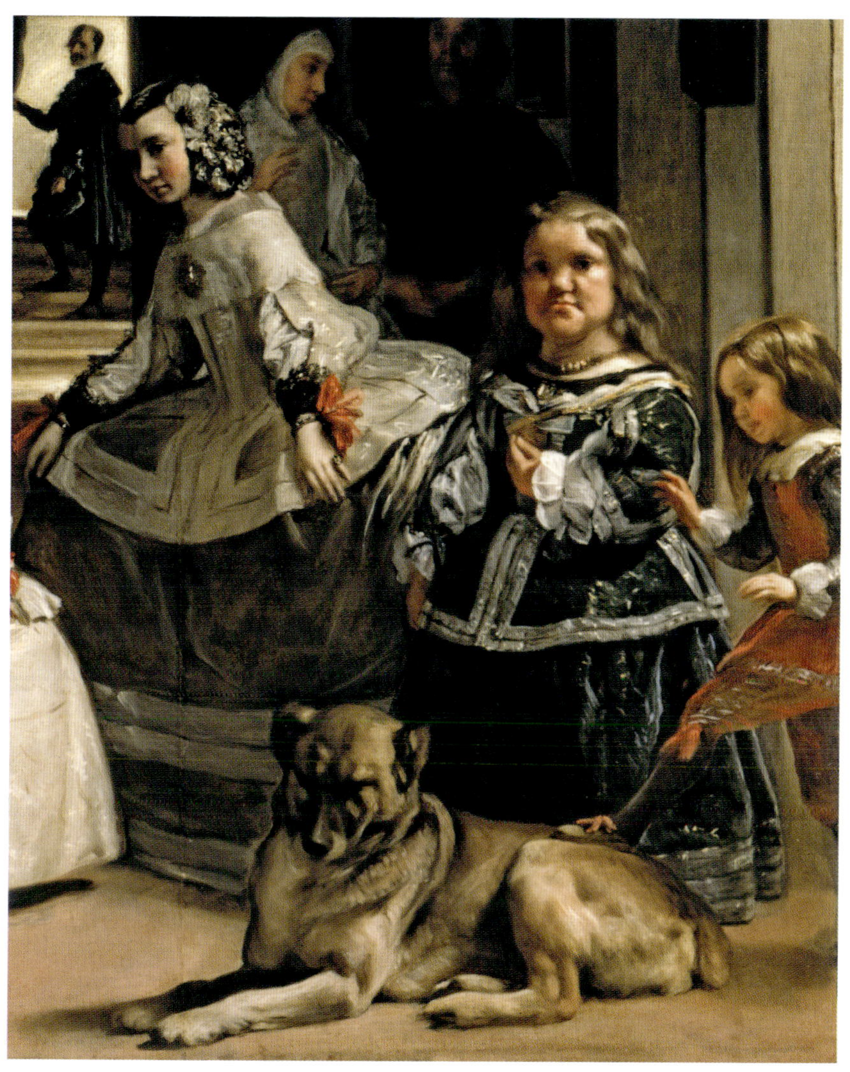

165 *Las Meninas*, 1656, detail

groups are all connected by their exchanging gazes; the Infanta and her entourage greet the King and Queen, who look on at them while Velázquez and the palace marshal in the doorway view them all.

What inspired this great picture will never be known but can be surmised. In carrying out his day-to-day duties in the royal household Velázquez must often have encountered the little princess dallying with her playmates and witnessed her parents looking admiringly on and her in turn greeting them. From these collective memories sprang the idea of a pictorial testimony to these occasions and of the artist's own abilities to immortalize them. For it cannot be denied that *Las Meninas* is ultimately a celebration of art – and the artist – as much as it is of his royal sitters. When one recalls the menial status accorded to Spanish painters in the seventeenth century, and Velázquez's lifelong pursuit to overcome it, this can be seen as a vindication of his own profession. Even royalty might fade from history unless immortalized by a painter, a mere artist outlasting a king.

However casual or commonplace the action of the picture may have been for the artist, the composition of *Las Meninas* is anything but. Uniquely in Velázquez's career, half of the painting is devoid of interest, depicting only the walls and ceiling of a darkened room. Such use of empty space above a group of figures may also be found in the late altarpieces of Caravaggio, where it serves as a kind of resonating space for the action depicted below. In Velázquez's use of it, too, it permits the figures to move and breathe, allowing them to stand in an ambient setting rather than just in a row. Articulating that empty space is a network of rectangles: the mirror, open doorway, framed pictures and window shutters on the right, and connecting them with the figures are the rectangles of the canvas and stretcher before which the artist is working. A counterpoint to all these straight lines and right angles is the lilting line of the figures themselves, which rises and falls in an undulating curve from the artist's hand and head at the top to that of the dozing dog across and below. It is the visual equivalent of a flowing melody soaring over a rhythmic ground bass. Viewed within the context of Old Master painting, however, it is a daring anomaly – and a masterstroke. Few artists of Velázquez's time or before – and least of all his favoured Venetian and Flemish painters – were known for leaving half their pictures virtually empty. To have done so would have deprived them of their decorative beauty and visual interest throughout. Moreover, it would have made them look more like real life. Every object that meets the eye, even in a single glance, is not equally of interest. Our attention wavers, our focus moves on, and gaps occur. It is this visual breathing space that Velázquez introduces into *Las Meninas* that gives it the semblance of reality.

Even more remarkable than the compositional strategies of this picture is its technical mastery. As it is not a traditional royal portrait confined to a single sitter, Velázquez could allow his brush freer rein here than usual, highlighting selected features and seemingly skirting over others – mirroring once again exactly the way the eye tends to see. Painted on three large strips of canvas vertically stitched together, *Las Meninas* (in the words of Jonathan Brown) 'can be thought of as the largest oil sketch ever painted'. Perhaps the most astonishing portions of the picture are those areas least emphasized: the ceiling and recesses of the room. Here, with little or no colour and only the dimmest of light, everything appears to swim in a subdued haze, yet the recession is perfectly convincing, individual forms and frames legible and the gradations of tone subtly modulated to create the perfect illusion of a deep space seen through a veil of light and air. Far from being a mere portrait of the Infanta and her attendants, on this level it is also the portrait of a room.

When one turns to the figures, Velázquez's lifelong quest to capture action in motion is eminently evident in his treatment of hands. As Doña Maria offers the princess the beaker of water, the fingers of her left hand appear to flutter in the air, while the hand bearing the tray is little more than a painterly smudge. The same is noticeable in those of Nicolasito prodding the dog or of the Infanta herself. As for the painting of the costumes throughout, no two strokes are ever the same. Some are daubed and speckled on, others meander and flow, some are even slashed. The one thing they never are is routinely or uniformly applied. No wonder Velázquez painted so relatively few pictures, given that each individual brushstroke amounted to a separate decision. Nor is the density of the paint texture remotely the same from one part of the picture to the next. On the right side of the Infanta's face it is dragged so thinly across the surface that the weave of the canvas itself creates a shadow across her cheek. But on the brooches and ribbons that adorn the dresses of the figures, a variety of strokes and daubs of colour are piled on top of one another, making them sparkle and dance before our eyes. Yet for all the freedom and spontaneity, the artist maintains a firm grip on the action. Notice, for instance, that eight figures are included in the picture, but only four head positions. The artist and Infanta gaze in the same direction, one *menina*'s profile mirrors that of the chaperone, the other,

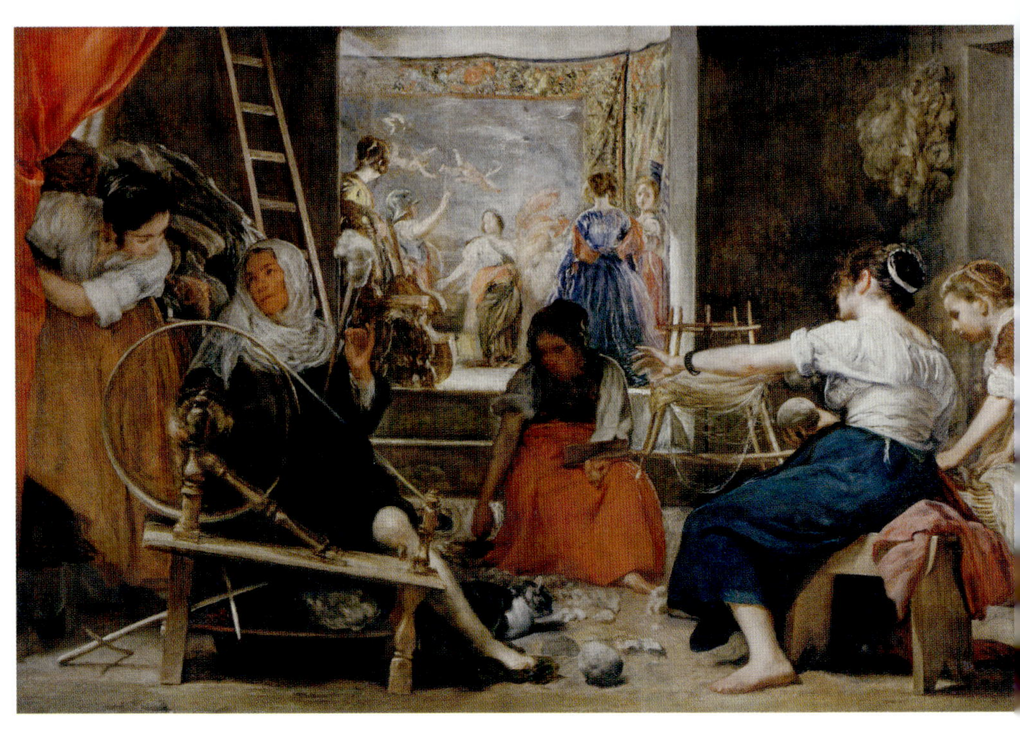

166 *Las Hilanderas* or *The Fable of Arachne*, c. 1657–58

that of the mischievous figure prodding the dog, and Mari
Bárbola's unashamed gaze that of the unnamed bodyguard
standing in the shadows behind her. Whether intentional or
not, there is also one passage in the picture that seems covertly
confessional, and that is the artist's own hand holding a brush.
His fingers melt into it, as though they are one. Here – above
all in Velázquez's career – they were.

The miraculous illusionism of this painting, which has
never been surpassed, will forever beguile viewers and defy
explanations. It is perhaps best summarized in the question
posed by the French writer and critic Théophile Gautier, who,
upon viewing the original on a visit to Madrid in 1840, asked
simply: 'Where, then, is the picture?'

This said, *Las Meninas* contains one final surprise for the
viewer who, if they were able to peer around the other side of
the stretch of canvas depicted on the left, would see exactly
what they see now: namely, the back of a picture.

Hanging at the top of the rear wall in *Las Meninas* are two
painted copies by Mazo of mythologies by Rubens and his
workshop, commissioned for the Torre de la Parada. One
depicts the Judgment of Midas and the other the contest
between Minerva and Arachne, both of them subjects in which
ordinary mortals dared to challenge the supremacy of the
gods. The latter became the subject of another of Velázquez's
greatest works, *Las Hilanderas* (or the *Spinners*), painted for a
private client and minor official of the palace, Pedro de Arce,
probably in 1657–58. Arce was presumably a friend of the artist
and owned a notable collection of paintings and Velázquez
rewarded him in this instance with one of his most learned
and sophisticated creations.

The subject is from Book VI (1–145) of Ovid's *Metamorphoses*
and concerns a contest between a goddess and a mortal.
Minerva, goddess of wisdom and patron of the arts, is
challenged by the Lydian maiden Arachne to a weaving
contest, the latter boasting that she can exceed the goddess
in this. Minerva appears disguised as an old woman and
warns Arachne not to presume so much, but Arachne persists.
Minerva then throws off her disguise to reveal her identity
and the contest begins. Arachne weaves a tapestry showing
the cruel acts performed by the gods on mere mortals, in the
form of the Rape of Europa. The contest completed, Arachne
is declared to have surpassed the goddess. Angered, Minerva
transforms Arachne into a spider, destined to weave for the rest
of her days. It is from this tale that the class of invertebrates
that includes the spiders – the Arachnida – derives its name.

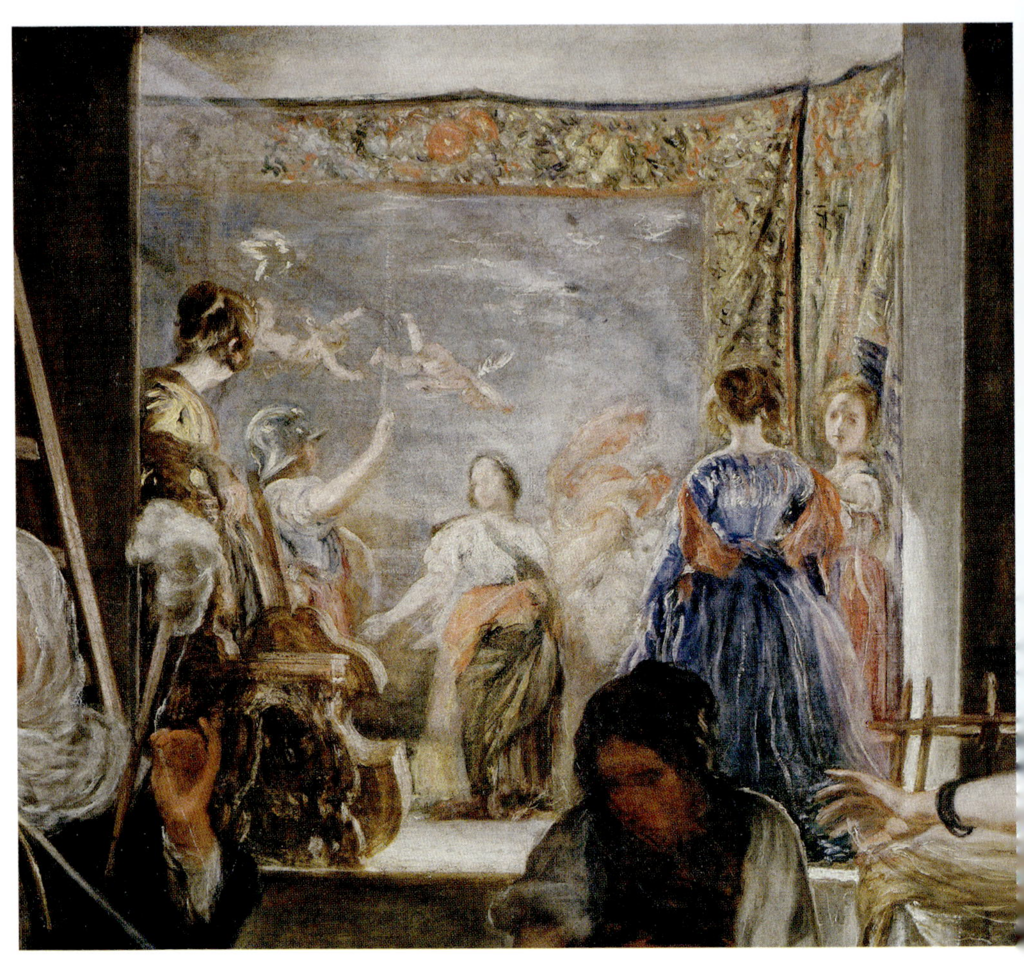

167 ABOVE *Las Hilanderas* or *The Fable of Arachne*, c. 1657–58, detail
168 OPPOSITE Titian, *Rape of Europa*, 1559–62

Velázquez divides his picture into two separate scenes in the manner of certain of his early *bodegones*. The judgment of the contest is depicted in a brightly illuminated scene in the background and the foreground is devoted to the dusky interior of a spinning workshop drawn from everyday life. The rear view depicts a tapestry showroom. Three women are visiting it, one of them standing alongside a bass viol, while before them stands Minerva, clad in her customary helmet and armour, her right arm raised to denounce Arachne, who implores the goddess to spare her. Behind Arachne hangs her winning tapestry of the Rape of Europa, which is based on Titian's painting of this subject, which was then in the collection of the Spanish king. The Venetian master had been the favourite painter of the Emperor Charles V, of King Philip II and also of Velázquez himself. To honour him here in this way may be seen as the Spanish master's bid to be acknowledged as a descendant of this exalted lineage and, above all, for the art of painting itself to be recognized as a noble profession. In a country and culture that still regarded painters as manual craftsmen, plying their trade alongside carpenters, ironmongers and picture restorers, Velázquez may have escaped this indignity through his sheer genius and service to the King. But the lowly status borne by his profession cannot entirely have escaped him, if only by association, and to pair his skills with those of the great Titian was one way of countering this injustice.

Characteristic of the undemonstrative nature of Velázquez's art is his decision to focus on Minerva's judgment of Arachne

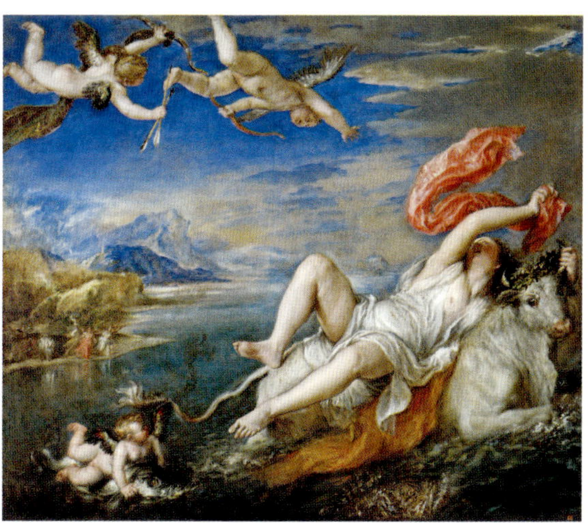

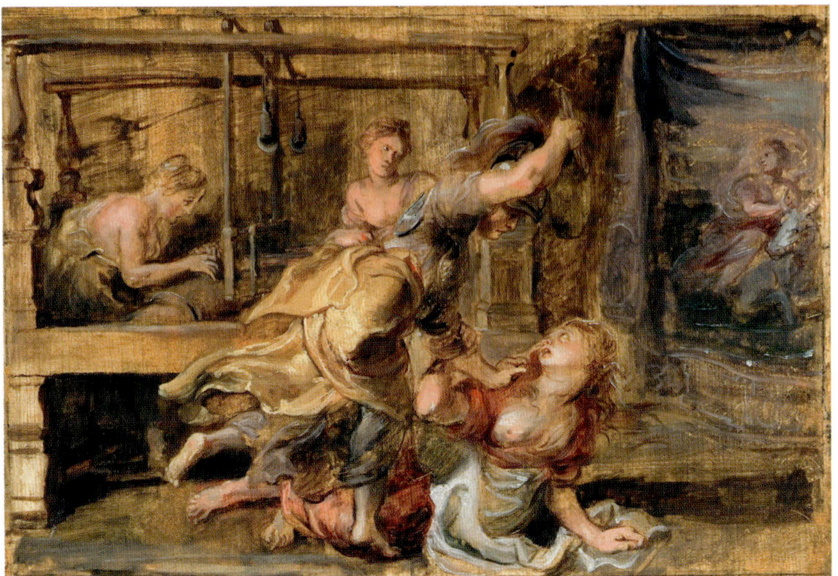

169 Peter Paul Rubens, *Pallas and Arachne, 1636–37*

rather than the latter's punishment. This contrasts with Rubens's treatment of the theme for Philip IV, which is preserved in an autograph oil sketch showing Arachne thrown to the ground and beaten by Minerva while the former's fellow weavers react with horror as they work at their looms.

The foreground scene in *Las Hilanderas* depicts a group of anonymous women engaged in the closely related activity of spinning. On the left an elderly woman wearing a headscarf works at her wheel as she turns to engage with a younger companion drawing a curtain aside. On the right a gracefully posed young girl, seen from the rear, winds wool as another puts a basket down by her side. In the centre, a kneeling woman cards tufts of wool, watched over by a curious cat, whose shape nearly rhymes with that of the ball of wool lying beside it.

Although the painting is poorly preserved, it is evident that all of these figures are very freely and summarily defined and selectively illuminated, the brightest light falling on the heroically posed woman winding wool and a more subdued one on her companion at the spinning wheel. Uniquely among all of Velázquez's multifigure pictures, none of the faces here appear to have been based on life models, which cannot be claimed for the *Borrachos*, *The Surrender of Breda* or *The Coronation of the Virgin*. Admittedly the artist may have relied on models to study their poses, but beyond this these women bear the most generic facial features thus far encountered in Velázquez's subject pictures.

Another unusual aspect of the painting is its apparent dependence on antique precedents. Jonathan Brown has astutely noted that one of the 154 books in Velázquez's library was the canonical sourcebook on ancient art (and much else) Pliny's *Natural History*. In it are recorded the legendary achievements of Antiphilus and Aristides. The former is praised 'for his picture of wool-weaving, where all the women busily ply their tasks', and the latter 'made a four-horse carriage, and so lifelike was it that one would swear that the wheels turned and rolled along'. The stroboscopic effects of the whirling spinning wheel in *Las Hilanderas* may have been Velázquez's attempt to rival these legendary achievements of ancient art.

It remains to consider how the two scenes in this picture may be connected. In the artist's early paintings with *Christ in the House of Martha and Mary* or *The Supper at Emmaus*, the biblical scene in the background serves as an example to the ordinary kitchen workers in front of them to serve their own masters as dutifully as Christ was served when he sat down to table on these two scriptural occasions. But can the foreground scene in *Las Hilanderas* be understood as an everyday equivalent of what is taking place in the rear? The short answer is only teasingly – and ambiguously – as is so often the case with Velázquez.

A parallelism between the two is immediately established by the fact that five women take part in each and that the two main figures in the foreground are strikingly contrasted, one old and the other young, one spinning as effortlessly as a goddess and the other winding as strenuously as a mortal. Yet this cannot literally be the contest between Minerva and Arachne. For one, they are spinning and not weaving, and the older one is not dressed as Minerva, as stipulated by Ovid. But she does appear disguised – or at least over-dressed for the occasion – and her bare, shapely leg may be taken as a hint that underneath all her garments is a woman younger than she first appears. And artistic licence may explain why Velázquez chose to depict them at work at a wheel rather than a loom, the large and cumbersome form of which would have distracted from the figures shown here.

Two other features of the picture link these figures with the background scene. The left hands of both foreground figures overlap with the showroom beyond, as though leading us naturally to it and – most tantalizingly of all – the Arachne figure in the showroom wears a white blouse, green skirt

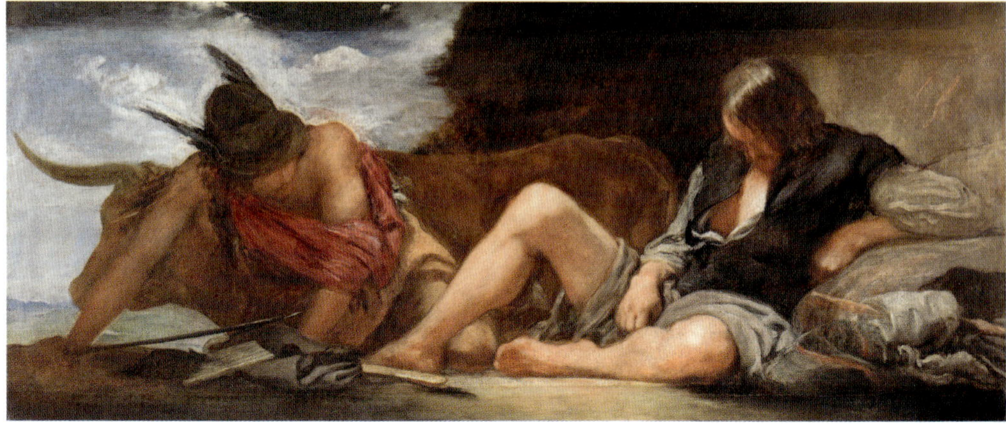

170 ABOVE *Mercury and Argus*, c. 1659
171 OPPOSITE Peter Paul Rubens, *Mercury and Argus*, 1636–38

and red sash, exactly the colours of her counterpart in the foreground. If Velázquez has not telescoped two episodes from the same tale into the picture, he has at least couched a moral message into the foreground group: namely, that maturity can often achieve effortlessly what youth must still strive to attain.

Around 1658, Velázquez was engaged in reinstalling the display of paintings in the Hall of Mirrors of the Alcázar. Pride of place was given to the great Venetian masters of the sixteenth century – Titian, Tintoretto and Veronese – and to Rubens, who was represented by no fewer than ten canvases. Velázquez's own works were also included in the scheme, among them *The Expulsion of the Moriscos* and four recent mythological paintings he had completed to hang between windows in the room. These depicted Apollo flaying Marsyas, Venus and Adonis, Cupid and Psyche and Mercury and Argus. On Christmas Day 1734 a fire raged through the west wing of the palace, eventually spreading beyond this, and despite the valiant efforts of many to rescue the most valued contents of the palace, nearly five hundred pictures perished in the flames. They included the *Moriscos* and three of the aforementioned mythologies by Velázquez, only the *Mercury and Argus* being spared. When one considers how relatively unproductive Velázquez was as a painter, together with the opportunities the lost pictures must have provided him with to portray nudity, butchery and carnal love, one gains a measure of how much of the scope of his genius remains forever lost.

Mercury and Argus depicts a subject recounted by Ovid (*Metamorphoses* Book I, 668–721). Jupiter is in love with Io, a princess of Argus, which incites his wife Juno to a fit of jealousy that leads her to transform Io into a heifer and entrust her to the care of the hundred-eyed giant Argus. Jupiter then sends Mercury to lull the giant to sleep and kill him, releasing Io.

Velázquez depicts Mercury creeping up on the slumbering Argus, bearing his pipes and a sword, with the heifer Io silhouetted behind him. The low-lying nature of all the protagonists is necessitated by the narrow dimensions of the canvas, which has added strips to the top and bottom, but Velázquez utilizes this limitation ingeniously to create a moment charged with suspense. In this he differs from Rubens's treatment of the same subject, which shows Mercury about to strike the fatal blow and is more straightforwardly dramatic. In Rubens's painting, all of the tension is finding release, whereas in Velázquez's it is steadily mounting.

Taking account of the distance from which his picture would be viewed, the artist executed it with the greatest degree of freedom and spontaneity of any of his works. Painting very thinly and often employing broad, sweeping strokes, he conjures forth individual forms, the most distinctly defined being the raised right knee of Argus, a focal point of the picture around which all else appears slightly blurred. The giant's face is a shadowed blob, no more than telling smears of darker pigment defining its features, and skeins of strokes hint at draperies while constantly also asserting their own autonomy. In any other master this might qualify as an oil sketch or a

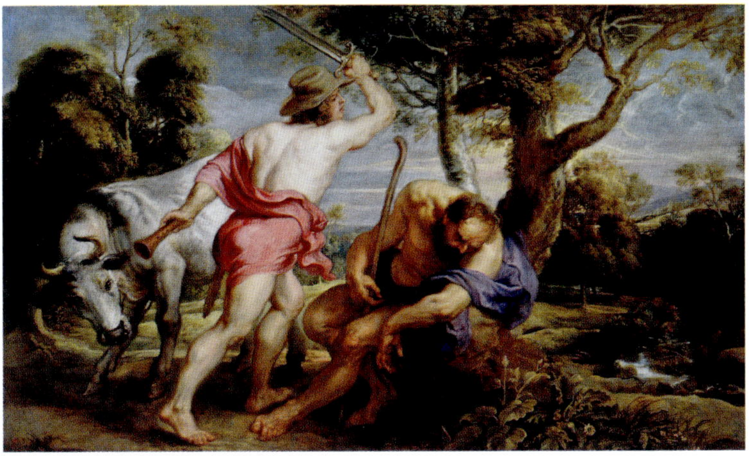

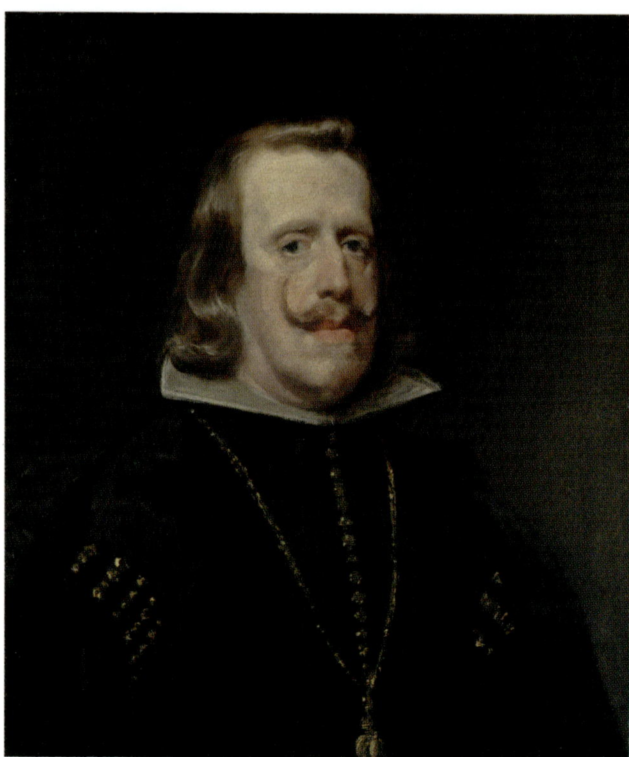

172 *Philip IV,*
1656–57

work in progress but in Velázquez it is simply a finished
painting in a style of the future.

172   The artist's last portrait of Philip IV, of around 1656, is closely
based on the similar bust-length portrait of three or four years
earlier and was reproduced not only in an engraving of that year
but also in nearly a dozen painted copies, making it one
of Velázquez's most widely imitated images of the monarch.
In contrast to the slightly earlier work, which shows him
in plain dress, the King now wears one of velvet or wool
decorated with gold buttons. Around his neck is the chain of
the Order of the Golden Fleece. The somewhat timid execution
of the costume coupled with the awkwardly sloping angle of
the shoulders have led most critics to conclude that all but
the King's head was entrusted to an assistant – yet another
inexplicable example of the apparent indifference with which
Velázquez regarded the overall authenticity of his works.
Can he really have been so overburdened with duties as to
have to delegate these final touches to an assistant in so
modest a work?

But the head of the monarch is masterful, although somewhat more taciturn than the earlier portrait. The drooping eyelids, impassive gaze and fleshier neck and chin convey a greater sense of sadness and world-weariness on the part of this declining and disillusioned monarch.

In 1659 Philip IV sent the last of three portraits of the Infanta Margarita by Velázquez to Emperor Leopold I in Vienna, to whom she had been promised as a child and would soon marry. It shows the Infanta aged eight wearing a blue silk dress elaborately trimmed in silver with an expansive hooped petticoat or *guardainfante*. She holds a large muff in her left hand.

The portrait was cut into an oval, probably in the eighteenth century, and its background severely damaged, but Palomino described its original state: 'on a small console table, there is an ebony clock of very elegant design, with bronze figures and animals; in the centre is a circle where the chariot of the sun is painted, and within the same circle there is a smaller one with the division of the Hours.' Although these details are much darkened and damaged, a reclining lion in bronze may still be discerned, painted in the abbreviated manner that distinguishes the entire painting, where dots, spots and cursory strokes of white and silver paint sparkle over the princess. Nor can one fail to notice that this tour de force of painterly dexterity all takes place within the restricted colour harmony of blue and silver.

Also sent to the Emperor with this portrait of the Infanta was another of the newly arrived heir to the throne, Philip Prospero, born on 28 November 1657. A frail and tender child with an enlarged head, which Velázquez minimizes, he stands resting his right hand on a chair and wearing a red dress over which is a white pinafore. Decorating it are an amulet to ward off the evil eye, an amber apple to guard against infections and bells to follow his passage around the royal household and ensure his protection. On the right is a stool with a crimson cushion and a plumed hat and, behind it, a view through an open door. On the chair by the prince sits a little lap dog, for which, Palomino tells us, 'Velázquez felt great affection'. Resting its head on the arm of the chair, its moist-eyed gaze and delicate age are a fitting accompaniment to the young prince, whose fragility is superbly conveyed by Velázquez without a trace of the sentimentality that can so often be encountered in portraits of young children. But the artist's sensitivity to his subject shines through, and if the portrait conveys an air of cheerlessness, this is somewhat mitigated by the harmony of reds and whites out of which it is created.

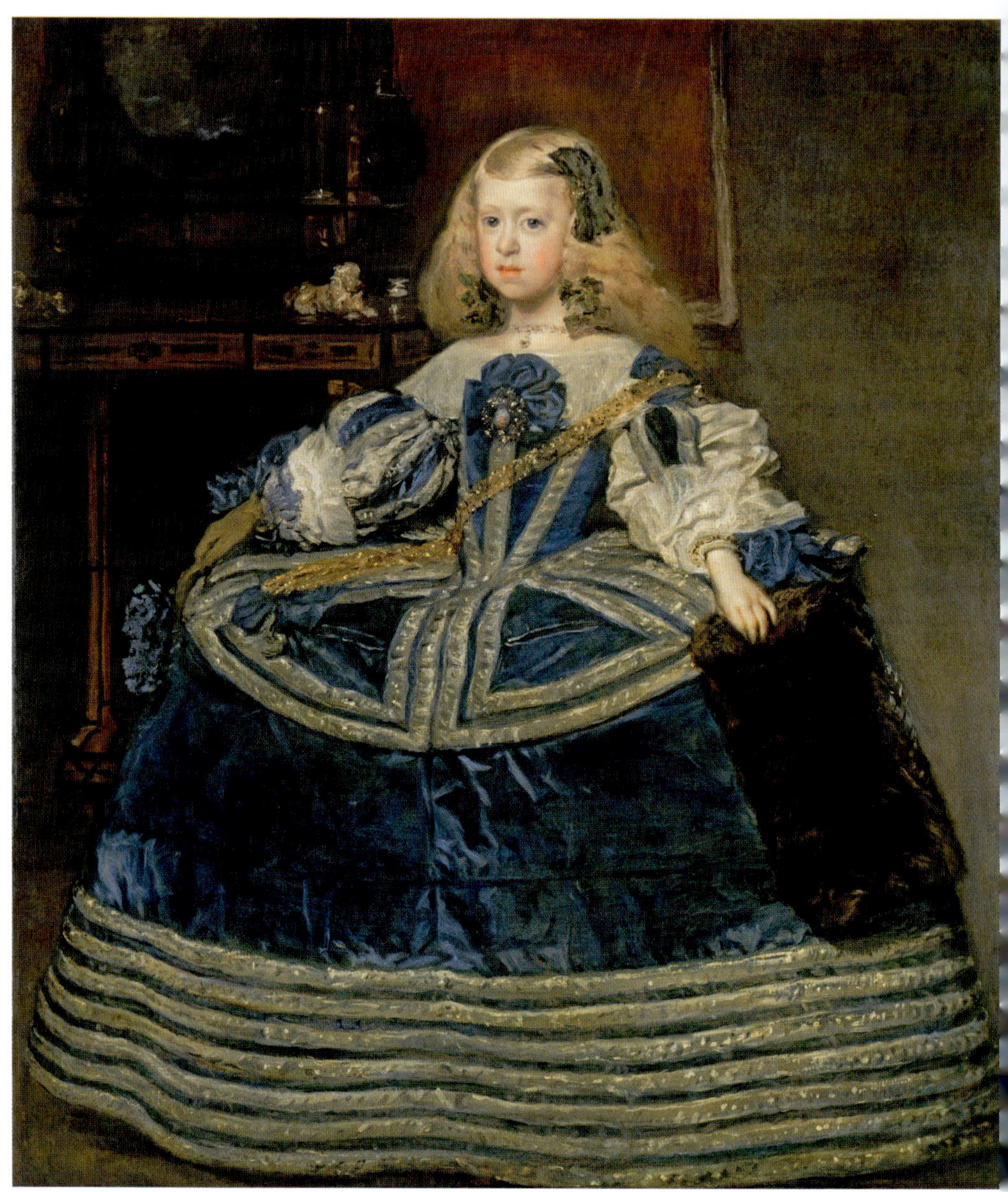

173 ABOVE *The Infanta Margarita Theresa in a Blue Dress, 1659*
174 OPPOSITE *Portrait of Prince Philip Prospero, 1659*

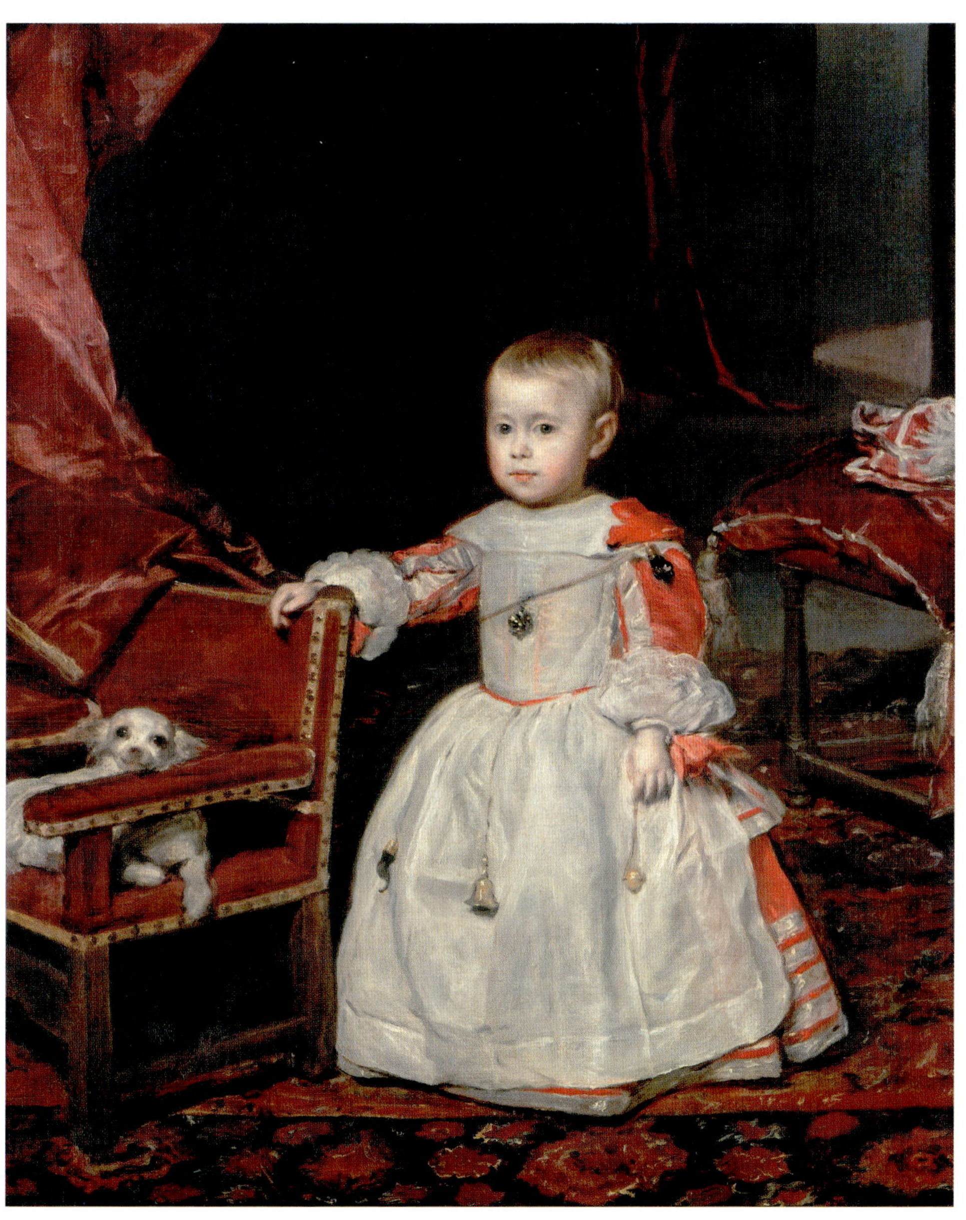

One year before these two royal portraits were dispatched, in June 1658, Velázquez's long-held ambition to join a military order and be recognized as a member of the nobility began to be realized in earnest with a nomination from the King. This had then to be reviewed by the Council of Military Orders to approve the candidate's eligibility, but its rules strictly forbade admission to anyone practising a manual occupation – for instance 'if he paints for a living'. Velázquez's credentials were subjected to repeated scrutiny, for although he had painted for a living, he was also descended from lesser nobility. After much opposition to the artist's admission and two interventions from the Pope, Velázquez was belatedly admitted to his chosen Order of Santiago in November 1659. Sometime after this the insignia of the order was added to the portrait of the artist in *Las Meninas*, according to some sources painted there by the King himself after the artist's death. Recent technical examination of the picture has concluded, however, that this passage is uniform with the rest of the canvas and may have been added by Velázquez himself about three years after the painting was completed.

In April 1660 Velázquez (and other royal courtiers) left Madrid for the Isle of Pheasants near Fuenterrabía on the border between Spain and France to prepare for the King's forthcoming journey and the ceremonies that would follow when he met the French king, Louis XIV, to present him with his daughter, Maria Theresa, whom the latter would marry a year later. Following a long journey northward which entailed twenty-three stops for the royal party, the event took place on 7 June, with Velázquez attending the ceremony splendidly attired. 'He was ennobled by many diamonds and precious stones,' Palomino relates. 'It is not surprising that he should surpass others in the colour of the cloth [of his suit], since he was exceptional in his knowledge of fabrics, for which he had always shown great taste... Also a heavy gold chain around his neck held by a badge set with many diamonds, on which the cross of Santiago was enamelled.' A 'knowledge of fabrics' is proclaimed by the paintings themselves and the cross of Santiago was a just reward for a lifetime of service to the King.

The royal party departed for Madrid the next day and returned to the capital on 26 June, Velázquez then resuming his court duties. But on the last day of July the artist fell ill with pains in his stomach and heart and, despite the efforts of several physicians, he died on 6 August 1660. He was buried on the following day, and his widow died a week later.

Chapter 8
After Velázquez

Left unfinished in Velázquez's studio at his death was his fourth and largest portrait of the Infanta Margarita. Aged about nine, she wears a silver and salmon pink dress with an expansive *guardainfante* and holds a large white handkerchief in one hand and a bunch of flowers in the other. Behind her hangs a deep red curtain with gold brocade and cascading above her is a brightly lit swag of the same fabric, the dynamic and convoluted folds of which contrast with the poise and fixity of the Infanta's pose. Lightning strokes of silver thread ignite as the light catches them, revealing a master 'exceptional in his knowledge of fabrics', Velázquez himself. But much of the rest of the portrait – and especially the obtrusive swag of drapery – is stiffer or more haphazard in handling, a kind of caricature of Velázquez's style by a less gifted master.

The artist's son-in-law, Mazo, is shown at work on this, or a very similar, picture in the background of his *Family Portrait* of about 1660. With his back to the viewer and dressed in courtly attire rather than studio garb, he inhabits a spacious high-ceilinged studio in which a nurse is leading an infant to inspect the painter's work. On a table outside sits a female bust before a portrait of Philip IV and lined up in the foreground (in Justi's words) 'are five children dispersed according to age and size just like organ-pipes'. Seated in profile amongst them is their mother and, on the left, two men and a young woman visiting the studio. Above them is an escutcheon depicting a raised arm holding a mace or mallet – in Spanish, a *mazo*, a pun on the artist's name.

Mazo most likely witnessed *Las Meninas* being painted and his own family portrait clearly reflects it in the informally posed figures, deeply recessional studio setting and (not least) portrait of the King on the back wall. In 1661, one year after

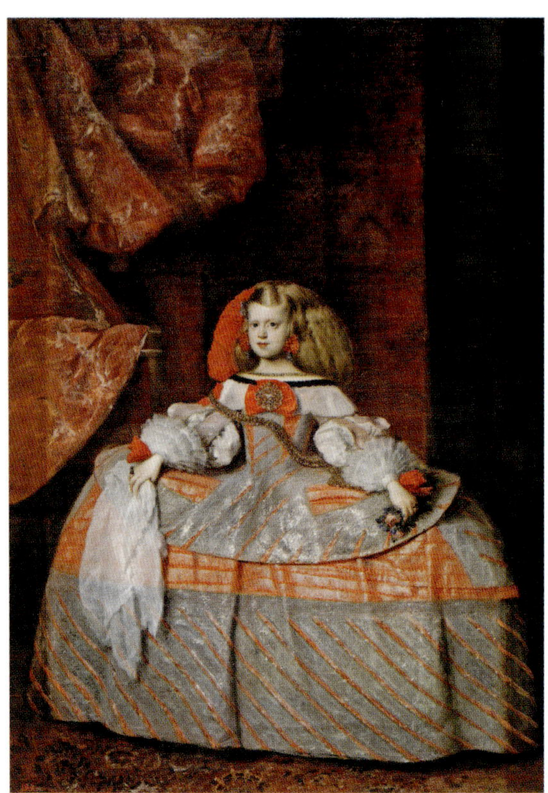

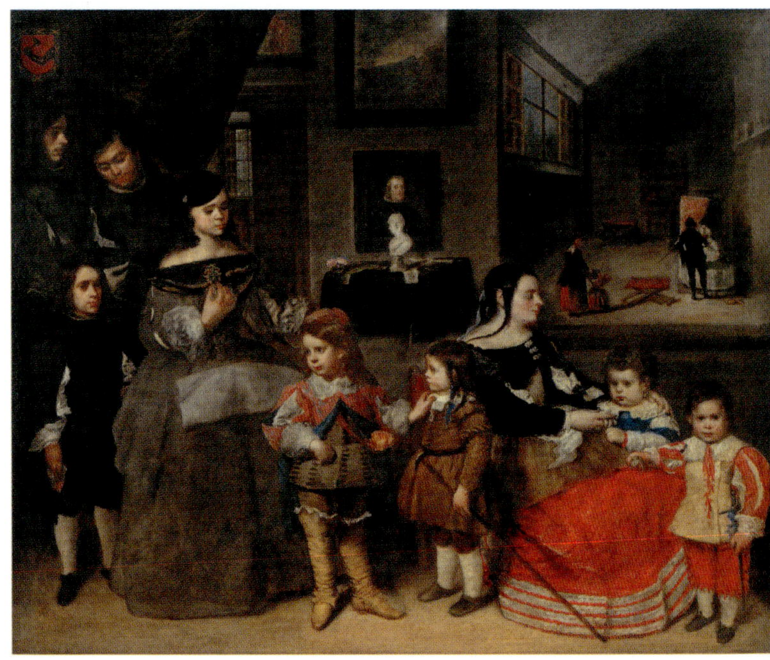

175 LEFT Velázquez/Juan Bautista Martínez del Mazo, *Margarita Theresa, Infanta of Spain*, c. 1660–65
176 BELOW Juan Bautista Martínez del Mazo, *Family of the Painter*, c. 1660

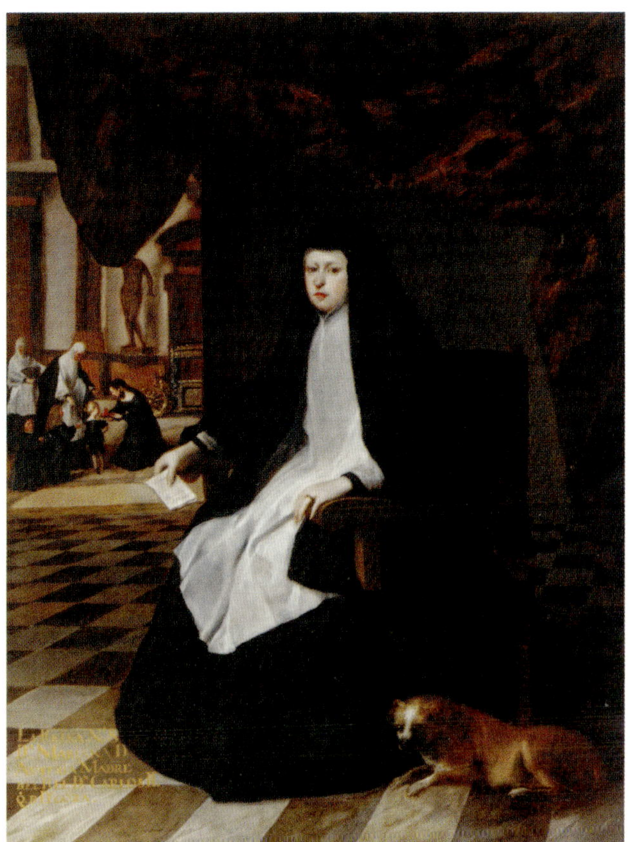

177 Juan Bautista
Martínez del
Mazo, *Queen
Mariana of Spain
in Mourning*, 1666

the death of Velázquez, Mazo was appointed Painter of the
Chamber in his master's place; and in the same year Philip
Prospero died and the degenerate and weak-minded Charles II
was born to Philip IV and Queen Mariana. With the death of the
King himself in 1665, the 4-year-old Charles became king under
the regency of his mother until 1677.

177   Mazo's portrait *Queen Mariana of Spain in Mourning* of
1666 shows her dressed in the habit of a nun, a custom of
noble Spanish widows. She is seated in a room in the south
wing of the Alcázar and in the background, a vignette of little
figures may be seen. It includes two court dwarfs and the
young Charles being guided on leading strings held by a nun.
Here too, there are reminiscences of *Las Meninas*, not least in
the bronze sculpture partly visible in the background which
stands in for Mazo's own copies after Rubens hanging on the
rear wall of *Las Meninas*.

An engaging portrait of a *Child in Ecclesiastical Dress* is widely attributed to Mazo and dated to the last years of his life, *c.* 1660–67. The sitter's identity and the circumstances of the commission are unknown, but what immediately strikes an admirer of Velázquez exploring his legacy is how it combines a veritable anthology of the master's favourite portrait devices and accessories into a single painting. The young boy resting his hand on a table with a vase of flowers recalls the first portrait of the Infanta Margarita, the dog that of her brother Philip Prospero, while the swag of overhanging drapery and landscape view beyond are reminiscent of any number of other Velázquez portraits. But what none of them ever does is combine all these elements together. For Velázquez himself, simplicity always reigned supreme – and less was always more. But minor masters do not always think that way, preferring instead to display all of their wares at once.

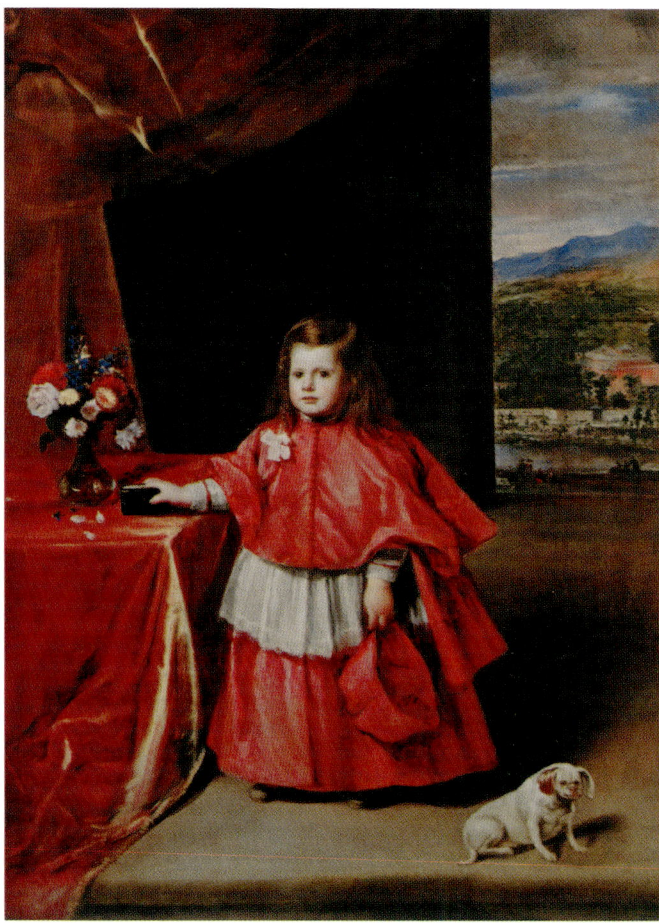

178 Juan Bautista Martínez del Mazo, *A Child in Ecclesiastical Dress, c.* 1660–67

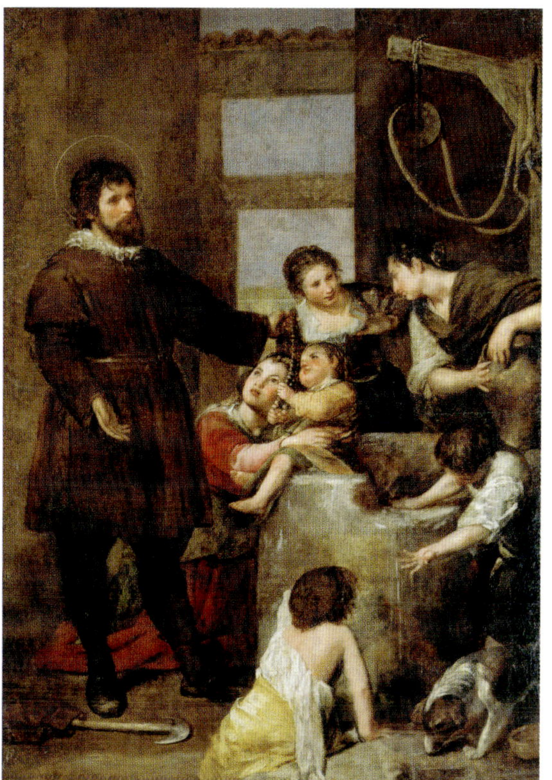

179 Alonso Cano,
*The Miracle of the
Well*, c. 1645–50

For obvious reasons – student, son-in-law and then studio
assistant – Mazo was the most devoted disciple of Velázquez
after the master's death. But other notable Spanish artists
were also touched by his influence, despite the fact that his
paintings were hidden away in the rooms of the Alcázar
Palace where only a privileged few could view them. One of
these was the Granada-born painter, sculptor and architect
Alonso Cano, born in 1601, whose family moved to Seville
in 1614, where he met Velázquez and became his lifelong
friend. In 1638, Cano moved to Madrid, where he renewed this
bond and was deeply influenced by the older master's work,
as seen in his extraordinary painting of *The Miracle of the Well*
of 1645–50, which shows St Isidore miraculously rescuing a
young boy who had fallen into a well. In its broken brushwork,
sonorous colour scheme and informal figure grouping it
reflects his knowledge of Velázquez's daring technique and
of such comparably off-centre compositions as *Balthasar
Carlos at the Riding School*.

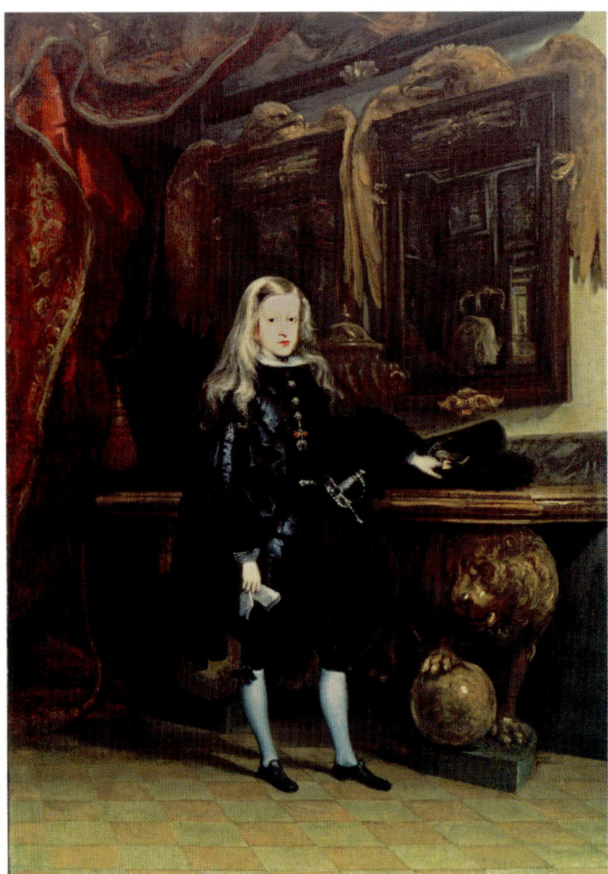

Cano left Madrid for his native Granada in 1652, having
never sought a royal appointment. After the death of Mazo
in 1667, that honour was soon after accorded to Juan Carreño
de Miranda on whom fell the increasingly unenviable task
of painting portraits of the ever more unattractive King.
180   One, of 1671, shows him standing with his hand on a table,
in virtually an identical pose to that painted by Velázquez
in his early full-length portraits of Charles's father. Whereas
those were always set against a plain background, however,
the 20-year-old Charles here poses in the magnificent Hall of
Mirrors in the Alcázar, where the reflections of the pictures
on the walls provide a welcome distraction from the King's
unfortunate appearance.

   Although subsequent royal and aristocratic portraiture in
Spain occasionally still adopted a diluted version of Velázquez's

sober style, it increasingly veered towards the more elegant and courtly manner of Flemish portraiture, especially that of Van Dyck. Claudio Coello was among the most gifted native painters at the end of the century and succeeded Carreño de Miranda as a painter to the King. He excelled in densely filled and theatrical religious paintings that are unashamedly showy. But when he dropped his guard, as in his little *Portrait of Padre Cabanillas*, much of the sincerity, simplicity and directness of Velázquez's comparable portraits (such as those of Cardinal Astalli or Ferdinando Brandani) still shines through, coupled with a greater human warmth reminiscent of Coello's more celebrated contemporary Murillo.

Velázquez's posthumous reputation took a decisive turn with the arrival in Madrid in 1692 of the Neapolitan painter Luca Giordano. Renowned for his remarkable technical facility and speed of working, Giordano was summoned by the King to execute frescoes glorifying the Habsburg dynasty on the Imperial Staircase of the Escorial. But in his ten years in Spain he also painted numerous other frescoes and countless easel paintings for the crown. When he was not engaged with these he was admiring the works of art in the royal collection, above all *Las Meninas*. According to Palomino, 'when Luca Giordano came – in our day – and got to see it, he was asked

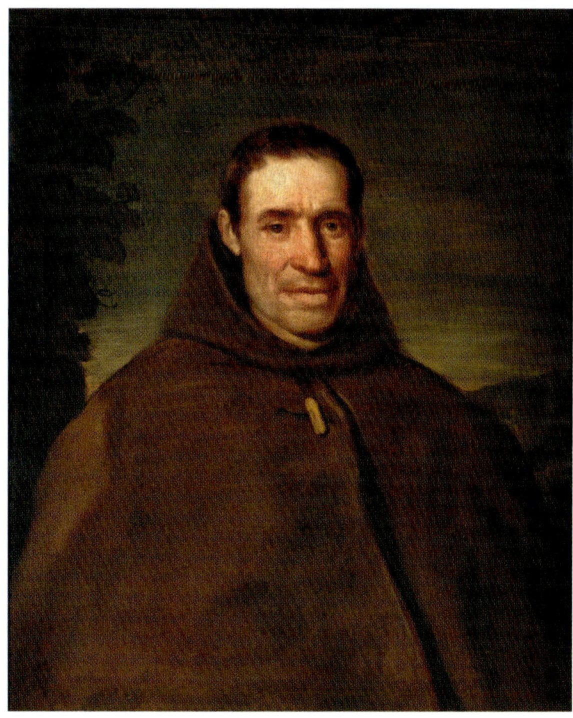

181 Claudio Coello,
*Portrait of Padre
Cabanillas*, 1689–93

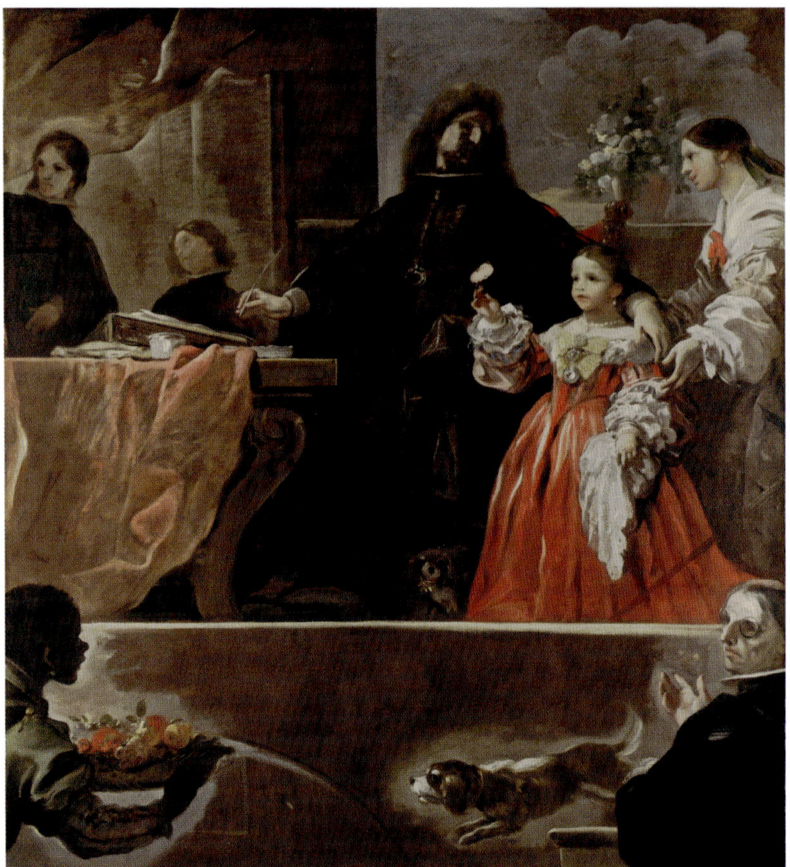

182 Luca Giordano, *A Homage to Velázquez*, c. 1692–95

by King Charles II, who saw him looking thunderstruck, "what do you think of it?". And he said, "Sire, this is the Theology of Painting". By which he meant that just as Theology is the highest among the branches of knowledge, so was that picture the best there was in Painting.'

Giordano's own artistic response to *Las Meninas* is his
182   *Homage to Velázquez*, which probably dates from his first years in Spain. This enigmatic picture, which has never been adequately explained, includes a self-portrait of the artist at the bottom right, directing the viewer towards a scene on an upper tier in which a male figure wearing the cross of the Order of Santiago, who might be Velázquez, is suddenly diverted from writing at his desk by an elegantly dressed young girl being ushered in by a female escort. Other elements in the

picture – the leaping dog, black servant and additional figures around the table – have so far defied identification. The picture is probably best considered a caprice woven out of reminiscences of Velázquez and especially of *Las Meninas*: the painter, the princess, the servants and attendants, the bystanders and not least the dog.

The next important artist to pay tribute to Velázquez was another international visitor to Madrid, the German neo-classical painter Anton Raffael Mengs. Called to the Spanish capital to decorate the newly erected Royal Palace with frescoes in 1761, Mengs had been trained in the idealizing style of the Italian Renaissance masters and the ancients, but in Velázquez's pictures he suddenly confronted an alternative. This was dedicated not to perfecting nature until it approached an ideal but instead to making it look real. Mengs called this the 'natural style'. 'The best models of the natural style', he wrote in 1776, 'are the works of Diego Velázquez, in their knowledge of light and shade, in the play of aerial effect, which are the most important features of this style because they give a reflection of the truth.'

Mengs was equally enthusiastic about works from all phases of Velázquez's career. Of *The Waterseller* he declared that here could be seen 'how Velázquez at first submitted to the imitation of nature itself, studying the essential difference between the lights and shades'. Of *The Surrender of Breda* he admitted that it 'contains all the perfection of which the subject was capable', implying by this that the master had made the very best of having to depict so many heads and bodies lined up in a row. Finally, *Las Meninas* represented for the German artist 'the proof that the perfect imitation of nature is something that equally satisfies all classes of observers'. The truth of this claim was to be proven by the enduring popularity of the works of some of Velázquez's greatest disciples – not least the French Impressionists of the following century.

Neither Mengs nor Giordano before him changed their own styles of painting following their revelations of the art of Velázquez. But their admiration for him signals nothing less than a fundamental shift from the classical norms of much of the great art of the past. For rather than striving to perfect nature in his art, the Spanish master had sought simply to reflect it – a challenge for his eyes as well as his mind.

In 1776, Velázquez's true successor among Spanish painters, Francisco Goya (1746–1828), entered royal employment, designing tapestry cartoons for King Charles III's manufactory. This brought with it access to the King's art collection and his first encounter with Velázquez, which was to prove decisive for

his own art. Goya's first act of homage to his great predecessor
was the creation of thirteen etchings after works by the master.
These were prepared with drawings in red or black chalk, which
are often more accomplished than the resultant etchings,
a technique in which Goya was still little experienced. They
included works after *Las Meninas*, the *Borrachos*, all of the
equestrian portraits and several of the court entertainers,
among them *Don Juan of Austria* and *Don Diego de Acedo or
'El Primo'*. Although the artistic significance of these works
may be marginal in the context of Goya's later career both as a
draughtsman and etcher, their historical significance cannot
be overestimated in regard to the dissemination of Velázquez's
art. Without them, for instance, an artist like Manet would have
been unaware of the *Borrachos* until his trip to Spain in 1865.

In addtion to producing these etchings, Goya made
four more red chalk drawings after works by the master,
including one of *The Waterseller*, and three painted copies
of *Aesop*, *Menippus* and *Innocent X*. Having partly served his
apprenticeship in dialogue with Velázquez, he could then
proceed to apply the lessons learned to his own art.

Following his appointment as painter to the King in 1786,
Goya advanced in stages until he became principal painter
to Charles IV in 1799. One year later he received his most
prestigious royal commission, to paint the entire royal family.
Inevitably, he looked back to the most celebrated of such
pictures to precede him, *Las Meninas*. Setting Queen Maria
Luisa in the centre of the group in a pose virtually identical to
that of the Infanta Margarita, he then placed himself behind
the easel at the extreme left, exactly as Velázquez had done.
Paintings adorn the back wall, in emulation of the *Meninas*,

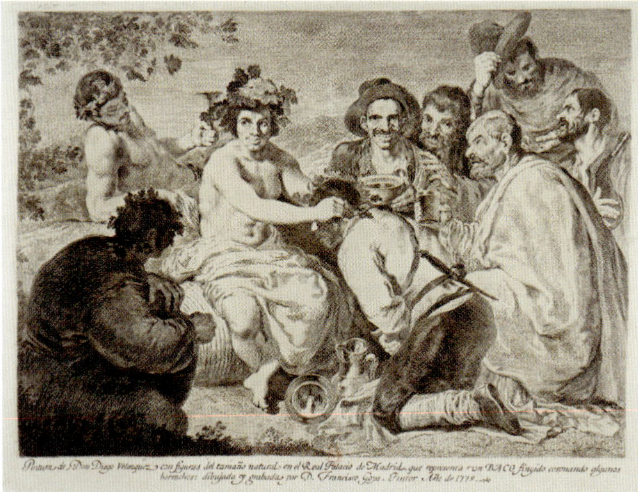

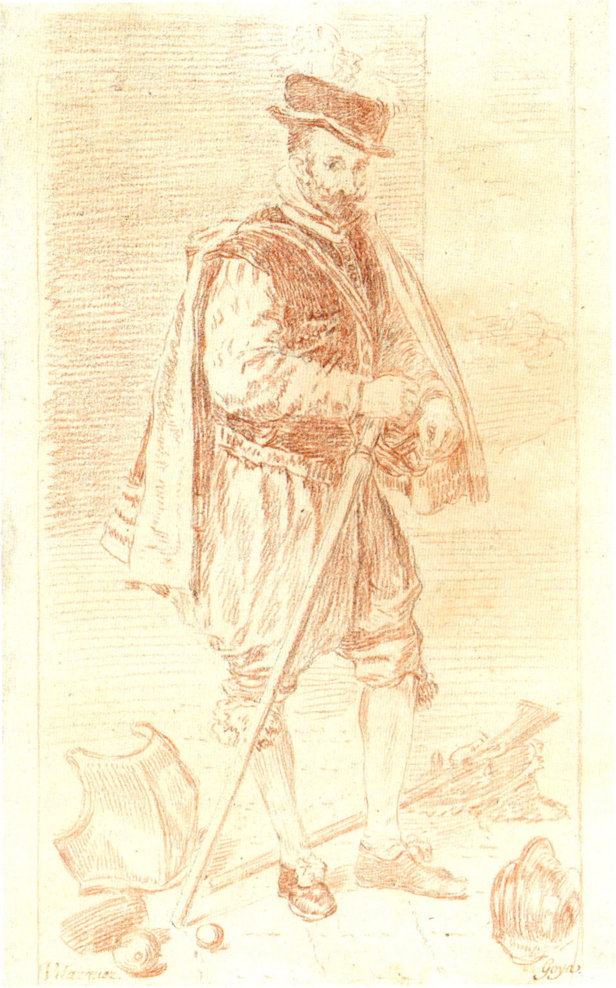

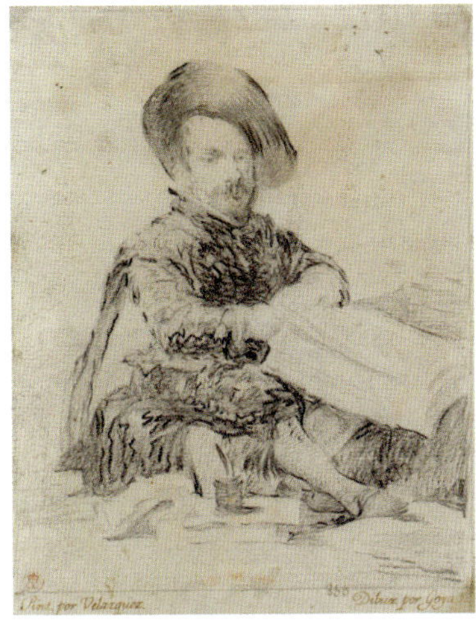

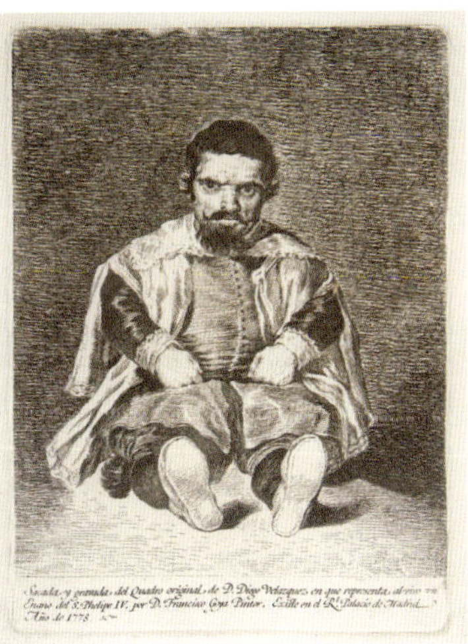

183 OPPOSITE Francisco Goya, etching after Velázquez, *Los Borrachos*, 1778
184 ABOVE LEFT Francisco Goya, drawing after *Don Juan of Austria*, 1778
185 TOP RIGHT Francisco Goya, drawing after Velázquez, *Portrait of Don Diego de Acedo, called 'El Primo'*, 1778
186 ABOVE RIGHT Francisco Goya, etching after Velázquez, *Portrait of Don Sebastián de Morra*, 1778

After Velázquez

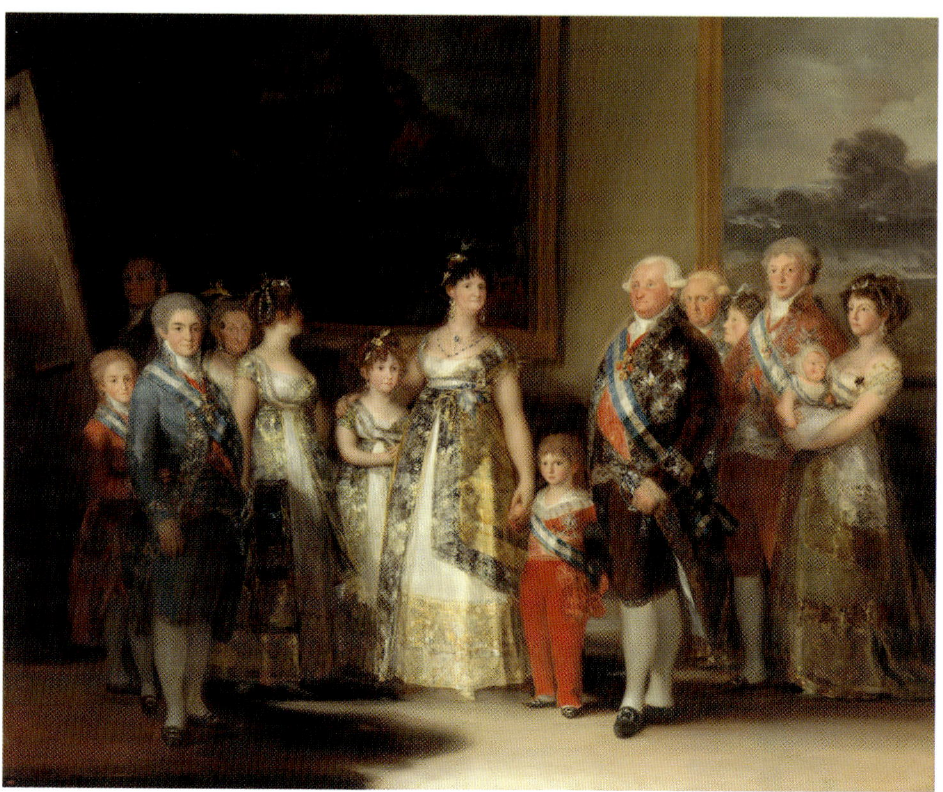

187 Francisco Goya, *Charles IV of Spain and his Family*, 1800

but the space is much shallower and the figures dominate the setting so that they effectively become all that the picture is about. Moreover, they are lined up in a row across the canvas with virtually no interaction between them. Velázquez himself confronted and increasingly overcame this difficulty from the *Borrachos* to *The Surrender of Breda* and eventually *Las Meninas* so that the picture moved away from being a row of faces and bodies until it became more of a dialogue between them – a dramatic encounter rather than a line-up of heads. But where Goya shows his indebtedness to Velázquez is in the scintillating brushwork throughout, not as daring or abbreviated as that of his seventeenth-century predecessor but striving its best to bring the royal family to life.

Goya's artistic isolation and fierce creative independence led him to retreat ever more in his later years into a world of his own private imagination peopled by demons and witches and images of unbearable carnage and cruelty. But in his

output as a portraitist at least he never entirely lost sight of
the achievement of his great predecessor and countryman,
Velázquez. This may even have haunted him in his daily
encounters with the blind singer and musician, Tio Paquete,
begging on the streets of Madrid, who became the subject of
one of his last portraits. Focusing on the coarsened features
and leering grin of this vagrant minstrel, Goya confronts
them unflinchingly. The result may be raw and unnerving,
but it is also utterly sincere. Had Goya confronted anything like
this in art before? He had, in Velázquez's portrait of the court
jester, Calabazas.

On 19 November 1819, during the reign of Ferdinand VII and
his second wife, Isabella de Braganza, the Royal Art Museum
was opened in Madrid. The myriad masterpieces of the
Spanish royal collection were suddenly available to the wider
world. Although Spanish art was already somewhat familiar to
artists and art lovers outside of Spain through engravings and
paintings acquired or pillaged from the country during the
Peninsular War, the creation of a public gallery that displayed
its full range and richness marked a decisive turning point
in the European artistic tradition. In contrast to the Italian,
French or Flemish schools of painting, which owed so much to
the classical art of the ancients, here was an alternative fount
of inspiration: an art rooted in the study and imitation of raw
nature. In the age of Constable and Corot and in the very year
of Courbet's birth, the creation of what would eventually be
known as the Prado Museum could not have been better timed.
For in its galleries had been planted many of the seeds of the
art of the future.

One of the first foreign artists to make the arduous journey
across the Pyrenees to visit the new museum was the Scottish
regency master Sir David Wilkie, a specialist in portraiture
and genre painting. He arrived in the Spanish capital in
October 1827 and remained there for six months, specifically
to study Titian and Velázquez, masters of the fluid and
painterly handling and rich colourism that was increasingly
becoming fashionable in British painting, especially that of Sir
Thomas Lawrence. Although Wilkie's art itself veered towards
historical Spanish subject matter and a freer application of
paint following his return to Britain, in common with many
of his contemporaries he was only able to assimilate the most
superficial aspects of Velázquez's style. But he was among the
earliest non-Spanish artists to acknowledge their significance.
In a letter to Lady Beaumont of 10 January 1828, he confessed
that Velázquez was 'the painter that every British artist must
in his heart admire. His art is the essence of painting as

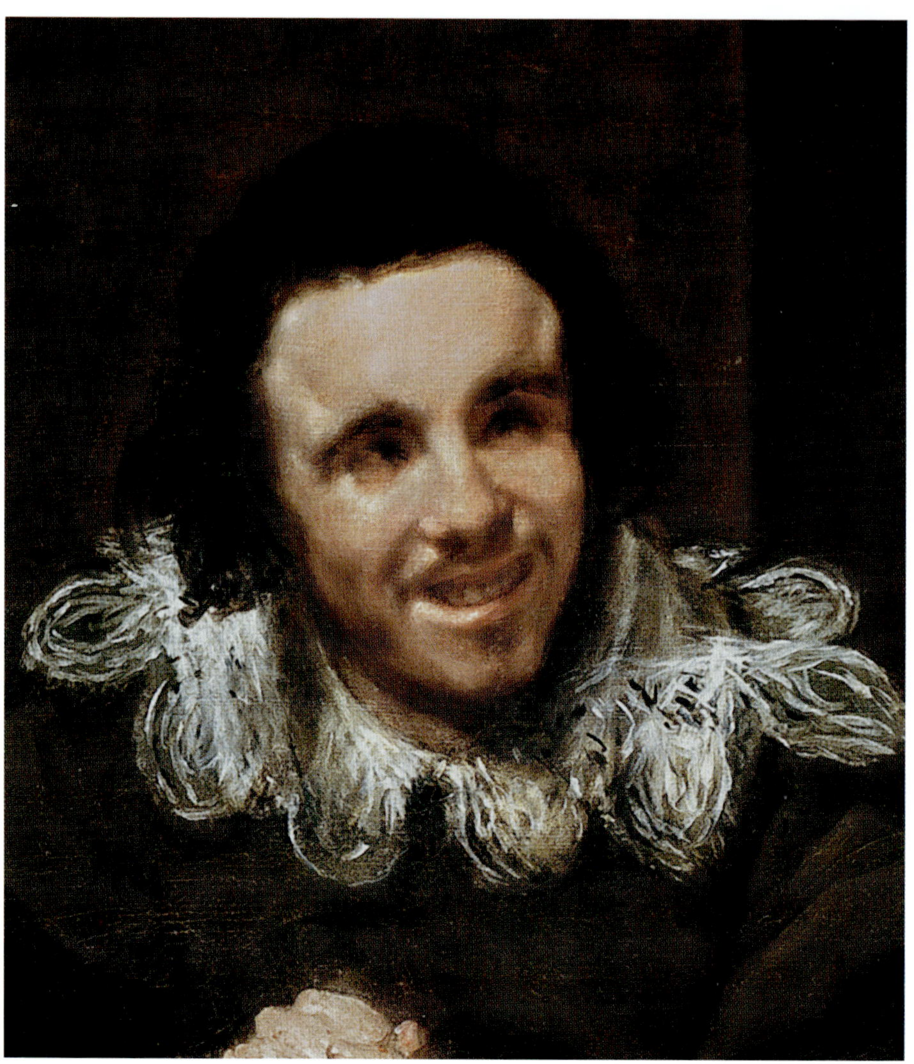

188 ABOVE *The Jester Calabazas*, 1635–39, detail
189 OPPOSITE Francisco Goya, *Tío Paquete*, c. 1819–20

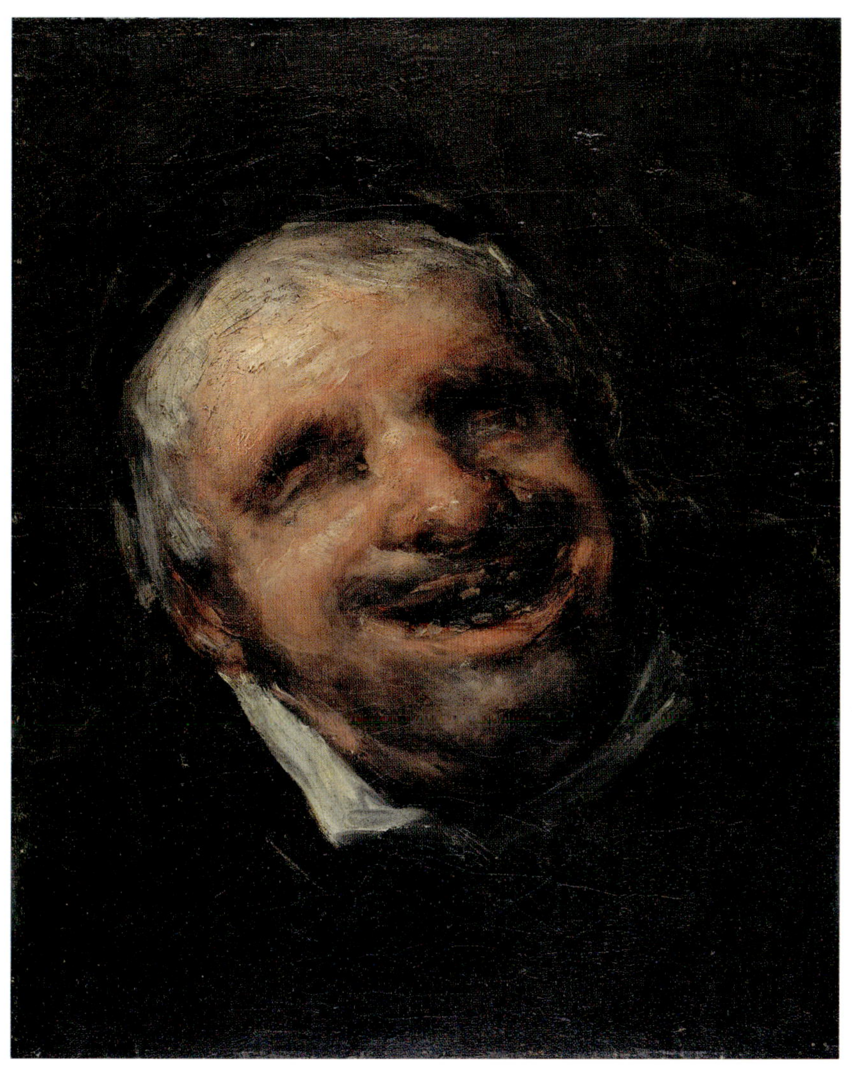

After Velázquez 237

opposed to sculpture, gives objects not as they are but as they appear – the aim of British art as distinguished from the art that prevails now all over the continent.' But unbeknown to Wilkie, that, too, was undergoing a similar change of direction.

While Wilkie was absorbing the lessons of Spanish art at its source, the greatest French romantic painter, Eugène Delacroix, was doing so at home. Among Delacroix's many copies after the Old Masters from his early years is one after a Velázquez portrait of Charles II which he made in 1824. (Although attributed to the Spanish master in Delacroix's day, it is in fact a workshop replica of Carreño de Miranda's portrait of Charles II.) 'Saw the Velázquez and got permission to copy it,' wrote the French artist in his diary on 10 April 1824. 'I am carried away with it completely. It has what I have been looking for so long – an impasto that is firm and yet blended. What I must chiefly remember are the hands. It seems to me that by combining this style of painting with firm and bold contours, one should be able to make some small pictures easily.'

Later in the same diary entry, Delacroix declared: 'A strange thing, and a very beautiful one, would be joining Michelangelo's style to that of Velázquez.' What he was seeking here was to reconcile the seemingly opposing forces of line and colour in painting. How can a form be defined and decorated at the same time – and by the same means? Delacroix never resolved this issue in relation to Velázquez's art, for he never visited Spain to witness its full force. Had he done so, he would have confronted an art that both coloured and contoured with the stroke of a brush.

When Delacroix made his copy after Carreño's *Charles II* in the early 1820s, knowledge and appreciation of Spanish art in France was still in its infancy, spurred principally by the small number of paintings of that school in the nation's collections and by prints after other works by its artists, among them those by Goya after Velázquez and (more importantly) Goya's own original etchings and aquatints. But this all changed dramatically in 1838 with the opening of the Musée espagnol in Paris under Louis Philippe. This consisted of 406 works by Spanish artists of all periods and schools, including among them 31 attributed to Velázquez and his school and 10 to those by Murillo. The Civil War in Spain and the dissolution of its convents and monasteries occasioned this mass exodus of works, which included Velázquez's *Adoration of the Magi, St Paul and St Anthony Abbot* and numerous court portraits. The exhibition closed ten years later with the coming of the 1848 revolution in France and its contents were dispersed and sold. But by this time the seeds of Hispanomania had been well

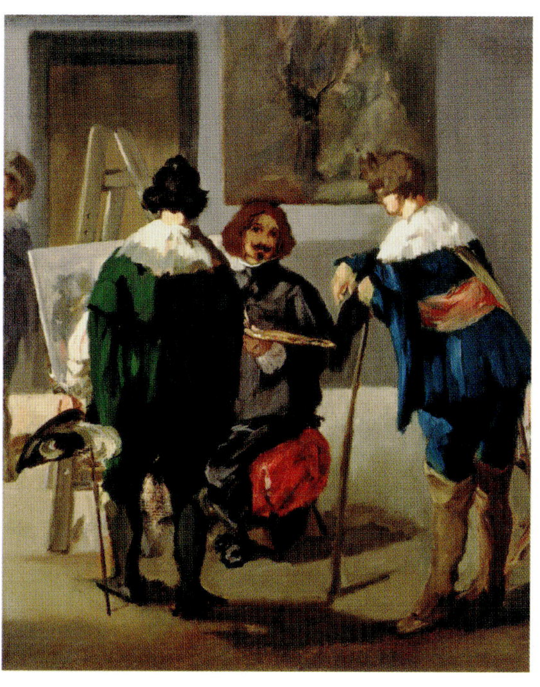

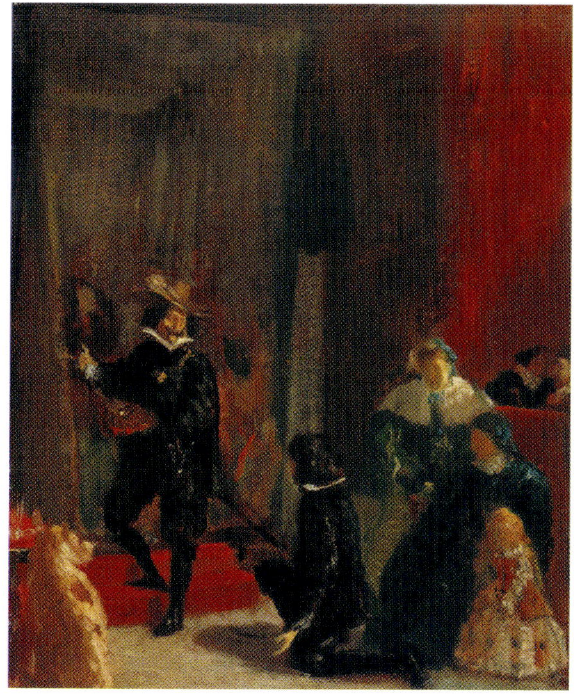

After Velázquez

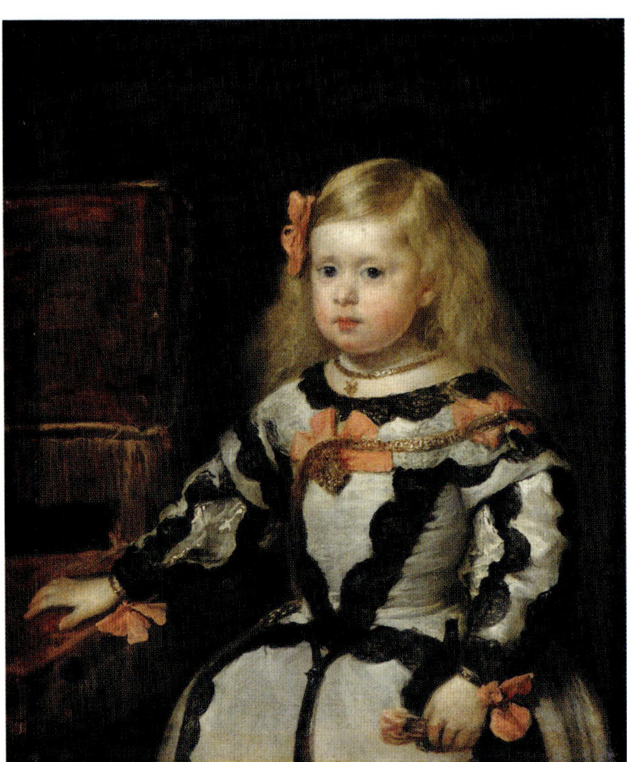

192 LEFT Workshop of Velázquez, *Infanta Margarita, c.* 1655
193 BELOW Workshop of Velázquez, *Thirteen Gentlemen, c.* 1645–50

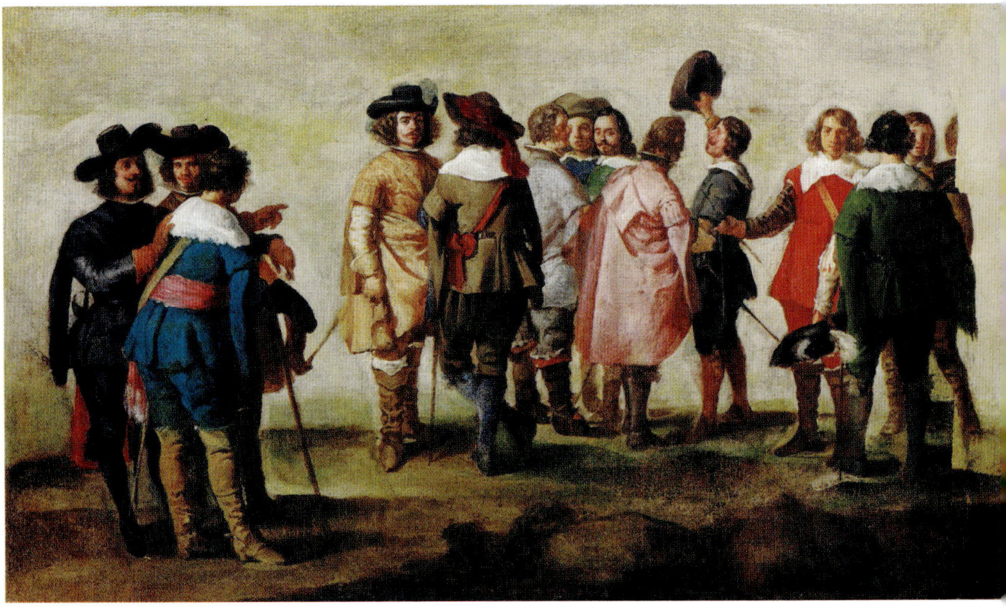

established in France, where its greatest admirers included
Balzac, Flaubert and Prosper Mérimée, the author of *Carmen*.

Two promising young artists also joined these ranks with
small private paintings celebrating Velázquez. Edgar Degas
executed a *Homage to Velázquez* in 1857–58 and Edouard Manet
a *Spanish Studio Scene (Velázquez Painting)* in 1859–60, along
with a painted copy of the Louvre's most celebrated 'Velázquez',
a portrait of the *Infanta Margarita*. With her name stencilled
in French at the top, this is only a workshop picture and one
of a handful of questionable works by the artist in the French
national collection. For the country's growing galaxy of major
painters, however, these were the only means of acquainting
themselves with the Spanish master's art unless they journeyed
to Spain.

Although Degas's interest in Velázquez appears to have been
short-lived, that of Manet lasted and deepened. It also predated
his *Studio Scene.* Around 1855 Manet made a copy of a painting
of *Thirteen Gentlemen* in the Louvre, which was then attributed
to Velázquez and bears obvious similarities to the small-scale
figures in animated conversation in the foreground of the *Tela
Real*, but is closer to Mazo in style. About five years later, Manet
placed this picture on Velázquez's easel in his painted homage
to the master at work, the aforementioned *Spanish Studio Scene.*
In the latter, two well-dressed connoisseurs of painting visit
the artist's studio to admire the picture on which he is putting
the finishing touches. Seated and turning to them in a pose
obviously inspired by his self-portrait in *Las Meninas*, Velázquez
greets his guests in a picture that itself marks a minor advance
in his acceptance into the canon of Western art. Scenes from the
lives of the great artists of the past figure prominently in the art
of the early nineteenth century, with both Ingres and Delacroix
contributing to them. But their subjects were invariably the
great masters of the Italian Renaissance – Masaccio, Leonardo,
Raphael, Michelangelo and Titian. Manet's *Spanish Studio* would
appear to be the first picture to elevate the greatest Spanish
painter into this company. Long overdue, this was where he
ultimately belonged, and would remain.

In 1862 Manet painted a large canvas of a motley assemblage
of dispossessed dwellers of the Petite Pologne district of Paris,
which had recently been destroyed in Baron Haussmann's
campaign to modernize the French capital. Entitled *The Old
Musician*, it is another homage to Velázquez, loosely modelled
on the *Borrachos*, which Manet presumably knew through
Goya's etching after the picture. Gathered around a bearded
gypsy violinist are a young girl with a baby in her arms, two
small boys, an absinthe drinker wearing a hat and an itinerant

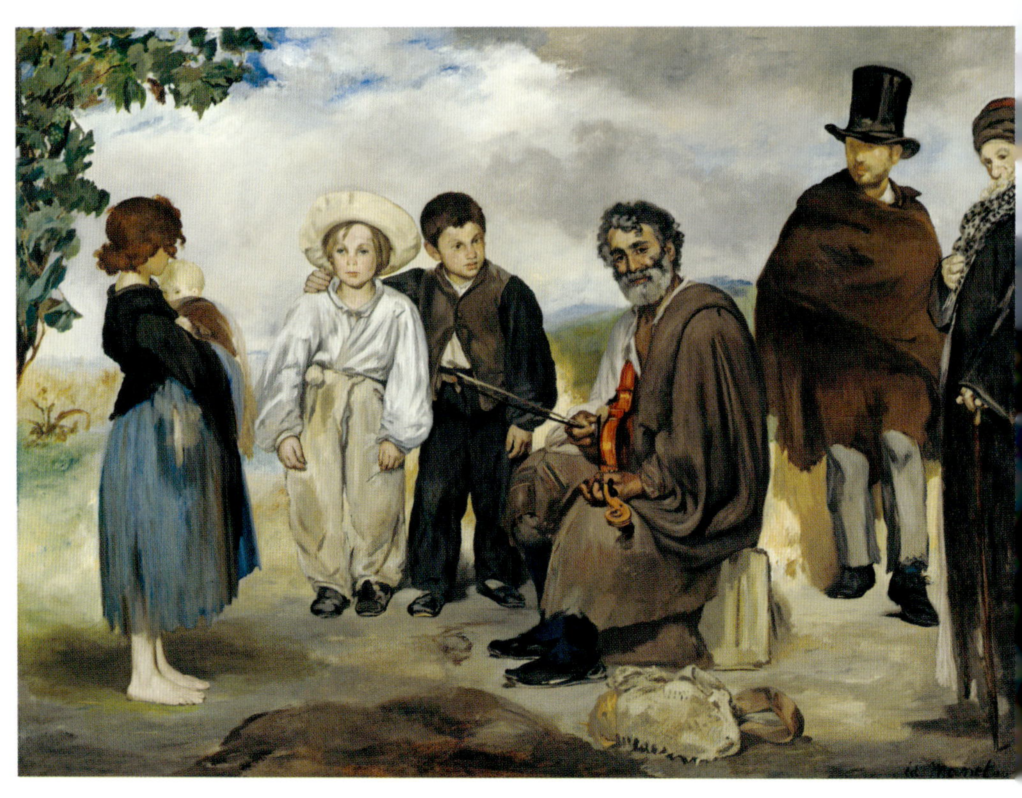

194 Edouard Manet, *The Old Musician*, 1862

beggar entering the picture at the right. All are clearly based on life studies and connected more by their proximity to one another than by any obvious interaction between them. In addition to the veracity of the individual likenesses, it is this sense of disengagement from one another that harks back to Velázquez's masterpiece, where individual identity likewise takes precedence over that of the group.

As a distant devotee of Velázquez's art, with very little of the Spanish master to study in the Louvre, Manet became the first major foreign artist to journey to Spain, in August 1865, visiting Burgos, Valladolid and Toledo before spending a week in Madrid. There he met his match, writing to his friend and fellow painter Henri Fantin-Latour from his hotel room in Madrid:

'What a joy it would have been for you to see Velázquez, which for him alone is worth the trip. The painters of every school who surround him in the museum of Madrid, and who are all very well represented, seem completely like fakes. He is the painter of painters, he has astonished me, he has ravished me. He is the supreme master... The most extraordinary piece in this splendid oeuvre and possibly the most extraordinary piece of painting that has ever been done is the picture described in the catalogue as a portrait of a famous actor at the time of Philip IV: the background disappears, there's nothing but air surrounding the fellow, who is all in black and appears alive.'

When he returned to Paris in September, Manet's immediate response to Velázquez's *Pablo de Valladolid* was *The Tragic Actor (Rouvière as Hamlet)*, which depicts this great Parisian actor playing Shakespeare's legendary hero in the season of 1846–47 but remained unfinished when Rouvière himself died in October 1865. The similarities are obvious – the black palette, splayed stance and shadowed legs upon the floor – but so, too, are the differences. Manet's blacks are broken up by stripes of greyish-white; his background darkens as it recedes, allowing Rouvière to stand back rather than leap out; and the abandoned sword on the ground introduces a spatial recession where Velázquez has no need of one. Finally, it is for readers themselves to decide which master is the more accomplished at painting air.

Manet's trip to Spain constituted a watershed in the history of Western art, resulting as it did in the almost immediate dissemination of Velázquez's subjects and style north of the Pyrenees. One year later, in 1866, another even more unknown master from the opposite end of Europe was rediscovered whose art bore much in common with that of the Spanish master. That artist was Johannes Vermeer (1632–75), the subject of a lengthy article published in that year by Théophile Thore-Bürger that effectively rescued this genre painter from Delft from two centuries of obscurity and recognized in him another of the greatest masters of European art. Intriguingly, Thore-Bürger was also an admirer of both Velázquez and Frans Hals and wrote extensively on them in these same years, thus paying tribute to these three precursors of Impressionism on the eve of the movement's emergence in France.

On the face of it there is little to link Velázquez and Vermeer. After all, one worked for a king and his court and the other for the open market. One painted exalted subjects and sitters and the other ordinary people. But both remained dedicated to an art based on life – and vision – rather than antiquity, the Renaissance or the ideal. Little wonder that their reputations soared simultaneously in the middle of the nineteenth century, when art was increasingly focused on the cult of the real.

Velázquez's unfinished *Needlewoman* of about 1640 and Vermeer's *Lacemaker* of the 1660s both depict anonymous women doing everyday things. Their heads bent and their eyes focused upon their needlework, both would appear to have been painted from life and seem oblivious of the artist's presence before them. He in turn captures them as though in a fleeting glance. No bounding lines describe their facial features or their separate strands of hair; their heads are seen through a gentle haze and their hands and wrists barely defined. Fingers resemble pincers – no anatomical textbook would have use for them. All that is shown is how they appear and not how they are. And the costumes, cushions and fabrics around them are there to be seen but not felt. This is an art of pure visuality by two artists who paint only what meets the eye and remain seemingly indifferent to the intrinsic significance of what they see. Hence its mysterious attraction for the viewer, for to gaze upon their pictures permits us, too, to recapture our originally innocent vision.

Velázquez's *Needlewoman* poses an additional challenge for the eye that was to become a central concern of many nineteenth-century painters. This is the matter of making subtle distinctions between closely related hues – in other words, tonal painting. Viewed as a whole, the picture may be seen as a harmony in browns, greys, creams and whites enlivened by accents of red. This is not the only work by the artist to be dominated by a colour chord, as we have seen. *Philip IV in Brown and Silver* may be Velázquez's sole painting

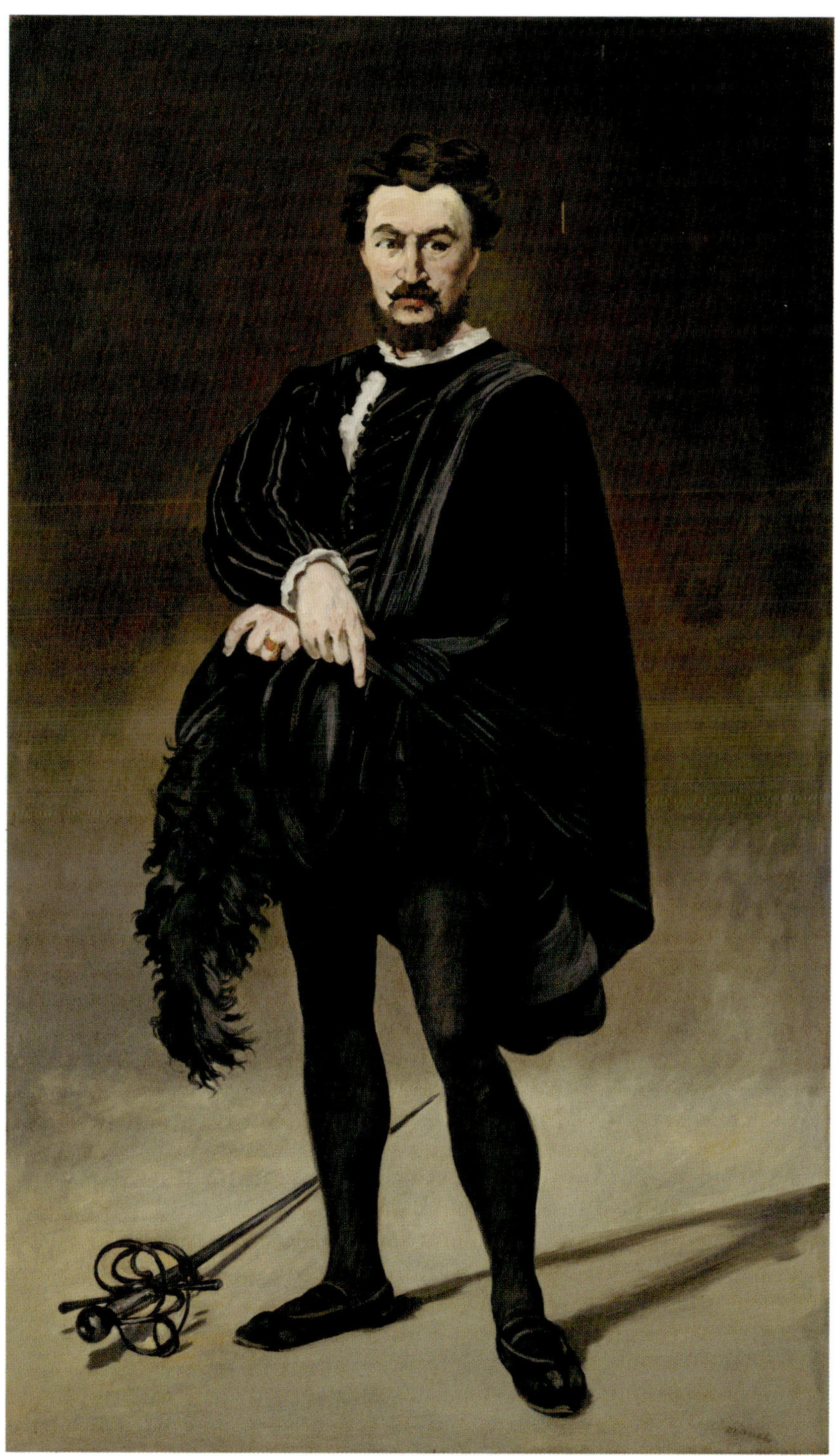

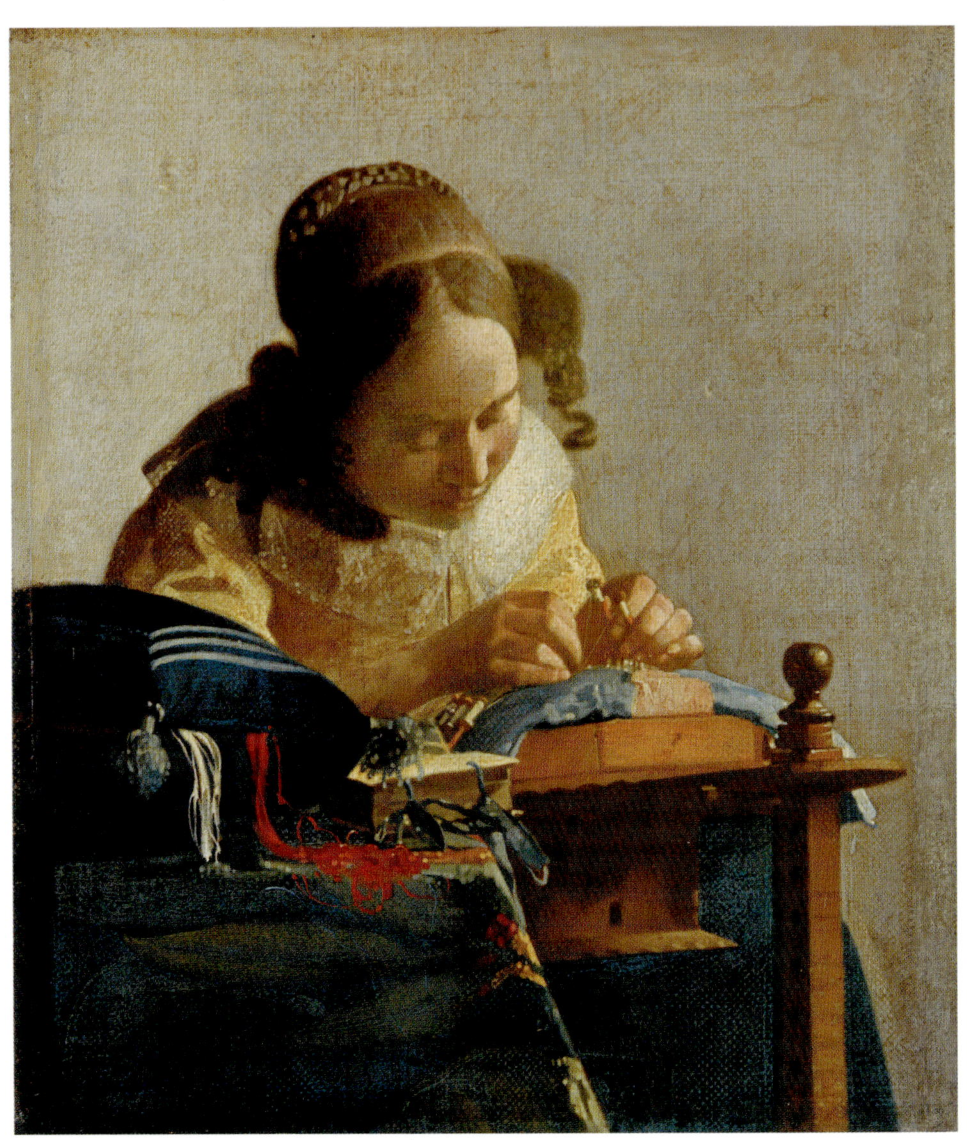

196 ABOVE Johannes Vermeer, *The Lacemaker*, c. 1660
197 OPPOSITE *The Needlewoman*, c. 1640

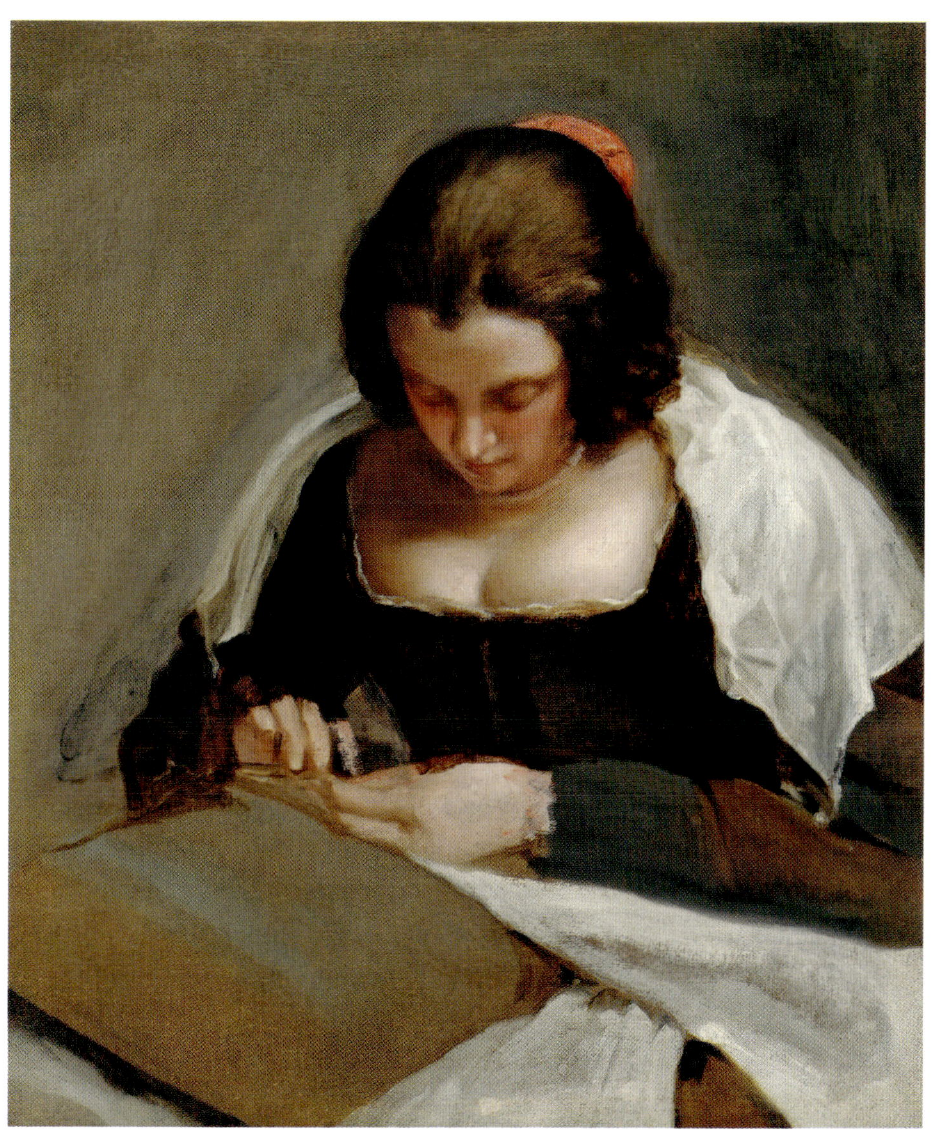

to admit to this in its title, but countless others have an equally good claim, and among their most distinguished successors are works like Manet's *Rouvière as Hamlet* and James McNeill Whistler's *Arrangement in Grey and Black, No. 2: Portrait of Thomas Carlyle.*

Whistler was a devotee and latter-day disciple of Velázquez's art throughout his career, despite the fact that he never realized his ambition to visit Spain, and his portrait of the historian and philosopher Carlyle bears witness to this. Pervaded by rectangular lines and nuanced tones of grey and black, it relegates the sitter to a motif in an arrangement dominated by aesthetic considerations, telling us less about Carlyle than it does about the harmony attainable in art. The parallels with Velázquez's portraits of the Infanta Margarita immediately come to mind, and for Whistler '[those] Infantas, clad in inaesthetic hoops, [were], as works of Art, of the same quality as the Elgin marbles'.

One of Whistler's own infantas was Miss Cicely Alexander, the 8-year-old daughter of a London banker and collector, who became the subject of one of the most exquisite portraits of his career in 1872–74. Entitled *Harmony in Grey and Green: Miss Cicely Alexander*, it depicts the sitter artfully posed against a grey wall subdivided by a brown dado and vertical strip and framed by a bunch of daisies on the right and two fluttering butterflies on the left. Between them stands Cicely dressed in white and greenish-grey muslin and holding her hat. Its rounded shape and feather initiate a sequence of curves that define her entire figure, from her hemline to her sleeve, and from her apron to the fall of her hair. A perfectionist's quest for absolute harmony dominates the whole and led the poor young girl to be subjected to more than seventy sittings. But the result is an undoubted masterpiece and one of Whistler's most overt homages to Velázquez in its ravishing colour harmony and pitch-perfect composition.

The last half of the nineteenth century and the early years of the twentieth witnessed the ascendancy of Velázquez's reputation, especially in Britain, where he enjoyed cult status amongst the most avant-garde artists and critics, including Whistler. It was during those years that the National Gallery acquired or was bequeathed five paintings by the master, including *The Rokeby Venus*, and that pictorial tributes to his art were paid by some of the most unlikely painters. One such was Sir John Everett Millais, a founding member of the Pre-Raphaelite Brotherhood, who in 1868 submitted as his diploma

piece to the Royal Academy of Arts *A Souvenir of Velázquez*. It depicts a young girl dressed in seventeenth-century Spanish

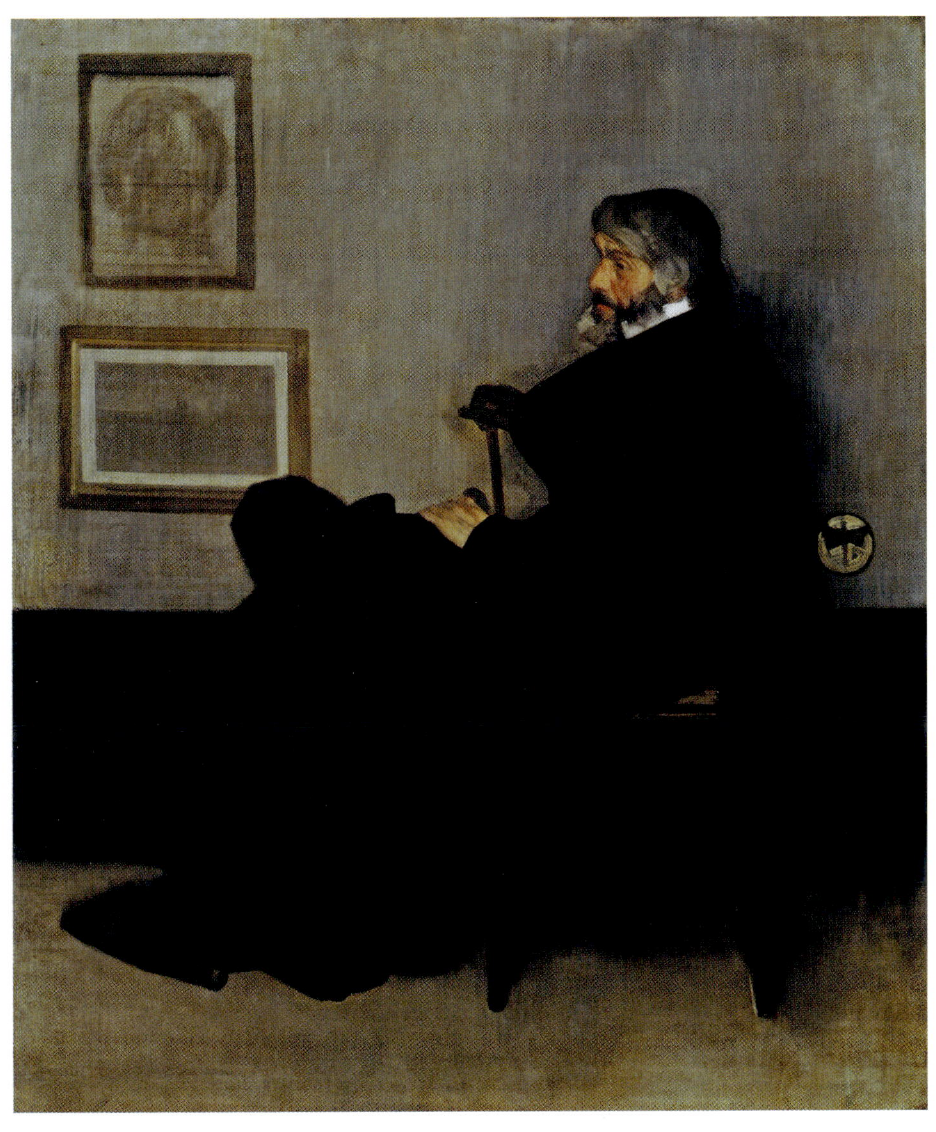

198 James McNeill Whistler, *Arrangement in Grey and Black, No. 2: Portrait of Thomas Carlyle*, 1872–73

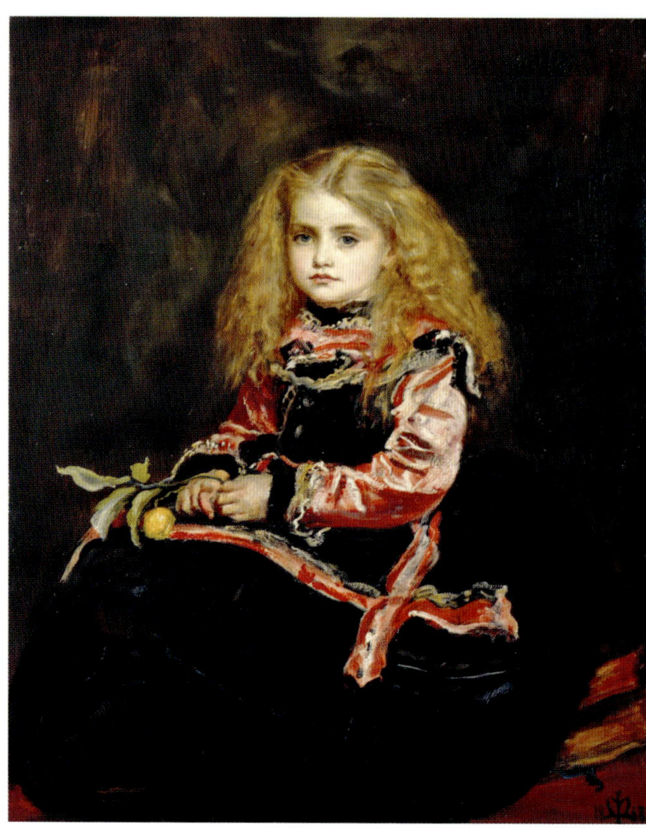

costume, seated and holding a branch of an orange tree.
Although the painting of the costume is vaguely reminiscent of
the Spanish master, the picture is utterly Victorian in mood, not
least because the sitter's expression in no way emulates that of
Velázquez's enchanting infantas. Rather than looking beguiling
as they do, Millais's heroine simply looks blank and bored.

Inevitably even more popular than Velázquez's infantas
was *Las Meninas* itself, regardless of how many of its admirers
actually made the arduous journey to Madrid to view the
original. Moreover, much of the picture's reputation rested not
on its technical wizardry but, rather, on the extent to which it
had anticipated that miracle of nineteenth-century invention:
the photograph. The seemingly impromptu arrangement of
the figures, and the sense that it was not simply a portrait of
a group of people but also a portrait of a room, added to its
veracity, while the availability of photographs of the picture
made familiarity with it ever easier. Whistler himself took its

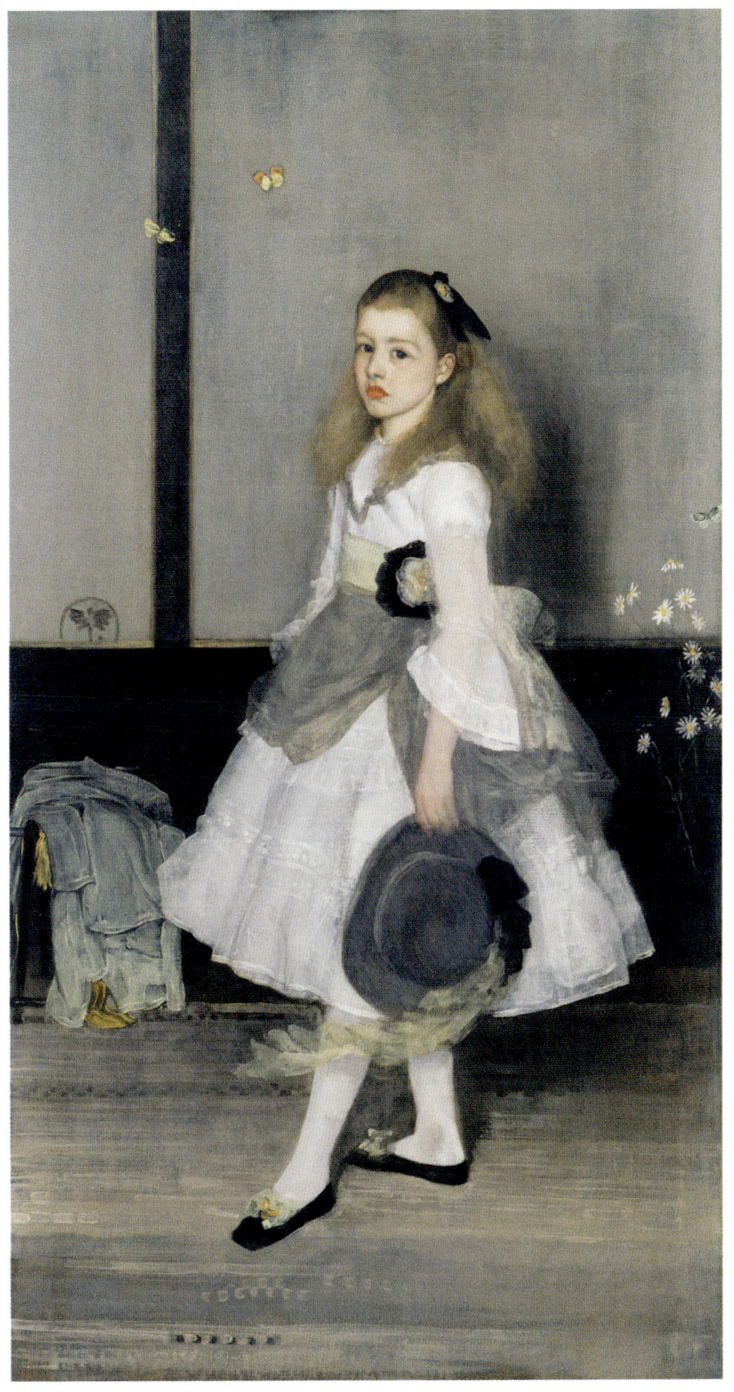

After Velázquez

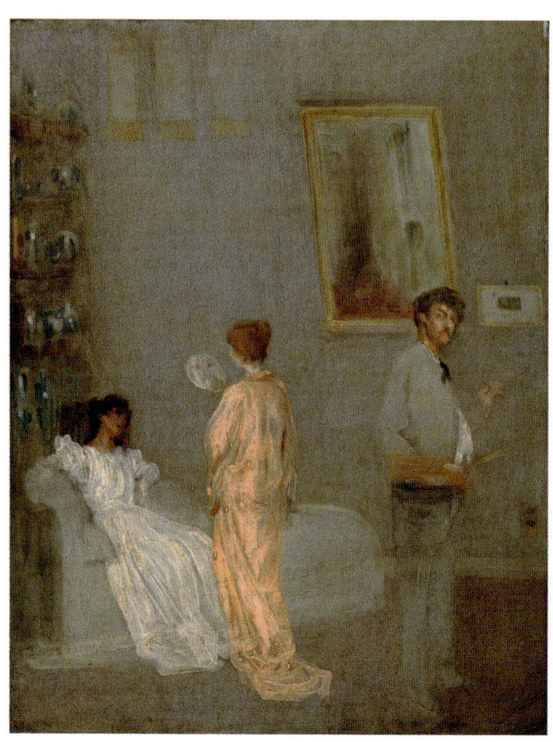

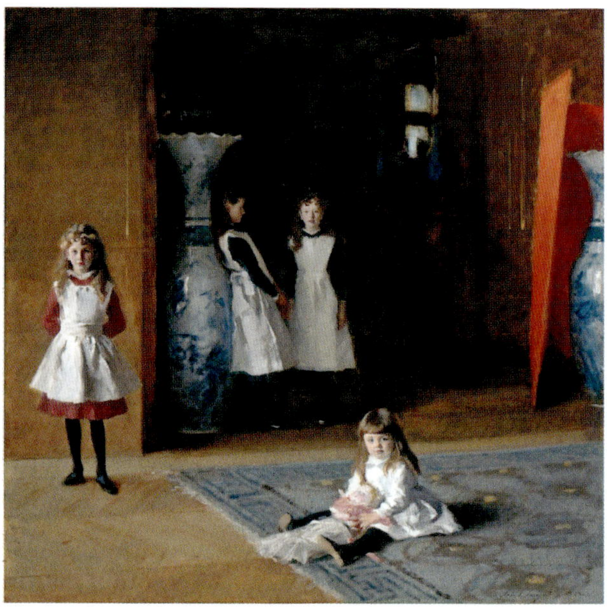

201 TOP James McNeill Whistler, *The Artist in his Studio*, 1865–66
202 ABOVE John Singer Sargent, *The Daughters of Edward Darley Boit*, 1882
203 OPPOSITE Sir John Lavery, *The Royal Family at Buckingham Palace*, 1913

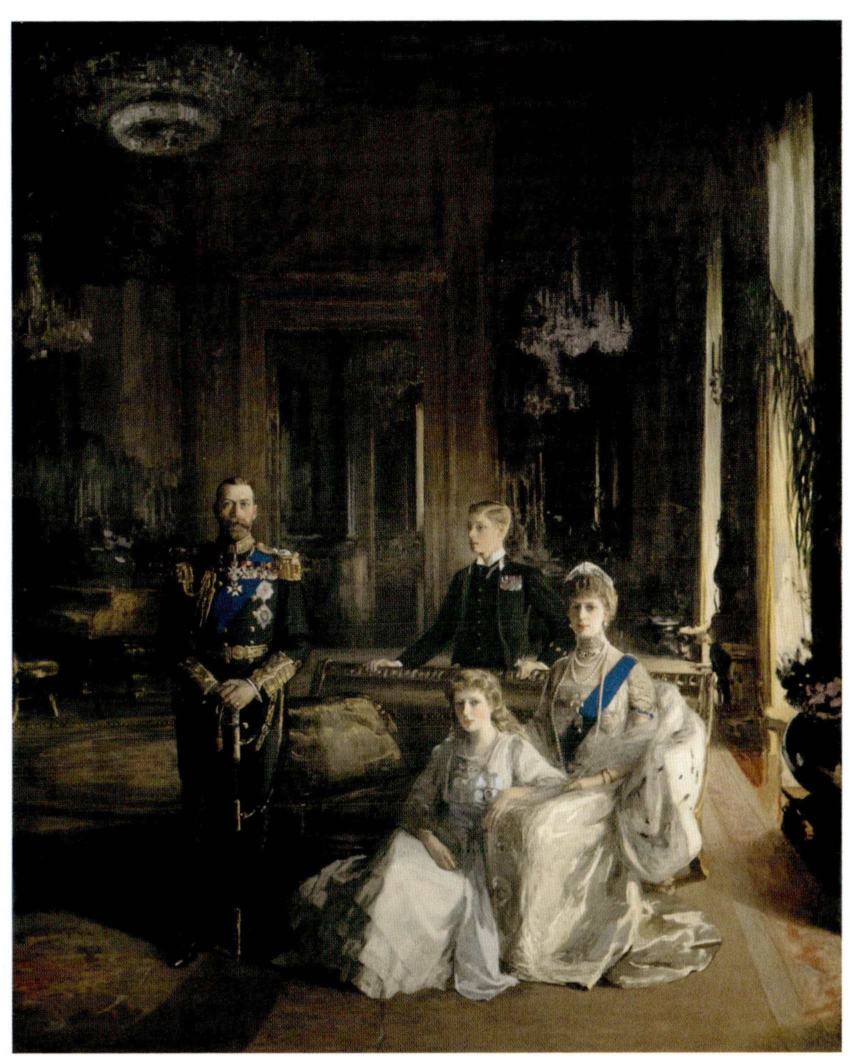

unrehearsed quality as inspiration for his *The Artist in his Studio* of 1865–66, although his narcissistic streak inevitably led him to switch places with the Velázquez of *Las Meninas* and position himself in the front of the room. The American virtuoso John Singer Sargent aped it even more in *The Daughters of Edward Darley Boit* of 1882, where the setting enjoys equal status with the sitters, who appear almost randomly positioned within it. Eventually, even the British royal family were subjected to this treatment in Sir John Lavery's portrait of them of 1913. The artist omitted his self-portrait and further departed from *Las Meninas* in subjecting King George V and his family to strictly formal poses set in a congestedly furnished interior. The spare and resonant space of Velázquez's original is, alas, sorely missed.

When Lavery executed this royal portrait, Cubism and its stylistic offspring represented the most avant-garde movement in European painting, and their leanings towards abstraction could hardly have been further from the naturalism of Velázquez. Instead, this generation rediscovered and praised the achievements of his great predecessor and diametric opposite among Spanish painters, El Greco. More than forty years later, however, one of the pioneers of Cubism – Picasso – returned to Velázquez to paint forty-four variations on *Las Meninas*, all between August and December 1957. Some of these encompass the entire picture, but the majority are after details from it, especially the Infanta herself, and while many are in colour, others are in grisaille.

The first of these, dated 17 August 1957, was left unfinished and is the largest of the series. It metamorphoses the entire ensemble into a medley of shapes, sizes and styles in monochrome. The Infanta is moved slightly off centre and her dress reduced to a flat, rectangular plane. The boy prodding the dog is left as a mere outline drawing and the mastiff of the original is replaced by Picasso's own dachshund, Lump. The chaperones become identical twins and the room a jigsaw of rods, rectangles and planes in which the artist himself becomes a towering figure who nearly touches the ceiling. His body is described in a rising column of Cubist shapes and his head made up of two profiles gazing at each other. He also now wields two palettes and formally is not only the tallest but also the most intricately constructed figure in the painting. This reminds us that one of the abiding attractions of *Las Meninas* for later artists was its inclusion of the painter himself in the picture, immortalizing with his brush the group around him. In short, he was the true master of ceremonies of the occasion, and in this case one presiding genius was paying homage to another.

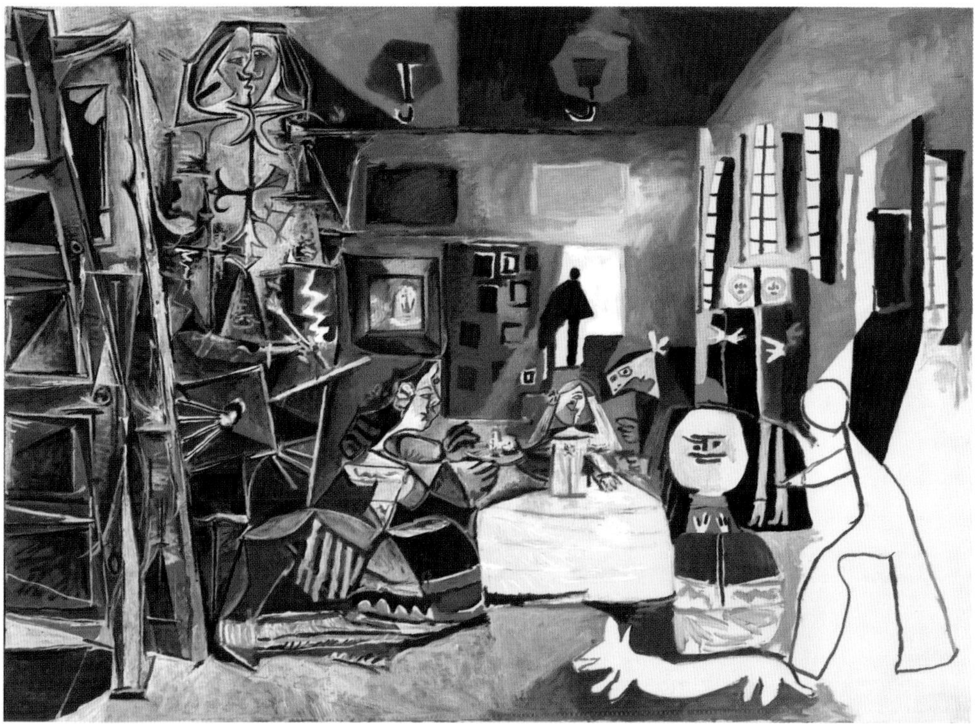

204 Pablo Picasso, *Las Meninas*, 17 August 1957

205   In a vibrantly coloured variation of the Infanta Margarita alone, executed on 14 September 1957, Picasso explores the duality of her original pose, which shows her turned to the right while her eyes swerve in the opposite direction. Once again he employs a Cubist dislocation of her face, her features facing both forward and to the left, while the rest of her seems to veer in both directions at once, her left hand and a bundle of hair weighting the right-hand side of the painting and the reaching gesture of her other hand and faceting of her face above it counterbalancing this.

206   Finally, in one of the most sheerly beautiful of all these variations, of 18 September 1957, Velázquez's subdued colour scheme is transformed into iridescent panes of stained glass. The Infanta reigns supreme as a stick-like figure in the centre, complemented by the black silhouette of the palace marshal in the doorway above. Around them is a kaleidoscopic array of red, blue and black planes of colour through which one can barely discern some of the actors of the original, for in this work space and figures commingle. The artist himself is reduced to an

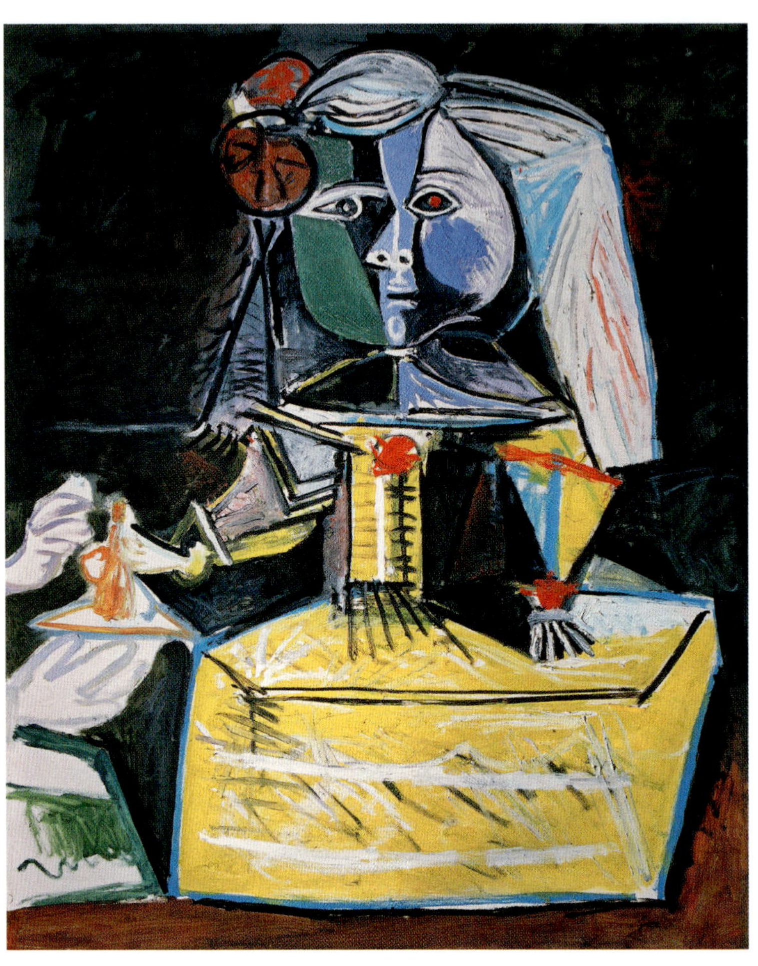

205 ABOVE Pablo Picasso, *Las Meninas (Infanta Margarita María)*, 14 September 1957
206 OPPOSITE Pablo Picasso, *Las Meninas*, 18 September 1957

ideogrammatic head contained in a palette-like plane akin to the one that he holds. The chaperones become two spooks and the mirror on the back wall reflects not the King and Queen but a receding grid of colour. Most playfully of all, at the bottom, Velázquez's slumbering mastiff reclines on his own shadow. Metamorphic possibilities are everywhere and anything can turn into something else.

Picasso's series of variations on *Las Meninas*, which constitute his most extensive body of works paying tribute to any earlier master, were themselves made the subject of a group of etchings by the English artist Richard Hamilton in the year of Picasso's death, 1973. Issued then in Berlin was an edition of prints entitled *Hommage à Pablo Picasso* by various artists, including among them Hamilton's *Picasso's Meninas*, an etching that remains faithful to Velázquez's original composition. Now, however, his cast of characters is depicted in the different styles adopted by Picasso himself throughout his long career. The Infanta Margarita emerges in Cubist-inspired planes,

207

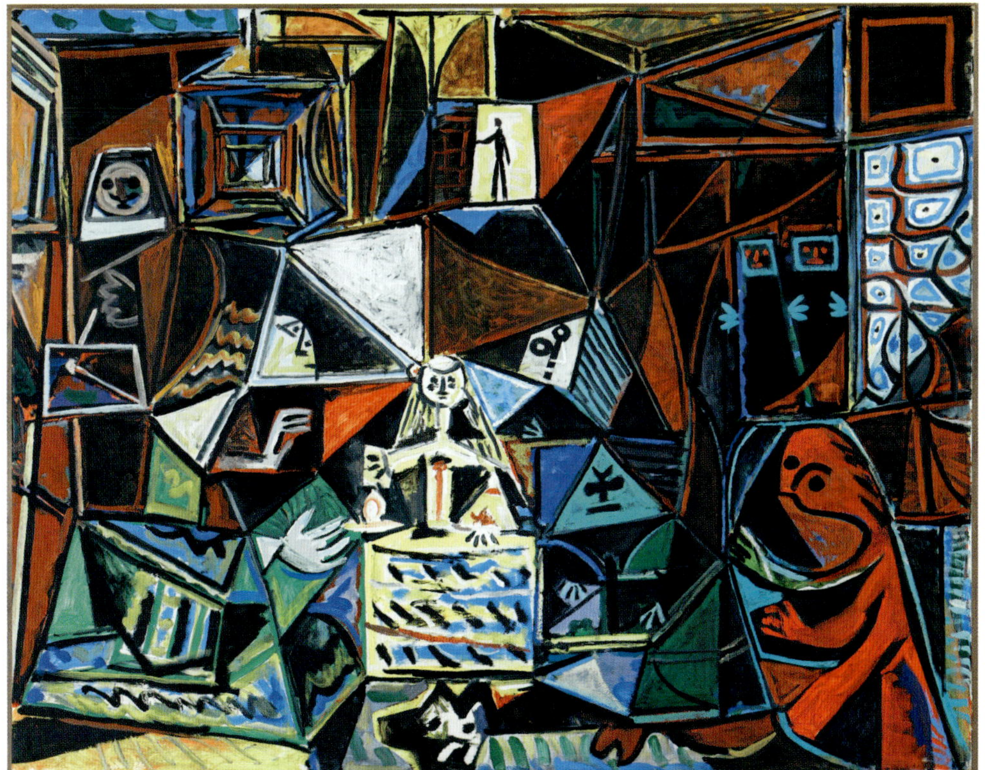

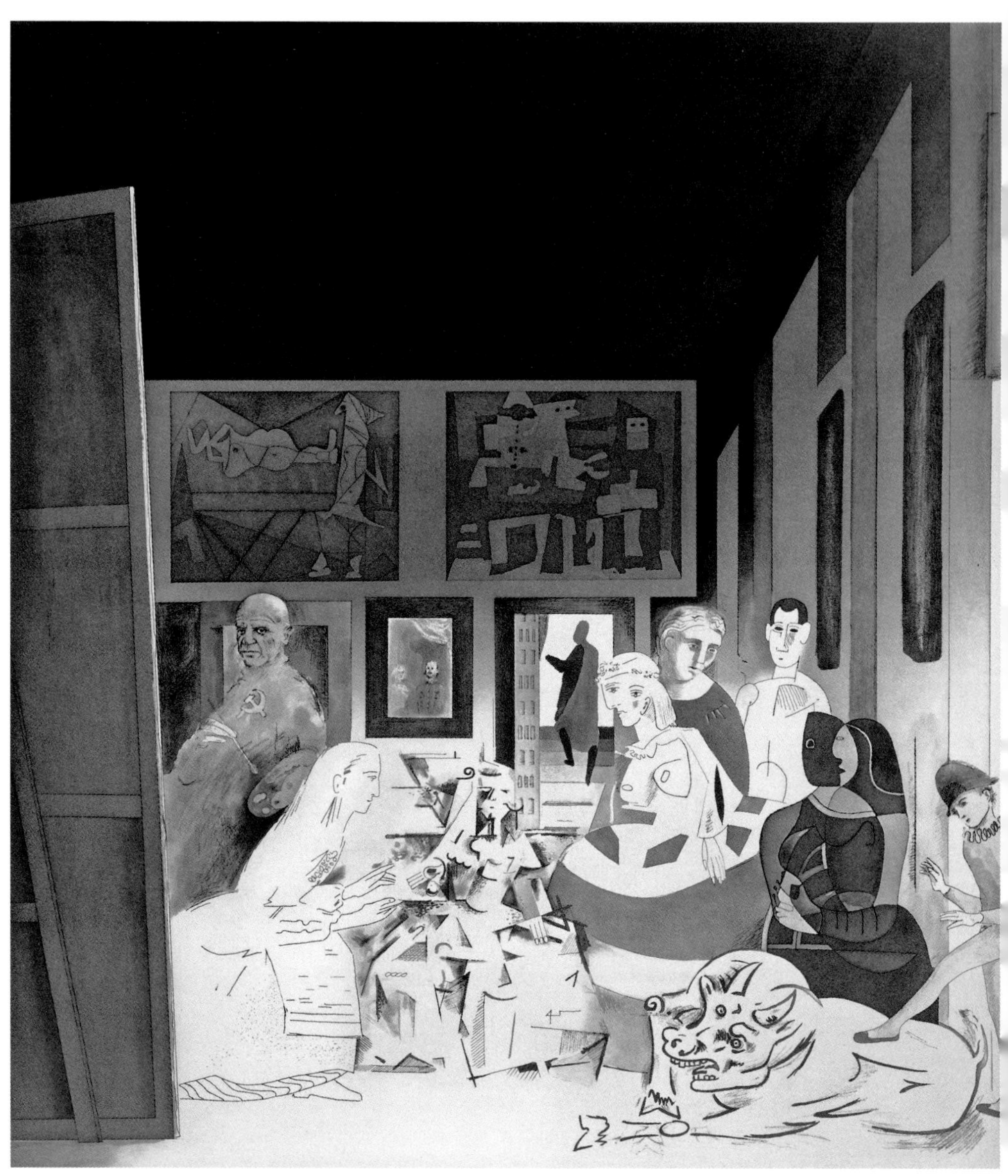

207 Richard Hamilton, *Picasso's Meninas*, 1973

Mari Bárbola in his style of the early 1930s, the dog is transformed into a reclining bull recalling his bull-fighting works and the artist himself is now decorated with a hammer and sickle to reflect Picasso's Communist sympathies. Even more ingeniously, the painted copies by Mazo once seen hanging on the back wall have now been transformed into synthetic Cubist compositions in Picasso's style of the early 1920s.

As one of the canonical images of Western art, *Las Meninas* is certain to inspire generations of artists to come, bewitched by its seemingly impromptu action and the artist's audacity in breaching the divisions between royal portraiture and genre painting. But it lacks one key quality of Velázquez's art that is found elsewhere – in the portraits of Mother Jerónima de la Fuente, Góngora, or certain of the court jesters and dwarfs. That is its pent-up emotional intensity, nowhere more in evidence than in his portrait of Innocent X.

Early in his career and for several years thereafter this picture became an obsession in the art of Francis Bacon, which itself ranks among the most anarchic and disturbing of any in recent years. An inveterate collector and pilferer of images – whether they be photographs, book covers or magazine illustrations – Bacon embarked upon a series of paintings inspired by Velázquez's pope in the late 1940s. None of these were done from the original, which Bacon even shied away from confronting on a trip to Rome in the 1960s. Instead he relied on postcards and other reproductions. Moreover, the vast majority of Bacon's variations avoid the most emotionally charged feature of the picture – the Pope's blazing red vestments and flushed complexion – in favour of less strident hues. But these they make up for in other ways.

In one, of 1951, the Pope has donned spectacles and perches at the edge of his chair, wielding his papal sceptre and wearing an inquisitorial expression, as though interrogating a miscreant or non-believer. Although the gilded contours of his throne proclaim his worldly splendour and authority, he sits ensnared by a curtained railing and cage, a symbol of power and prestige trapped and corrupted. In another of two years later, the gilt throne and railing remain and the Pope utters an unbearable cry, as though screaming for deliverance from this prison. Such a visceral outburst may be alien to Velázquez, of course, however much the red cap and cape of his own papal portrait themselves silently scream. But it is exactly this throttled emotionalism that Bacon found most compelling in Velázquez's art. His singular position among the portrait painters of his time was characterized by Bacon in an astute

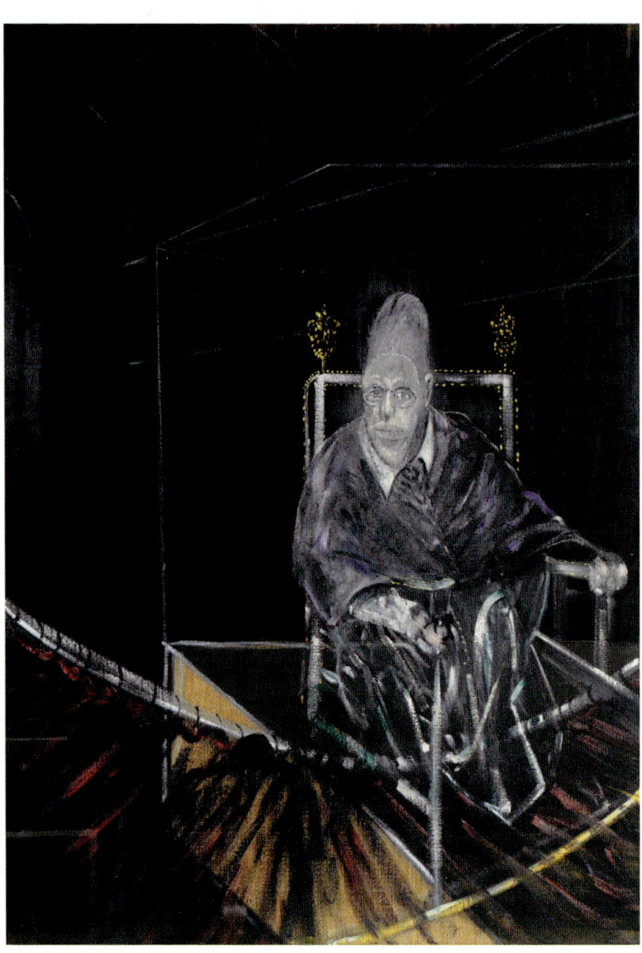

208 ABOVE Francis Bacon, *Pope I*, 1951
209 OPPOSITE Francis Bacon, *Study after Velázquez's Portrait of Pope Innocent X*, 1953

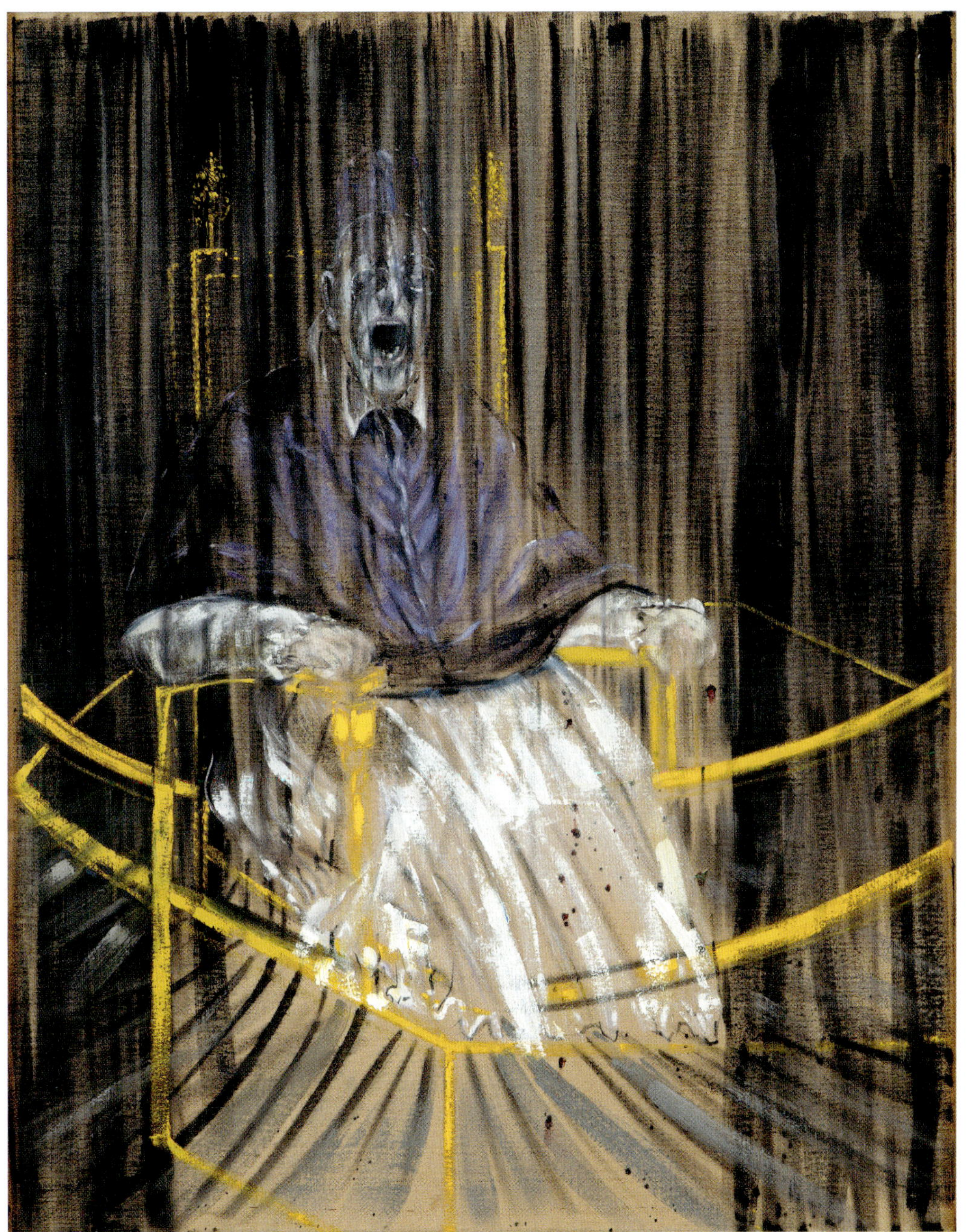

After Velázquez

comparison between his works in this form and those of his great contemporary, Rembrandt. In the paintings of the latter, Bacon noted, 'the whole contour of a face changes time after time… and by this difference it involves you in different areas of feeling.' Thus the Dutchman felt free not simply to describe the outward appearance of nature, which Bacon regarded as the task of pure 'illustration', but to alter and interpret this in order to convey different emotional states in his subjects or sitters. 'But with Velázquez it's more controlled and, of course, I believe, more miraculous.' Bacon continued:

Because one wants to do this thing of just walking along the edge of the precipice, and in Velázquez it's a very, very extraordinary thing that he has been able to keep it so near to what we call illustration and at the same time so deeply unlock the greatest and deepest things that man can feel. Which makes him such an amazingly mysterious painter.

The mystery remains through all these later transformations, while Velázquez lives on as one of the greatest of painters.

Select Bibliography

Oeuvre Catalogues

Yves Bottineau and P. M. Bardi, *Tout l'ouvre peint de Velázquez*, Paris, 1969

José López-Rey, *Velázquez, A Catalogue Raisonné of his Oeuvre*, London, 1963, (the most comprehensive and fully illustrated catalogue of works by or attributed to the artist)

José López-Rey, *Velázquez, The Complete Works*, updated by Odile Delenda, Cologne, 2020

August L. Mayer, *Velázquez, A catalogue raisonné of the pictures and drawings*, London, 1936

Monographs

J. Camón Aznar, *Velázquez*, Madrid, 1964

A. de Beruete, *Velázquez*, London, 1906

Jonathan Brown, *Velázquez, Painter and Courtier*, New Haven and London, 1986

Julián Gállego, *Velázquez*, Madrid, 1983

Kurt Gerstenberg, *Diego Velázquez*, Munich and Berlin, 1957

José Gudiol, *Velázquez*, London, 1974

Enriqueta Harris, *Velázquez*, Oxford, 1982

C. Lewis Hind, *Days with Velasquez*, London, 1906

Carl Justi, *Diego Velazquez and his time*, London, 1889

Madlyn Millner Kahr, *Velázquez, The Art of Painting*, New York, 1976

José López-Rey, *Velázquez' Work and World*, London, 1968

José López-Rey, *Velázquez, Painter of Painters*, Cologne, 1996, 2 vols

August L. Mayer, *Diego Velázquez*, Berlin, 1924

R. A. M. Stevenson, *Velázquez*, London, 1962 (orig. 1895)

William Stirling, *Velázquez and his Works* (with a catalogue of the paintings by W. Thoré-Bürger), London, 1855

Elisabeth de Gué Trapier, *Velázquez*, New York, 1948

Background

Jonathan Brown, *Painting in Spain, 1500–1700*, New Haven and London, 1999

Jonathan Brown, *The Golden Age of Painting in Spain*, London, 1990

Jonathan Brown and J. H. Elliot, *A Palace for a King, The Buen Retiro and the Court of Philip IV*, New Haven and London, 1980

J. H. Elliot, *Spain and its World 1500–1700*, New Haven and London, 1989

Oskar Hagen, *Patterns and Principles of Spanish Art*, Madison, Wisconsin, 1943

Marianna Haraszti-Takács, *Spanish Genre Painting in the Seventeenth Century*, Budapest, 1983

George Kubler and Martin Soria, *Art and Architecture in Spain and Portugal and their American Dominions*, Harmondsworth, 1959

Michael Levey, *Painting at Court*, New York, 1971

William Stirling-Maxwell, *Annals of the Artists of Spain*, London, 1848, 3 vols

Primary Sources

Instituto Diego Velázquez, *Velázquez, Homenaje en el tercer centenario de su muerte*, Madrid, 1960 (early biographies, commentaries, documents and inventories)

Francisco Pacheco and Antonio Palomino, *Lives of Velázquez*, trans. Nina Ayala Mallory, London, 2018

J. M. Pita Andrade and Á. Aterido (eds), *Corpus Velazqueño: Documentos y textos*, Madrid, 2000, 2 vols

Varia Velazqueña: homenaje a Velázquez en el III centenaria de su muerte, 1660–1960, Madrid, 1960, 2 vols

Specialized Studies

Anthony Bailey, *Velázquez and 'The Surrender of Breda'*, New York, 2011

A. Braham, *The Rokeby Venus*, London, 1960

Jonathan Brown and Carmen Garrido, *Velázquez, The Technique of Genius*, New Haven and London, 1998

Gustaf Cavallius, *Velázquez' 'Las Hilanderas', An Explication of a Picture Regarding Structure and Associations*, Uppsala, 1972

Aneta Georgierska-Shine and Larry Silver, *Rubens, Velázquez, and the King of Spain*, London and New York, 2014

Giles Knox, *The Late Paintings of Velázquez*, Farnham, 2009

Jacques Lassaigne, *Vélasquez, Les Ménines*,
    Fribourg, 1973
Gridley McKim-Smith, Greta Andersen-Bergdoll
    and Richard Newman, *Examining Velázquez*,
    New Haven and London, 1988
Steven N. Orso, *Velázquez: 'Los Borrachos' and
    Painting at the Court of Philip IV*, Cambridge,
    Mass, 1993
A. Prater, *Venus at her Mirror*, Munich, 2002
Suzanne L. Stratton-Pruitt (ed.), *Velázquez's
    'Las Meninas'*, Cambridge, 2003
Barry Wind, *Velázquez's 'Bodegones'*, Fairfax,
    VA, 1987

Exhibition and Museum Catalogues

Velázquez y lo Velázqueño, Dirección General de
    Bellas Artes, Madrid, 1960
The Golden Age of Spanish Painting, Royal
    Academy of Arts, London, 1976
Vladimir Kemenov, *Velázquez in Soviet Museums*,
    Leningrad, 1977
Velázquez, Antonio Domínguez Ortiz, Alfonso E.
    Pérez Sánchez, Julián Gállego, Metropolitan
    Museum of Art, New York, 1989
Velázquez, Antonio Domínguez Ortiz, Alfonso
    E. Pérez Sánchez, Julián Gállego, Museo del
    Prado, Madrid, 1990
Spanish Still Life from Velázquez to Goya, William
    B. Jordan and Peter Cherry, National Gallery,
    London, 1995
Velázquez in Seville, David Davies, Enriqueta
    Harris et al., National Gallery of Scotland,
    1996
Velázquez a Roma, ed. A. Coliva, Galleria
    Borghese, Rome, 1999
*Manet/Velázquez: The French Taste for Spanish
    Painting*, ed. Gary Tinterow and Genevieve
    Lacambre, Musée d'Orsay, Paris and
    Metropolitan Museum of Art, New York,
    2002–3
*Paintings for the Planet King, Philip IV and the Buen
    Retiro Palace*, Museo del Prado, Madrid, 2005
Velázquez, Dawson W. Carr et al., National
    Gallery, London, 2006
*Velázquez's Fables, Mythology and Sacred History
    in the Golden Age*, Museo del Prado, Madrid,
    2007

Essays and Articles

Jonathan Brown, 'On the Meaning of *Las
    Meninas', Images and Ideas in Seventeenth-
    Century Spanish Painting*, Princeton, NJ, 1978
Ortega y Gasset, *Velázquez, Goya, The
    Dehumanization of Art and other essays*, trans.
    by Alexis Brown, London, 1972

Fritz Saxl, 'Velázquez and Philip IV', *Lectures I*,
    London, 1957, pp. 311–24
Suzanne L. Stratton-Pruitt (ed.), *The Cambridge
    Companion to Velázquez*, Cambridge, 2002
Charles de Tolnay, 'Velázquez' "Las Hilanderas"
    and "Las Meninas", An Interpretation', *Gazette
    des Beaux-Arts*, 35, 1949, pp. 21–38

Imagining Velázquez

Velázquez and his works have been the subject
    of several books which combine fact with
    fiction in an imaginative attempt to fill some
    of the many gaps in our knowledge of them,
    a selection of which are listed here.
Elizabeth Borton de Treviño, *I, Juan de Pareja*,
    New York, 1965
Laura Cumming, *The Vanishing Man, In Pursuit
    of Velázquez*, London, 2016
Santiago Garcia and Javier Olivares, *The Ladies-in-
    Waiting*, Seattle, 2017
Antoinette James, *Son of Spain, Diego Velázquez*,
    New Zealand, 2017
Amy Sackville, *Painter to the King*, London, 2018

List of Illustrations

Measurements are given in centimetres and inches, height before width before depth, where applicable

All works are by Velázquez unless otherwise stated

1 *Las Meninas*, 1656 (detail). Oil on canvas, 320 × 281.5 (126 × 110⅞). Museo Nacional del Prado, Madrid. Photo Bridgeman Images
2 *Old Woman Cooking Eggs*, 1618 (detail). Oil on canvas, 100.5 × 119.5 (39⅝ × 47⅛). Scottish National Gallery (National Galleries Scotland), Edinburgh. Purchased with the aid of the Art Fund and a Treasury Grant 1955
3 *The Musical Trio*, c. 1617. Oil on canvas, 90.4 × 113.2 (35⅝ × 44⅝). Gemäldegalerie, Staatliche Museen zu Berlin
4 *Three Men at a Table*, 1617–18. Oil on canvas, 108.5 × 102 (42¾ × 40¼). State Hermitage Museum, Saint Petersburg
5 *Old Woman Cooking Eggs*, 1618. Oil on canvas, 100.5 × 119.5 (39⅝ × 47⅛). Scottish National Gallery (National Galleries Scotland), Edinburgh. Purchased with the aid of the Art Fund and a Treasury Grant 1955
6 *Christ in the House of Martha and Mary*, 1618. Oil on canvas, 60 × 103.5 (23⅝ × 40¾). The National Gallery, London. Bequeathed by Sir William H. Gregory, 1892
7 Jacob Matham after Pieter Aertsen, *Kitchen Scene with the Supper at Emmaus*, c. 1603. Engraving, 24.5 × 32.5 (9¾ × 12⅞). Harvard Art Museums/Fogg Museum. Gray Collection of Engravings Fund. Photo President and Fellows of Harvard College
8 *Kitchen Maid with the Supper at Emmaus*, 1618–19. Oil on canvas, 55 × 118 (21¾ × 46½). National Gallery of Ireland, Dublin
9 *The Waterseller of Seville*, c. 1620. Oil on canvas, 107.7 × 81.3 (42½ × 32⅛). Apsley House, London

10 *Two Young Men at a Table*, c. 1620. Oil on canvas, 65.3 × 104 (25¾ × 41). Apsley House, London
11 *The Immaculate Conception*, c. 1619. Oil on canvas, 135 × 101.6 (53¼ × 40). The National Gallery, London. Bought with the aid of the Art Fund, 1974. Photo The National Gallery, London/Scala, Florence
12 *St John the Evangelist on the Island of Patmos*, c. 1619. Oil on canvas, 135.5 × 102.2 (53⅜ × 40¼). The National Gallery, London. Bought with a special grant and contributions from The Pilgrim Trust and the Art Fund, 1956. Photo The National Gallery, London/Scala, Florence
13 Juan Martínez Montañés, *The Virgin of the Immaculate Conception*, 1606. Painted and gilded wood, h. 155 (61). Church of the Annunciation, Seville. Photo Album/Alamy Stock Photo
14 Francisco Pacheco, *Immaculate Conception with Miguel del Cid*, c. 1616. Oil on canvas, 160 × 110 (63 × 43⅜). Seville Cathedral
15 *The Tears of St Peter*, 1618–19. Oil on canvas, 132 × 98.5 (52 × 38⅞). Fundación Juan-Miguel Villar Mir, Madrid
16 *The Adoration of the Magi*, 1619. Oil on canvas, 203 × 125 (80 × 49¼). Museo Nacional del Prado, Madrid. Photo Museo Nacional del Prado/Scala, Florence
17 *St Paul*, 1619–20. Oil on canvas, 99.5 × 80 (39¼ × 31½). Museu Nacional d'Art de Catalunya, Barcelona
18 *St Thomas*, 1619–20. Oil on canvas, 95 × 73 (37½ × 28¾). Musée des Beaux-Arts Orléans
19 *St Ildefonso Receiving the Chasuble from the Virgin*, 1622–23. Oil on canvas, 166 × 120 (65⅜ × 47¼). Ayuntamiento, Seville (Depot of the Centro de Investigacion Diego Velázquez, Seville)
20 *Don Cristóbal Suárez de Ribera*, 1620. Oil on canvas, 207 × 148 (81½ × 58⅜). Museo de Bellas Artes de Sevilla. Photo Archivart/Alamy Stock Photo
21 *The Venerable Mother Jerónima de la Fuente*, 1620. Oil on canvas, 160 × 110 (63 × 43⅜). Museo Nacional del Prado, Madrid
22 *The Venerable Mother Jerónima de la Fuente*, 1620. Oil on canvas, 162.5 × 105 (64 × 41⅜). Fernández de Araoz collection, Madrid
23 *Portrait of a Man with a Ruff Collar*, 1620–22. Oil on canvas, 41 × 36. Museo Nacional del Prado, Madrid
24 Francisco Pacheco, *Man Wearing a Laurel Wreath*, undated. Black and red chalk over wash, 18.4 × 15 (7¼ × 6). Biblioteca Nacional de España, Madrid

25 *Portrait of Don Luis de Góngora*, 1622. Oil on canvas, 50.2 × 40.6 (19⅞ × 16). Museum of Fine Arts, Boston

26 *Philip IV*, 1623–24. Oil on canvas, 61.9 × 48.9 (24⅜ × 19⅜). Meadows Museum, Dallas. Photo Bridgeman Images

27 *Philip IV*, 1624. Oil on canvas, 200 × 102.9 (78¾ × 40⅝). The Metropolitan Museum of Art, New York. Bequest of Benjamin Altman, 1913

28 *Philip IV*, 1623–28. Oil on canvas, 198 × 101.5 (78 × 40). Museo Nacional del Prado, Madrid. Photo Museo Nacional del Prado/Scala, Florence

29 *Portrait of Philip IV in Armour*, c. 1628. Oil on canvas, 57 × 44 (22½ × 17⅜). Museo Nacional del Prado, Madrid

30 *Portrait of the Count-Duke of Olivares*, 1624. Oil on canvas, 202 × 105.5 (79⅝ × 41⅝). São Paulo Museum of Art

31 *The Count-Duke of Olivares*, c. 1625–26. Oil on canvas, 222 × 137.8 (87½ × 54⅜). Hispanic Society of America, New York. Gift of Mrs Collis P. Huntington (née Arabella Duval; subsequently Mrs Henry E. Huntington), in memory of Collis P. Huntington, 1910. Photo akg-images/Joseph Martin

32 *Portrait of the Infante Don Carlos*, 1626–27. Oil on canvas, 209 × 125 (82⅜ × 49¼). Museo Nacional del Prado, Madrid. Photo Museo Nacional del Prado/Scala, Florence

33 *Portrait of St Simon de Rojas Dead*, 1624. Oil on canvas, 101 × 121 (39⅞ × 47¾). Collection of the Dukes of Infantado, on deposit at the Museo de Bellas Artes de Valencia

34 *Portrait of a Young Man*, 1627–28. Oil on canvas, 89.2 × 69.5 (35⅛ × 27⅜). Alte Pinakothek, Bayerische Staatsgemäldesammlungen, Munich. Photo Scala, Florence/bpk, Bildagentur für Kunst, Kultur und Geschichte

35 *Democritus*, 1628–29. Oil on canvas, 101 × 81 (39⅞ × 32). Musée des Beaux-Arts de Rouen

36 Vicente Carducho, *The Expulsion of the Moriscos*, 1627. Wash, pencil and pen on paper, 38 × 50.4 (15 × 19⅞). Museo Nacional del Prado, Madrid

37 *Christ after the Flagellation Contemplated by the Christian Soul*, 1626–28. Oil on canvas, 165.1 × 206.4 (65 × 81⅜). The National Gallery, London. Presented by John Savile Lumley (later Baron Savile), 1883. Photo The National Gallery, London/Scala, Florence

38 *The Supper at Emmaus*, 1628–29. Oil on canvas, 123.2 × 132.7 (48⅝ × 52¼). The Metropolitan Museum of Art, New York. Bequest of Benjamin Altman, 1913

39 *The Triumph of Bacchus*, 1628–29. Oil on canvas, 165 × 225 (65 × 88⅝). Museo Nacional del Prado, Madrid

40 *The Triumph of Bacchus*, 1628–29 (detail). Oil on canvas, 165 × 225 (65 × 88⅝). Museo Nacional del Prado, Madrid

41 Peter Paul Rubens, *The Adoration of the Magi*, 1609/1628–29 (detail). Oil on canvas, 355.5 × 493 (140 × 194⅛). Museo Nacional del Prado, Madrid. Photo Museo Nacional del Prado/Scala, Florence

42 Peter Paul Rubens, *The Adoration of the Magi*, 1609/1628–29. Oil on canvas, 355.5 × 493 (140 × 194⅛). Museo Nacional del Prado, Madrid. Photo Museo Nacional del Prado/Scala, Florence

43 *The Forge of Vulcan*, 1630. Oil on canvas, 223 × 290 (87⅞ × 114¼). Museo Nacional del Prado, Madrid. Photo Museo Nacional del Prado/Scala, Florence

44 *Joseph's Bloody Coat Brought to Jacob*, 1630. Oil on canvas, 223 × 250 (87⅞ × 98½). El Real Monasterio de San Lorenzo de El Escorial

45 *Head of Apollo*, 1630. Oil on canvas, 36.3 × 25.2 (14⅜ × 10). Private collection

46 *The Forge of Vulcan*, 1630 (detail). Oil on canvas, 223 × 290 (87⅞ × 114¼). Museo Nacional del Prado, Madrid. Photo Museo Nacional del Prado/Scala, Florence

47 *View of the Gardens of the Villa Medici, Rome, with a Statue of Ariadne*, 1630. Oil on canvas, 44 × 38 (17⅜ × 15). Museo Nacional del Prado, Madrid

48 *View of the Gardens of the Villa Medici, Rome*, 1630. Oil on canvas, 48.5 × 43 (19⅛ × 17). Museo Nacional del Prado, Madrid

49 *Portrait of Doña Maria, Queen of Hungary*, c. 1630. Oil on canvas, 59.5 × 45.5 (23½ × 18). Museo Nacional del Prado, Madrid. Photo Museo Nacional del Prado/Scala, Florence

50 *Prince Balthasar Carlos with a Dwarf*, 1631. Oil on canvas, 128 × 101.9 (50½ × 40⅛). Museum of Fine Arts, Boston. Henry Lillie Pierce Fund

51 *Portrait of the Prince Balthasar Carlos*, 1633. Oil on canvas, 117.8 × 95.9 (46½ × 37⅞). Wallace Collection, London

52 *Philip IV in Brown and Silver*, 1631–32. Oil on canvas, 195 × 110 (7½ × 43⅜). The National Gallery, London. Photo The National Gallery, London/Scala, Florence

53 *Philip IV*, c. 1632. Oil on canvas, 127.5 × 86 (50¼ × 37⅞). Kunsthistorisches Museum, Vienna. Photo Album/Alamy Stock Photo

54 *Isabella of Bourbon, c.* 1632. Oil on canvas, 153.5 × 123.6 (60½ × 48¾). Kunsthistorisches Museum, Vienna. Photo akg-images

55 *Doña Antonia de Ipeñarrieta y Galdós and Her Son Don Luis*, 1631–32. Oil on canvas, 215 × 110 (84¾ × 43⅜). Museo Nacional del Prado, Madrid. Photo Museo Nacional del Prado/Scala, Florence

56 *Don Diego del Corral y Arellano*, 1631–32. Oil on canvas, 215 × 110 (84¾ × 43⅜). Museo Nacional del Prado, Madrid. Photo Museo Nacional del Prado/Scala, Florence

57 *Don Pedro de Barberana y Aparregui, c.* 1631–32. Oil on canvas, 198.1 × 111.4 (78 × 43⅞). Kimbell Art Museum, Fort Worth, Texas

58 *Don Juan Mateos, c.* 1634. Oil on canvas, 109 × 90.5 (43 × 35¾). Gemäldegalerie Alte Meister, Staatliche Kunstsammlungen Dresden

59 *A Sybil, c.* 1632. Oil on canvas, 62 × 50 (24½ × 19¾). Museo Nacional del Prado, Madrid. Photo Museo Nacional del Prado/Scala, Florence

60 Guido Reni, *Sibyl*, 1635–36. Oil on canvas, 74.2 × 58.3 (29¼ × 23). Pinacoteca Nazionale, Bologna. Photo Scala, Florence

61 *St Rufina*, 1632–34. Oil on canvas, 79 × 64 (31⅛ × 25¼). Fundación Focus-Abengoa, Seville

62 *The Temptation of St Thomas Aquinas*, 1631–33. Oil on canvas, 240 × 203 (94½ × 80). Museo Diocesano de Arte Sacro de Orihuela

63 *Christ on the Cross, c.* 1632. Oil on canvas, 248 × 169 (97¾ × 66⅝). Museo Nacional del Prado, Madrid. Photo Museo Nacional del Prado/Scala, Florence

64 Francisco de Zurbarán, *The Crucifixion*, 1627. Oil on canvas, 290.3 × 165.5 (114⅜ × 65¼). Art Institute of Chicago. Robert A. Waller Memorial Fund

65 *The Coronation of the Virgin*, 1635–36. Oil on canvas, 178.5 × 134.5 (70⅜ × 53). Museo Nacional del Prado, Madrid. Photo Museo Nacional del Prado/Scala, Florence

66 El Greco, *The Coronation of the Virgin, c.* 1590. Oil on canvas, 99 × 101 (39 × 39⅞). Museo Nacional del Prado, Madrid. Photo Museo Nacional del Prado/Scala, Florence

67 Claude Lorrain, *Landscape with St Mary Magdalene*, 1637. Oil on canvas, 162 × 241 (63⅞ × 95). Museo Nacional del Prado, Madrid. Photo Museo Nacional del Prado/Scala, Florence

68 Nicolas Poussin, *Landscape with St Paul the Hermit*, 1637. Oil on canvas, 155 × 234 (61⅛ × 92¼). Museo Nacional del Prado, Madrid. Photo Museo Nacional del Prado/Scala, Florence

69 Peter Paul Rubens, *Judgment of Paris, c.* 1638. Oil on canvas, 199 × 381 (78⅜ × 150). Museo Nacional del Prado, Madrid. Photo Museo Nacional del Prado/Scala, Florence

70 Francisco de Zurbarán, *Death of Hercules*, 1634. Oil on canvas, 136 × 167 (53⅝ × 65¾). Museo Nacional del Prado, Madrid. Photo Museo Nacional del Prado/Scala, Florence

71 *Equestrian Portrait of Philip III, c.* 1635. Oil on canvas, 305.5 × 317.5 (120⅜ × 125). Museo Nacional del Prado, Madrid. Photo Museo Nacional del Prado/Scala, Florence

72 *Equestrian Portrait of Margaret of Austria, c.* 1635. Oil on canvas, 302 × 311.5 (119 × 122¾). Museo Nacional del Prado, Madrid

73 *Equestrian Portrait of Philip IV, c.* 1635. Oil on canvas, 303 × 317 (119⅜ × 124⅞). Museo Nacional del Prado, Madrid. Photo Museo Nacional del Prado/Scala, Florence

74 *Equestrian Portrait of Isabella of Bourbon, c.* 1635. Oil on canvas, 301 × 314 (118⅝ × 123⅝). Museo Nacional del Prado, Madrid

75 *Equestrian Portrait of Philip IV, c.* 1635 (detail). Oil on canvas, 303 × 317 (119⅜ × 124⅞). Museo Nacional del Prado, Madrid. Photo Museo Nacional del Prado/Scala, Florence

76 *Equestrian Portrait of Prince Balthasar Carlos*, 1634–35. Oil on canvas, 211.5 × 177 (83⅜ × 69¾). Museo Nacional del Prado, Madrid

77 *The Surrender of Breda, c.* 1635. Oil on canvas, 307.3 × 371.5 (121 × 146⅜). Museo Nacional del Prado, Madrid. Photo Museo Nacional del Prado/Scala, Florence

78 *The Surrender of Breda, c.* 1635 (detail). Oil on canvas, 307.3 × 371.5 (121 × 146⅜). Museo Nacional del Prado, Madrid. Photo Museo Nacional del Prado/Scala, Florence

79 Francisco de Zurbarán, *The Defence of Cádiz*, 1634–35. Oil on canvas, 302 × 323 (119 × 127¼). Museo Nacional del Prado, Madrid

80 Juan Bautista Maíno, *The Recapture of Bahía*, 1634–35. Oil on canvas, 309 × 381 (121¾ × 150). Museo Nacional del Prado, Madrid. Photo Museo Nacional del Prado/Scala, Florence

81 Jusepe Leonardo, *The Surrender at Jülich*, 1634–35. Oil on canvas, 307 × 381 (120⅞ × 150). Museo Nacional del Prado, Madrid. Photo Museo Nacional del Prado/Scala, Florence

82 Study for the figure of Spinola in *The Surrender of Breda*, 1634–35. Biblioteca Nacional, Madrid

83 Study for *The Surrender of Breda*, 1634–35.
Biblioteca Nacional, Madrid
84 *Equestrian Portrait of the Count-Duke of
Olivares*, c. 1636. Oil on canvas, 313 × 242.5 (123¼ ×
95½). Museo Nacional del Prado, Madrid. Photo
Museo Nacional del Prado/Scala, Florence
85 *White Horse*, 1634–38. Oil on canvas, 310 × 243
(122⅛ × 95¾). Palacio Real (Patrimonio Nacional),
Madrid
86 *Philip IV as a Hunter*, 1632–34. Oil on canvas,
189 × 124 (74½ × 95¾). Museo Nacional del Prado,
Madrid. Photo Museo Nacional del Prado/Scala,
Florence
87 *Cardinal Infante Don Fernando as a Hunter*,
1632–34. Oil on canvas, 191 × 107 (75¼ × 42¼).
Museo Nacional del Prado, Madrid. Photo Museo
Nacional del Prado/Scala, Florence
88 *Head of a Stag*, 1626–28. Oil on canvas,
66 × 52 (26 × 20½). Museo Nacional del Prado,
Madrid
89 *Prince Balthasar Carlos as a Hunter*, 1635–36.
Oil on canvas, 191 × 103 (75¼ × 40⅝). Museo
Nacional del Prado, Madrid. Photo Museo
Nacional del Prado/Scala, Florence
90 *Prince Balthasar Carlos in the Riding School*,
c. 1636. Oil on canvas, 144 × 96.5 (56¾ × 38).
Collection of the Duke of Westminster, London.
Photo Bridgeman Images
91 *Portrait of Juan Martínez Montañés*, 1635. Oil
on canvas, 109 × 88 (43 × 34¾). Museo Nacional
del Prado, Madrid
92 Pietro Tacca, *Equestrian Bronze of Philip IV*,
1634–40. Plaza de Oriente, Madrid. Photo Album/
Alamy Stock Photo
93 *Francesco d'Este*, 1638. Oil on canvas, 68 × 51
(26⅞ × 20⅛). Galleria Estense, Modena
94 *Portrait of a Man (possibly José Nieto)*,
c. 1635–45. Oil on canvas, 76.3 × 65.3 (30⅛ × 25¾).
Apsley House, London
95 *The Lady with a Fan*, c. 1635. Oil on canvas,
122.5 × 99 (48¼ × 39). Wallace Collection,
London
96 *The Jester Named Don Juan of Austria*,
c. 1632–33. Oil on canvas, 210 × 123 (82¾ × 48½).
Museo Nacional del Prado, Madrid. Photo Museo
Nacional del Prado/Scala, Florence
97 *The Jester Barbarroja or Don Cristóbal de
Castañeda y Pernia*, c. 1637–40. Oil on canvas,
198 × 121 (78 × 47¾). Museo Nacional del Prado,
Madrid. Photo Museo Nacional del Prado/Scala,
Florence
98 Peter Paul Rubens, *Democritus*, 1636–38. Oil
on canvas, 180.5 × 66 (71⅛ × 26). Museo Nacional
del Prado, Madrid. Photo Museo Nacional del
Prado/Scala, Florence

99 Peter Paul Rubens, *Heraclitus*, 1636–38. Oil on
canvas, 183 × 64.5 (72⅛ × 25½). Museo Nacional
del Prado, Madrid. Photo Museo Nacional del
Prado/Scala, Florence
100 *Menippus*, c. 1638. Oil on canvas, 179 × 94
(70½ × 37⅛). Museo Nacional del Prado,
Madrid. Photo Museo Nacional del Prado/Scala,
Florence
101 *Aesop*, c. 1638. Oil on canvas, 179 × 94
(70½ × 37⅛). Museo Nacional del Prado,
Madrid. Photo Museo Nacional del Prado/Scala,
Florence
102 *Mars Resting*, c. 1638. Oil on canvas,
179 × 95 (70½ × 37½). Museo Nacional del Prado,
Madrid. Photo Museo Nacional del Prado/Scala,
Florence
103 *Portrait of Pablo de Valladolid*, c. 1636–37.
Oil on canvas, 209 × 123 (82⅜ × 48½). Museo
Nacional del Prado, Madrid
104 *St Anthony Abbot Visits St Paul the Hermit*,
c. 1634. Oil on canvas, 261 × 192.5 (102⅞ × 75⅞).
Museo Nacional del Prado, Madrid. Photo Museo
Nacional del Prado/Scala, Florence
105 Albrecht Dürer, *The Hermits St Anthony
and St Paul*, c. 1503. Woodcut, 21.1 × 14
(8⅜ × 5⅝). Minneapolis Institute of Art.
The William M. Ladd Collection Gift of Herschel
V. Jones, 1916
106 *Head of a Young Girl*, c. 1638–42. Oil on
canvas, 51.5 × 41 (20⅜ × 16¼). The Hispanic
Society of America, New York. Photo Heritage
Image Partnership Ltd /Alamy Stock Photo
107 *The Prince Balthasar Carlos*, 1638–39.
Oil on canvas, 130 × 99.5 (51¼ × 39¼).
Kunsthistorisches Museum, Vienna
108 *Portrait of the Count-Duke of Olivares*,
c. 1638. Oil on canvas, 67 × 54.5 (26½ × 21½).
State Hermitage Museum, Saint Petersburg
109 *Portrait of Philip IV at Fraga*, 1644. Oil on
canvas, 129.9 × 99.4 (51¼ × 39¼). Frick Collection,
New York
110 Anthony van Dyck, *Cardinal Infante
Ferdinand of Austria*, 1634. Oil on canvas,
107 × 106 (42¼ × 41¾). Museo Nacional del Prado,
Madrid. Photo Museo Nacional del Prado/Scala,
Florence
111 *Portrait of Philip IV at Fraga*, 1644 (detail).
Oil on canvas, 129.9 × 99.4 (51¼ × 39¼). Frick
Collection, New York
112 Frans Hals, *Jasper Schade van Westrum*,
1645 (detail). Oil on canvas, 114 × 98 (45 × 38⅝).
National Gallery, Prague
113 Frans Hals, *Jasper Schade van Westrum*,
1645. Oil on canvas, 114 × 98 (45 × 38⅝). National
Gallery, Prague

114 Workshop of Peter Paul Rubens, *Philip IV on Horseback* (copy), *c.* 1645. Oil on canvas, 337 × 262 (132¾ × 103¼). Uffizi, Florence
115 Rodrigo de Villandrando, *Prince Philip and the Dwarf, Miguel Soplillo, c.* 1620. Oil on canvas, 204 × 110 (80⅜ × 43⅜). Museo Nacional del Prado, Madrid. Photo Museo Nacional del Prado/Scala, Florence
116 Anthony van Dyck, *Queen Henrietta Maria with Sir Jeffrey Hudson*, 1633. Oil on canvas, 219.1 × 134.8 (86⅜ × 53⅛). National Gallery of Art, Washington, D.C. Samuel H. Kress Collection
117 *The Jester Calabazas*, 1635–39. Oil on canvas, 106 × 83 (41¾ × 32¾). Museo Nacional del Prado, Madrid. Photo Museo Nacional del Prado/Scala, Florence
118 *Portrait of Sebastián de Morra, c.* 1645. Oil on canvas, 106.5 × 82.5 (42 × 32½). Museo Nacional del Prado, Madrid. Photo Museo Nacional del Prado/Scala, Florence
119 *Portrait of Francisco Lezcano, c.* 1645. Oil on canvas, 107 × 83 (42¼ × 32¾). Museo Nacional del Prado, Madrid. Photo Museo Nacional del Prado/Scala, Florence
120 *The Jester Don Diego de Acedo or 'El Primo', c.* 1645. Oil on canvas, 107 × 82 (42¼ × 32⅜). Museo Nacional del Prado, Madrid. Photo Museo Nacional del Prado/Scala, Florence
121 *Portrait of Cardinal Gaspar de Borja y Velasco*, 1643–45. Pencil and watercolour on paper, 18.8 × 11.6 (7½ × 4⅝). Real Academia de Bellas Artes de San Fernando, Madrid
122 *Knight of the Order of Santiago*, 1645–50. Oil on canvas, 67 × 56 (26½ × 22⅛). Gemäldegalerie Alte Meister, Staatlichen Kunstsammlungen Dresden
123 *María Theresa, Infanta of Spain, c.* 1648. Oil on canvas, 48 × 37 (19 × 14⅝). The Metropolitan Museum of Art, New York. Robert Lehman Collection, 1975
124 *Female Figure (Sibyl with Tabula Rasa), c.* 1648. Oil on canvas, 64.8 × 58.4 (25⅝ × 23). Meadows Museum, Dallas. Algur H. Meadows Collection
125 *The Toilet of Venus (The Rokeby Venus), c.* 1647–51. Oil on canvas, 122.5 × 177 (48¼ × 69¾). The National Gallery, London. Photo The National Gallery, London/Scala, Florence
126 Giorgione, *Sleeping Venus, c.* 1510. Oil on canvas, 108.5 × 175 (42¾ × 69). Gemäldegalerie Alte Meister, Staatlichen Kunstsammlungen Dresden
127 Titian, *Venus of Urbino*, 1538. Oil on canvas, 119 × 165 (46⅞ × 65). The Uffizi, Florence
128 Anonymous, *Venus Reclining in a Landscape*, 16th century. Oil on canvas, 121 × 175 (47¾ × 69). Location unknown
129 Alonso Cano, *Christ's Descent into Limbo*, 1645–50. Oil on canvas, 167.6 × 120.6 (66 × 47½). Los Angeles County Museum of Art. Gift of Bella Mabury
130 Titian, *Venus with a Mirror, c.* 1555. Oil on canvas, 124.5 × 105.5 (49⅛ × 41⅝). National Gallery of Art, Washington, D.C. Andrew W. Mellon Collection
131 Jan van Eyck, *Arnolfini Portrait*, 1434. Oil on oak, 82.2 × 60 (32¼ × 41⅝). The National Gallery, London
132 *The Toilet of Venus (The Rokeby Venus), c.* 1647–51 (detail). Oil on canvas, 122.5 × 177 (48¼ × 69¾). The National Gallery, London. Photo The National Gallery, London/Scala, Florence
133 After Velázquez, *Francisco de Ocáriz y Ochoa*, 18th century. Oil on canvas, 196 × 84 (77¼ × 33⅛). Museo Nacional del Prado, Madrid. Photo Museo Nacional del Prado/Scala, Florence
134 After Velázquez, *Portrait of Francisco de Quevedo*, mid-17th century. Oil on canvas, 60.5 × 48 (23⅞ × 19). Instituto Valencia de Don Juan, Madrid
135 After Velázquez, *Archbishop Fernando de Valdés*, undated. Oil on canvas. Colección Conde de Toreno, Madrid. Photo Instituto del Patrimonio Cultural de España, Madrid, Ministerio de Cultura y Deporte
136 Attributed to Velázquez, *Portrait of Archbishop Fernando de Valdés*, 1640–45. Oil on canvas, 63.5 × 59.6 (25 × 23½). The National Gallery, London
137 Fragment of a hand *c.* 1630. Oil on canvas, 27 × 24 (10¾ × 9½). Location unknown since August 1989
138 Attributed to Velázquez, *Tavern Scene with Two Men and a Girl, c.* 1618–19. Oil on canvas, 96 × 112 (37⅞ × 44⅛). Museum of Fine Arts, Budapest
139 *Head of a Young Man, c.* 1618–19. Oil on canvas, 39.5 × 35.5 (15⅝ × 14). State Hermitage Museum, Saint Petersburg. Photo The State Hermitage Museum/Vladimir Terebenin
140 *Philip IV Hunting Wild Boar (La Tela Real)*, probably 1632–37. Oil on canvas, 182 × 302 (71¾ × 119). The National Gallery, London
141 *Philip IV Hunting Wild Boar (La Tela Real)*, probably 1632–37 (detail). Oil on canvas, 182 × 302 (71¾ × 119). The National Gallery, London

142 *Sleeping Ariadne*, Roman version of a 2nd-century BC Greek sculpture, 150–75 AD. Marble, 99 × 238 × 95 (39 × 93¾ × 37½). Museo Nacional del Prado, Madrid. Photo Museo Nacional del Prado/Scala, Florence
143 Matteo Bonarelli, *Sleeping Hermaphrodite*, 1652. Bronze, 36 × 160 (14¼ × 63). Museo Nacional del Prado, Madrid. Photo Museo Nacional del Prado/Scala, Florence
144 *Camillo Astalli*, 1650. Oil on canvas, 61 × 48.5 (24⅛ × 19⅛). Hispanic Society of America, New York
145 *Camillo Massimi*, 1650. Oil on canvas, 75.9 × 61 (30 × 24⅛). Kingston Lacy Estate, Dorset
146 *Ferdinando Brandani*, 1650. Oil on canvas, 50.5 × 47 (20 × 18⅝). Museo Nacional del Prado, Madrid. Photo Museo Nacional del Prado/Scala, Florence
147 *Portrait of Juan de Pareja*, 1649–50. Oil on canvas, 81.3 × 69.9 (32⅛ × 27⅝). The Metropolitan Museum of Art, New York. Purchase, Fletcher and Rogers Funds, and Bequest of Miss Adelaide Milton de Groot (1876–1967), by exchange, supplemented by gifts from friends of the Museum, 1971
148 Juan de Pareja, *The Calling of St Matthew*, 1661 (detail). Oil on canvas, 225 × 325 (88⅝ × 128). Museo Nacional del Prado, Madrid. Photo Museo Nacional del Prado/Scala, Florence
149 Juan de Pareja, *The Calling of St Matthew*, 1661. Oil on canvas, 225 × 325 (88⅝ × 128). Museo Nacional del Prado, Madrid. Photo Museo Nacional del Prado/Scala, Florence
150 Raphael, *Portrait of Pope Julius II*, 1511–12. Oil on poplar, 108.7 × 81 (42⅞ × 32). The National Gallery, London
151 Titian, *Portrait of Pope Paul III*, 1543. Oil on canvas, 113.7 × 88.8 (44⅞ × 35). National Museum of Capodimonte, Naples
152 *Pope of Innocent X*, 1650. Oil on canvas, 140 × 120 (55⅛ × 47¼). Galleria Doria Pamphilj, Rome. Photo akg-images
153 Gianlorenzo Bernini, *Bust of Pope Innocent X*, *c.* 1650. White Carrara marble, height 95 (37½). Galleria Doria Pamphilj, Rome. Photo Araldo De Luca/Getty Images
154 Alessandro Algardi, *Bust of Pope Innocent X*, 1647–48. Marble, 97 × 81 × 29 (38¼ × 32 × 11½). Photo © Stefano Baldini/Bridgeman Images
155 *Pope Innocent X*, 1650. Oil on canvas, 82 × 71.5 (32⅜ × 28¼). Apsley House, London. Photo Historic England/Bridgeman Images
156 *Bust of Philip IV*, *c.* 1653. Oil on canvas, 69.3 × 56.5 (27⅜ × 22¼). Museo Nacional del Prado, Madrid. Photo Museo Nacional del Prado/Scala, Florence
157 *Maria Theresa, Infanta of Spain*, 1652–53. Oil on canvas, 32.7 × 38.4 (12⅞ × 15⅛). The Metropolitan Museum of Art, New York. The Jules Bache Collection, 1949
158 *Portrait of the Infanta Maria Theresa of Spain*, *c.* 1652–53. Oil on canvas, 127 × 98.5 (50 × 38⅞). Kunsthistorisches Museum, Vienna. Photo Artefact/Alamy Stock Photo
159 *Portrait of Mariana of Austria*, 1652–53. Oil on canvas, 234.2 × 132 (92¼ × 52). Museo Nacional del Prado, Madrid
160 Workshop of Velázquez, *Philip IV in Armour, with a Lion at his Feet*, *c.* 1653. Oil on canvas, 234 × 131.5 (92¼ × 51⅞). Museo Nacional del Prado, Madrid. Photo Museo Nacional del Prado/Scala, Florence
161 *The Infanta Margarita*, 1653. Oil on canvas, 128 × 99.6 (50½ × 39¼). Kunsthistorisches Museum, Vienna. Photo Heritage Image Partnership Ltd/Alamy Stock Photo
162 *The Infanta Margarita*, *c.* 1656. Oil on canvas, 105 × 88 (41⅜ × 34¾). Kunsthistorisches Museum, Vienna. Photo Artefact/Alamy Stock Photo
163 *Las Meninas*, 1656. Oil on canvas, 320 × 281.5 (126 × 110⅞). Museo Nacional del Prado, Madrid. Photo akg-images
164 *Las Meninas*, 1656 (detail). Oil on canvas, 320 × 281.5 (126 × 110⅞). Museo Nacional del Prado, Madrid. Photo akg-images
165 *Las Meninas*, 1656 (detail). Oil on canvas, 320 × 281.5 (126 × 110⅞). Museo Nacional del Prado, Madrid. Photo akg-images
166 *Las Hilanderas* or *The Fable of Arachne*, *c.* 1657–58. Oil on canvas, 220 × 290 (86⅝ × 114¼). Museo Nacional del Prado, Madrid. Photo Museo Nacional del Prado/Scala, Florence
167 *Las Hilanderas* or *The Fable of Arachne*, *c.* 1657–58 (detail). Oil on canvas, 220 × 290 (86⅝ × 114¼). Museo Nacional del Prado, Madrid. Photo Museo Nacional del Prado/Scala, Florence
168 Titian, *Rape of Europa*, 1559–62. Oil on canvas, 178 × 205 (70⅛ × 80¾). Isabella Stewart Gardner Museum, Boston
169 Peter Paul Rubens, *Pallas and Arachne*, 1636–37. Oil on wood, 26.7 × 38.1 (10⅝ × 15). Virginia Museum of Fine Arts, Richmond, VA
170 *Mercury and Argus*, *c.* 1659. Oil on canvas, 127 × 250 (50 × 98½). Museo Nacional del Prado, Madrid. Photo Museo Nacional del Prado/Scala, Florence
171 Peter Paul Rubens, *Mercury and Argus*, 1636–38. Oil on canvas, 180 × 298 (70⅞ × 117⅜).

Museo Nacional del Prado, Madrid. Photo Museo Nacional del Prado/Scala, Florence
172 *Philip IV*, 1656–57. Oil on canvas, 64.1 × 53.7 (25¼ × 21¼). The National Gallery, London. Photo The National Gallery, London/Scala, Florence
173 *The Infanta Margarita Theresa in a Blue Dress*, 1659. Oil on canvas, 125.5 × 106 (49½ × 41¾). Kunsthistorisches Museum, Vienna
174 *Portrait of Prince Philip Prospero*, 1659. Oil on canvas, 129 × 100 (50⅞ × 39⅜). Kunsthistorisches Museum, Vienna
175 Velázquez/Juan Bautista Martínez del Mazo, *Margarita Theresa, Infanta of Spain*, c. 1660–65. Oil on canvas, 212 × 147 (83½ × 54). Museo Nacional del Prado, Madrid. Photo Museo Nacional del Prado/Scala, Florence
176 Juan Bautista Martínez del Mazo, *Family of the Painter*, c. 1660. Oil on canvas, 149.5 × 174.5 (58⅞ × 68¾). Kunsthistorisches Museum, Vienna
177 Juan Bautista Martínez del Mazo, *Queen Mariana of Spain in Mourning*, 1666. Oil on canvas, 196.8 × 146 (77½ × 57½). The National Gallery, London. Presented by Rosalind, Countess of Carlisle, 1913
178 Juan Bautista Martínez del Mazo, *A Child in Ecclesiastical Dress*, c. 1660–67. Oil on canvas, 167.3 × 121.9 (65⅞ × 48). Toledo Museum of Art, Ohio
179 Alonso Cano, *The Miracle of the Well*, c. 1645–50. Oil on canvas, 216 × 149 (85⅛ × 58¾). Museo Nacional del Prado, Madrid. Photo Museo Nacional del Prado/Scala, Florence
180 Juan Carreño de Miranda, *Portrait of Charles II*, 1671. Oil on canvas, 210 × 147 (82¾ × 57⅞). Museo de Bellas Artes de Asturias, Oviedo. Photo Album/Alamy Stock Photo
181 Claudio Coello, *Portrait of Padre Cabanillas*, 1689–93. Oil on canvas, 76 × 62 (30 × 24½). Museo Nacional del Prado, Madrid. Photo Museo Nacional del Prado/Scala, Florence
182 Luca Giordano, *A Homage to Velázquez*, c. 1692–95. Oil on canvas, 205.2 × 182.2 (80⅞ × 71¾). The National Gallery, London. Photo The National Gallery, London/Scala, Florence
183 Francisco Goya, after Velázquez, *Los Borrachos*, 1778. Etching, 32.2 × 43.8 (12¾ × 17¼). Bibliothèque nationale de France, Paris
184 Francisco Goya, after Velázquez, *Don Juan of Austria*, 1778. Red chalk drawing, 26.7 × 16.5 (10⅝ × 6½). Hamburger Kunsthalle. Photo Scala, Florence/bpk, Bildagentur für Kunst, Kultur und Geschichte/Christoph Irrgang

185 Francisco Goya, after Velázquez, *Portrait of Don Diego de Acedo, called 'El Primo'*, 1778. Black chalk, 20 × 15.3 (7⅞ × 6⅛). Victoria and Albert Museum, London
186 Francisco Goya, after Velázquez, *Portrait of Don Sebastián de Morra*, 1778. Etching, 20.8 × 14.9 (8¼ × 5⅞). The Metropolitan Museum of Art, New York. Harris Brisbane Dick Fund, Rogers Fund, and Gift of Theodore De Witt, by exchange, 1931
187 Francisco Goya, *Charles IV of Spain and his Family*, 1800. Oil on canvas, 280 × 336 (110¼ × 132⅜). Museo Nacional del Prado, Madrid
188 *The Jester Calabazas*, 1635–39 (detail). Oil on canvas, 106 × 83 (41¾ × 32¾). Museo Nacional del Prado, Madrid. Photo Museo Nacional del Prado/Scala, Florence
189 Francisco Goya, *Tio Paquete*, c. 1819–20. Oil on canvas, 39 × 31 (15⅜ × 12¼). Museo Nacional Thyssen-Bornemisza, Madrid.
190 Edouard Manet, *Spanish Studio Scene*, 1859–60. Oil on canvas, 45.7 × 38.1 (18 × 15). Private collection. Photo Christie's Images/Bridgeman Images
191 Edgar Degas, *Homage to Velázquez*, 1857–58. Oil on canvas, 31 × 25.2 (12¼ × 10). Neue Pinakothek, Bayerische Staatsgemäldesammlungen, Munich. Photo Scala, Florence/bpk, Bildagentur für Kunst, Kultur und Geschichte
192 Workshop of Velázquez, *Infanta Margarita*, c. 1655. Oil on canvas, 70 × 58 (27⅝ × 22⅞). Musée du Louvre, Paris. Photo RMN-Grand Palais (musée du Louvre)/Gérard Blot
193 Workshop of Velázquez, *Thirteen Gentlemen*, c. 1645–50. Oil on canvas, 47 × 77 (18⅝ × 30⅜). Musée du Louvre, Paris. Photo RMN-Grand Palais (musée du Louvre)/Thierry Ollivier
194 Edouard Manet, *The Old Musician*, 1862. Oil on canvas, 187.4 × 248.2 (73⅞ × 97¾). National Gallery of Art, Washington, D.C. Chester Dale Collection
195 Edouard Manet, *The Tragic Actor (Rouvière as Hamlet)*, 1866. Oil on canvas, 187.2 × 108.1 (73¾ × 42⅝). National Gallery of Art, Washington, D.C. Chester Dale Collection
196 Johannes Vermeer, *The Lacemaker*, c. 1660. Oil on canvas, 24 × 21 (9½ × 8⅜). Musée du Louvre, Paris
197 *The Needlewoman*, c. 1640. Oil on canvas, 74 × 60 (29¼ × 23⅝). National Gallery of Art, Washington, D.C. Andrew W. Mellon Collection
198 James McNeill Whistler, *Arrangement in Grey and Black, No. 2: Portrait of Thomas Carlyle*,

1872–73. Oil on canvas, 171.1 × 143.5 (67⅜ × 56½). Kelvingrove Art Gallery and Museum. Photo CSG CIC Glasgow Museums Collection/Bridgeman Images

199 John Everett Millais, *A Souvenir of Velázquez*, 1868. Oil on canvas, 102.7 × 82.4 (40½ × 32½). Royal Academy, London. Photo Bridgeman Images

200 James McNeill Whistler, *Harmony in Grey and Green: Miss Cicely Alexander*, 1872–74. Oil on canvas, 190.2 × 97.8 (75 × 38⅝). Tate. Photo Tate

201 James McNeill Whistler, *The Artist in his Studio*, 1865–66. Oil on board mounted on wood panel, 62 × 46.5 (24½ × 18⅜). Art Institute of Chicago. Friends of American Art Collection

202 John Singer Sargent, *The Daughters of Edward Darley Boit*, 1882. Oil on canvas, 221.9 × 222.6 (87⅜ × 87¾). Museum of Fine Arts, Boston. Gift of Mary Louisa Boit, Julia Overing Boit, Jane Hubbard Boit, and Florence D. Boit in memory of their father, Edward Darley Boit

203 Sir John Lavery, *The Royal Family at Buckingham Palace*, 1913. Oil on canvas, 340.3 × 271.8 (134 × 107⅛). National Portrait Gallery, London. Photo Stefano Baldini/ Bridgeman Images

204 Pablo Picasso, *Las Meninas*, 1957. Oil on canvas, 194 × 260 (76½ × 102⅜). Museu Picasso, Barcelona. Donated by the artist, 1968. Photo Javier Larrea/age fotostock/Superstock. © Succession Picasso/DACS, London 2023

205 Pablo Picasso, *Las Meninas (Infanta Margarita María)*, 1957. Oil on canvas, 100 × 81 (39⅜ × 32). Museu Picasso, Barcelona. Donated by the artist, 1968. Photo Album/sfgp/Album Archivo/ Superstock. © Succession Picasso/DACS, London 2023

206 Pablo Picasso, *Las Meninas*, 1957. Oil on canvas, 129 × 161 (50⅞ × 63½). Museu Picasso, Barcelona. Donated by the artist, 1968. Photo akg-images/Album/Kocinsky. © Succession Picasso/ DACS, London 2023

207 Richard Hamilton, *Picasso's Meninas*, 1973. Etching on paper, 57 × 49 (22½ × 19⅜). Tate Britain, London. Photo Tate © R. Hamilton. All rights reserved, DACS 2023

208 Francis Bacon, *Pope I*, 1951. Oil on canvas, 198 × 137 (78 × 54). Aberdeen Art Gallery and Museums Collection. © The Estate of Francis Bacon. All rights reserved, DACS/ Artimage 2023. Photo Prudence Cuming Associates Ltd

209 Francis Bacon, *Study after Velázquez's Portrait of Pope Innocent X*, 1953. Oil on canvas, 153 × 118 (60¼ × 46½). Des Moines Art Centre. © The Estate of Francis Bacon. All rights reserved, DACS/Artimage 2023. Photo Prudence Cuming Associates Ltd

Index

References in italics indicate
illustration figure numbers

A

Acedo, Don Diego de, jester
149, 154; *120, 185*
Aertsen, Pieter 13–15; *7*
Aesop 129; *101*
Alcázar Palace, Madrid 51–2,
90, 91, 169, 177–8, 216, 227
Alexander, Cicely 248; *200*
Algardi, Alessandro 180, 191;
154
Astalli, Camillo, Cardinal
180–3; *144*

B

Bacon, Francis 259–60; *208,
209*
Balthasar Carlos, Prince 47,
70–3, 78, 94, 98–9, 115–17,
140, 151, 155, 178; *50–1, 76,
89, 90, 107*
Barberana y Aparregui, Don
Pedro de 78–81; *57*
Barberini, Francesco 60
Bárbola, Mari 204, 209
Bernini, Gian Lorenzo 60, 180,
191; *153*
Beuckelaer, Joachim 13
bodegones 8–16, 56, 128, 174–7,
213; *2–6, 8–10*
Bonarelli, Matteo *143*
Borja y Velasco, Gaspar de,
Cardinal 90, 155; *121*
*Borrachos (The Triumph of
Bacchus)* (1628–29) 55–6, 133,
241; *39, 40*
Brandani, Ferdinando 184; *146*
Brown, Jonathan 135, 209, 215

Buen Retiro, Madrid 91–4, 117,
123, 135, 177

C

Cajés, Eugenio 51
Calabazas, Juan de, jester 151,
235; *117, 188*
Calderón de la Barca 103
Cano, Alonso 163, 227–8; *129,
179*
Caravaggio 51, 54, 208
Carducho, Vincente 51, 52;
36
Carlos, Infante Don 47–8;
32
Carlyle, Thomas 248; *198*
Carreño de Miranda, Juan 228,
238; *180*
Castañeda y Pernia, Don
Cristóbal de, jester 123,
127–8; *97*
Charles I of England 38,
178
Charles II 223, 228, 238; *1
80*
Charles III 231
Charles IV 231; *187*
Christ on the Cross (c. 1632)
88; *63*
Claude Lorrain 60, 93, 177;
67
Coello, Claudio 229; *181*
The Coronation of the Virgin
(1635–36) 90–1; *65*
Corral, Don Diego de 78;
56
Corral, Don Luis de *55*
Correggio 178
Cortona, Pietro da 60, 180
Crescenzi, Juan Bautista 51

D

de la Fuente, Jerónima 29–31;
21, 22
Degas, Edgar 241; *191*
Delacroix, Eugène 238, 241
Democritus 50, 128–9; *35,
98*
Dürer, Albrecht 54, 135; *105*

E

El Escorial 91, 178, 195, 228,
229
El Greco 91, 254; *66*
Este, Francesco d' 119; *93*

F

Ferdinand of Austria, Cardinal
Infante (Don Fernando) 112,
145, 151; *87, 110*
Ferdinand VII 235
Figueroa, Juan de Fonseca y
16, 37, 38
The Forge of Vulcan (1630) 60–2,
84, 88, 94, 133; *43, 46*

G

Gautier, Théophile 211
Gentileschi, Artemisia 93
Giordano, Luca 229–30; *182*
Giorgione 163; *126*
Girón, Fernando 100
Góngora, Don Luis de 35–7; *25*
Goya, Francisco 231–5, 238; *183,
184, 185, 186, 187, 189*
Guercino 58

H

Hals, Frans 50, 145–6, 244;
112, 113
Hamilton, Richard 257–9;
207
Haro y Guzmán, Gaspar de
161
Henrietta Maria, Queen of
England 150; *116*
Heraclitus 128; *99*
Hercules 94–5; *70*
Hudson, Jeffrey 150; *116*

I

The Immaculate Conception
(c. 1619) 91; *11*
Innocent X, Pope 185–93,
259–60; *152, 153, 154, 155,
208, 209*
Ipeñarrieta, Doña Antonia de
47, 78; *55*
Isabella of Bourbon 90, 94,
95–7, 119, 178; *54, 74*

J

*Joseph's Bloody Coat Brought
to Jacob* (1630) 60–3, 94;
44
Juan of Austria, Don, jester 123,
150; *96, 184*
Julius II, Pope 185; *150*
Justi, Carl 137, 191, 223
Justin of Nassau 103–5

L

La Tela Real (prob. 1632–37) 81,
177; *140–1*
The Lady with a Fan (*c.* 1635)
121–3; *95*
Lanfranco, Giovanni 93
Las Hilanderas (*c.* 1657–58)
211–16; *166, 167*
Las Meninas (1656) 117, 119,
204–11, 222, 223, 229–30,
231, 250–54; *163–5*
Lavery, John 254; *203*
Lawrence, Thomas 235
Leonardo, Jusepe 103; *81*
Lezcano, Francisco 154;
119
Louis XIV of France 196,
222

M

Maíno, Juan Bautista 51, 100,
103; *80*
Manet, Edouard 241–3, 248;
190, 194, 195
Mantegna, Andrea 178
Margaret of Austria 94, 95–6;
72
Margarita, Infanta 202–4, 219,
223, 241; *161, 162, 173, 175,
192, 205*
Maria, Doña (sister of Philip IV)
38, 69, 163, 202; *49*
Maria Theresa, Infanta of Spain
119, 155–60, 195–6, 222; *123,
157, 158*
Mariana of Austria/Spain 178,
202, 204, 223; *159, 177*
Massimi, Camillo 183–4;
145
Mateos, Don Juan 81, 115–17;
58
Matham, Jacob *7*
Mazo, Juan Bautista Martínez
del 117, 204, 211, 223–7; *175,
176, 177, 178*
Medici Villa *47, 48*
Méndez de Haro, Gaspar 83
Mengs, Anton Raffael 231
Menippus 129; *100*
Mercury and Argus (*c.* 1659)
216–17; *170*
Mérimée, Prosper 241
Michelangelo 60
Millais, John Everett 248–50;
199

Montañés, Juan Martínez 19,
29, 117–19; *13, 91*
Morra, Sebastián de 151–4;
118, 186
Murillo, Bartolomé Esteban
238

N

Nardi, Angelo 51
Nieto, José de 119, 204; *94*

O

Ocáriz y Ochoa, Francisco de
169–70; *133*
Olivares, Count-Duke of 37,
43–7, 108–10, 117, 119, 141–2,
171; *30–1, 84, 108*

P

Pacheco, Francisco 8, 18–19, 31,
35–7, 38, 70; *14, 24*
Pacheco, Juana 7, 29
Palomino, Antonio 8, 52, 55,
119, 141, 142, 143, 171, 178,
180, 185, 204, 219, 222,
229–30
Paquete, Tio 235; *189*
Pareja, Juan de 184–5, 193; *147,
148, 149*
Patinir, Joachim 135
Paul III, Pope 185; *151*
Pertusato, Nicolasito 204,
209
Philip III 94, 95–6; *71*
Philip IV 7, 37, 51, 73–5, 94,
97–8, 100, 111, 112, 141,
143, 149–50, 177, 178,
199, 204, 218–19, 223;
*26–9, 52–3, 73, 75, 86, 92,
109, 111, 114–15, 140–1, 156,
160, 172*
Philip Prospero, Prince 219;
174
Picasso, Pablo 254–7; *204, 205,
206*
Pliny the Elder 215
Poussin, Nicolas 60, 93, 169,
180, 184; *68*
Prado Museum 235
Preti, Mattia 180

Q

Quevedo y Villegas, Francisco
de 171; *134*

R

Raphael 60, 178, 185; *150*
Rembrandt 169, 262
Reni, Guido 83; *60*
Reynolds, Joshua 193
Ribera, Jusepe de 180
Rodríguez de Silva, Juan 7
Rokeby Venus (*c.* 1647–51) 161–8,
180, 248; *125, 132*
Rouviére, Philibert 243; *195*
Rubens, Peter Paul 55, 56, 93,
111, 128, 149, 178, 204, 211,
214, 216, 217; *41, 42, 69, 98,
99, 114, 169, 171*

S

Sacchetti, Giulio 58
Sacchi, Andrea 60
Sargent, John Singer 254;
202
Sarmiento, Maria, Doña 204,
209
Snyders, Frans 111
Soplillo, Miguel 149; *115*
Sotomayor, Antonio de 84
Spinola, Ambrogio 58, 103–7
*St Anthony Abbot Visits St Paul
the Hermit* (*c.* 1634) 135–7;
104
St Simón de Rojas 49–50; *33*
St Thomas Aquinas 84; *62*
Stanzione, Massimo 93
Suárez de Ribera, Don Cristóbal
29; *20*
The Supper at Emmaus (1628–29)
54, 56; *38*
The Surrender of Breda (*c.* 1635)
53, 100, 103–8; *77, 78, 82, 83*

T

Tacca, Pietro 117, 119; *92*
*The Temptation of St Thomas
Aquinas* (1631–33) 84–8;
62
Thore-Bürger, Théophile
244
Tintoretto 58, 180
Titian 54, 55, 58, 163, 178, 185,
213; *127, 130, 151, 168*
Torre de la Parada, Madrid 111,
128–9, 178
Turchi, Alessandro 90–1

U

Ulloa, Marcela de, Doña 204

V

Valdés, Fernando de,
    Archbishop 172; *135*, *136*,
    137
Valladolid, Pablo de 133–5, 150,
    170, 243; *103*
Van Dyck, Anthony 38, 141, 145,
    178, 229; *110*, *116*
Van Eyck, Jan 163; *131*
Velasco, Isabel de, Doña 204
Velázquez, Diego de
    biographical details 7–8,
    222
    lost works 169–74
Velázquez, Jerónima 7
*The Venerable Mother Jerónima
    de la Fuente* (1620) 31; *21*,
    22
Venus 161–8; *125*, *126*, *127*, *128*,
    130, *132*
Vermeer, Johannes 244; *196*
Veronese 58
Villandrando, Rodrigo de *115*

W

Whistler, James McNeill 163,
    196, 248–54; *198*, *200*, *201*
Wilkie, David 235–8

Z

Zurbarán, Francisco de 88–90,
    94, 100; *64*, *70*, *79*

'The single most influential series of art books
ever published' *Apollo*

'Outstanding ... exceptionally authoritative and
well-illustrated' *Sunday Times*

'World of Art delivers real knowledge with crisp,
useful clarity' *Guardian*

Comprehensive in coverage and accessible to all,
the World of Art series explores both the newest
and the perennial in all the arts, covering themes,
artists and movements that straddle the centuries
and the gamut of visual culture around the globe.

You may also like:

William Blake
Kathleen Raine
Preface by Colin Trodd

Cézanne
Richard Verdi

Gainsborough
William Vaughan

Gauguin
Belinda Thomson

Hogarth
David Bindman

Monet
James H. Rubin

Raphael
Paul Joannides

Rembrandt
Christopher White

Turner
Graham Reynolds
Introduction by David
Blayney Brown

World of Art